The Permanence of the Political

The Permanence of
the Political

A DEMOCRATIC CRITIQUE
OF THE RADICAL IMPULSE TO
TRANSCEND POLITICS

• *JOSEPH M. SCHWARTZ* •

PRINCETON UNIVERSITY PRESS

PRINCETON, NEW JERSEY

Copyright © 1995 by Princeton University Press
Published by Princeton University Press, 41 William Street, Princeton, New Jersey 08540
In the United Kingdom: Princeton University Press, Chichester, West Sussex
All Rights Reserved

Library of Congress Cataloging-in-Publication Data

Schwartz, Joseph M., 1954–
The permanence of the political :
a democratic critique of the radical impulse
to transcend politics / Joseph M. Schwartz.
p.   cm.
Includes bibliographical references (p.   ) and index.
ISBN 0-691-03357-9 (cloth)
1. Socialism.   2. Social conflict.   3. Social justice.
4. Democracy.   5. Pluralism (Social sciences).
6. Radicalism.   I. Title.
HX73.S385   1995
335—dc20   95-3045

This book has been composed in Laser Galliard

Princeton University Press books are printed on acid-free paper, and meet the guidelines
for permanence and durability of the Committee on Production Guidelines for Book
Longevity of the Council on Library Resources

Printed in the United States of America by Princeton Academic Press

1   3   5   7   9   10   8   6   4   2

• IN MEMORY OF •

MICHAEL HARRINGTON (1928–1989)

COMRADE, TEACHER, FRIEND

• C O N T E N T S •

ACKNOWLEDGMENTS   ix

CHAPTER 1
Introduction: The Radical Impulse to Transcend Politics   3

CHAPTER 2
The Threat of Interests to the General Will: Rousseau's
Critique of Particularism   33

CHAPTER 3
The Hegelian State: Mediating Away the Political   70

CHAPTER 4
The Origins of Marx's Hostility to Politics: The Devaluation
of Rights and Justice   104

CHAPTER 5
Lenin (and Marx) on the Sciences of Consciousness and
Production: The Abolition of Political Judgment   146

CHAPTER 6
Hannah Arendt's Politics of "Action": The Elusive Search for
Political Substance   189

CHAPTER 7
Conclusion: Redressing the Radical Tradition's Antipolitical
Legacy—Toward a Radical Democratic Pluralist Politics   217

NOTES   251

BIBLIOGRAPHY   311

INDEX   325

• A C K N O W L E D G M E N T S •

My work in political theory grew out of my practical concerns as a radical democratic activist and intellectual in a liberal democratic capitalist society. Radical theory and practice, in my experience, has been crippled by its often-unbridled hostility to both social pluralism and rights-based liberalism. This book seeks to mediate the radical critique of democratic capitalist societies with the concern for pluralism evidenced in both liberal and postmodern thought. It also aims to retain for radical political theory a commitment to the solidarity of socialism without embracing those parts of the socialist tradition characterized by an overly comprehensive conception of true universal human interests that have violated not only in theory, but also in brutal practice, the plural nature of humanity.

I wish to thank many individuals who over my life have helped develop my capacity for moral and political reflection. To my parents, David and Anita Schwartz, I am grateful for an upbringing rooted in a critical but tolerant tradition of social concern. My older sisters Rebecca Schwartz Greene and Adina Beth Schwartz helped introduce me to the world of politics, moral philosophy, history, and the law.

I was fortunate to enter graduate school in the Department of Government at Harvard University just in time to sign on Michael Walzer as my dissertation supervisor before he moved to the Institute for Advanced Study. I remain grateful for his intellectual advice, encouragement, and patience as I made the transition from political organizing to sustained intellectual work. In an era when hyperspecialization threatens to render the university irrelevant to public life, Walzer is a rigorous political theorist who makes a significant contribution to public deliberation, particularly through his editing of *Dissent* magazine. Professor Walzer's generous offer of a year's "research assistantship" at the Institute in 1984–85 enabled me to begin work on my dissertation. Much of the critique of the radical tradition outlined in this work was initially sketched out in our periodic postprandial strolls in the Institute woods. They were then developed with the help of a Charlotte W. Newcombe dissertation fellowship from the Woodrow Wilson National Fellowship Foundation.

By serving on my dissertation committee, Professors Harvey C. Mansfield and Michael Sandel rendered my committee an exemplar of political pluralism. While pressing me on salient points where we disagreed, they also strove to understand my project on its own terms. Michael Sandel's receptivity to my differences with aspects of his work indicates that my conception of him as a democratic, pluralist communitarian may not be far off the mark.

I wrote the dissertation that initiated this book project while teaching for four years in the 1980s as a graduate teaching fellow and Instructor in the Committee on Degrees in Social Studies at Harvard University. The community life of this program enabled me to share my concerns with faculty and graduate students from across the social sciences. I owe the committee's chair, Professor David Landes, and the program's head tutor, Judith Vichniac, a special debt for creating an atmosphere in which both teaching and scholarship were strongly supported. Many colleagues listened to formal talks based on my research or read parts or all of the dissertation and made innumerable helpful suggestions. My graduate school housemate Jeff Goodwin provided particularly invaluable feedback. To my friend Debra Satz I owe a special debt of gratitude. Her abilities as a moral philosopher and her generosity as a person contributed much to this work and my own personal growth. Beyond the Social Studies community, my friendship with U.S. politics specialists Margaret Weir, Jim Shoch, and Cathie Martin demonstrated to me that political theorists have no monopoly on being theoretical and that social theory would benefit from greater empirical and historical knowledge of politics. In the past three years, Elizabeth Kiss and Jeff Holzgrefe have helped to rekindle my faith that there remain insightful, caring, and engaged intellectuals within the academy.

The transformation of this work from a dissertation primarily grounded in critical exegesis to a book that also advances a prescriptive vision of radical democratic politics would not have been possible without the generous support of a Mellon Postdoctoral Fellowship in 1990–91 under the auspices of the Cornell University Humanities Council and the Department of Government. The transformation from dissertation to book began on a 1989 summer faculty research fellowship from Temple University.

The Mellon fellowship also allowed me to become reacquainted with an old undergraduate friend, Marilyn Migiel, who teaches Italian literature at Cornell. For the past two years she has shared the trials, tribulations, and joys of a commuting marriage mediated by our success in having a first child in our late thirties. Marilyn's exemplary energy, intellectual discipline, skills at university governance and mentoring of graduate students, as well as her parenting abilities, are attributes that I try to emulate.

As I prepared the book to go to press in the fall and winter of 1993–94, I was on leave courtesy of a yearlong fellowship from the American Council of Learned Societies. The grant supported work on a second book that aims to reconceptualize a politics of social solidarity in globally integrated yet socially fragmented late-industrial polities. The grant not only provided time for sustained scholarship but also spared me a year of weekly driving from Ithaca to Philadelphia. I have also had the inestimable pleasure of being with my son Michael Benjamin Migiel-Schwartz full-time during his second enthusiastic year of life.

I cannot say enough about the supportive atmosphere of my home department at Temple University. Not only do my senior colleagues endorse a balanced commitment to serious research and teaching, but they have offered the friendship and encouragement for which junior faculty can usually only hope. Both of my department chairs, Professors Robert Osborn and

Lynn Miller, created a nurturing atmosphere for junior members of the department. In his five years as chair, Lynn Miller has utilized his superb talent as an administrator and his sense of moral fairness to improve the department's cohesiveness as an intellectual and academic community. I am particularly grateful that my fellow junior faculty colleagues, Robin Kolodny, Richard Deeg, and Gary Mucciaroni, are not only engaged intellectuals but also good human beings.

Teaching at an urban, public, commuter school is not only in accord with the values defended in this book but is also a great pleasure to which I hope to make a lifetime commitment. I have gained considerable insight into many of the arguments of this work in conversation, both in and out of class, with former Temple undergraduates Andy Buckman, Virginia Coughlin, Mytri Singh, Kish Enstice, Karen Gohdes, Cindy Chmielewski, Nancy Wiefek, James Kelly, Pat Burke, Shinya Niato, David Gross, and Kelly Osborne and with graduate students Joseph McLaughlin, Dan Good, Sang Joon Choi, Jasper LiCalzi, Dan Dileo, Bruce Lapenson, Andre Leighton, Ric Kolenda, Sharon Gramby, Pat Cannon, Sonja Moore, Donald Rieck, James Heasley, Chris Speicher, Brigid Callaghan, Donghyun Kim, Beverly Al-Greene, Carol Jenkins, Anita Skogland, Carole Porter, and Xia Ming.

To those friends with whom I have been active in Democratic Socialists of America (DSA) over the past fifteen years, I owe a special thanks for demonstrating a real-world commitment to the values defended in this book. Listing all the political friends to whom I am indebted would challenge the standard length of acknowledgments, so I will uncharacteristically demure. But you know who you are, and all of you serve as a constant reminder that "organic intellectuals" are as likely to be located outside of the academy as inside. Mark Levinson, Guy Molyneux, and Peter Mandler are "comrades" in the truest sense of the word—for by working with me as friends, political allies, and intellectual colleagues, they have come to mean more to me than a simple amalgamation of those roles. They have seen this book (and its author) through all its metamorphoses.

Finally, I wish to thank Ann Wald, my editor at Princeton University Press, for her unflappable support, beginning with her decision to send the manuscript out for external evaluation through her guiding it to final production. She has shepherded an initiate through the world of university publishing. The readers' reports she solicited were noteworthy for their intelligence and critical acumen and have significantly informed my final revisions. I owe particular gratitude to social and political theorists Don Herzog, Alan Gilbert, Jeffrey Isaac, and Carmen Sirianni, all of whom read the manuscript with care and commented on it at great length and with sustained insight. My reflection on and response to their comments, I hope, have significantly improved the final version. In final production, my copyeditor at Princeton University Press, Marta Steele, significantly improved the manuscript's writing and documentation. Whatever shortcomings remain are, needless to say, my own responsibility.

Two final editorial notes. Whenever possible, I have attempted to use gender-inclusive language. In cases, however, where an author consciously excluded women from full participation in political life (Rousseau and Hegel contend that women's concern for the familial and private preclude their status as public citizens), I have not tried to exclude the gender bias, anachronistically, from their politics and discourse. In the notes I document, in analyzing a specific theorist, why and when it is necessary to use gender-exclusive language for reasons of historical and intellectual accuracy.

As to editions and translations I cite in cases of multiple translations, I have tried, particularly in the case of Marx, to use both reputable and accessible translations (those found in most decent college and university libraries). For notes and unfinished manuscripts such as *The Economic and Philosophical Manuscripts of 1844*, I chose what I considered to be the best translation of the relevant passage (because the manuscripts are only printed in full in the rather cumbersome and stilted translation of *The Marx-Engels Works* [Moscow: Progress Publishers, 1975]). In the case of the *Grundrisse*, Marx's notes for the first volume of *Capital*, I have used the translation from the entire work, *Grundrisse*, translated by Martin Nicolaus (Baltimore: Penguin, 1973), except in a few instances where the translation in the earlier *Grundrisse: Selections* (ed. David McClellan, New York: Harper and Row, 1971) provides a more compelling and felicitous translation based on my own reading knowledge of German.

The Arendt chapter draws on material that initially appeared as "Arendt's Politics: The Elusive Search for Substance," *Praxis International* 9:1/2 (April and July 1989): 25–47 copyright © 1989 Basil Blackwell Ltd., and I am grateful for their permission to reprint it here.

Joseph M. Schwartz
Slaterville Springs, New York
January 1995

The Permanence of the Political

Introduction

THE RADICAL IMPULSE TO TRANSCEND POLITICS

RADICAL THEORY AND RADICAL PRACTICE: AN ANTIPOLITICAL ELECTIVE AFFINITY

This book explores the paradox that radical political theorists, whose work inspired mass movements for democracy, were themselves hostile to the very conditions that give rise to democratic politics—a plurality of social interests and diverse conceptions of the good life. Only the most cynical or conservative students of history would deny that the popular ideological versions of radical thought, particularly Rousseau's ideal of a self-sovereign people and Marx's conception of democratic control over social life, informed the moral and political vision of nineteenth- and twentieth-century democratic mass movements, as well as populist, nondemocratic variants thereof. But radical theorists, rather than envisioning the democratization of political life, sought to transcend politics through the creation of conflict-free societies. The social practices of these societies would fulfill a universal conception of "true human interests," thereby eliminating social conflict and the need for politics. This work hopes not to engage in a crude intellectual history that contends that ideas solely determine historical development—as if ideas determine human action apart from the complex interrelationship between ideas (the layperson's conception of how the world works) and ideal (normative values) and material interests. Rather, the book explores how the radical tradition's intellectual hostility to pluralism and conflict helped preclude, until very recently, the development of a coherent theory and practice of radical democratic politics. This hostility also rendered the task of democratic critics of authoritarian left regimes more difficult, because there existed, at best, only ambiguous internal resources within an overly canonical radical theoretical tradition to mobilize in critique of such regimes.

Most contemporary radical theorists would claim that their vision places a high value on political participation. But did the central figures in the radical political tradition envision a flowering of political life? Or did these theorists long for the abolition of social conflict and of politics itself? If they aimed to transcend politics, then contemporary theorists interested in developing a radical democratic theory of *politics* need to confront this legacy. There are questions that radical democratic theorists still must answer: Can one envision—both theoretically and practically—a relatively egalitarian distribution of political and economic power which would still embrace tension and conflict among diverse social groups and conceptions of the good? Is a *politics* more egalitarian and democratic than that which exists in liberal democratic capitalist societies possible?

Since the collapse of authoritarian communism as the dominant intellectual paradigm within the Western ideological left after the Khrushchev revelations of 1956, there has developed a significant corpus of radical democratic political theory. The insights of these writers informs this work, though I am also indirectly involved in a critical dialogue with them. Admirers of the early-twentieth-century work of the democratic socialist R. H. Tawney and the guild-socialist G.D.H. Cole could well argue that a dissident pluralist socialist tradition existed throughout the twentieth century, which drew also on the insights of such independent communists as Rosa Luxemburg, Victor Serge, and advocates of council communism.[1] In terms of the constructive argument advanced herein for a radical democratic theory and practice of politics, a reader will discern the influence of contemporary theorists such as Carole Pateman, Robert Dahl, Michael Walzer, Jane Mansbrige, Benjamin Barber, Amy Gutmann, Iris Marion Young, Chantal Mouffe and Ernesto Laclau, Joshua Cohen and Joel Rogers, Roberto Ungar, and Samuel Bowles and Herbert Gintis among others.[2] Admirers of one or more of these theorists might make the case that contemporary radical democratic political philosophy is well on its way to constructing a coherent *theory of radical pluralist politics.*

Without commenting in detail here on the promise or problems of each of these works, I would note that most of them represent a significant break with the "classical" radical tradition because they openly embrace, as central to a democratic society, social pluralism and a civil society relatively autonomous from a functioning, democratic state. In addition, most of these authors argue that the radical tradition should build on liberalism's recognition of the essential role of individual liberties and rights as a barrier against unjust state or societal interference in free associational life. Even contemporary radical democratic theorists who embrace the traditional radical critique of individual rights as promoting an atomized and competitive society, such as Benjamin Barber, or who dismiss the theory of rights as dependent on fallacious, "foundational" metadiscourses, such as Laclau and Mouffe, implicitly admit that a "strong" or radical democratic society would still incorporate liberal rights that guarantee equal voice to each member of the polity.[3] What unites these theorists as radical democrats is that they build on the radical tradition's criticism of liberal pluralism for conflating citizenship rights and, in some liberal analyses, the right to own one's labor, with the rights of corporate property. According to this radical critique, corporations are, in reality, not the outcome of free and individual contracts—to be treated as legal persons—but socially created institutions that must be socially and democratically regulated.

On the other hand, the work of the central theorists examined in this work—Rousseau, Hegel, Marx, and Lenin—had a predominant influence on the left's critique of democratic capitalist societies until the 1970s, when radical pluralist theory emerged as a major left intellectual trend. Those who might be loosely termed the "classical" radical theorists all embraced a critique of liberal rights as being, in essence, a defense of the prerogatives of private property and of an atomized society of competing interests. Each of these theorists criticized the dominant role that particular interests play in liberal marketplace society. They all feared that strife among particular interests would tear society apart and inevitably engender the domination of some interests over others. Thus, they tried to subsume these interests under a universal conception of human identity and a monistic conception of the good. Although they insightfully perceived the difficulty in a liberal democracy of constructing a shared sense of the public good, Rousseau, Hegel, Marx, and Lenin, in their mutual desire to overcome the centrifugal tendencies of social pluralism, conflated agreement on the common good—the basic rules of a political regime—with universal adherence to one set of true interests.

There is a profound difference, however, between free and sovereign individuals establishing the institutions and rules of their mutual political association and the belief that such a system yields one "true" set of interests common to all individuals. That is, the radical tradition failed to distinguish between the common bonds of a political community—what in liberal discourse is termed the social contract or the public good—and the particular conceptions of the good that distinct social groups within that political community may hold. These three recurrent motifs within radical thought—1) the hostility to particular interests, 2) the belief in a set of universal true interests, and 3) the inability to conceive of cohesive political bonds coexisting with plural conceptions of the good—crippled the radical tradition's ability to develop a viable vision of postrevolutionary politics. In addition, the radical tradition has always been torn between the Enlightenment's desire to develop a deterministic science of society (the positivist side of the Enlightenment) and its desire to promote the transcendent value of human freedom (its voluntarist side).[4] The postpolitical vision of the radical tradition attempted to transcend this tension by holding that in a truly free society human beings would no longer be dominated by social institutions but would spontaneously and continuously reshape these institutions in accordance with their collective will. In a nonalienated world, human destiny would not be determined by institutional structures; rather, social structures would be permanently malleable to the desires of a conscious, collective human will.

Any student of contemporary radical political practice cannot avoid noting the pervasive hold of this desire to transcend conflict and politics on radical political movements, including the "new" post-Marxist social movements of "identity politics." Prefiguring the social harmony of a good society informs many activists' obsession with "consensus" decision-making, even in groups larger and more diverse in interests than the small, solidaristic communities that Jane Mansbridge argues are necessary in order for consensus decision-making not to coerce dissident minorities or narrow majorities.[5] Internal political argument or sharp debate is frequently viewed by participants in these movements as unnecessarily divisive or elitist. On the basis of admittedly subjective, personal experience in contemporary movement politics, I have been struck by the difficulty many activists experience in acknowledging the logical possibility that all could sincerely share the movement's overall goal—say, nuclear disarmament or an environmentally sustainable universe—while differing, in what should be a sororal and fraternal manner, over the best strategy and tactics to achieve that goal.

THE MYTH OF THE TRANSCENDENCE OF SCARCITY: A RATIONALE FOR REPRESSIVE ANTIPOLITICS

Both classical liberalism and Marxism held that economic abundance would diminish, perhaps even abolish, the need for political authority. Although the collapse of the Soviet Union, growing world capitalist integration, and the abject failure of forced collectivization of agriculture have led most Third World revolutionary movements to abandon classical Marxist-Leninism, many still embrace a Marxist or increasingly free-market vision of economic abundance as the ultimate solution to all social problems. Either due to the wonders of a planned, postscarcity communism or to those of the capitalist market's invisible hand, by abolishing scarcity these societies would transcend the need for the political structuring of social choice and social organization. The belief that all politics inherently involves human domination not only hindered Marxist reformers' search for democratic institutional reforms within Communist regimes. The cultural legacy of such a worldview now influences many contemporary Eastern European intellectuals, often former Marxist-Leninists, to romanticize the unfettered market as a *deus ex machina* capable of resolving all societal ills. Such a faith uncannily inverts Marxist-Leninism's belief that in a classless society social conflict would be abolished and there would be no need for political institutions to mediate conflict. Nor is it a wonder that postcommunist societies experiencing the pain of International Monetary Fund-style shock therapy engender mass nationalist movements that, without the egalitarian and universalist pretenses of Communism, reproduce its search for a holistic identity and comprehensive, shared interests. According to nationalist doctrine, of course, this humanity is shared by only those with correct bloodlines rather than those adhering to a proper ideology or class pedigree. Yet neither classical liberalism's faith in the market nor traditional radicalism's (nor nationalism's) belief in the harmony of "true human interests" enables its adherents to envision an institutional matrix of political, civil, and market mechanisms capable of mediating between the diverse interests of a free society. As Charles Lindblom has demonstrated, although markets help to allocate resources efficiently and register consumer demand, leaving the establishment of social priorities solely to the market inordinately enhances the power of those who control investment.[6]

Historical analysis may enable us to comprehend, though not condone, the reasons why Marxist-Leninist regimes governing under conditions of economic scarcity engaged in brutal politics of "primitive accumulation," aimed at extracting resources for capital accumulation from their own populations—usually, but not exclusively, from the peasantry. Some radicals still excuse this injustice by ascribing it solely to the exigencies of economic scarcity and the imperatives of economic development. In reality, however, most political repression in developing nations did not arise from the exigencies of "fixed laws" of economic development, but from the desire of narrowly based political elites to monopolize political power by obliterating the social basis for political pluralism, such as a small-holding peasantry or independent trade unions.

The rationale offered by narrowly based, repressive, "modernizing" bureaucracies for their monopolization of power invariably involved the claim that a hostile, "backward" class (e.g., the peasantry) must be eliminated because it hindered the achievement of a postscarcity economy and the elimination of political conflict, which allegedly is inherently class-based. To incorporate small-holding peasants or voluntary cooperatives into the social and political landscape of a Soviet Union or People's Republic of China would have permitted a social pluralism that violated the classless ethos of socialism. The tragic legacy of this outlook is that the prescribed means, the rapid collectivization of agriculture, failed even to achieve the alleged end, rapid industrialization. As Alec Nove's and Alexander Erlich's definitive work on the economic history of the Soviet Union demonstrates, attempts to extract "surplus" from a repressed peasantry did not accelerate economic growth in the 1930s but helped to retard it, even in the short run, because of its disastrous adverse impact on agricultural productivity.[7]

Even if collectivization indirectly contributed to the rapid growth of heavy industry in the 1930s through the shifting of scarce resources away from consumption, the main source of surplus for investment derived from massive cuts in both working-class and peasant living standards and severe cutbacks in investment in agricultural and consumer industries. The economic legacy of such an overemphasis on heavy industry would have long-run disastrous implications for Soviet economic development. Pre–World War I industrial growth under the Tsars, as well as the recovery of economic productivity during the 1923–1928 New Economic Program, indicates that forced collectivization may not have been the most effective means for accelerating industrial development. But it was an effective—and conscious—means of eliminating a class that had demanded independent political representation by its overwhelming support of the autonomous and peasant-based

Social Revolutionary Party during the early years of the Bolshevik revolution. Neither Lenin nor Bukharin ever held that their New Economic Program (NEP) would necessitate independent political representation for a peasantry whose economic contributions were solicited by NEP's pluralist economic, but not political, strategy. The contemporary embrace by the Chinese Communist Party of "authoritarian capitalist" development as the current stage of Chinese "socialism" may further indicate that Communist elites fear political pluralism more than they do a statist capitalism dominated by Communist elites.

Political theory's unfortunate turn away from social theory's enterprise of integrating normative and empirical analysis may mean that the recurrent historical and sociological references in this work may strike some traditional students of political philosophy as unusual, at best, or irrelevant, at worst. But not only does responding to the strong historicist mode of argumentation within the radical tradition demand knowledge of historical development. In addition, the ineluctable, "dialectical" relationship between "facts" and "values" in all normative evaluation of political history and political possiblities precludes any traditional, positivist social-scientific drawing of a radical fact-value distinction. This is reflected in the way we argue politically and ethically in everyday life—marshaling alleged historical and empirical evidence, which our values sometimes permit or deny us the ability to take into account, but which we hope will shake both the empirical and normative orientation of our interlocutors.

Toward a Definition of Politics

Although this work is primarily a critical evaluation of the theoretical and practical legacy of the radical tradition in political thought, I also aim to outline a viable radical democratic conception of politics, to be more fully developed in future work. In the course of the work, I implicitly hold to a multilayered conception of democratic politics, contending that on one level politics involves the general community establishing comprehensive norms, backed by state power, for the authoritative allocation of social roles and goods that are not simply economic but also political, positional, and cultural. On another level, politics involves particular groups participating in public life in order to pursue their own interests. In imperfect liberal democracies, this struggle often involves groups who have fewer social resources than others, demanding greater access to public goods and social opportunities in order to reequilibrate their social power relative to other interests.

In a democratic polity these interests may also reshape their self-conception through public dialogue—and, at times, conflict—with other groups. But democratic politics also involves the public evaluation of the legitimacy of particular interests. Those particular interests deemed by the democratic polity as a whole to be undemocratic or in violation of the public good can be regulated, restructured, or abolished. Thus, imperfect democracies have abolished the interests of slaveholders, social democracies have curtailed the prerogatives of corporate power, and the U.S. polity may eventually restructure the private health-care industry. A democratic society to our north, Canada, between 1960 and 1970 chose to abolish the private health insurance industry. During that time Canada's provincial governments became the single public insurer, contracting for health care provision with independent medical professionals and nonprofit hospitals.

"Politics" may well be the most underdefined and undertheorized concept in political science, perhaps because metareflection on the nature of one's discipline is inherently contestable. Although I do not offer a comprehensive treatise on the nature of politics, to clarify my critique of the radical tradition's desire to transcend politics, an explicit discussion of how I utilize the term *politics* may be in order. Perhaps the best-known "political science" definition of politics is that it is those activities by which a society authoritatively allocates its values—moral, economic, and cultural—through conflict and cooperation among social groups with both shared and divergent interests.[8] Yet does such a definition threaten to render politics synonymous with all human social activity?[9] The uniqueness of political activity lies in its *authoritative* allocation of values. Political action renders judgments that are legally—ultimately, forcibly—binding on the members of that community. Such activity, when carried out democratically, involves the citizens of a polity engaging in a public allocation of goods which takes precedence over social relations deemed to be voluntary or private.[10] (Of course, the expansion of democracy has involved—and still involves—the reconceptualization of who counts as a full citizen and what the rights of citizens are.)

In the vast majority of societies and historical epochs, the authoritative allocation of social values has been carried out undemocratically. Political decision-making has more often than not been limited to a narrow stratum of society. Even the very Greek city-states that invented the term "rule of the people," *democracy*, excluded slaves, women, propertyless laborers, and *metics* (the ancient Greek equivalent of "guest workers") from membership in the polity. In part, the radical critique of liberal democracy is an immanent one, exposing how imperfect liberal democracies exclude the less privileged from full political voice, and more centrally, critiquing the relegation of certain crucial spheres of social life to the realm of the "private." Such a relegation is political in and of itself and excludes those who create such institutions from having a political voice in the very decisions that are binding on them. Thus, as critique, the radical tradition appeared to demand the expansion of the realm of politics, as well as the full democratization of that realm.

But when one closely examines the radical vision of a truly humane (frequently referred to as "social") society, it more often than not appears to be a peculiarly postpolitical society, in which both diverse social interests and the need for political mediation among them would "wither away" amid the spontaneous self-creation of a solidaristic society. This work attempts to rescue the spirit of the radical critique of the imperfections of liberal democracy from its dangerous prescriptive aim of transcending the very need for politics—either through the stifling solidaristic general will of Rousseau, the spontaneous postscarcity anarchism of Marx's "full communism," or the technocratic, scientistic rule of Lenin's vanguard party. Put succinctly, my prescriptive argument is that politics is unavoidable in any society that is more than minimally complex and diverse in social structure and that the only just way of making such political decisions is through democratic politics—and democratic disagreement. The radical vision's desire to transcend the messy business of democratic disagreement through the instantiation of a solidaristic society embodying truly universal human interests not only is profoundly antipolitical; it also violates the very democratic impulses that inspired the radical critique of not only authoritarian, but also less-than-fully democratic regimes. Thus, this work desires not only to highlight the necessity or unavoidability of politics but also to affirm radical democratic pluralism as the most desirable of political regimes. Tragically, this goal was not the uneqivocal one of the radical tradition in both theory and practice.[11]

The determination of what is to be decided voluntarily or privately is itself political, as is the question of whether public binding decisions will be made democratically or not. That is, what is personal and what is public is politically constructed. But to obliterate any and all distinctions between public and private would be to totalize politics. Matters that are justly politicized are only those that a majority of the polity believes should be subject to the binding institutional decisions of the community. Only political decisions have binding claims on the behavior of all community members. Undoubtedly, cultural, aesthetic, and sexual relations are crucially affected by the relationships of political power. And liberal democratic capitalist societies have historically "privatized" not only economic but also gender relations that have coercive and binding influence on their subjects, such as violence against women within the family. Thus, democratic social movements—the labor movement and the feminist movement—have argued that the capital-labor relationship and *aspects* of the romantic and physical relationship between individuals should be democratically and publicly regulated. The purpose of this is to give equal power to parties who have traditionally been denied a say in the very social relationships that they work to create. And today both gay male and lesbian couples contend for the same legal recognition and child-rearing rights that straight couples enjoy. Such a demand, if won, will inevitably involve similar public, political regulation of child rearing currently applicable to straight child-rearing individuals and couples.

But would a democratic society choose to regulate politically all social relationships? For example, although democrats might wish that a polity regulate, by means of state edicts and actions, guardian-child relations (e.g., bar the sexual abuse or physical battering of children), should a democratic state politically regulate the imparting of all religious, moral, and sexual values by guardians to children? Of course public schools inevitably impart values. But a pluralist democrat would argue that schools should impart a minimalist, democratic ideology to students, involving a capacity for critical reasoning (even about democracy itself) and a commitment to the equal rights of democratic citizens. To inculcate a thicker, more comprehensive political ideology would cross the line between democratic schooling and ideological indoctrination. While recognizing that the inability to draw definitive boundaries between the public and the private is characteristic of democratic politics, one cannot deny that such boundary drawing is essential. That is, a democratic political society depends on a democratic delimitation of the political realm, if individuals and the particular associations in which they develop their identities are to live in civil society relatively free from political interference.

WHY DOES DEMOCRATIC POLITICS DIFFER FROM ALL OTHER POLITICS?

How might one distinguish democratic politics from other forms of politics? Democratic politics necessitates contestation between divergent interests and groups who constitute their identity through social relationships in a civil society relatively autonomous from state control. But democratic politics also demands a shared commitment on the part of these relatively autonomous interests to the democratic political process and to those public goods that the polity determines to be essential to ensure the equal worth of citizenship. I term this shared agreement a minimalist, or thin, conception of the democratic social contract or public good. The contention of some postmodern theorists that a commitment to a shared, universal conception of citizenship negates the meaningful, particular identities of "difference" fails to comprehend that democratic pluralism can exist only if particularity is mediated by a delimited but definite sense of shared citizenship. If particular groups are to have an equal potential to develop their unique conceptions of the good life, they must have a sufficient claim on common resources to ensure their proportionate share of economic, social, and political power. As the plight of many inner-city Americans indicates, not all "difference" is unambiguously emancipatory.

Ironically, the postmodern celebration of radical plurality shares a strikingly similar limitation to the liberal pluralism that radicals criticize. Both postmodernist and liberal pluralists often fail to comprehend that interests are structured on a terrain of social power in which privileged groups have greater resources. Nor does either tradition advance coherent principles by which a democratic polity can critique certain interests for being hierarchically or undemocratically constituted, for to do so would be to violate the celebration of particularism at the expense of universal standards of justice.

Yet democratic societies continually alter the boundaries of acceptable democratic interests. The nature of a democratic interest or of the public provision necessary for equal citizenship, however, is not a predetermined, given concept, but rather determined through democratic political conflict.

Thus, democratic principles can at times be in conflict or tension with those of an unqualified libertarianism. For example, is it undemocratic for a democratic polity to ban voluntary associations that aim to abolish democracy, say, a Nazi party? Is Germany clearly undemocratic for doing so? Should a democratic polity ban voluntary associations that are structured in antidemocratic ways if their constituents voluntarily consent to such practices? Could a radical democratic polity ban a Catholic Church or an orthodox Judaism that continued to be both patriarchal and undemocratic in its social practices, or would this be an unjustified interference in consensual voluntary associational life? Of course, there are alternatives to a hard-and-fast yes or no answer to these queries, such as cutting off state funds or subsidies to undemocratic but voluntarily constituted institutions.

The above examples should give pause to any radical democrat who advances an imperious conception of the personal as political. The assertion that all voluntary associational life should be politically regulated in accord with the values of democracy might threaten the very plurality of social practices that radical democratic pluralists claim to value. That is, should a political majority in a democratic pluralist society be allowed to ban either the communal rearing of children or nuclear-structured families? Or should state subsidy or financing of diverse forms of child care be defended as facilitating the greatest choice in child-rearing practices, particularly when accompanied by generous paternity and maternity leave policies? A tension will always exist in a democracy between providing resources that facilitate choice and precluding choices deemed to be undemocratic or in violation of individual rights. For example, would a "democratic" defender of a "politics of difference" condemn the French state's decision to ban the ritual genital mutilation of the daughters of recent African immigrants? What of wearing veils in public schools? To judge with confidence that certain choices are definitively undemocratic may be to adhere to a conception of social solidarity and shared mores so thick that it precludes social difference, political conflict, and individual choice. But to deny that democracies have a right to construct shared norms and to defend themselves against practices that violate the equal moral worth of persons is to embrace a moral relativism incapable of defending democratic pluralism.

A radical democrat cannot claim, as do a few remaining Western advocates of an unreconstructed Marxism, that the classical Marxist tradition unambiguously values social pluralism and political contestation. A governing assumption of my book is that the inherent scarcity of time and the socially structured nature of all cooperative activity means that neither scarcity nor the division of labor will *ever* be entirely eliminated. This assumption may be viewed as an inherent "conservative" bias by some radical theorists. Nevertheless, as an antiutopian, realistic understanding of how any conceivable democratic society would be structured, it motivates my sympathetic but critical evaluation of the radical tradition. Much of the political deliberation in a society more democratic than our own would still revolve around how to curtail or reconceptualize scarcity and how to restructure the division of labor so that it can promote greater life-choice and self-realization.[12]

TOWARD A MORE NUANCED RADICAL DEMOCRATIC CONCEPTION OF LIBERALISM

A recurrent theme of my argument is that the radical tradition's rejection of politics ironically turned on its narrow interpretation of the liberal conception of politics, according to which both the liberal social contract and utilitarian traditions construed politics to be an instrumental means for satisfying private ends. In reality the classical liberalism of the seventeenth and eighteenth centuries was not solely a theory of "possessive individualism" but rather contributed to the growth of human freedom through its critique of absolutism and established religion. But the "Smithian," minimalist-government, ideological version of liberalism, which has been a powerful strand within a diverse liberal tradition, is wary of the value of politics-in-itself. According to this worldview, the desired minimalist, "nightwatchman" state facilitates the individual pursuit of particular interests in civil society, free of interference from politics and the state. Even many social-welfare liberals, who favor state intervention to promote greater equality and social security, often affirm that it is primarily in "the private realm" that human beings truly fulfill themselves.

The work of Samuel Bowles and Herbert Gintis astutely examines the mutually reinforcing weaknesses of the liberal and classical radical (particularly Marxist) conception of human interests. Bowles and Gintis contend that both liberalism and radicalism advance inadequate conceptions of agency and choice in a democratic society. Most liberal and radical analyses assume that political interests are exogenously determined and that people participate in politics to advance those pregiven interests. Both traditions fail to see how the concept of interests—what we desire or choose—is endogenously shaped by our learning experience through the political and social process. The classical liberal tradition often "naturalizes" human interests, assuming that the desire for personal accumulation and self-advancement is determined by an inherent human nature or unalterable social predicament, such as scarcity or insecurity. According to Bowles and Gintis, while liberalism offers a rich tradition of limiting the power of despotic regimes and promoting individual choice, classical liberalism offers little analysis of exploitation and fails to recognize the necessity of not just a liberal, but also a democratic community to secure human freedom. But the authors are equally scathing in their critique of the Marxist tradition's inattentiveness to the question whether or not interests are produced through democratic and free social life. In *Democracy and Capitalism*, Bowles and Gintis downplay the pluralist neo-Marxism of the 1970s to which their own work significantly contributed, choosing to emphasize that Marxism as a whole has denigrated the role of democratic learning and choice in the shaping of interests. Marxism, in their view, has usually assumed that the interests of a class are structurally predetermined by its position in the means of production. The role of politics is simply to promote the discovery and consolidation of a class consciousness that can be "read-off" from the structure of society. In the analysis of Bowles and Gintis, neither liberalism nor Marxism comprehends the dialectical manner in which social structure constrains choice, although that very constraining structure can also be transformed by human choice and collective action itself.[13]

Beyond the pursuit of particular interests and the setting of overall social distribution and norms, democratic politics is also a potential arena for the development of human capacities. Through conflict and mediation over how to organize common life, particular individuals and groups learn how to reason, imagine, and evaluate regarding both their own and the public good. As Bowles and Gintis put it, politics at its best is not just about "who gets what from whom" but it is also about "who we become." That is, politics produces people through a process of learning and choosing.[14] Benjamin Barber has eloquently articulated how a vigorous democratic politics can lead to the transformation of individual and group interests through the self-reflective, evaluative nature of human dialogue.[15] *Strong Democracy*'s attack on the narrow individualism of liberal-rights discourse shares, however, the radical tradition's underestimation of the importance of civil, political, and social rights as both procedural and substantive guarantees that each citizen can participate equally in the transformative process of "democratic talk."[16]

The radical acceptance of an instrumental liberal conception of politics led to the assumption that when the intensity of particular interests is curtailed by the general will (Rousseau), mediated by a neutral state (Hegel), or eliminated by the abolition of classes (Marx and Lenin), then the need for politics will wither away. But would regional, ethnic, racial, or sexual conceptions of social identity—and thereby social interests—necessarily decline in a world of decreased economic inequality? Even in the most egalitarian of radical democracies, in which differentials in power among individuals and groups would have been decreased by previous democratic struggles, public disputes would remain over both public policy and social values. Is there one true radical democratic answer to the policy issues posed by euthanasia or surrogate motherhood? Although radical democrats would agree that the public/ private distinction is a social construct, would all concur as to how to draw the boundary between action that should be publicly regulated and action best left to the choice of individuals or autonomous groups in civil society? And although universal agreement on such social dilemmas probably will never be achieved, even if it were, would it not eliminate the potential for human self-development through democratic participation? That is, would not such a consensus achieve the static society of boring equilibrium which both Mill and de Tocqueville feared liberal materialism, without a vigorous public life, would engender? If one views participation as not only a means for achieving a good society but also an end-in-itself that enables people to deliberate collectively about the nature of their public life, then why would a postpolitical society be desirable?

In contrast to both the predominant liberal and radical conceptions, politics cannot adequately be understood as a simple reflection of given material interests. Not only do "ideal interests" play a critical role in politics (e.g., normative values and sexual, racial, or national conceptions of identity); but as Max Weber argued in "The Sociology of World Religions," it is often our *ideas*, the layperson's ontology of how the world works, that structure both our ideal and material interests: "Not ideas, but material and ideal interests directly govern men's conduct. . . . Yet very frequently the 'world images' that have been created by 'ideas' have like switchmen, determined the tracks along which action has been pushed by the dynamic of interest."[17] For example, although both Protestants and Hindus have an ideal interest in salvation—and in acquiring the material status necessary for salvation—their distinct "ideas" of salvation, Protestant predestination versus Hindu reincarnation, lead to radically divergent conceptions of the type of social action commensurate with the individual's ideal interests. Likewise, democratic politics involves not just collective deliberation on our own material and ideal interests, but also deliberation about public ideas and how those values can best be institutionalized. That is, we argue politically about how the world functions and what moral purposes those functions should serve.

Since Aristotle's *Politics*, many political analysts have conceived politics as the master "science" of all other social practices and group interests because it orders their rival claims over scarce resources (e.g., material, status, or positional goods). Modern political rule itself arises from the problems posed by the diversity of social interests in a functionally differentiated society. The problem of political obligation in part develops out of the dilemma of how to achieve relative social cohesion amid social diversity. How can wide agreement on the common rules of the political game be achieved when the players are so diverse in background? Only through democratic political activity can distinct collectivities be reconciled and occasionally reshaped, by according them recognition and access to resources proportionate to their politically negotiated status within the social order as a whole. Nor do democracies tolerate all interests as being in accord with the principles of a democratic society. Democracies, by formal or informal constitutional means, often ban the interests of a majority in dictatorship or in the oppression of minorities because the tolerance of such interests would preclude the future exercise of democratic choice itself.[18] Today the American polity is reconceptualizing the relative interests and responsibilities of mothers, fathers, and the community as a whole in the rearing of children. Political struggles also center on the state's role in preventing the battering of women by men. Although democratic societies continually debate whether the structure of certain interests or social relationships in civil society violates core democratic values (and therefore should be restructured or abolished), democratic theory has yet to reflect systematically on what structure "autonomous" interests in civil society must have if they are to be accorded the legal protection of a liberal democratic state.

Intuitively, such reflection would begin with the traditional radical critique of liberal pluralism's defense of all existing "interests," which, however, fails to recognize the inequalities of political power generated by a social order that defines as "private" social relationships that undemocratically give power to some over others. The radical critique of these relationships is that they are undemocratic because the social actors involved have not freely deliberated on the structure of those institutions nor freely chosen their positions within them (whether those relationships be the structural subordination of workers to capitalists in the economy or of women to men in a patriarchal family). The democratic justification for the alteration or elimination of a particular interest is that it thwarts an identifiable social group's capacity for self-development and political participation. But the democratization of a previously undemocratically structured interest must also rest on the conviction that the decisions of that organization or interest are binding on the members that constitute that association and that options for exit from that association are severely limited or have dire consequences. Thus, Robert Dahl, Michael Walzer, and other advocates of workplace democracy contend that a corporation is not constituted by voluntary acts of free contract among managers and workers but by binding systems of power and authority that should be subject to democratic deliberation by the firms' employees.[19]

An attractive and plausible radical democracy would need to overcome mainstream liberalism's blindness to both the inequality of power among interests and to the internally undemocratic structure of many social interests. But radical democratic theory and practice would also need to borrow significantly from the liberal tradition in order to develop sufficient guarantees for the relative autonomy of those interests deemed to be in minimal accord with basic democratic principles. Without a guarantee that the social projects in which individuals have voluntarily invested themselves will be respected and protected by the democratic state, it is hard to imagine how a risk-taking, industrious citizenship would develop. In order for a society to be able to provide a sense of security for its members and for the associational projects in which they invest their energies, a relatively stable consensus must exist regarding its constitutional norms and the permissible internal structure of social interests.

THE POTENTIAL LIBERAL CONTRIBUTION TO
RADICAL DEMOCRATIC POLITICS

Radical democrats often underestimate how, beginning in the seventeenth century, the emergence in Western Europe of liberal conceptions of religious, associational, and economic freedoms grounded in a civil society independent of the state, not only promoted human freedom but also engendered a social dynamic that would lead the disenfranchised to demand the suffrage in the name of individual rights.[20] But, as Marx contended in *On the Jewish Question*, emancipating religious, economic, and cultural relations from direct state control did not necessarily democratize these social relations of civil society. The core difference between a radical and liberal pluralism is that the former acknowledges how inequalities of social and economic power erode the democratic principle that each voice counts for one and only one. Too often in liberal democratic capitalist societies, interests have influence proportionate to their economic or cultural resources rather than to their democratic numbers.

But the politics of one dollar-one vote is not the only manner in which liberal pluralism finds itself at odds with a more democratic pluralism. Liberal pluralism also fails to critique as undemocratic hierarchical power relations within the institutions of civil society. By accepting economic contracts as purely voluntary acts and by ignoring the constraints that unequal access to resources places on contractual bargainers, liberal pluralism limits politics too narrowly to the formal realm of representative state authority. It fails to recognize, for example, that corporate firms are hierarchical institutions whose decisions have binding authority over their members. The relationships among members of a firm are not determined by voluntary contract, except for the initial hiring of an employee who then works at the will of the employer. Even traditional neoclassical economic theories of the firm admit that although firms relate externally to one another through contractual bargaining, internally they are organized by hierarchical chains of command. Capitalist firms, by their very social organization, implicitly admit that planning and relations of authority are more efficient than the use of market mechanisms to govern investment and the organization of the labor process. That is, private corporate firms plan their investments and structure their labor process through a command structure rather than myriad numbers of individual contractual bargains.[21] Apologists for workplace hierarchy contend that workers can always choose to exit from a given firm (assuming the existence of a tight labor market). But what this analysis ignores is that workers can never opt out of the structural relationship of being subordinate to corporate managers who control the very capital that permits the worker to labor.

Of course, as the command economies of Eastern Europe discovered, markets can be effective mechanisms for ascertaining supply and demand and comparative costs of production. But the chaos of these allegedly "planned" economies, which failed to make intelligent use of markets and economic incentives, does not mean that complex economies do not need to plan. As Keynes definitively demonstrated, no set of present prices and interest rates can determine future economic behavior. Therefore, all investment—the planning of the future structure of a firm—involves calculated risk-taking rather than certain bargains. Decisions that are both risky and binding should involve a considerable say by those they affect. That is, a political and economic democrat is committed to the proposition that workers should have a strong voice in firm management, while other citizens influence production through demand in the product market and through the macro-economic and monetary policy of representative governments that heavily influence overall economic behavior. The precise nature and balance among these institutions would, of course, be subject to democratic choice and periodic reordering.

Carole Pateman makes a similar argument regarding the absence of democratic participation in contractual arrangements, focusing on the alleged "voluntary" nature of the traditional marriage contract. Such contracts assume that women marry voluntarily. Yet the absence of female economic independence and publicly financed child care, combined with continued legal and moral defense of male economic and physical dominance within marriage, denies many women an equal voice in the constitution of social relations within marriage and family life.[22]

But Rousseau and Marx went beyond democratic critique of relations of power within civil society by assuming that if such relations were democratized social conflict would wither away—or at least recede to the point where formal legal or state institutions would no longer be needed to mediate conflict. Yet there is a profound difference between democratizing social relationships and freeing them from divergent interests and conflict. By conflating a shared interest in democratic decision-making with transparent, consensual modes of agreement, the radical tradition conflated social democracy with social unity. At a minimum, it envisioned sororal and fraternal bonds sufficiently strong that differences could be mediated by spontaneous social relations, analogous to the idealized operation of a healthy family, rather than by formal legal and political institutions.

Such a rejection of the need for any fixed institutional structure characterizes Roberto Ungar's excessively antiinstitutionalist conception of a fluid, "anti-necessitarian" politics in which the distinction between structure-maintaining and structure-transforming behavior is completely abolished.[23] Ungar's vision of a permanent politics of transformation, though explicitly breaking with the postpolitical project of the radical tradition, eerily resembles the hostility of radical theorists toward reflection on the need for a basic institutional and constitutional structure through which conflict can be mediated. That is, the democratic or general will cannot be spontaneously and continuously reinvented; it must be embodied in shared norms regarding democratic procedures and public goods. Not only does Ungar's project of permanent revolution threaten the security of the particular associational projects in which people invest themselves; it also fails to comprehend the role of stable democratic institutions in facilitating social learning through the institutionalization of memory. Time will always be scarce and the transference of knowledge about social roles through political and social institutions is an economy of scale that a radical democratic society would probably choose not to forego in its entirety.

Of course, as Bruce Ackerman has argued, there will always be "republican" moments within relatively stable constitutional regimes in which a majority chooses to transform certain constitutional norms.[24] But if there are no such norms to transform with caution, then it is hard to imagine a democratic populace living under conditions of restrained conflict. Such basic rules of the democratic game can only be transformed when a constitutionally determined majority or supra-majority deems them a barrier to the future of the democratic regime. The incessant democratic self-transformation that Ungar desires threatens to engender the very insecurity of a politics of permanent revolution that he claims to reject.

Thus, the radical critique of liberal pluralism did not give birth to a coherent vision of radical pluralism because radical theorists conflated the shared commitment to democratic norms with universal agreement on a comprehensive set of human interests. Yet, as anyone knows who has participated in a relatively egalitarian political community, such as a union local, school board, or community organization, while political equality may attenuate the brutality of political conflict, these outposts of democratic participation are often characterized by spirited political disagreement and contestation. What makes a democratic political regime distinct from such voluntary associations is that members of a polity frequently do not have the ability to exit voluntarily. Of if they do, the costs in social dislocation and the breaking of communal ties is far greater those of leaving a voluntary association within that society. Thus democrats contend that decisions that have binding influence over the members of an association should be made democratically. But contending that, say, citizens should have an equal political voice in the determination of transportation policy in no way implies that the citizenry will agree on whether or not mass transit is preferable to private passenger vehicles. That is, a polity could eliminate the structural bias that the auto corporations and highway lobby have over energy and transportation policy and still disagree over the most desirable transit policy.

Of course, such equal voice can only be established *in potentia* in a democratic society, because some citizens will prove more persuasive than others within the arena of democratic politics. Some will take a more active interest in politics than will others. Ironically a passage that traditional Marxists cite from Trotsky as evidence of the postpolitical nature of life under communism, renders self-evident the reductionist fallacy of equating all politics with class conflict. What Trotsky describes as the postpolitical conflicts of a classless communist society might more aptly be described as highly political, and likely to give rise to disagreement between identifiable social and political interests. Trotksy argued that under communism, although politics would not exist, conflict would:

> There will be the struggle for one's opinion, for one's project, for one's taste. In the measure in which political struggles will be eliminated—and in a society where there are no classes, there will be no such struggles—the liberated passions will be channelized into techniques, into construction which also includes art. . . . All forms of life, such as the cultivation of land, the planning of human habitations, the building of theaters, the methods of socially educating children, the solution of scientific problems, the creation of new styles will vitally engross all and everybody. People will divide into "parties" over the question of a new gigantic canal, or the distribution of oases in the Sahara (such a question will exist too), over the regulation of the weather and the climate, over a new theater, over chemical hypotheses, over two competing tendencies in music, and over a best system in sports.[25]

Considering that environmental policy, the location and financing of sports and cultural facilities, and the nature of public works all involve the authoritative allocation of social goods and values, it is no wonder that in both less and more affluent societies such issues are central to politics, even if the attendant conflicts do not always neatly cleave along class lines. That is, equal political voice does not eliminate political choice among positional and status, as well as economic, goods, although it might yield more equitable and humane democratic choice. All political scientists in the Department of Political Science at the People's University of Berkeley might be tenured and thereby equally empowered. But not all of them would be able to have offices with full views of San Francisco Bay, unless the nature of space and architecture were transformed beyond our current imagination—or at great cost or inefficient space utilization (e.g., a building with only bay-facing windows.) At best, the greater base-line social equality provided by democratic provision of public goods would yield the mutual respect necessary for the stable functioning of a democracy. But in such a relatively egalitarian society, polyarchy would truly rule, as ever-shifting majorities would rule on the immediate questions of the day while the resultant, temporary minorities would endeavor to create new alliances and fight on for another day and another issue.

Radical democratic pluralism envisions a more egalitarian distribution of resources and education and the democratization of "private" decisions that are clearly social in their consequences. But to remain political, a radical conception of democracy must meet three conditions: first, it must grant a relative autonomy to particular social interests; second, it must develop, by democratic means, regulating principles of the social order; and third, it must allow for plural conceptions of the good. These are the conditions necessary for any democratic politics, radical or otherwise. Finally, any radical democratic theory of *politics* must strive toward a democratic consensus on the structure of democratic and undemocratic interests. Although such a consensus will shift over time, it should be relatively stable and subject only to gradual and deliberate transformation. Citizens would be reluctant to invest time and energy in particular associational projects if such projects were easily transformed or obliterated by a temporary majority or an interventionist state that frequently changed its definition of what constitutes a democratic interest.

THE RADICAL CANON'S HOSTILITY TO PLURALISM

This book treats the radical impulse to transcend politics historically through an examination of the postpolitical visions held by major figures in that tradition. It claims neither to offer an exhaustive exegesis of each theorist's work nor to offer completely innovative readings. Rather, critical exegesis serves a different, dual purpose: first, of illuminating a common anti-political thematic, manifested in distinct ways, which has been ignored or denied by radical theorists; and second, to inform the project of reconstructing a radical democratic theory of politics which advances a realistic conception of politics in a feasible society more democratic and egalitarian than our own.

Rousseau, Hegel, Marx, and Lenin concurred that classical liberalism naturalizes the atomized and acquisitive individualism of modern marketplace societies into a static conception of human nature. They believed that the social institutions that human interdependence creates, but that human beings do not democratically control, alienated the human potential for more cooperative modes of social organization. But although viewed by some as patron saints of "radical democracy," these theorists did not conceptualize a further democratization of political life but rather the transcendence of politics through the creation of societies characterized by minimal social conflict and universally shared conceptions of the public or human good.

These theorists shared a hostility to the pluralism of modern society, or in Hegel's case, a profound ambivalence toward that pluralism. Their deep concern for social harmony entailed the erosion, if not eradication, of the particular communities and projects in which people invest themselves and develop their particular identities. In addition to these four figures in the radical canon, the book considers Hannah Arendt as an unacknowledged but powerful and influential precursor of strands of contemporary "communitarian" and "republican" political theory. Authors such as Arendt, Michael Sandel, and Alasdair MacIntyre pose a special case for my argument. On the one hand, Arendt and the communitarians join the radical tradition in rejecting the priority liberalism places on the defense of individual rights and private interests. On the other hand, the communitarians break with the radical tradition by claiming to value most highly the life of politics. I argue, however, that Arendt and, in a similar fashion, most communitarians fail to advance a plausible conception of democratic politics precisely because they share the radical tradition's hostility to particular interests, as well the radical tradition's proclivity for monistic conceptions of the good.

I focus on the radical tradition's hostility to politics partly because of the unique antinomy between radicalism's democratic critique of the undemocratic structure of liberal society and radicalism's vision of a solidaristic society that would transcend the need for political institutions. My purpose is to explore why "it is no accident," to borrow a phrase from teleological Marxists, that the radical tradition, despite its democratic critique of liberalism, never succeeded in envisioning and instantiating a freer and more democratic society than that of liberal democratic capitalism. Obviously, the accidents of history partly explain this failure. Socialist revolutions succeeded only in less developed nations where, as Michael Walzer has pointed out, the revolutionary party substituted itself for a weak or barely existing working class. In countries where a powerful working-class movement existed, social democratic, labor, and communist parties achieved reforms that enriched the democratic practices of liberal democratic capitalist regimes but partly demobilized radical democratic impulses.[26]

There certainly have been dissident radical voices that differed with the dominant radical, postpolitical vision. The pluralist values of the British ethical socialists R. H. Tawney, George Orwell, and Harold Laski come immediately to mind.[27] Thus, the weakness of the Marxist intellectual tradition in Britain may not have been the tragedy that Perry Anderson believes it to have been.[28] The pluralist critique of classical Marxism offered by Ernesto Laclau and Chantal Mouffe, drawing on the "anti-essentialism" of discourse theory to critique Marxian teleological theories of history and structuralist theories of consciousness, illuminates the authoritarian implications of imputing objective class consciousness from an allegedly objective class structure.[29] But it took the simultaneous conjuncture of the crisis of traditional social democracy (engendered by the slowdown in the post-World War II boom that began in the early 1970s), the emergence of mass social movements based on identities of race, gender, ethnicity, and sexual preference, and the collapse of authoritarian communism to create social space for the growth of radical pluralist thought. Ironically, a significant wing of this emerging radical pluralist current, which advocates an unqualified "politics of difference," questions the "enlightenment" project of universal citizenship and thereby the desirability, or even possibility, of developing a moral vision and strategy for a new majoritarian left politics. If the radical tradition tragically affirmed solidarity over difference, the postmodern radical celebration of difference eschews the limited but real forms of social solidarity that must be constructed politically if a democratic polity is to empower different social groups equally.

A reductive caricature of my argument might place it within a line of neoconservative criticism, which runs from Jacob Talmon to the French *nouvelle philosophes*. Talmon, Bernard-Henri Lévy, and André Glucksmann contend that the radical tradition was never committed to a democratic project, but only to the authoritarian imposition of elite values on ordinary people.[30] But even a cursory reading of Rousseau and Marx illuminates the emancipatory impulse behind their critique of absolutism, the dehumanization of hierarchical forms of production, and inequality's evisceration of democratic deliberation. The critical problem in these works is not one of intent or motivation, but of conceiving of a reductionist version of liberalism as the only possible form of pluralism. That is, Rousseau and Marx never asked the question that challenges democratic theorists and activists to this day: Can pluralism and solidarity coexist, or must society choose between difference and universality?

Rousseau's social contract cannot simply be dismissed as a vision of authoritarian political suppression. Rather, it represents the most rigorous but problematic investigation of the procedural nature of democratic deliberation and democratic legitimacy. Rousseau openly asks the question, Why should members of a democratic polity voluntarily obey laws that they themselves have opposed? Nor is Rousseau's concern with a regime's inculcation of shared democratic values irrelevant in an age where the fragmentation of liberal polities threatens to render a politics of democratic equality impossible. But in assessing those procedural, cultural, and economic preconditions of democracy, Rousseau overemphasized the threat of particularity to democratic identity. Fearing the centrifugal impulses of an emerging marketplace society, Rousseau opted for the bonds of a solidaristic, small-scale community instead of the mediated and partially shared identity that citizens of a complex postindustrial polity can only construct through democratic public life.

Marx well understood that an absence of democracy in the authoritative institutions of civil society, particularly the workplace, would produce a society of freedom of contract and equal formal suffrage which obfuscated despotism in the workplace and the veto-power of capital over democratic politics. Yet his ultimate vision of a communism that transcended all forms of scarcity, thereby creating a society of spontaneous mutualism, prevented Marx from realizing that political conflict is inherent to the purposive structuring of democratic and egalitarian social institutions. Only if one assumes that time is not scarce, that intergenerational memory needs no institutionalization, and that any task can be performed by anyone, without any need for sustained training or specialization, can one argue that political deliberation can be eliminated from the organization of social life. It is doubtful that the human species could ever achieve all these preconditions for a postpolitical society. Marx's vision of full communism goes beyond that of democratizing control over the division of labor and of the allocation of time, to a society where both the scarcity of time and the specificity of social roles are eliminated. This excessive utopianism led one of Marx's more brilliant and orthodox disciples, Leon Trotsky, to contend that "the social construction" of the individual under communism would enable "the average human type

[to] rise to the heights of an Aristotle, a Goethe, or Marx."[31] But would we deem such beings, even if "created" by human effort, to be human? Is this genetically engineered, cyborg utopia "a world more attractive?"

The radical tradition constructively highlighted the difficulties modern pluralism confronts in attempting to construct a strong sense of the public good. But in a functionally differentiated society, the common good cannot be imposed through the obliteration of society's constituent parts if freedom and politics are to be sustained. Rather, the defining of what we share as citizens can develop only through political negotiation, confrontation, and conciliation among particular interests, subcommunities, and distinct conceptions of the public good—all of which can themselves be transformed through political participation. This is the very stuff of politics.

THE ANTIPOLITICS OF EVEN "POLITICAL" THEORY

Contemporary theorists as diverse as Hannah Arendt, John Gunnell, Sheldon Wolin, Benjamin Barber, and Bonnie Honig have developed a similar theme that political theory is profoundly ambivalent toward the very subject—politics—about which it claims to theorize (be it conservative, liberal, or radical political theory).[32] Most political traditions' vision of a good society, according to the common themes of these analyses, involves the devaluation of politics because political theorists too often endeavor to discover fixed, foundational principles that will ground a stable—and therefore antipolitical—regime. There is considerable merit to this argument, because the temptation to locate fixed, permanent principles or laws of politics is an inevitable danger in theorizing about a practical activity that involves more the *phronesis* of contextualized judgment than the simplistic application of abstract principles to static situations.

The antipolitical impulse in political theory may be traced back to the founding classical patriarchs. Plato's adherence to an objective conception of the good continually threatens to reduce politics to philosophical contemplation. Aristotle rejects Plato's conception of a philosopher-king determining both the division of labor and the educational system—the very means of social reproduction—but largely because Aristotle deems these practices to be politically unsustainable. But his alternative of "the polity" or mixed regime as a second-best solution envisions a stable political equilibrium between the wealthy few and the small property-owning many, thus excluding women, male laborers, and slaves from the political regime. Aristotle desires to approximate, realistically, Plato's politics of objective virtue. Although he hints at the developmental potential of political participation, he is primarily concerned with the legitimacy such participation confers on a political aristocracy chosen by small property-owners who have only a limited electoral voice in the elite's selection.

The liberal tradition undoubtedly widened the arena of political activity by protecting freedom of thought and association from the suppression of absolutist regimes. Contemporary radical theorists must be careful not to caricature liberalism as solely a defense of marketplace "possessive individualism," if they are to be decent intellectual historians and if they are to appropriate the best of the liberal tradition.[33] The social strata that fought for a liberal political regime cared more about freedom of religion and limited government than about narrowly preserving property rights—though the freeing of property rights from feudal and monarchical interference played an important role in the rise of liberalism.

Because there can be no possibility for democratic politics unless the power of the state is circumscribed by institutionally guaranteed rights, within the logic of liberalism there has been (a sometimes muted) *leitmotiv* that inspired subsequent democratic social movements: if government's legitimacy can be derived only from the voluntary consent of the people, then the people eventually will desire not only the guarantees of civil freedoms but also an equal voice in the making of the laws that govern them. Thus John Stuart Mill's evolution toward participatory democracy grew out of his liberal convictions and, as Richard Aschraft and James Tully demonstrate in their rich intellectual history of Lockeian liberalism, the logic of Rousseau's social contract is not as radically divergent from the logic of Locke's as has been traditionally conceived. After all, the Levellers and Diggers emerged simultaneously with liberal movements to circumscribe the power of the Crown.[34] Nevertheless, the dominant "Smithian" ideological form of liberalism, which remained the hegemonic form of liberalism through the nineteenth century, conceived of voluntary transactions in civil society as constituting the good life, with politics as a necessary condition for the preservation of the freedom of nonpolitical associational life.

The conservative tradition, particularly in its cultural guise beginning with Burke, urged elites to bear the dreary burdens of politics, even within decadent democracies, so that the prescriptive traditions of a religious and paternal order could be upheld. The burden is to be borne because leaving politics to the *demos* would threaten the existence of higher philosophical and cultural values. But this work of political prophylaxis against an incipient democratic order is continually threatened by the inexorable democratic sociological tide it aims to forestall. The conservative search for moral and religious unity, epitomized by Thomas Hooker, depended on mass, deferential acceptance of a hierarchical order ordained by God and a belief that social status neatly mirrored a natural distribution of abilities. The radical search for a universal human identity that would transcend conflict stood the conservative view of accepted hierarchy on its head. The radical vision of a postpolitical society is grounded not in conservative respect of hierarchy and tradition, but in a faith that a society free of domination would enable radical individualism to be in spontaneous accord with collective self-determination ("the free development of each is the precondition for the free development of all"). The radical search for transcendent unity engages in a democratic inversion (a "standing-on-its-head" in Marxian terms) of the conservative longing for a consensual moral and social hierarchy.[35]

According to Barber, Honig, and other critics of Rawls, social welfare liberals attempt to discover fixed distributive principles in accord with allegedly universal principles that any disinterested, autonomous reasoner about justice would discern. That such a reasoning procedure could be performed by any representative citizen violates the agonal essence of politics itself. This heuristic procedure, the critics argue, contradicts the social reality that the struggle for political justice occurs among groups who do not share agreement on a comprehensive scheme of distributive justice.[36]

Among theorists of the antipolitical nature of political theory, the radical tradition usually is criticized more gently. Arendt eschews Marx's alleged economism but praises the syndicalist and council communist tradition of workers' councils. Barber draws heavily on Rousseau's critique of rights-based liberalism and representative government, though he cautions against Rousseau's "unitary" conception of solidarity. And Nietzsche is frequently appropriated by postmodern theorists as the theoretical fountainhead for a radical politics of a nonessentialized, decentered, self-constructed political will. Not that this softer critique of Rousseau and Marx is completely unjustified, though, as I discuss in the conclusion, I doubt whether Nietzsche can be uncritically appropriated for a radical *democratic* project. The radical critique of liberalism has deep roots in Rousseau's commitment to self-determination through collective sovereignty. Contrary to uninformed ideological critiques of Marx, his project was not one of promoting human homogenization but of a flowering of individuality through communal participation. Alan Gilbert terms this project the search for "democratic individuality."[37] Rousseau did not advocate a Talmonesque totalitarian subservience to an omnipotent state but rather the creation of a democratic state in which citizens actively concurred in—if not originated—the basic constitutional norms of their existence. Thus, not only have participatory democratic theorists drawn on Rousseau's and Marx's conception of democratic individuality, but the democratic revolutions of the late-eighteenth and nineteenth centuries and the subsequent labor and socialist movements explicitly acknowledged these theorists as inspirations. The relationship between mass social movements and intellectual currents is a complex one. But if democratic social movements are, in part, intellectually indebted to Rousseau and Marx, so, at least indirectly, were the self-proclaimed radical regimes that contended that political conflict no longer existed in their virtuous societies. In the name of that assertion, dissent was repressed by a party or state that claimed to instantiate true human interests.

Thus, the historical legacy of Rousseau's democratic vision and Marx's concept of emancipated labor is Janus-faced. Both theorists came down too heavily on the side of shared identity and common interests within the democratic dialectic of diversity and unity. In an age of growing social fragmentation, one of the most undertheorized issues in contemporary democratic theory is how extensive shared values, norms, and interests must be in order to underpin a functioning democratic order. Rousseau's analysis of the social contract represents the most sustained investigation of this issue. His emphasis on the shared commitment to communal norms and decisions renders almost mute his occasional recognition that the very necessity for democratic politics arises from divergent interests and opinions. Rousseau feared the centrifugal force of the division of labor and the proliferation of social roles characteristic of an emergent commercial modernity. In reaction to this fear, he offered a vision of social solidarity as an undifferentiated society of self-sufficient artisans and peasants whose intense sense of citizenship outweighs whatever minor differences in individual opinion they might have. These potential differences, Rousseau argued, should not be exacerbated by active membership in strong secondary associations. Rousseau's overly solidaristic vision of democracy culminates in citizens periodically gathering in a pastoral setting—preferably peasants resting under a tree—to reaffirm their commitment to shared but simple communal norms. This picture of solidarity starkly contrasts with his analysis of the liberal social contract as an instrumental agreement in which members pledge to obey a neutral sovereign because it enables them to advance their particular, private interests.

Any sophisticated analyst of Marx knows that he considered the desire for economic equality a product of bourgeois society's commodification of human value. Marx did not believe that each human being had a true need to possess the same amount of material goods as did everyone else; rather, they had a true need to have equal control over their creative labor. Marx envisioned an emancipatory society as transcending bourgeois notions of economic equality. But he also argued that an emancipated society would move beyond the need for formal legal and political institutions, a utopian vision that would have dystopian consequences. Not that Marx believed that all mediation of social disputes would disappear, but he held that in a truly human society these disputes could be solved through a spontaneous, mutual accommodation that eschewed the need for formal state institutions. Decisions would be made in a communist society; but such authority would result from a spontaneous process of mediation, similar to the way that close friends and family ideally work out their problems. For Marx, the need for permanent mediating institutions resulted only from the functional need of a dominant class to manage conflict in accord with its narrow interests. In the absence of an identifiable and permanent ruling class, there would be no need for a falsely universal set of norms or laws to legitimate a non-existent dominant class. Thus the state—and the law—would wither away.

This posing of a sharp disjunction between an intensely solidaristic society and a crudely instrumental liberalism in certain ways prefigures the overly polarized contemporary debate between communitarians and Rawlsian liberals, a significant cottage industry in political theory that largely rests on an unproductive mutual caricature of positions. The false dichotomy between individual liberty and community is evidenced by neither side consistently adhering to its own ideological or methodological commitments. Communitarians dismiss the instrumental, anticommunal nature of liberal rights. But communitarians who are committed to a modern, pluralist, democratic community (not all communitarians are) cannot politically avoid a concern for the rights that protect the particular subcommunities in which we partially develop ourselves.[38] Rawlsian liberals, on the other hand, sometimes argue as if they can deduce a theory of rights from foundational metaphysical or ontological truths about the nature of the self. But Rawls himself quickly responded to his critics by arguing that the original position is simply a heuristic for explaining the commitment to individual rights implicit in our own democratic community. Thus Rawls appears to admit that rights cannot be ontologically or metaphysically grounded apart from the pragmatic practices of a democratic community.[39]

In the final analysis, Rawls claims to be explicating the situated, shared understandings of a democratic community, while democratic communitarians have never explicitly denied the need for rights to guarantee the existence of a plurality of self-constituted communities. This "overlapping consensus" among democrats—both communitarian and liberal—reflects the fact that democracy involves a continual political redefinition of the relationship between the shared values of citizenship and the interests and identities individuals develop within the particular subcommunities of the polity. Such identities, in a pluralist democracy, need to be protected, to some politically determined degree, from interference by the state and majoritarian decisions. Despite its explicit hostility to liberalism's universalist and "homogenizing" conception of human rights, much of postmodern theory, which recently has supplanted communitarianism as the cutting edge practice of self-defined "political" theorists, remains, as Seyla Benhabib argues, parasitic on a supraliberal tolerance of diversity.[40] In addition to this hidden affinity with liberal pluralism, many postmodern advocates of a "politics of difference" further reproduce liberalism's lack of concern about the shared commitments and public goods necessary for an equally empowering citizenship.

The practice of celebrating one's theoretical craft at the expense of concrete normative reflection on historical and empirical political developments is, unfortunately, indulged in even by many theorists who claim to rescue politics for political theory. Whether it is Sandel's search for the good, Arendt's longing for agonal discourse, Barber's proposals for "strong democratic talk," or Honig's promotion of a politics of *virtù* which "desituates" and politicizes the self, these "political" theorists often conflate metaphilosophical discourse about the nature of politics with the real world of politics. That is, they often substitute a love of their own *virtù* (theoretical discourse) for a theoretical-practical analysis and critique of institutions of power. Any such viable critique must be grounded in an understanding of the structure of social institutions and the potential for change they embody, as well as the obstacles they pose for democratic agency. Political theory must ask in whose interest it is to transform political power relations and institutions. To say that existing institutions should be decentered or reconstructed on behalf of the politics of "the committed" does not tell us who will do the reconstructing—and why and how they will transform existing structures of domination.

These theorists of "the political" generally express an affinity for a republican, Machiavellian vision of a constantly shifting politics of necessity which, at its best, promotes the public good. Yet, as is true for Machiavelli, these theorists are often more intrigued by the rhetoric of politics than with advancing a substantive vision of a workable democratic order. Machiavelli clearly underdefined the good regime—is it one where a skillful prince benefits himself or the many—or both? Is popular benefit promoted by the checks and balances of the republic or by the untrammeled skill of the prince? In similar fashion, contemporary republican and postmodern defenders of "politics" offer at best a vague concept of a good regime. Too often the rhetorical brilliance of a metapolitics of "decentered" discursive practices overwhelms any concrete political practice that addresses the needs and desires of ordinary people. Most citizens, if not completely turned off from an overly instrumental, self-interested politics, tend to be politically concerned with this-worldly political and economic issues rather than purely metaphysical and ontological questions. Unless political theory rejoins the tradition of social theory in which normative analysis is informed by a sensitivity to history, social structure, and public policy, political philosophy will remain a specialized—and nonpublic—branch of academic life.

THE STRUCTURE AND PURPOSE OF THE PROJECT

In this book's examination of the radical hostility to politics, Chapter 2 investigates Rousseau's fear that the emerging marketplace of particular interests would strip citizens of the ability to comprehend the general interest of society. Rousseau's belief that the modern individual's involvement in particular projects and associations would have to be radically curtailed if the general will were to be upheld, would have a profound effect on future radical ambivalence toward social particularism.

The inclusion of Hegel as a theorist who influenced, but was not of, the radical tradition may be dismissed by some readers. Hegel is often conceived by the radical tradition itself as simply a defender of the "rationality" of the Prussian bureaucratic state, or at best a defender of autonomous life in civil society against the Enlightenment impulse toward universal identity. But such a reading ignores how much Marx, for his teleology of history, critique of the market, and concept of the universal class, owed to Hegel. One need only have a cursory knowledge of contemporary communitarian thought to recognize the often-unacknowledged Hegelian legacy. Hegel not only dismissed as an intellectual myth the social contract conception of a society constructed by free and rational choosers, but he also rejected as liberal ideology the belief that contracts could "go all the way down" and provide the moral foundation of a free society. Contemporary communitarian critiques of individualistic conceptions of identity are parasitic on Hegel's social conception of moral development. In this conception individuals are not born free and rational choosers but are products of the cultural and moral ethos—the *Sittlichkeit*—of their times. Thus, Chapter 3 analyzes Hegel's belief that the particular interests and communities within civil society could coexist and identify with a properly structured universal state, but only if these particular associations were regulated by a corporatist state bureaucracy that vigilantly guarded the state's universal interest. Participation in corporate bodies in civil society, Hegel hoped, would enable the average citizen to discern a social purpose within the pursuit of their private interests. But Hegel believed that only a small "universal class" of state functionaries could truly perceive the common good. The democratic interplay among particular interests could never achieve, on its own accord, a coherent sense of the public good.

Chapter 4 examines Marx's contention that the final victory of the truly universal class, the proletariat, would eliminate not only class conflict but also, with the transcendence of scarcity, the need for any political deliberation about social roles. Defenders of a "democratic" Marx claim that the Paris Commune—a radical, decentralized democracy in which the state served society as a whole rather than the interests of a dominant class—embodies Marx's vision of the state under first-stage communism, a society in which scarcity and thus standards of justice persist. Even if this is the case, Marx never openly acknowledged that particular social interests and associational life would persist under *either stage of communism*. Nor did he ever explicitly call for institutional guarantees—in socialist or communist societies—for freedom of association and a plurality of social identities. Although Marx asserted that individuals would develop their individuality to its fullness under communism, he also envisioned that they would share a common, unambiguous set of comprehensive human interests. Nor did Marx develop a theory of postrevolutionary politics and rights which would enable particular communities and individuals to participate in defining the social order as a whole.

Chapter 5 examines Lenin's conception of postrevolutionary society and his "scientific" conception of class consciousness and postrevolutionary administration. Contrary to most readings of Lenin, the chapter does not view *State and Revolution* as a utopian deviation from the corpus of Lenin's work, written on the eve of state power to provide the Bolshevik conception of the state a radical democratic veneer. Rather, the withering away of politics in *State and Revolution*, the chapter holds, derives from the same "scientific" view of revolutionary consciousness which informs Lenin's writings on democratic centralism and the vanguard party. Postrevolutionary administration could be performed by anyone because its tasks are technically determined by the requirements of advanced industrial production. Technicians and experts will be needed, but their work will be guided by the undivided proletarian will—a will that can only be discerned by the vanguard party.

Chapter 6 examines the work of Hannah Arendt, particularly as it prefigures many of the themes of contemporary "communitarian" and "republican" criticisms of liberalism. In contrast to the other theorists studied, Arendt defends the virtue of politics, as do most self-defined "communitarians," contending that a revival of modern politics requires the abandonment of interest-group liberalism and a return to classical conceptions of political virtue. The chapter contends that her hostility to political deliberation about the structure of socioeconomic interests—and her belief that such "social questions" should be solved by "experts"—prevents her "republican" vision of politics from being relevant to the workings of a modern democratic society.

In this work political philosophy serves, in part, as political therapy. For it will remain difficult for radical democrats to develop an adequate theory and practice of politics as long as they fail to confront their own tradition's hostility to both associational life and politics in "harmonious" or "postrevolutionary" societies. Whenever one criticizes the canonical figures in a tradition, the more subtle of their self-professed descendants discover alleged counterarguments embedded in the text of the masters themselves. If this book provokes renewed debate, particularly among those sympathetic to the radical tradition, as to whether an adequate theory of radical democratic political life can be discerned in the texts of the "founders," then it will have accomplished one of its primary tasks.

The recovery of a compelling radical vision of a just, democratic, and pluralist society is particularly urgent at a time when dominant conservative ideology claims that interference with the "natural" workings of the market can only yield greater inefficiency and inequality. At the same time, some extreme versions of a postmodern "politics of difference" imply that there can be no dialogue between radically different "identities," let alone the construction of common democratic interests. The defense of any commonly shared moral value is sometimes crudely reduced to a metaphorical attempt at establishing another power/knowledge discourse of human domination.[41] Particularist strategies of "resistance" are all that remain politically possible. But if "particular" groups or identities share nothing with "others" who have different "particular" identities, then how can a just polity be constructed? How can subordinated groups construct any moral or political alliances with one another unless they share certain common interests or human identity? Or are the concepts of emancipation or shared humanity just two more "rationalist" illusions? The political challenge in an era of growing racial, gender, and class inequalities is to develop a political project of democratic "unity through diversity." Only by reestablishing a commitment to the universal values of democratic citizenship—those civil, political, and social rights that facilitate equal participation in public life—can the diversity of human identities and of associational life in civil society be truly enriched.[42]

Such a politics of "unity through diversity," or radical democratic pluralism, remains not only the means to challenge the continued structural injustices of liberal democracy. It is also the only politics by which to challenge the lassitude of former radicals who have recently abandoned the struggle for the expansion of democracy, dispirited by two decades of conservative hegemony and left fragmentation, a fragmentation that the "politics of difference" defensively celebrates. We live in a peculiar political and cultural interregnum in which the right's project of economic deregulation and cultural conservatism has failed to engender stable growth and full employment. The paradigm of Reagan-Thatcherism is exhausted, and the end of the Cold War denies the right the option of a politics of anticommunism that papered over the emerging tensions between the core constituencies of the new right: upper-middle-class economic and social libertarians and working- and lower-middle-class cultural conservatives. But the democratic left, indirectly tarnished by the collapse of authoritarian communism and confronted by the globalization of capital which renders past Keynesian, social democratic practices of the welfare state in one nation impractical, can only be reconstructed if new forms of international solidarity and transnational political and economic institutions are constructed. In the short run, the collapse of communism has discredited the entire left in mainstream democratic politics. But in the long run, this collapse will free a pluralist left from the burden of guilt by association with the concrete manifestation of the antipluralist legacy of the radical tradition.

The Threat of Interests to the General Will

ROUSSEAU'S CRITIQUE OF PARTICULARISM

ROUSSEAU'S QUEST TO TRANSCEND POLITICAL CONFLICT

Rousseau's hostility to politics centers on his aversion to the competitive, particular interests of the emerging marketplace societies of the eighteenth century. Whereas his defense of equality primarily involves a critique of the injustices of status-based, monarchical regimes, Rousseau also criticized the inclination of the emerging interest groups of commercial society to treat politics as an instrumental means for advancing their interests at the expense of the common good. Such awareness led Rousseau to reject the liberal conception of the social contract as universal adherence to those minimally necessary sovereign laws that enable individuals to pursue their self-interest without violating the essential rights of others to life, liberty, and property. Instead of conceiving the social contract to be those universally accepted laws that maximize the individual's freedom to pursue his or her self-interest, Rousseau envisioned a social contract that would maximize the individual's capacity for autonomous self-government. Conceiving of modern individuals as socially interdependent beings who desire self-rule, Rousseau argued that the only just social order was one in which each and every citizen had an equal voice in making the basic laws.[1] Modern citizens could be truly free, Rousseau held, only if they live under such conditions of civil freedom. Yet, while astutely criticizing economic and status inequality for eroding the equal worth of a citizen's voice, Rousseau, fearing the centrifugal dynamics of an emerging pluralist, market society, devalued the importance of associational life and group rights as the primary means by which individuals develop their particular identity.

This structure of Rousseau's civil freedom—human beings obeying laws of which they are the sovereign authors—has led contemporary political theorists such as Joshua Cohen, Carole Pateman, and Jim Miller to conceive of Rousseau as the founder of modern democratic theory.[2] Although Rousseau may have been the first political theorist to outline *the form* of a democratic social contract, his obsession with social solidarity precluded his conceptualizing *the content* of modern democratic political life.[3] In a modern democratic polity the construction of the general will involves the establishment of a democratic consensus, among divergent social interests and distinct moral conceptions of the good, on those shared constitutional practices and public goods that reach beyond one's identity with a particular subcommunity.

Rousseau was the first political theorist to comprehend that if democracy were to be a stable and viable order, a commitment to its political practices and public goods would have to be an integral part of the will of each of its citizens, regardless of their propertied status. Although Rousseau acknowledged that in a free society the existence of such a shared "general will" should not obliterate individual wills, his attitude toward the role of associational life in a democratic order was profoundly ambivalent. Perhaps because he never witnessed a functioning pluralist democracy and vigorously opposed the status and economic inequalities of a commercial, monarchical society, Rousseau could not envision a democracy in which the political interactions of divergent interests forged a commitment to a common political life. In his day, status-based interests were a profound barrier to the creation of an egalitarian, democratic order; thus Rousseau never witnessed free associations playing a central role in the life of a democratic polity.

Nor did Rousseau believe that individual voluntary contractual judgments would, absent the individual's proper acculturation by extrapolitical institutions, be capable of willing a democratic order. Only through inculcation of the solidaristic mores of "the morality of the common good" would each citizen become capable of willing such an order.[4] This Catch-22—that only members of a democratic culture are capable of willing a democratic order—could be read, as Joshua Cohen has interpreted it, to be simply Rousseau's sociological insight that a democratic social order best encourages those motivations and self-understandings that would lead citizens to will a just, democratic social contract.[5] Yet both the acculturating function of the founding Legislator and the solidaristic mores of patriotism and civil religion do more than construct the cultural norms of an egalitarian pluralist democracy. They also promote a stifling social solidarity that would banish particular interests unless they were so weak, numerous, relatively equal in power, and dispersed that they could have no effect on democratic political life and state policy.[6]

Richard Fralin contends that the major role for democratic participation in Rousseau is to check the potentially self-interested behavior of government officials.[7] Rousseau makes a critical distinction between sovereignty, the approval by the people of a regime's basic laws, and government, the application of those basic laws to specific cases. This is not necessarily a radical break with subsequent democratic thought; as John Dewey argued in *The Public and Its Problems*, in representative democracy the critical question is whether the sovereign people have final say over the actions of their government.[8] Although Rousseau places ultimate sovereignty in the people, he fears that direct democratic "government" will lead citizens to advance their self-interest at the expense of the general will. If ordinary citizens were to govern, they would be overwhelmed by the temptation to apply universal laws in ways biased by their particular interests. His preferred "aristocratic" government of the dispassionate few is elected by the people, though the candidates are nominated by the government, and the universal laws this government applies in specific cases are periodically reviewed by the democratic sovereign assemblies. In form this is a thicker conception of democratic participation than envisioned by representative democracy, but it is not as direct a democracy as popular conceptions of Rousseau would have. What is strikingly absent in Rousseau is any substantive description of how the sovereign assembly makes new laws or amends existing ones.[9] Rather than describe such a process in detail, Rousseau explicitly states that lengthy deliberation on the part of the assembly would be a manifestation of a fractious decaying of social solidarity.[10]

Although Rousseau is theoretically committed to the sovereign authority of the people, he severely curtails the arena for democratic politics by denying any role for particular interests groups or subcommunities in political deliberation. A democratic society is partly constituted through popular participation in the election of government and in popular deliberation about the constitutional structure of society, the nature of the basic laws. But it is also shaped by particular interests defending their concerns in both civil society and the political arena. In a vigorous and egalitarian democratic order, a complex dialectic would persist between the activities of secondary associations and their regulation by broader democratic cultural norms and legislative practices. Although the citizens of a democracy must at times achieve a measure of reflective distance from their particular attachments in order to reason about shared institutions and practices, a complete distancing from particular identities will never be fully achieved. This mediation between particular and collective identities, and between partial interests and the common good, can only occur politically. There is no Archimedean resolution to this inherent democratic dilemma.

An exploration of Rousseau's effort to overcome the centrifugal effects of social pluralism must address the tension in his thought between grounding the modern regime in a rational social contract and his belief that such a contract must be bolstered by nonrational, emotive appeals to the passions, particularly through the mores of patriotism and civil religion. Reason, for Rousseau, is a Janus-faced quality: it alone cannot sustain the modern regime because this capacity for rational self-perfection is the very human ability that enables citizens to calculate how best to advance their own particular interest at the expense of the general will. The creative force that engenders humanity's emergence from natural freedom, reason enables the forging of the common bonds of civil freedom. But reason is also the human capacity that fosters the competitive individualism that threatens to tear civil society asunder. In Rousseau's view only the inculcation of the solidaristic mores of patriotism and civil religion can delay the inevitable declension of modern, rational citizens into competitive individuals. These mores must be institutionalized by a founding Legislator—a suprahuman being who comprehends social beings' competitive nature but transcends it by his total devotion to the common good. Without the proper founding of the Legislator, political life among competitive social beings would never give rise to the harmonious social mores essential for social cohesion.

For Rousseau the essence of both "natural freedom" and "civil freedom" is the absence of personal dependence on others. In a society characterized by a healthy civic culture, all constantly adhere to the general will, regardless of their specific interests. This civic culture of conflict-free social solidarity is best facilitated by a relatively undifferentiated political economy. Anachronistic terms such as *artisanal, pastoral,* and *petty bourgeois* best describe this economy in which "wealth should never be so great that a man can buy his neighbor, nor so lacking that a man is compelled to sell himself."[11] Personal independence can only be restored in civil society by the conscious, voluntary acceptance of the equal dependence of each on all, i.e., the social contract. "Man"[12] can only liberate himself from the chains of a competitive, particularist civil society by the conscious authorship of a solidaristic, legitimate "civil freedom": "whoso gives himself to all gives himself to none."[13]

But does Rousseau's obsession with the healthy polity's need for social solidarity—a strong and binding general will—permit him to conceptualize a compelling vision of modern politics as mediation, debate, judgment, and resolution among diverse social interests and divergent conceptions of the good? The healthy Rousseauian "citizen" appears to be a human being stripped of all his concerns for particular associations, activities, and interests, perhaps even devoid of his own personal conception of the common good. Rousseau argues that individuals would best comprehend the general will if they were so radically detached from their specific social roles that they could not communicate politically with their fellow citizens in between meetings of the sovereign assembly: "If the People, engaged in deliberation, were adequately informed, and if no means existed by which the citizens could communicate one with another, from the great number of small differences the general will would result, and the decisions reached would always be good."[14] But could such radical disinterestedness ever characterize the citizens of an actual polity—would citizens so distanced from their particular identities be recognizable as similar to ourselves? A detailed examination of what transpires in Rousseau's "periodic sovereign assemblies of the people," often interpreted as the embodiment of radical "participatory democracy," reveals that they serve as ritualistic reaffirmations of the legitimacy of the modern regime. Disputes between particular interests and individuals are relegated to the realm of "government," a realm that Rousseau contends is best run by "aristocratic" experts. He explicitly states that extensive debate and disagreement within the sovereign assemblies is a sign that particular interests pose an imminent threat to the general will.

Rousseau presciently envisioned the threats that privatism and unrestrained social pluralism posed to the social solidarity and legitimacy of the modern democratic regime. And his work remains a powerful rhetorical critique of the role inequality plays in thwarting democratic deliberation. Perhaps because he wrote at a time when the diversity of modern marketplace society still appeared preventable, Rousseau did not adequately reflect on a central modern democratic dilemma: creating unity out of diversity and vice-versa. His hostility to political conflict precluded his outlining a realistic path by which a citizenry's sense of collective obligation could develop through a vibrant, diverse, "interested" political culture.

THE DIALECTIC OF SENTIMENT AND REASON: THE HARBINGER OF CIVIL SOCIETY

Some Rousseau scholars, most recently Allan Bloom, argue that a tension exists between two Rousseaus—the "Kantian" one who grounds political legitimacy in the rational institutionalization of the categoral imperative in the general will and the "romantic" who pessimistically abandons the political project for a philosophic and aesthetic recreation of the sweet sentiment of natural existence.[15] But to draw such a radical dichotomy between "two Rousseaus" is to ignore Rousseau's explicit construction of a symbiotic relationship between sentiment and reason in the just political regime. Though Ernst Cassirer argues persuasively that the *form* of obligation in *The Social Contract* closely resembles that of Kant's categorical imperative, Cassirer is wrong to hold that Rousseau considered the rational, categorical imperative to be the form of all political will and decision.[16] Nor did Kant believe this to be so, because he recognized that moral judgment and social justice depended on particular historical and material circumstances and therefore that political judgment could not take the form of transhistorical, universal rules. Establishing a viable regime, in Rousseau's view, necessarily involves a consideration of a nation's geography, customs, and circumstances. Rousseau grounded his ideal state on conventional sentiments rather than natural reason because he did not trust the self-sufficient political power of reason. In contrast to a rationalist universalism, Rousseau's vigorous defense of patriotism against cosmopolitanism manifests his appreciation of the importance of sentiment and parochialism for the stability of a regime.

The Second Discourse rejects life in the state of nature as a model to which modern citizens can hope to return.[17] Rousseau's natural beings are "prehuman" animals whose lack of reason and the social passions, later acquired through human artifice's struggle with accident, sets them radically apart from their modern descendants. Although the prerational human animals cannot recognize the natural right in which they participate, the independence of natural freedom serves as an external standard by which to evaluate an illegitimate civil society of domination and subordination. Only rational human beings can delineate the natural rights that natural beings experience unconsciously. A central irony in Rousseau's work is that the very development of human reason—which allows humans to perceive consciously the prerational sensibilities of *amour de soi-même*—also promotes the vanity and pride that subverts the practice of natural right.[18]

This dialectical interaction of passion and reason drives human beings out of the state of nature. In the very process of satisfying human needs, which initially expand because of accidental historical developments such as population growth, reason produces new desires and needs. The beatific repose of the natural being "given over to the sole sentiment of its present existence without any idea of the future" gives way to the "petulant activity" of vanity and reason.[19] The historical growth of reason, though abolishing the "natural" mode of human existence which unconsciously fulfills the precepts of natural law, enables the modern philosopher to found in theory a regime in which the precepts of "political right" recreate, in a qualitatively new form, the independence of natural beings. Through "meditating on the first and simplest operations of the human soul,"[20] modern citizens can discover both "the two principles anterior to reason" at the foundation of natural right and how these rules of natural right can be transubstantiated into political right: "It is from these two principles, without the necessity of introducing that of sociability, that all the rules of natural right appear to me to flow: rules which reason is later forced to reestablish upon other foundations *when, by its successive developments, it had succeeded in stifling nature*" (emphases added).[21] Reason is both a "state contrary to nature," the source of modernity's depravity, and the ultimate means for the philosophical—if not the political—construction of the just regime.

Reason, however, can only serve as a sufficient political guide for a few "true philosophers" and legislators. Humans, according to Rousseau, are not by nature social beings; nor can political life alone generate a commitment by democratic citizens to the general will. Unrestrained reason is likely to promote schemes for personal gratification at the expense of the common good. Thus, the will of the many must be properly constrained and conditioned if it is to be generalized—that is, if humans are to recognize the rights of others as equal to their own. Politics, in Rousseau's conception, is an "unnatural" practice that can promote the common good only with the aid of mores such as patriotism and civil religion. These mores aim to promote civic integration by transforming *amour propre* (egoistic love of self) into love of the regime. In the state of nature, pity moderates love of oneself into a benign desire for self-preservation, *amour de soi-même*, which one extends to all other humans; whereas the competitive love of oneself of modernity, *amour propre*, leads one to view all others as threatening competitors.

Rousseau ultimately grounds his hopes for a legitimate order in which each wills the general will on the transformation of the natural sentiment of pity into the civic virtue of patriotism. In the state of nature, pity makes possible an unthinking natural goodness distinct from those forms of virtue dependent on reason. Hobbes, who believed that feelings could be communicated only by language, contended that even a regime properly grounded in the passions would degenerate into the chaos of conflicting linguistic and political interpretation, if not for the arbitration of a final judge, the sovereign. For Rousseau, although sentiment alone is insufficient to establish a just or even stable regime, the universal sense of pity, when properly rechanneled into patriotism, can check those disputatious passions that erode community. For the untutored many, only socially constructed healthy passions can ensure social cohesion. Rousseau rejects the need for a Hobbesian final arbiter, but only if there exists previously an initial Legislator who establishes cultural practices that will properly shape the passions: "Instead of that sublime maxim of reasoned justice, Do unto others as you would have them do unto you, [pity] inspires all men with this other maxim of natural goodness, much less perfect but perhaps more useful than the preceding one: Do what is good for you with the least possible harm to others."[22] Philosophic wisdom can defend the virtue of the "science of the simple souls," the conscience, by constructing a regime in which legal and political equality replaces natural inequality. The sophistry of popularized science must be combated by the true philosophers because its cultivation of "talents" reinforces natural inequality. Only a society pervaded by a patriotic esprit can weaken reason's promotion of *amour propre*.

Cosmopolitanism's undifferentiated compassion for humanity, which simply "civilizes" natural pity, cannot curtail the venal behavior of modern man. Rousseau holds that the universal veil of cosmopolitanism is often used by civilized men to rationalize unprincipled individualism. In Rousseau's view, it is an irony of political life that the public good can only be achieved within a specific national community—where a communal identity supercedes the individualism that lurks behind the facade of cosmopolitan universalism: "There are no such things nowadays as Frenchmen, Germans, Spaniards, or even Englishmen—only Europeans. All have the same tastes, the same passions, the same customs and for good reason: Not one of them has even been formed nationally, by distinctive legislation. . . . They will all tell you how unselfish they are, and act like scoundrels. They will all go on about the public good, and think only of themselves."[23]

Patriotism is both a more intense and more discriminating sentiment than natural pity. Natural pity is the benign indifference that natural beings exhibit toward those humans they randomly encounter in their relatively autonomous existence. Patriotism limits man's benign sentiments to his fellow countrymen. At most, patriotic civilized humans are indifferent to foreigners; if they threaten his compatriots, then civilized man is outrightly hostile to them. The emergence of civilized nation-states means humans can no longer afford to be benignly indifferent to all their fellows. One must either be friend or foe, compatriot or foreigner. Once the state has made the fatherland the citizens' central preoccupation, there exists not only less time for the venal pursuits but also less need for them. In order, however, for civil man to feel for his fellow citizens, he must lose whatever latent pity he feels for foreigners. The conventional establishment of national customs is the key to establishing national fellowship. These customs are so essential that in *The Government of Poland* Rousseau openly states that their existence is more important then their specific moral quality and content: "Let those new customs be neither here nor there as far as good and bad are concerned; let them even have their bad points; they would unless bad in principle, still afford this advantage: they would endear Poland to its citizens and develop in them an instinctive distaste for mingling with the peoples of other countries."[24] In contrast to the internationalism of Kant, Rousseau's attack on universalism presages the trenchant defense of parochialism rendered by Nietzsche in *The Use and Abuse of History*.[25] The first step in overcoming individual particularism is to make men love their country more than themselves. Thus, Rousseau intuited the sociological relationship between the rise of nationalism and the rise of democracy. But, as a world of resurgent nationalism reminds us today, uncritical love of country can also constrain political diversity by placing the highest value on internal political unity and intolerance of "others," both within and without.

From Natural to Civil Freedom:
The Humanization of Social Chains

Freedom in Rousseau's state of nature is an underdefined quality, consisting in the negative quality of the absence of dependence on other human beings. Freedom, which in Rousseau's opinion differentiates humans from other animals, consists in our ability to make conscious choices. Whereas the animal is a slave to instinct, human beings can resist "human" instinct and appropriate the instincts of any other species.

This natural freedom, however, also engenders humanity's tragic emergence from the state of nature. The ability to choose enables human beings to solve the survival problems posed by the external forces of accident and growth which occur over a glacial period of time. These solutions facilitate the perpetuation of the species, but at the price of individual misery. The ability to reason develops with the satisfaction of bodily needs. Reason, however, also promotes vanity and *amour propre* by making us acutely conscious of the opinion of others. Thus natural freedom's development of reason, the faculty of self-perfection, is the source of all human misfortune, "drawing him out of that original condition in which he would pass tranquil and innocent days."[26]

Yet natural freedom's success story, its coping with adversity, engenders its own demise. As the human species progresses by means of cooperation, a pernicious division of labor develops in which both master and slave become dependent on each other:

> But from the moment one needed the help of another . . . property was introduced, labor became necessary, and vast forests were changed to smiling fields

which had to be watered with the sweat of men . . . having formerly been free and independent, behold man, due to a multitude of new needs, subjected so to speak to all of nature and especially to his fellow men, whose slave he becomes in a sense even in becoming their master; rich, he needs their services; poor, he needs their help; and mediocrity cannot enable him to do without them.[27]

Natural freedom cannot be restored in civil society because such freedom's demise is an integral part of the "civilizing" process of the division of labor. Civil freedom can only emerge in a society where citizens consciously construct and embrace their bonds of dependence. This humanization of humanity's chains through the conscious collective construction of them can occur only when all are equally dependent on all. Civil freedom, as defined by Rousseau, is essentially democratic self-legislation, but with the critical caveat that each individual prescribes for himself the universal law, the same law proclaimed by each and all—the social contract. Universal adherence to the social contract, to the community, is the essence of civil freedom:

> Each when united to his fellows, renders obedience to his own will and remains as free as he was before . . . the complete alienation by each associate member to the community of all his rights . . . since each has made surrender of himself without reservation, the resultant conditions are the same for all: and because they are the same for all, it is in the interest of none to make them onerous to his fellows. *In short, whoso gives himself to all gives himself to none.*(emphases added)[28]

This Rousseauian relationship between natural and civil freedom is less than intuitively evident. Civil freedom combats the social differentiation and competition that, unrestrained, is promoted by individual reason, a talent of natural freedom. The competitive behavior of nascent civil society—where property lines are first drawn and where men compete around the fire to be the most-liked dancer—must be curtailed by the social contract. Under the social contract man's equality as a citizen is primary, his differentiated talents secondary, to his self-definition. In contrast to the bonds of equal dependence that define civil freedom, the natural freedom of the state of nature appears to be a condition of near-total independence. Encounters with one's fellows are few; relationships of dependence are nonexistent. Pity is a form of benign indifference rather than a strong emotional commitment to one's fellows. Civil man, however, can no longer choose to run away from encounters with his fellows. He is imprisoned by an infinitely thicker web of social relations. Civil freedom consists in the willful acceptance of equal dependence. Ironically, civil man, whose rational bondage is the product of his natural predecessors "freely" dealing with blind fate, becomes civilly free only when he willfully reconstructs that fate by means of an egalitarian bondage of each to all—the social contract.

But the modern patriotism that underlies the general will rests on a less stable, conventional basis than does its prerational ancestor, natural pity. The pity of the savage is innate; it is a prerational principle equivalent "to the repugnance of horses to trample a living thing underfoot."[29] Given the reality of modern egoism, the individual who contracts into civil society constantly threatens to become a "free rider," deriving private benefits from civil society while escaping his obligations to community whenever societal vigilance wanes. The self-interested calculating skills acquired over the centuries of living in both precontractual, nascent civil society and in regimes of unjust social contracts are not a natural ally of fellow-feeling. These skills are destructive of the construction of a civil community. They militate against the newly acquired sense of duty and patriotism which uneasily coexists with calculation in a propertied society.[30]

An acute awareness of the potential for "free-riding" leads Rousseau to advocate the cultural revolution of a founding Legislator and the institutionalization of a strong civil religion. Unlike contemporary rational choice theorists, Rousseau did not believe a democratic society could cohere on the basis of rational self-interest and "side-payments." A moral sense of social solidarity would be necessary to bind the community. Only proper customs and opinions can reign in rational man's self-interest and vanity. In *The Government of Poland*, Rousseau goes even further than in *The Social Contract*, in institutionally promoting public-interested behavior by ensuring that the only means for satisfying one's *amour propre*, the only means for gaining esteem, is through public service. *The Government of Poland*'s advocacy of state control of education is a critical addition to the support structure for the regime of the general will outlined in *The Social Contract*.

The self-interested behavior of a newly liberated constituency threatens the freedom of already functionally integrated citizens. The more functionally complex a society—the more constituencies with particular grievances and interests—the less likely it is, in Rousseau's view, that a political regime will remain cohesive. The legacy of oppression means, however, that newly liberated groups are unlikely to be self-restrained. It is no accident that the alleged founder of participatory democracy, in *The Government of Poland*, cautions against the immediate emancipation of the Polish serfs. The laws of liberty are stern, but their "yoke" is imposed by the sovereign people themselves. The relative strictness or laxity of the laws has little to do with the extent of liberty. A "tyrannous yoke" emerges only when the fundamental law is made by particular individuals rather than by the entire community:

> Liberty is a food that is good to taste but hard to digest: it sets well only on a good strong stomach. I laugh at those debased peoples . . . with their hearts still heavy with the vices of slaves, they imagine that they have only to be mutinous in order to be free. Proud, sacred liberty! If they but knew her, those wretched men: if they but understood the price at which she is won and held; if they but realized that her laws are stern as the tyrant's yoke is never hard, their sickly souls, the slaves of passions that would have to be hauled out by the roots, would fear liberty a hundred times as much as they fear servitude.[31]

Rousseau employs the independence of natural freedom as a benchmark by which to criticize humanity's slavish dependence on acquisition and public recognition. But the strict requirements of Rousseau's natural freedom deem that modern independence can only come through a strict interdependence. Rousseau employed a conception of voluntary, unconditional duty and nonmercenary virtue to negate the Hobbesian conception of the primacy of the natural right to life, a primacy that posed severe problems for Hobbes's theory of obligation. Acutely aware of the moral declension of modern acquisitive citizens, in comparison to the mutual indifference of pre-rational natural human beings, Rousseau rejected social contract liberalism's claim that ordinary people, guided by reason and calculated self-interest, could construct a stable, modern regime. Without the *esprit* of the patriotic polis and the socialization of the private will, civil society would inevitably degenerate into the private, fragmented competition for vainglory. Rousseau's description of the emergence of modern society in *The Second Discourse* presages *The Social Contract*'s explicit position that a developed social pluralism precludes social solidarity.

History as Declension: Reason's Failure to Solve the Problems It Poses

Human history, as described in Part Two of *The Second Discourse*, is a tragedy in which the sweetest sentiments known to human beings, conjugal and paternal love, inevitably give way to the jealousy and discord of civil society. Rousseau did not glorify the indolence and ignorance of the primitive state of nature. His Golden Age of the self-sufficient family is situated at the beginning of civil society. Such families develop immediately after human beings emerge from the state of nature, when the "first revolution" engendered by rapid population growth forces human beings to form communities centered on the division of labor within the family. Here humans first develop the faculties of language and comparative judgment. But the absence of a highly differentiated division of labor and of a developed system of property and exchange salutarily limits one's dependence on others.

Rousseau's vision of a cohesive society, the Golden Age family, prefigures Durkheim's description of "mechanical solidarity"—a society in which the bonds among human beings are created by their sharing the same simple lifestyle. Such societies are characterized by little social differentiation and an absence of serious social conflict.[32] Civil religion and patriotism aim to recreate this prepolitical human solidarity. Rousseau does not praise the Golden Age family because it is a truly voluntary and democratic institution. Children are born into the family; they do not choose their parents nor the bonds of affection and obligation that develop between parent and child. Rather, the family is a "free" institution because conjugal and paternal love, by their very nature, collapse when they are no longer freely willed. Love cannot be coerced, whereas human beings' relationships in both the economic and political marketplace can be. Within the Golden Age family, human beings do not live "outside" themselves. Their needs and desires are not imposed from without by social imperatives. Within the family humans are insulated from the continually escalating struggle for the esteem of others. The most pernicious aspect of the modern division of labor, in Rousseau's opinion, is not humans' material dependence on others but their psychological dependence on their fellows' judgments. In the ideal family of the Golden Age, men and women love their brothers and sisters for what they truly are, not for their public image or external achievements. Rousseau conceives of civil religion and patriotism as a modern surrogate for the freely willed social solidarity of the long-lost Golden Age family. As with familial love, the social solidarity of enlightened patriotism can only be freely willed; and it too is inculcated by habit and upbringing.

The Golden Age family, however, cannot serve for long as a "haven in a heartless world." The internal social dynamics of the Golden Age render the family susceptible to the "fatal accidents" that institutionalize already-nascent bonds of dependence. The sexual division of labor, already present in the Golden Age, provides leisure for surplus production, which promotes the multiplication of needs. As language develops, people gain the ability to make comparisons. Notions of merit and beauty emerge, as does the need for sociability. Romantic love, the desire for a particular mate, threatens the reciprocal "natural" affection of the family. Once people truly "choose" their partners, the unquestioning bonds of family life are continually threatened. Romantic love and familial affections cannot peacefully coexist in Rousseau's opinion: "A tender and gentle sentiment is gradually introduced into the soul and at the least obstacle becomes an impetuous fury. Jealousy awakens with love, discord triumphs and the gentlest of the passions receives sacrifices of human blood."[33]

The equality of natural autonomy—the human ability to be a free chooser—is the quality that Rousseau strives to instantiate in the social contract. Rousseau consistently rejected crude, leveling conceptions of equality. Contrary to conservative stereotypes, most radical egalitarians, Marx included, recognize that human beings are not the same in talents and capacities; that is, one can uphold the equal moral worth of human beings without homogenizing or denying their distinct individual natures. This inequality of talents, however, in Rousseau's view, is irrelevant to the lives of prerational natural beings because of the absence of the dependent relations of the division of labor. In the allegorical descent of *The Second Discourse* from pre-social contract society into conflictual civil society, the metallurgical revolution—occasioned by humanity's accidental observation of volcanic action fusing metal objects—radically expands the division of labor beyond its original sexual basis in the Golden Age household. Only when some human beings become laborers, rather than self-sufficient farmers, do they become dependent on others for satisfying their most basic needs—including nourishment.

Developed social relations destroy natural "equality" because they eliminate the equality of natural autonomy—benign independence—which individuals of divergent innate capacities all share. Different talents become unequal talents only when they are valued by the marketplace of an interdependent, socially differentiated society. The ambitious and clever capture the market for scarce commodities. Under conditions of unequal exchange, Rousseau's rich get richer and his poor get poorer. For example, because iron may be more difficult to extract than food is to produce, those who have access to the rarer skills and resources needed to extract iron have a structural economic advantage over the less skilled.[34] Rousseau does not believe in unconstrained social mobility; the privileged conspire to establish a monopoly on the higher-priced, skilled crafts. Therefore, the possessors of scarce skills are likely to preserve their marketplace advantage. Ordinary human beings begin to comprehend these laws of the market and start to feign the talents of the advantaged or attempt to substitute force for skill. Because there exists no final arbiter in pre-social contract society, everyone invents their own rules of competition. The strong bank on their physical prowess, the clever on their sighting of new opportunities, the poor on the power of collective action. All share in the natural right of appropriation for self-preservation. On the eve of the social contract, Golden Age civil society degenerates into the Hobbesian war of all against all.[35]

Whereas the Hobbesian contract renders all men equally subject to an omnipotent sovereign, Rousseau's "historical" contract, as described in *The Second Discourse*, perpetuates the dominance of the rich over the poor. As with any economic contract between legal, but not material, "equals," the "historical" social contract provides unequal benefits for its contractees. The rhetoric of the contract, however, is egalitarian: "to protect the weak from oppression, restrain the ambitious and secure for everyone the possession of what belongs to him, let us institute regulations of justice and peace to which all are obliged to conform."[36] Both rich and poor voluntarily enter the contract. The poor do receive tangible benefits—the protection of their meager but direly needed property. The real winners, however, are the rich, who have the most to lose in the war of all against all. The poor are duped because they are more numerous and have difficulty in collectively organizing against the rich. But the poor's inability to organize is not only a function of the dominant ideology of the rich; Rousseau also believes that the atomizing, competitive race of the market poses a structural barrier to the emergence of democratic resistance.

Thus, Rousseau depicts the historical origins of political rule as a product of social domination. The rich are the authors and initiators of the "historical" contract because it provides them with "institutions which were as favorable to [them] as natural right was adverse. It gave new fetters to the weak and new forces to the rich, destroyed natural freedom for all time, established forever the law of property and inequality, changed clever usurpation into an irrevocable right."[37] In contrast to the "historical" contract's promotion of inequality, the ideal contract of *The Social Contract* eliminates extremes of wealth.

Rousseau delineates a clear distinction between the imperfection of this "historical" contract and the possible construction of a just contract by a wise lawgiver. In the final pages of *The Second Discourse*, Rousseau outlines the kernel of the argument of *The Social Contract*. The "historical" political regime, in Rousseau's analysis, has "remained ever imperfect because it has almost always been the work of chance." Political reformers, by trying to mend a structurally imperfect system, fail to comprehend the necessity for a *tabula rasa* on which the Legislator can create the legitimate state: "trying to mend whereas it is necessary to begin by clearing the area and setting aside all the old materials as Lycurgus did in Sparta."[38]

Civil man's desire to command leads him to accept inequality, as domination becomes dearer to him than independence. Thus, Rousseau's self-defined task is to construct a model political regime grounded on the interdependence of individual autonomy and social solidarity. Such an ideal regime can serve as a critique of all previous political regimes that embody relations of dependence and conflict. The political hierarchy found in "historical" regimes only accentuates dependence in societies where people judge others by comparison. A society dominated by wealth and the desire for reputation, honor, and preference can never hope to produce a virtuous regime. Tyranny, however, returns political life to a new state of nature. Here "the notions of good and the principles of justice vanish once again"[39] and the rule of the strongest, which the ideal social contract aims to transcend, returns in the form of the will of the despot. Human beings, by forfeiting the natural gifts of life and freedom, return to a primitive state of equality— political impotence.[40]

Rousseau is ultimately pessimistic about the prospect for a just, stable social contract because its creation necessitates nothing less than a fundamental transformation of human nature. Contrary to Marx and Hegel, Rousseau does not believe that such a transformation is inscribed in the teleology of history; it is not history's fated culmination. Human history is a story of declension, not of rejuvenation. Yet in particularly fortuitous circumstances, such as a new society uncorrupted by the market economy (Corsica) or a weak, pariah state whose only remaining virtue is its intense, if inefficacious, patriotism (Poland), the philosopher may contribute to the restoration of virtue. Neither of these societies has yet been infected by the competitive individualism of the market or the status-hierarchies of a long-standing monarchy. Yet Rousseau is aware that the road to modernity cannot be permanently avoided; to ward off foreign invaders, regimes will be forced to modernize. But until then, humans may recreate a "premodern" nation-state version of the Golden Age family of early civil society. In these instances political theorists who comprehend the moral price of modernity can use their rational capacity for historical reflection to help a premodern society control the vain passions produced by modernity's struggle for self-perfection. The student of history, when given a fortuitous chance by a premodern regime, may use the lessons of history to deter temporarily the downward spiral of civilization. Like the ancient philosophers of natural right, Rousseau advances a model of the just regime while simultaneously doubting its plausibility.

Far from being a philosopher of revolution, Rousseau maintains in *The Second Discourse* that if "the fatal right of disposing the government" were to rest with citizens' reason alone, constant disorder would be the result. Rousseau extols religion and the citizen's belief in divine will because it "spares even more blood than fanaticism caused to be shed": "But the frightful dissension, the infinite disorders that this dangerous power would necessarily entail demonstrate more than anything else *how much human governments needed a basis more solid than reason alone*, and how necessary it was for public repose that divine will intervened to give sovereign authority a sacred inviolable character which took from the subjects the fatal right of disposing of it."(emphases added)[41] Morality, which cannot be legislated, is the key element to preserving a healthy, stable polis. The magistrate should judge only whether or not citizens' actions violate the written code. Public opinion, on the other hand, should judge the moral quality of the citizenry: "It is up to the public esteem to establish the differences between evil and good men. The magistrate is the judge only of rigorous right; but the people are the true judges of morals."[42] Rousseau's denial that the state should directly legislate virtuous behavior should not, however, hearten modern advocates of tolerance. The virtuous citizens of Rousseau's model polis live "within themselves" because they *internalize* the values of a small, solidaristic community. Rousseau's patriotic, parochial polis is not the diverse, expansive state of modern liberalism.

During those precious periods when solidaristic patriotism erodes the competitive ethos of market society, Rousseau urges that not the market but the state reward citizens according to their contributions to public life. Whereas the market rewards humans according to their ability to sell themselves by "appearances," the vigilant state rewards them according to their real public contributions, and not by their reputations. Rousseau adamantly opposes economic inequalities extensive enough to render some dependent on others. But he rejects a stringent equality of results. In the notes to *The Second Discourse*, he writes, "Distributive justice would still be opposed to this rigorous equality of the state of nature, even if it were practicable in civil society; and as all members of the state owe it services proportionate to their talents and strengths, the citizens in their turn ought to be distinguished and favored in proportion to their services."[43]

Rousseau does not offer a political program for the transformation of the degenerate regime's moral ethos, because corrupt human beings cannot create virtuous opinion. This vicious circle underlies the pessimism of *The Social Contract*, a book that Rousseau believed would rarely guide actual practice but would serve as a standard against which to judge the practice of existing regimes. The pessimism that underlies the "history" of humanity's decline in *The Second Discourse* is also reflected in *The Social Contract's* analysis that the only just regime that can survive is one that is not only just from birth, but born with the proper educational and cultural institutions provided by a founding Legislator.[44]

The Legislator, who combines the roles of public tutor, demigod, and philosopher, is given the job of transforming human nature. But Rousseau is noticeably silent as to how the Legislator achieves power. As Judith Shklar wrote, "The Great Legislator practices a preventive politics in much the same way as the tutor gives Emile a negative education. Both create an external environment that will forestall moral deformation."[45] Rousseau believed that only in extraordinary circumstances would such instruction be politically possible. Perhaps because of these doubts about the possibility of public moral tuition, Rousseau's later writings turned to the issues of private moral education and solitary reflection. A political philosopher who was ultimately pessimistic about the possibility of a "virtuous" political life, Rousseau eventually focused his work on the education of those "few fortunate souls" capable of recreating in their philosophic life the self-sufficient *amour de soi-même* of natural beings. Rousseau found little solace in the prospects of modern politics. Rather than being a manifesto on behalf of participatory democracy, *The Social Contract* represents a best-case scenario for temporarily forestalling the inevitable decline of public life engendered by modern vanity, calculation, and interest.

REASON AND THE GENERAL WILL: THE CONVENTIONAL
BOUNDARIES OF SOVEREIGN POWER

Significantly, Rousseau opens *The Social Contract* by arguing that a legitimate and stable regime must be founded on conventional and not natural right: "The social order is a sacred right which serves as a foundation for all other rights. This right, however, since it comes not by nature, must have been built upon conventions."[46] Although Rousseau may be hostile to pluralism, he was the first political theorist to advocate political sovereignty based on universal male suffrage. There are no external moral standards by which to judge the legitimacy of a political regime; sovereignty rests in the conscious, conventional agreement of the people. Although Rousseau outlines the structure of democratic legitimacy, he feared that the free interplay of interests in civil society would continually threaten that agreement.

Rousseau contends that a legitimate social compact must be in the equal interest of each participant. Contrary to Hobbes, he contends that this contract cannot be founded on a conventional surrender of freedom to an omnipotent sovereign because such an agreement, which authorizes all the acts of the sovereign as if they were authored by each citizen, is the equivalent of slavery: "When a man renounces his liberty he renounces his essential manhood, his rights and even his duty as a human being." Initially Rousseau's criterion of legitimacy, that individual self-interest and social obligation be in accord, seems too lofty, given his description of the *amour propre* of modern citizens. He desires that there be a "constant [connection] between what right permits and interest demands," while acknowledging that "man's personal interests may dictate a line of action quite other than that demanded by the interest of all." He contends that humans cannot renounce their freedom without destroying their nature as human beings; yet he also describes the essence of the social contract as "the complete alienation by each associate member to the community of all his rights."[47]

Rousseau endeavors to reconcile the seeming contradiction between personal and social interests and between individual freedom and the social contract by distinguishing between natural and civil freedom. This distinction also lies at the heart of Rousseau's conception of the General Will. As in *The Second Discourse*, Rousseau conceives that natural man contracts into civil society when his security of person and property are no longer assured in the state of nature. Civil society is able to protect each member's person and property only when each individual sacrifices to the community an essential aspect of natural freedom—the right to be the sole judge of the means to self-preservation. At this point the resemblance to the Hobbesian contract is striking. But whereas Hobbes believes the contractee surrenders all claims of political independence, except the right to preserve one's life, to an omnipotent sovereign, Rousseau argues that by personally willing obedience to the common good the citizen maintains his personal freedom. By resting sovereignty in all the citizens, rather than in a government that makes specific laws, Rousseau claims that civil society is a willful, "free" creation of each individual. This "free" act is reaffirmed by recurrent assemblies of the sovereign people.

Rousseau is careful to differentiate this civil freedom from natural freedom. The essence of both "freedoms" is the absence of personal dependence. Natural freedom is achieved through humans' self-sufficient autonomy in the state of nature and their natural right to judge their means of self-preservation. On the eve of the social contract, the remnants of natural freedom in nascent civil society produce civil war and the dependence of the weak on the strong. Personal independence can be restored only by the voluntary acceptance of the equal dependence of each on all (i.e., civic freedom). Male citizens liberate themselves from the chains of illegitimate civil society by becoming the conscious authors of the chains of legitimate civil society.[48]

Conventional freedom is an artificial and fragile right that is threatened whenever a citizen places personal interest before the interest of all. Civil freedom is possible only in a society where all obey the general will, a condition that can exist only when the sovereign people has the necessary power to be sole judge of all conflicts between the rights and duties of citizens. In order to preserve civil freedom, the individual must therefore alienate to the collective sovereign all natural rights, including the right of male citizens to determine when to risk their lives for the state.[49] Rousseau's collective sovereign has a more authoritative claim on the life of its citizens than does Hobbes's Leviathan. According to the internal logic of Rousseau's argument, the infamous maxim that "man must be forced to be free" is not a pernicious oxymoron, because anyone who violates the general will threatens the civil freedom of every citizen, including himself. In order to preserve a free society, it is rational for each individual to will that any violator of those freely prescribed laws—including him- or herself—be adequately punished. Only by retaining the ultimate right to "force people to be free" can the collective sovereign enforce a solution to the free-rider problem posed by individual self-interest. Any disgruntled citizen retains the natural right to flee into exile; though if the state needs his talent, it can detain any citizen who initially recognized its legitimacy. But once he voluntarily remains, the citizen must obey the fundamental laws that are the bulwarks of civil freedom. Quoting the famous maxim in context demonstrates that Rousseau believed that one who disobeyed the general will must be "forced to be free" because his violation threatens the very basis of the political regime and thereby every citizen's civil freedom: "Whoever shall refuse to obey the general will must be constrained by the whole body of his fellow citizens to do so: which is no more than to say that *it may be necessary to compel a man to be free—freedom being that condition which, by giving each citizen to his country, guarantees him from personal dependence, and is the foundation upon which the whole political machine rests*, and supplies the power which works it." (emphases added)[50]

Rousseau contends that those free riders who initially assent to the democratic laws of civil freedom but then disobey them can be forced to be free— for their disobedience threatens the social solidarity at the heart of civil freedom. Rousseau did not confuse democratic liberty with unrestrained libertarianism. He is the first political theorist to comprehend the centrality of social solidarity to democratic legitimacy. Democratic citizens must be willing to obey all laws that they have an equal voice in making. Even if a citizen disagrees with a specific law, he must obey it if it has been made according to a democratic process that he originally helped to shape. But to achieve such an equal voice in self-legislation, Rousseau believed that particular interests had to be prevented from expressing themselves politically. He failed to comprehend that the very possibility of democratic legitimacy depends on the ability of particular interests to construct politically what they share in common. If they cannot, then the regime will not hold. Universally obeyed democratic institutions permit social interests to pursue their particular goals, constrained by their commitment to the constitutional norms of a polity that is, in John Rawls's term, a "supraunion" of these particular communities.

Theorists as diverse as Karl Popper, John Plamenatz, and Jacob Talmon have condemned Rousseau for failing to recognize the critical relationship between minority rights and political freedom. What they fail to recognize is that Rousseau clearly distinguished between isolated, individual opinions and group interests. Rousseau understood that absent the existence of distinct human interests and different opinions about public matters there would be no need for politics—the discernment of what distinct individuals share in common. But whereas Rousseau defended individual rights and affirmed individual difference, he feared strong associational life in civil society as a hindrance to the discernment of the general will. Rousseau believed that constraining the freedom of interest groups would not constrain the development of individuality. Thus, he rejected any conception of group or associational rights to political voice or representation. Organized interest groups, he believed, would oppose their own narrow "general interest" (shared only by members of a specific association) to the general will of all. If interest groups must exist, it would be preferable for the maintenance of the general will if they were weak, numerous, dispersed, and relatively equal in power: "But where subsidiary groups do exist their numbers should be made as large as possible, and none should be more powerful than its fellows."[51] Only under such sociological conditions could the influence of interest groups on politics be adequately restrained and the general will be discerned.

Rousseau believed that the general will would be most readily known when the greatest number of different *individual* opinions were expressed. Such a situation would be facilitated by restricting the influence of secondary associations on politics and by encouraging each citizen to voice his own individual opinion in regard to the general will: "If then the general will is to be truly expressed it is essential that there be no subsidiary groups within the State, and that each citizen voice his own opinion *and nothing but his own opinion*."(emphases mine)[52] Rousseau conceives the general will to be that kernel of the common interest which remains when all conflicting particular, *individual* wills cancel out, leaving behind only that interest common to each and every individual: "There is often considerable difference between the will of all and the general will. The latter is concerned only with the common interest, the former with interests that are partial, being itself but the sum of the individual wills. But take from the expression of these separate wills the pluses and minuses—which cancel out—the sum of the differences is left, and that is the general will."[53]

Implicit in Rousseau's analysis is an intense concern with the problems of cohesion and social legitimacy engendered by functionally differentiated complex societies. Rousseau believed that an economically "primitive" society characterized by what Durkheim would later term "mechanical" solidarity would be more conducive to the development of the general will. But Rousseau recognized that increased social differentiation was part and parcel of an inevitable emergence of modernity. Although Rousseau would have rejected Durkheim's optimistic analysis in *The Division of Labor in Society* that a well-functioning, highly articulated division of labor could create its own "organic" social bonds of functional unity, Durkheim's depiction in his later writings of the central role of the civil "religion of the individual" in promoting "organic solidarity" strikingly resembles Rousseau's civil religion.[54]

Rousseau did not share Madison's later faith that by "extending the sphere" of the geographical regime, and thereby multiplying interests, one could prevent the domination of the state by any permanent majority or fixed coalition of interests. Rather, Rousseau favored banning interest-group representation in politics, in contrast, respectively, to *Federalist* 10 and to Durkheim's corporatism. To ensure that each and every citizen expresses his personal conception of the general will, interest groups should be suppressed, at least in terms of their voice in politics: "But when intriguing groups and partial associations are formed to the disadvantage of the whole, then the will of each of such groups is general only in respect of its own members, but partial in respect of the State. When such a situation arises it may be said there are no longer as many votes as men, but only as many votes as there are groups. Differences of interest are fewer in number, and the result is less general."[55]

Rousseau did not advocate the unlimited sovereignty of an omnipotent state that crushed independent life in civil society. He defended individual autonomy within civil society but opposed civil associations having any political influence on the state. Although Rousseau held that "the social compact gives to the body politic complete power over its members," he later argued that sovereign power should not be absolute. Rousseau can uphold both ends of this seeming paradox because his test for the legitimacy of duties imposed by the sovereign is the rational certitude that these duties serve the well-being of the community. The sovereign people should make no laws that are not essential to the promotion of the interests of the commonwealth. If the sovereign makes demands that extend beyond this reasonable limit, the state will lose legitimacy in the eyes of rational men.[56] Thus, the principles of political right, in Rousseau, appear to be self-enforcing. If the political community exceeds the bounds of legitimate law, then the social contract is justly destroyed.

A generous reading of Rousseau might claim that in this implicit description of individual rights he advances the truism that rights do not have an independent ontological existence; rather, human rights are socially created by human communities. But this sociological reality should not prevent a democratic political theorist from outlining those minimal rights necessary for the perpetuation of a democratic community. What are the legitimate bounds of sovereign power, the reader may ask, other than what the majority of the sovereign people claim them to be? What if the body politic is not a healthy one and the majority does not will the general will but instead laws that discriminate against a permanently excluded, identifiable minority? What should the rights of voluntary associations, as well as individuals, be? Any such concepts of constitutionally guaranteed rights are strikingly absent from Rousseau's analysis, perhaps because Rousseau believed that the only means by which individuals could regain their natural freedom against despotic regimes would be to exercise their natural right to flee. But Rousseau also contends that a legitimate political community may justly "coerce" the citizens it has nurtured to contribute to the common good. If the criteria for judging such a regime legitimate is that each citizen has had an equal voice in the shaping of its basic laws, then institutional guarantees against repression and discrimination would seem to be essential to the structure of democratic liberty. One might hold that a commitment to individual rights is implicit in Rousseau's argument that each voice should count once and only once in determining the sovereign laws. But Rousseau's desire for deliberation by monistic, individual wills prevented him from recognizing the group-based nature of identity in complex, differentiated societies. This Rousseau-ian tradition has contributed to an association of the democratic concept of social solidarity with a monolithic, populist conception of nationalism and a hostility to secondary, associational forms of identity. In addition, many conservative theorists, building on Rousseau's silence, argue that democracy inevitably exists in tension with liberty. But as Amy Gutmann and others have argued, democracy's guarantee of the equal worth of individual political voice necessitates a commitment to those rights that guarantee freedom of speech and assembly.[57]

Rousseau provides no clear criteria for judging a citizen's claim that the fundamental laws do not accord with the general will. Obviously not every objection is legitimate, because some can be legitimately "forced to be free" and be justly constrained from emigrating if their services are needed by society. Might one surmise that a significant minority objecting to the fundamental laws would be *prima facie* evidence that the sovereign power is illegitimate? Not according to Book 4, section 2, "Of Voting," where Rousseau contends that in a healthy political society the general will is always grounded in the majority: "When that ceases to be the case, no matter what side we are on, liberty has ceased to exist."[58] In a healthy civic culture, Rousseau assumes that a minority readily accedes to the will of the majority because all constantly will the general will. But what if an identifiable group finds itself a permanently excluded minority and refuses to accede to the majority's will? Are they morally right or wrong? Would it be just to "force them to be free?"

Rousseau thus failed to distinguish between temporary democratic majorities, which consist of shifting majority coalitions of minority groups focused on specific policy issues, and the broader social consensus on the democratic rules of the regime. This failure gave rise to an unfortunate tendency within the radical tradition to associate democracy with a populist, homogeneous will in favor of a broad range of specific policies rather than a "thinner," shared, general will limited to the universal embrace of democratic norms and procedures and those politically established public goods that aim to achieve the equal individual worth of those norms. That is, a strong, universal democratic and egalitarian political regime will coexist with ever-shifting polyarchal majorities (majority coalitions of minorities) in favor of specific policy outcomes.

In criticizing private interests for fouling the "Common-Weal," Rousseau implicitly employs a normative conception of the common good. The violation of this criterion might serve as a yardstick by which to judge the majority's alleged definition of the general will. Yet as much as one searches in *The Social Contract* for such a "thin" conception of the general will, such as the basic civil, political, and social rights of a democratic regime, one can only discern an even more minimal, proceduralist conception of how the general will is formed. Rather than being the just constitutional and social structure of a legitimate democracy, the general will appears to be purely the procedural norms of consensual choice. The fundamental laws of the social contact need only fulfill several *formal* requirements: each vote must count as one and only one; all basic laws must be willed by all; and all laws must be applied fairly to all members of society. These criteria speak neither to the desired norms of a just political regime nor to the distribution of power and resources among the diverse social and economic interest groups that Rousseau disdains.

The free act of the initial contract is reaffirmed by periodic assemblies of the sovereign people. But, as will be discussed shortly, it remains unclear what—if anything—political transpires at these assemblies, other than the reaffirmation of the social contract. Conflicts among specific citizens are relegated to the sphere of "government" and not considered by the "sovereign" assembly. The structure of Rousseau's government resembles that of a modern administrative bureaucracy. In the periodic assemblies, the citizenry is asked to reaffirm its commitment to the basic laws and to approve the current holders of government office. While reforming the basic laws and replacing officeholders is theoretically possible, Rousseau never outlines substantive procedures for achieving such reforms. Degeneration, chaos, and social revolution seem the only alternative in *The Social Contract* to the reaffirmation of the general will and the reelection of government officials by a healthy, undifferentiated citizenry that repeatedly will the general will. Instead of hotbeds of participatory, agonal political argument, the sovereign assemblies are depicted as periodic, momentary affirmations of consensual support for the governing regime.

The existence of appropriate moral customs and traditions crucially affects the chances for the political realization of this consensual general will. In Book 4, section 1 of *The Social Contract*, "That the General Will is Indestructible," Rousseau holds that the common interest will be most readily manifest to all in a simple, rural, closed society, unencumbered by the conflicting interests of an expanding modern state. Judith Shklar emphasizes this dependence of political unity on the moral character of the citizenry when she construes the general will to be itself a principle of moral regulation, rather than the norms of democratic political deliberation: "The general will, like any will, is that faculty, possessed by all men, that defends them against destructive impulses and influences. It is general because each citizen can guard himself and his fellow citizens against the dangers of *amour propre*, the empire of opinion and institutionalized inequality."[59]

To describe the general will as a defensive force that protects the individual against inevitable moral degeneration may, however, conflate the moral and political realms to a greater extent than Rousseau did. In Rousseau's analysis *every* political regime fights a long-term losing battle against the forces of particularism. A simple egalitarian society possessing a relatively undeveloped division of labor is likely to withstand the onslaught longer. But it too will witness the day when its sovereign people are no longer vigilant, thereby allowing the tyranny of private interests to rule. Book 3 of *The Social Contract*, Rousseau's lengthy disquisition on the three forms of government, Democracy, Aristocracy, and Monarchy, provides ample evidence that Rousseau believed that the general will could be realized, but only temporarily, in even a large, commercial, enlightened monarchy. Book 3, section 8 is significantly entitled "That Every Form of Government Is Not Suited to Every Country."[60] Any government that protects the property and safety of its citizens can gain the assent of the periodic assemblies. Despite the emphasis elsewhere on individual autonomy and voice as the source of political legitimacy, here Rousseau's criteria for political legitimacy appear quite similar to those of Lockeian liberalism. In *The Second Discourse* Rousseau goes so far as to admit that historically the initial motivation for individuals to form government was a desire to secure life and property rather than the autonomy of self-government. Most "stable" regimes ensure security and property, as defined by the state, for the mass of their people.

The above criteria set only a very minimal standard by which to judge a regime just or unjust, legitimate or illegitimate. In *The Social Contract* Rousseau explores the conditions for a just regime in which each citizen has equal voice in the making of the laws. Yet when he finally describes the actual workings of regimes that fulfill the general will, he depicts regimes that are stable and legitimate in the eyes of their members. But it is not clear if they are truly democratic regimes in which citizens have access to the education and information necessary for autonomous deliberation. In conditions of modernity Rousseau believes few "legitimate" governments can also be virtuous. "Legitimacy" queries only whether the people assent to the basic constitutional structure of the regime. It does not ask whether the specific laws, those acts of "government" that affect the populace in a differentiated manner, promote a fair distribution of burdens and benefits among social groups.

"Government," the creation of specific laws, is a technical enterprise for Rousseau. The founding of regimes and the institutionalization of healthy mores and opinions are the central questions of political concern for Rousseau in *The Social Contract*. Hence the reader should not be surprised that Rousseau praises Machiavelli, the great theoretical founder of modern, "mixed" republican regimes—but no advocate of egalitarian democracy—as a true lover of republican liberty.[61]

Book 3 of *The Social Contract*'s *leitmotiv* of the inevitable decline of civil society into competitive particularism reflects Rousseau's pessimism that all political regimes are ultimately unnatural. Rousseau thought that the personal interests of the citizens and the private interests of the magistrates would eventually assert themselves against the general will. The "teleology" of Rousseau's politics is the eventual "death" of the body politic: "As particular wills act constantly in opposition to the general will, so does Government make an incessant effort against Sovereignty. As this strife becomes more marked, the constitution changes for the worse . . . sooner or later, the Prince will oppress the Sovereign and break the social treaty . . . just as old age and death ultimately destroy the human body."[62] Representative government serves only as a modern way-station on the natural path of political declension that results from the emerging bourgeois preoccupation with commerce, the arts, and personal gain. This preoccupation occurs at the expense of patriotic fervor and public spiritedness. Rather than serve the state by personal effort, modern citizens offer alms to the state in the form of taxes. To avoid the inconvenience of attending sovereign assemblies, they delegate representatives. In Rousseau's conception both taxation *and* representation threaten the sovereignty of the people.

Rousseau believed that historical development conspired against the stability of all political regimes; thus the healthy state can only be temporarily sustained by unnatural means. Rousseau praises the Athenians for having dared to admit that the polis could only be sustained by the denial of the slaves' natural rights. The Athenians recognized that the polis, being a product of human convention, could not hope to be morally perfect: "What! Can liberty be maintained only on a basis of slavery? Perhaps. Extremes meet. Everything that is not part of the natural order has its disadvantage, and civil society more than most. There are some situations so unhappy that liberty can be maintained by those who live in them only at the expense of the liberty of others."[63] Rousseau does not counsel that modern citizens reinstitute slavery. Rather, he urges them to make sacrifices, not just of their time but also of their narrow individualism, in order to reinstitute popular assemblies and abandon representative sovereignty. Modern citizens have no slaves, but they are slaves to the representatives to whom they alienate their sovereignty.[64]

Not only does Rousseau fail to outline a vibrant politics of participatory democracy; his desire to forestall the social differentiation of modernity meant that he gave little thought to the proper balance between direct and representative institutions. Even if relative material equality and well-being were to be achieved, the inherent scarcity of time, the efficiency promoted by institutional memory, and the need to aggregate and conciliate diverse interests would require representative political institutions to operate at a level above those of grassroots, participatory democracy. Within the radical democratic tradition, the relationship between direct and representative institutions has, since Rousseau's day, been posed as a stark choice. This either/or tradition, however, limited radical movements' ability to comprehend that in any large-scale, advanced industrial society a democratic order would necessitate a democratically determined, shifting relationship between direct and representative political institutions.[65]

Rousseau's general will describes the spirit of a democratic society—a regime in which we recognize ourselves to be the sovereign authors of the laws we obey. A shared conception of fairness and of the public good is necessary if citizens are to achieve some reflective distance from their particular interests when they deliberate about public matters. Nor must a democratic polity assume that the structures of particular interests are sacrosanct. If a democratic polity believes that a given interest's structure violates the governing principles of democratic legitimacy, it can use the power of the state to regulate or restructure that interest. But if the recognized, legitimate interests within a democratic polity are prohibited from making political claims on the polity as a whole, particularly when the pursuit of their particular needs demands a share in communal resources, then it is unlikely that members of this interest or association will feel that they have been given a fair hearing by their fellow citizens. Democratic societies inevitably involve a struggle over the social definition of fairness. Individuals, and the ever-changing associational interests through which they develop their identities, demand equal respect and consideration from other members and groups within the polity. Such a commitment to justice requires from citizens some degree of reflective distancing from their particular group commitments and identities. But such reflection will never happen behind an actual veil of ignorance. Rather, the concept can only be employed as a heuristic to describe the limited empathy that members of one group must have if they are not only to tolerate but also to comprehend the claims of others on common resources. This struggle for group recognition is a continuous dynamic in a self-transforming democratic society. Such equality can never be accomplished by suppressing or abandoning particular group identities. Rather, the democratic project necessitates the continual expansion and reconstitution of the social horizons of those subcommunities that constitute the polity. But stripping ourselves completely of the particularist attachments to family, neighborhood, and workplace whenever we deliberate politically will not make us better citizens—rather, it would render us beings whom we could not recognize to be ourselves.

REGIME LEGITIMATION: WHAT ACTUALLY TRANSPIRES IN ROUSSEAU'S "SOVEREIGN ASSEMBLIES OF THE PEOPLE"

Few Rousseau scholars have adequately examined what really takes place in Rousseau's periodic "sovereign assemblies of the people" in *The Social Contract*, perhaps because a plausible answer, derived from a close reading of the text, would be, not much. Essentially the sovereign assemblies are periodic, ritual gatherings to reaffirm the loyalty of citizens to the regime. The required, periodic assemblies reaffirm each and every one's commitment to the social contract, and, in theory, do allow for the reconstruction of the sovereign laws of the general will. The meetings also determine whether there should be any change in both the structure and membership of "the government." But when one investigates Rousseau's distinction between "sovereignty" and "government," it becomes apparent why politics—deliberation, judgment, and resolution of conflict—is located in the realm limited to some, the "government," rather than in the assembly open to all.

Sovereignty, for Rousseau, is the promulgation by every member of society of laws that apply equally to all. These laws must be "general, not only in their origins . . . but in its [*sic*] objects, applicable to all as well as operated by all . . ." The social contract represents an affirmation of political equality: "establishing between all the citizens of a State the degree of equality that all undertake to observe the same obligations and to observe the same rights."[66] But when a "fundamental law" of the general will must be applied to a specific case involving particular individuals, it is a matter for "government," "the realm of debate" where universal laws are applied to particular cases by "magistrates" or "princes." As noted previously, there is nothing antidemocratic about government being distinct from the sovereign people, as long as the people ultimately control those who legislate and administrate. But in Rousseau's healthy regime, there appears to be neither a desirability or probability that the sovereign people will exercise such a right of control.

Government acts according to the instructions of the general will; it is the "minister" of the sovereign. But the government is an intermediate body distinct from both the sovereign people as a whole and individual subjects. Government deliberates, applying laws to cases and dealing "with particular acts which do not fall within the competence of the law." Hence, to adjudicate specific cases, the government must have "assemblies, councils, a competence to deliberate issues and to make resolutions, rights, titles and privileges, all belonging to the prince exclusively."[67] Rousseau fears, however, that assuring the government sufficient power to enforce its decisions may facilitate the usurpation of sovereign power by self-interested magistrates. Forestalling this usurpation is one of the major charges of the periodic assemblies.

Government is created by an act of the sovereign people—by an act of law. But this choice of leaders cannot be a "sovereign law" because "the people" are judging differentially among individuals, rather than proclaiming universal laws: "The People nominate those leaders who shall be charged with the administration of the government by law established. Now this nomination, being in itself a particular act, is not a second law, but only a consequence of the first and a function of government. What transpires is a 'sudden conversion of sovereignty into democracy . . . the citizens having become magistrates, pass from general acts to particular acts, from the law to the execution of the law.' "[68] To achieve legitimacy, every government must first be established by a democratic government, "a magistrate of the whole people," created by "the simple act of the general will."

Rousseau believed elected aristocracy to be the best form of government because of its more expert and efficient magistrates. Democratic government, he contends, can only work in a small nation where all can assemble together easily and frequently. But because democratic government's success depends on each citizen being a good magistrate, Rousseau judges it to be ultimately a utopian vision: "Were there such a thing as a nation of Gods, it would be a democracy. So perfect a form of government is not suited to mere men." Monarchy is best suited for large nations, where a concentrated executive power is needed, and where there is likely to be a surplus of wealth whose consumption by a lavish monarch would help to avoid distributional conflicts.[69]

Rousseau's opposition to "direct democracy," the combining of legislative and executive authority in the hands of the sovereign people, and his advocacy of separation of powers is rarely noted by those who claim Rousseau as a "participatory democrat." But this opposition plays an integral role in the depoliticization of the sovereign assembly. Discussion of it in the secondary literature may be absent because many scholars view the periodic assemblies as proof that Rousseau was an advocate of "direct democracy."[70] Rousseau wishes the sovereign people to approve the basic laws; but he opposes popular involvement in the administration of these laws because the people are likely to be biased in their judgments. Nowhere, however, does he describe the process by which the sovereign people deliberate on and make sovereign laws. Nor does he wish the body politic, as a whole, to be involved in settling disputes among particular interests. This separation between a government that applies universal laws to specific cases and a sovereign people that has ultimate say as to the content of these laws is integral to much of representative democratic theory and practice. But nowhere does Rousseau suggest in which local assemblies—whether neighborhood or workplace councils—popular political participation, disagreement, and conciliation will occur. If anything, Rousseau, admittedly on a smaller geographic and demographic scale, prefigures the Jacobin's centralist, populist conception of political will rather than the decentralist, participatory conception of French anarcho-syndicalism.

Whereas the periodic reapproval of the basic constitutional structure of a regime is an element of democratic political life, more central to day-to-day democratic reality is the making of new laws, which often involves the polity's evaluation of particular interests' demands on common resources. As Hegel would later do, Rousseau searches for a body of experts, admittedly approved by the sovereign people, who can apply the sovereign laws fairly and adjudicate disputes among particular interests. The role of the government includes making "special" laws that affect specific, rather than general, interests. But Rousseau's desire to separate radically considerations of particular interests from considerations of the common good denudes the deliberations of the sovereign people of significant political content, by denying the assembly any opportunity to respond to the political demands of particular interests.[71]

Rousseau's argument in *The Social Contract* that the constitutional rules of a democratic regime be made by all and not advantage any particular group justifiably remains a central tenet of democratic theory. But whether or not a formally democratic society is just and held to be legitimate by a broad range of citizens also depends on how it allocates goods among diverse and often competing interests. If the "general will" may be translated into modern political vernacular, the equally underspecified term "common good" readily comes to mind. The "common good" of a democratic society is constituted both by the agreed-upon constitutional rules of the polity and by those political, civil, and social rights deemed essential to creating a citizenship equally valuable to all.

Metaphorically, Rousseau's distinction between the executive ("government") and the legislative ("sovereign") function might be put thus: the sovereign makes the rules of the game; the government serves as the referee. The periodic, required meetings of the sovereign people serve several functions, but none of them are political in the sense of mediating among conflicting interests or deciding among competing conceptions of the general will. The first function Rousseau mentions for the sovereign assembly is to ensure that the government does not usurp the sovereign power of the people, thus ensuring that "the referees" do not take it on themselves to alter the rules of the game:

> As particular wills act constantly in opposition to the general will, so does Government make an incessant effort against Sovereignty. . . . Sooner or later, the Prince will oppress the Sovereign and break the social treaty. . . . Thus the periodic assemblies of which I spoke above are peculiarly fitted to prevent or defer this evil, especially when they need no formal act of convening. For the prince cannot then put obstacles in the way of their meeting without openly showing that he is infringing the law and is an enemy of the State.[72]

But Rousseau cautions against a sovereign people altering their form of government frequently. Stability is a prudential maxim almost as important to Rousseau as legitimacy: "Changes of this kind are always dangerous. . . . Violent hands should not be laid upon an established government save when it has become incompatible with the public good."[73]

The primary purpose of Rousseau's assemblies is to reaffirm the rules of the game and those serving as referees, the government's personnel. Rousseau's sovereign assemblies are primarily vehicles for periodically relegitimating a healthy regime; they are not political bodies that adjudicate and mediate social conflict. More damaging to the conception of Rousseau as a proponent of direct democracy, nowhere in the text does he describe the sovereign assemblies actually deliberating on and making a general law. Rather, the sovereign assemblies reaffirm their commitment to the existing basic laws (perhaps given in full and final form by an omniscient Legislator?). As Rousseau continually associates political argument and debate with political upheaval and degeneration, he does not even outline the procedures to be followed if and when the sovereign people reject the existing social treaty of basic laws and/or the government personnel. He only outlines the behavior of the sovereign assemblies of a healthy, solidaristic regime:

> The opening of these meetings, *whose only object is the maintenance of the social treaty*, should always take the form of enunciating two propositions which may not be suppressed and should be made the objects of two separate votes.
>
> The first is this: "That it please the sovereign to uphold the present form of Government."
>
> And the second: "That it please the People to leave the administration in the hands of those who at present conduct it."[74] (emphasis added)

Rousseau implies that these assemblies can, in theory, revoke the fundamental social pact and temporarily act as a supreme democratic "committee of the whole" to replace the rulers and alter the form of government. But nowhere in *The Social Contract* does Rousseau outline how such transformations would occur. The operative assumption is that in a good society the sovereign people would normally choose to "uphold the present form of Government" and "leave the administration in the hands of those who at present conduct it."[75] In Rousseau's brief outline of the activity of the periodic assemblies there is no description of activity comparable to the "deliberation, council and resolution" that he describes government engaging in when it applies universal laws to particular cases. The main purpose of the sovereign assembly, according to Rousseau's actual description of its activities, is to reaffirm periodically the legitimacy of the regime. The assemblies reaffirm the people's willingness to abide by the contract and their belief that they have equal sovereignty over one another, regardless of the form of government. The assemblies are ritual institutions that promote moral education and rejuvenation. They do not engage in political debate and decision making.

It is not surprising that in *The Social Contract*, a utopian description of an ideal contract by which conventional regimes can be judged, Rousseau does not highlight what might transpire in the assemblies if there were social discord. For, in Rousseau's view, it is precisely the absence of conflict in the sovereign assembly which manifests the existence of civic well-being and a healthy general will. Conflict in the assembly is *prima facie* evidence of the decline of the strength of the general will: "When the social bond begins to grow slack, and the State to become weaker, when the interests of the individuals begin to make themselves felt . . . then the common interest suffers a change for the worst and breeds opposition. No longer do men speak with a single voice, no longer is the general will the will of all. *Contradictions appear, discussions arise, and even the best advice is not allowed to pass unchallenged.*"[76] (emphasis added) In the section of *The Social Contract* where Rousseau explicitly describes the method of voting in the assembly, he reiterates that dissension and debate are repugnant signs of the growth of private interest and the decline of the common good: "The manner in which public affairs are conducted can give a pretty good indication of the state of a society's morale and public health. The greater the harmony when the citizens are assembled the more predominant is the general will. *But long debates, dissension and uproar all point to the fact that private interests are in the ascendant and that the state as a whole has entered on a period of decline.*"[77] (emphasis added) Every citizen being born free, none can give himself to all without his explicit, voluntary consent. The social contract is thus the only law that must be passed by unanimous consent. Those who dissent from the compact, in a free state, have only one option—voluntary exile, because "residence implies consent."[78] Nowhere does Rousseau describe how alternative conceptions of the social contract—nor reforms of the existing basic laws—might be politically considered.

Rousseau refers to other general laws, besides the social contract and the choice of government officials, which might be willed by the periodic assemblies. But it is never clear from the text what these laws are. When such a general law is proposed, the citizens do not vote on whether they personally approve or reject the proposal in question, "but whether it is or is not in conformity with the general will, which is their will."[79] In a healthy regime, majority vote "objectively" determines the general will. The minority concedes that it mistook its true interests and assents to the majority's conception of the general will. Only in a society characterized by an absence of liberty would the majority err in its judgment of the general will:

> When therefore a view which is at odds with my own wins the day it proves only that I was deceived and that what I took to be the general will was no such thing. Had my own opinion won, I should have done something other than what I wished to do, and in that case it should not have been free. True, this assumes that all the characteristics of the general will are still in the majority. When that ceases to be the case, no matter what side we are on, liberty has ceased to exist.[80]

Rousseau fails to advance a normative conception of the general will; instead, he only offers the procedural conception that its universal laws must be made by all and apply equally to all. In a virtuous society the majority omnisciently discerns the general interest, including that of a minority that initially objects. Rousseau might be defended from the charge that he advocated a form of majoritarian "vanguardism" by interpreting his faith in the majority as an *ex post facto* rather than an *a priori* claim about the nature of the general will in a healthy polity. When and if the minority accedes to the majority's view, the general will is visible to all. If the minority does not accede, then there is conflict and fragmentation regarding the basic constitutional structure of the regime. And, in Rousseau's analysis, a house divided among itself (*after reflection on the initial vote regarding a general law*) cannot sustain the general will. Under these conditions, however, there is no reason to believe that either the majority or the minority are truly voting their general rather than particular interests. The minority refuses to acquiesce to the majority's will because they honestly believe that the majority is biased in favor of its own interests.

But then is it fair to ask if Rousseau's general will consists of nothing more than those common agreements needed to sustain any "legitimate" regime? Is the general will no more than a tautology—those common political procedures that exist in stable regimes? If this be the case, then the question remains: How do we know if those subscribing to the general will are truly voluntary, autonomous choosers? Nowhere does Rousseau explicitly reflect on the cultural and economic prerequisites of a democratic *political* culture that facilitates the development of citizens into self-reflective, critical choosers. Perhaps Rousseau cannot answer this question because, in distinction to Kant, he rejects the concept of a voluntary, rational autonomous chooser. For Rousseau, rational agents always act in narrow, self-interested ways unless acculturated from above by proper, restraining mores. Rousseau had little faith that democratic polities could generate these cultural prerequisites from within; they needed to be legislated from without.

The antipolitical tone of Rousseau's harmonious regime is strikingly evinced by his pastoral description of the just regime in the opening of Book 4, section 1, "That the General Will Is Indestructible." In the idyllic repose of this "happiest nation in the world" where peasants decide the affairs of state beneath an oak tree, "peace, equality, and unity" render "political subtlety" and mystifying rhetoric superfluous. The self-sufficient peasants of Rousseau's utopia possess a "constancy of wisdom" denied to those "encumbered with confused or conflicting interests." In this healthy society in which all are "concerned with their common preservation and with the well-being of all," the principles of state are "plain and clear-cut." There is no need here for the talented rhetoricians produced by complex political societies that are both "illustrious and wretched." In a healthy polity there is no need for the tumult of debate because the common interest is readily manifest to all. On the crucial issue of the few general laws needed to legitimate a society, consensus forms rapidly: "A state thus governed has need of very few laws, and when it is found necessary to promulgate new ones, the necessity will be obvious to all. He who actually voices the proposal does but put into words what all have felt, and neither intrigue nor eloquence are needed to ensure the passing into law of what each has already determined to do as soon as he can be assured that his fellows will follow suit."[81]

Does Rousseau's fear of social fragmentation and his obsessive search for consensus regarding the basic rules of society make him, as Jacob Talmon argued, a precursor of modern totalitarianism?[82] Rousseau is hostile to organized social interests, but not to individual diversity. Rousseau argues, in fact, that it is precisely the persistence of the conflict of individual interests which necessitates the search for a legitimate social contract: "Did individual interests not exist, the idea of a common interest could scarcely be entertained for there would be nothing to oppose it. Society would become automatic, and politics would cease to be an art."[83] Contrary to the practices of totalitarian regimes, every individual in the Rousseauian polity retains the right to opt out of the social contract and to enter voluntary exile. And each individual must openly and consciously contract into civil society.

Rousseau is more concerned with sustaining the legitimacy and cohesion of a modern society of diverse individuals than he is with promoting the ideological uniformity and frenzied mobilization characteristic of totalitarian regimes. He explicitly opposes a civic religion of intolerance, favoring one that tolerates religious differences while promoting a secular religion of allegiance to the social contract. Good citizens need not zealously subscribe to an overbearing ideology; they need only refrain from fomenting any rejection of the general will: "In the Republic . . . each man is perfectly free in all things that do no harm to others."[84] Though not a nascent totalitarian, Rousseau's fear of tumult led him to a conception of uniform adherence to the social contract which cannot, by his own implicit admission, be easily distinguished from the political unanimity produced by tyranny.[85]

Rousseau recognized the importance of deliberation to considered political judgment. But he relegates such activity to the realm of "government"— the realm of prudential calculation which applies the general laws to specific cases and individuals. He did not believe that political deliberation could help solve the crisis of constitutional legitimacy he found in modern regimes. The tumult of interests always threatens the general will. The social contract cannot be grounded on a common belief in the value of political democracy, social pluralism, and individual and associational rights because these liberal democratic values are not sufficiently solidaristic to restrain the abuse of the general will by particular interests. Ultimately, the social contract can only be renewed by a solidaristic reaffirmation of each and every citizen's loyalty to the general will. Rousseau understood the critical import of common values and mores in perpetuating that periodic reaffirmation. But his description of how a community reaffirms its sense of solidarity is too formalistic—too devoid of substantive content—to be termed political. Nor did Rousseau comprehend that the true challenge for a just polity is to develop bonds of social solidarity which do not obliterate those very social differences that necessitate the construction of a limited but substantive common identity. This social solidarity of citizens can be promoted only by a shared democratic political life—fraught with conflict, but also with compromise and reconciliation among citizens who possess relatively equal resources and equal potential political voice.

THE LEGISLATOR AND CIVIL RELIGION: BULWARKS AGAINST MAN'S APOLITICAL NATURE

Unassisted human reason, Rousseau believes, is not strong enough to engender consistent obedience to the general will. Personal passion prevents individuals from promoting the general will consistently, even when their intellect recognizes the need to do so. Only a suprahuman being, uncorrupted by human passions, can both discover and implement the general will: "In order to discover what social regulations are best suited to nations, there is needed a superior intelligence which can survey all the passions of mankind, though itself exposed to none: an intelligence having no contact with our nature, yet knowing it to the full."[86] If human beings are to remain sovereign, however, the Legislator cannot be a permanent political fixture. He must be the father of his country, a Lycurgus who constitutes the state but plays no further role in its political life. In order to have this permanent effect on the regime, the Legislator must "change the very stuff of human nature." He must transform the moral character of "his people" from naturally private, apolitical individuals into conventionally public-spirited citizens: "The giver of institutions undertakes to change the very stuff of human nature, *substituting a communal and moral existence for his purely physical and independent life with which we are all endowed by nature*. He must take from man his own proper powers and give to them foreign ones which he can use only if he is helped by the rest of the community."(emphasis added)[87]

In order to transform mere mortals, the wise Legislator must learn to speak the language of the "vulgar herd." An appeal to their individual reason will not convince citizens to be public spirited. As calculating beings, humans are narrowly self-interested. The citizens must be mystified by the Legislator's appeal to heaven if they are to "bear with docility the yoke of public happiness." In order to act unnaturally (i.e., be public-spirited), humanity must be overawed by the supranatural: "The legislators, by putting into the mouths of the immortals that sublime reasoning which is far beyond the reach of poor mankind, will, under the banner of divine authority, lead those to whom mere moral prudence would ever be a stumbling block."[88] The Legislator is the *deus ex machina* of the legitimate regime. His visible role is limited to the founding of the regime. His influence lives on, however, through the mores, customs, and religion that he bequeaths his people. In order to transform his people, he must reach them in their youth, when their customs and prejudices are still tractable. The Legislator cannot operate on the rigidified customs of an aged nation. Only in the rare instances of the founding of a regime in a newly civilized region, or a revolution that eliminates a nation's memory, would Rousseau's Legislator have the opportunity to mold a people.[89]

In political circumstances less auspicious than a founding or revolutionary creation of a *tabula rasa*, Rousseau counsels a politics of gradual reform. The laws must be adapted to the degenerate moral state of the people. Measures should be taken to promote patriotism and reinvigorate public life. In *The Government of Poland*, Rousseau contends that a hierarchical, meritocratic civil service should be made the most prestigious vocation. State-controlled education should inculcate patriotic values. Strictly mandated, regionally elected officials are to be subject not simply to recall, but also to death if they disobey instructions from the people they represent. Such a strict conception of political mandates strengthens the ties between the sovereign people and their delegates. Gradual emancipation of the serfs will render the people truly sovereign. But Rousseau warns that precipitous emancipation without adequate preparation of the serfs for freedom would threaten subsequent social chaos.[90] Nowhere in *The Government of Poland* is there a call for regular meetings of the sovereign assembly or for a radical change in the structure of Polish government. The monarchy, the regional structures, and even the regional veto all remain, though in a slightly reformed manner. In terms of actual political practice, Rousseau turned out to be a gradual reformist, perhaps because his theoretical belief in the inevitable degeneration of the political regime made him less than sanguine about the political project of building a solidaristic regime.

The major bulwark of the General Will is the civil religion. Rousseau founds a new civil religion, because in his analysis modern Christianity subverts rather than supports the nation state. The few simple, "unexplained" dogmas of the civil religion all promote loyalty to the state and tolerance toward one's fellow citizens. Rousseau's civil religion teaches the citizen that a powerful, beneficent God rewards those who act justly, those who obey the social contract, with an afterlife. Because theological intolerance inevitably challenges sovereign authority, Rousseau's civil religion promotes tolerance toward all religious beliefs, provided their tenets do not violate the few "simple dogmas" of the civil religion. The state cannot compel anyone to obey these; it cannot banish citizens solely for religious impiety. But it can exile them "for a lack of social sense," for the absence of secular allegiance to the nation's laws, exhibited by their refusal to adhere publicly to the few secular tenets of the civil religion. No one should be killed for refusing to adhere to them; if they are open about their lack of fealty they will simply be banished. The greatest crime, according to the patriotic Rousseau, is not impiety but treason. He who professes the civil religion in public but then acts unpatriotically deserves death.[91] Rousseau claims this punishment is justified because lying before the law is the greatest of crimes. But unpatriotic actions are the evidence for this lying. Violating the social compact is for Rousseau a greater crime than violating an oath made to god.

CONCLUDING REMARKS: ROUSSEAU'S HOSTILITY TO POLITICS

It is significant that Rousseau concludes *The Social Contract* with the chapter on civil religion. Though the modern polity is to be grounded rationally in conventional right, reason alone cannot engender the communal bonds needed to keep modern citizens from placing their group interests above those of the general will. Rousseau's hostility to pluralism arises from his belief that humans are not by nature political beings. Sociability in civil society breeds allegiance to one's particular group identity; only a strong civil religion and a curtailment of associational activity by a vigilant state can promote individual identity with the interests of the polity. The ineluctable Rousseauian political ideal of a small, relatively egalitarian society of primary producers is peculiarly apolitical. In that pastoral idyll the stuff of politics—deliberation about priorities, moral values, and social roles—is conspicuously absent. In an undifferentiated society, the common interest is readily discerned by—and comprehensively shared by—each individual. To appropriate Jane Mansbridge's terminology, Rousseau is the theoretical founder of "unitary democracy." He explicitly critiques pluralist societies that engender the need for institutions of "adversary democracy."[92]

The major political activity of Rousseau's citizenry appears to be a periodic reaffirmation of their loyalty to the regime. Unlike Plato's and Aristotle's criticisms of social pluralism, which also emphasized the polis's educational role in inculcating virtue in the citizenry, Rousseau's healthy mores and civil religion aim primarily to bolster the conventional political regime rather than to improve individual moral character. The search for moral excellence is a solitary endeavor, best achieved through a private philosophical education that protects one from the depravities of modern politics. Those who look to Rousseau as the founder of modern democratic theory cite the periodic assemblies of the people as the arena in which the community determines its destiny. But nowhere does Rousseau detail the democratic political practices of these assemblies, beyond their permitting each individual to reaffirm his loyalty to the basic constitutional structure of the regime. Actual political judgment is best left to an aristocratic government, preferably selected on the basis of merit.

Interest group politics in an egalitarian democracy would undoubtedly have a different character than it does in contemporary liberal pluralist polities in which the voice of each citizen allegedly counts for one and only one, but where, in reality, the distribution of economic and cultural resources too often decides policy matters. The stifling of autonomous political life under authoritarian communism has taught radical democrats that a democratic society involves not only a universal commitment to the public good but also the vigorous pursuit of citizens' interests within associational life in civil society.[93] Democratic political participation cannot exist solely through an unmediated individual concern with the public good. In part, the public good is constituted by political struggle and bargaining among distinct interests; through this democratic process citizens discover what interests they share in common, as well as what interests remain distinct and contested.

As central as particular identities and interests may be to the shared life of a pluralist democracy, Rousseau affirmed an important political truth at times forgotten by contemporary advocates of both a politics of "autonomous civil society" and a "politics of difference": democratic political life must nurture a commitment by individual citizens, particular communities, and specific interests to a common public life and to those public goods that can make such a life equally accessible to all. In a democratic polity neither the state nor common interests can wither away. A major aspect of the crisis of contemporary liberal democratic societies is the weakness of such shared common interests, regarding both the shared good of political participation and support for those public goods and public spaces that facilitate widespread participation in common affairs. Whether such a shared commitment to democratic norms is termed "the public interest," "the common good," or "the general will," such a popular sensibility must influence the behavior of the particular subcommunities of a pluralist democracy if the social solidarity requisite for a democratic society is to exist.[94]

Such a sense of social solidarity, however, cannot be imposed from above or from without by an externally created solidaristic political culture. Rather, such a culture of democratic social solidarity and pluralism will emerge only from the shared experiences and struggles of a practicing democracy. Rousseau believed that this culture of social solidarity must be externally nurtured because social interests left to their own devices would favor their own particular interests at the expense of the general will. The morality of the common good could not develop through the internal political practices of a pluralist society; rather, in Rousseau's conception, such a morality could only be cultivated by extrapolitical means. Although the form of Rousseau's social contract has inspired democratic theory and practice for two centuries, his specific vision of public life in a solidaristic society is an integral part of that other lineage of the radical tradition—its hostility to social pluralism and political conflict.

Rousseau presciently envisioned the decline of public spirit and the privatism characteristic of modern pluralist societies, not to mention former state collectivist ones. He did not, however, outline a manner in which patriotism and a spirit of collective obligations could sustain—often through a creative tension—a vibrant, diverse political culture. Hegel, in contrast, acknowledged that in modern society human beings would develop their particular identities through associational life in civil society. His universal class of state bureaucrats guard the common interest and promote social harmony through regulating competition among social interests. His bureaucracy strives to curtail the centrifugal forces in civil society which Rousseau so feared, but which Hegel partially affirmed. Whether such a universal class would facilitate the existence of a vigorous democratic political life among the citizenry is the subject to which the next chapter turns.

The Hegelian State

MEDIATING AWAY THE POLITICAL

THE HEGELIAN INFLUENCE ON
RADICAL THOUGHT

Including Hegel in a work on the radical tradition's hostility to politics may at first seem anomalous, because Hegel's operative politics can best be described as a *sui generis* form of corporatist conservatism. Far from being a radical democrat, Hegel defended the "rationality" of conservative but modernizing Napoleonic and Prussian bureaucracies. In a slightly more liberal guise, he advocated moderate reforms in the British constitution, primarily aimed at mitigating class conflict.[1] But simply dismissing Hegel as a political conservative ignores the profound influence of his epistemological and historicist critique of liberal individualism on both the Marxist tradition and contemporary radical thought. The way in which the radical tradition appropriated Hegel's thought contributed to its desire to overcome the social differentiation at the heart of politics. In particular this appropriation accentuated the radical tradition's desire to abolish the tensions between universal and particular forms of identity and between decentralized and centralized forms of social organization.

Any reading of Hegel's major political work, *The Philosophy of Right*, must be informed by his larger philosophic project of analyzing history as the unfolding of human freedom. Thus contextualized, *The Philosophy of Right* is best read not as a polemical justification for the extant Prussian bureaucracy, but as a conceptualization of a "universal" state that would "end history" by mediating away conflict among particular interests in the service of a totalistic reconciliation of universal and particular. Some contemporary democratic theorists, implicitly or explicitly, see Hegel as prefiguring a relatively autonomous politics of civil society and advocating a communitarian conception of identity. According to this analysis, Hegel's vision of autonomous life in civil society prefigures the defense of modern social movements against the encroachment by the bureaucratic rationality of both corporate and state institutions on the moral and emotional bonds of a threatened, noninstrumental "life-world."[2] But Hegel's conception of the end of history in a liberal, corporatist bureaucratic state precludes a democratic challenge to the structure of associations within civil society and to the structure of power within "ethical communities" such as the family. Hegel did not envision an ongoing democratic dialectic between the politics of a democratic state and the politics of the particular communities that constitute that polity. Rather, foreshadowing radicalism's tragic attraction to false antinomies between direct and representative democracy, and between centralized and decentralized forms of power, Hegel opted for political dominance by a universal state that arbitrated away the centrifugal conflicts of civil society.

Hegel's vision of the end of history is most plausibly described in non-metaphysical language as the creation of a liberal, legal state, if not a democracy, in which citizens mutually recognize each other as autonomous, desiring beings and in which the universal value of the state is recognized by each citizen. The liberal, legal state successfully overcomes the tension between a hitherto excessively particularist bourgeois civil society[3] and a hitherto falsely universal legal state. Prior to the modern era, this false universal legal state had culminated in its premature Roman republican incarnation (and degeneration) as the private property of its rulers.[4] Only when the laws truly treat each citizen equally could the individuality of the modern citizen be achieved. The citizens of a legal, rational state transcend the distinction between particular and universal forms of identity, thereby eliminating the historic tension between the thwarted particularity of civil society and the false universality of the unrestrained state.

Although Alexander Kojève's influential reading of Hegel excessively construes Hegel's historicism as a materialist precursor of Marx, Kojève brilliantly elucidates how the master-slave dialectic serves as a metaphor underpinning Hegel's phenomenological description of history.[5] Hegel envisions historical development as a dialectic conflict between the master's purely universal desire to rule and the slave's purely particular action or work. Masters are those who are willing to risk their lives to rule; slaves are those who agree to labor for others in return for the security of life.[6] Only when the bourgeoisie, having achieved equality of particularity in postmedieval, commercial civil society, risk their lives in the bourgeois political revolution, can freedom be realized by a self-governing community of creators who are also rulers.[7] This state Hegel deems universal and homogenous, because it can no longer be expanded and it need no longer be transformed because all "men" are recognized by it.[8] Thus the history of fighting and action (work), the realm of necessity, is transcended and yields to a realm of freedom of art, love, and play. Kojève misreads, perhaps intentionally, *The Phenomenology* when he fails to analyze Hegel's contention that it is not through action and work that the end-of-history is consummated, but only when absolute freedom ceases its volitional attempt to transform the material world (an effort that engendered the terror of the French Revolution) and adapts the contemplative perspective of Absolute Spirit. In Hegel's own words, only when humanity seeks refuge in the "land of self-conscious spirit" can peace be achieved through human philosophic self-comprehension:

Just as the realm of the real and actual world passes over into that of belief and insight, absolute freedom leaves its self-destructive sphere of reality, and passes over into another land of self-conscious spirit, where in this unreality freedom is taken to be and is accepted as the truth. In the thought of this truth spirit refreshes and revives itself (so far as spirit is thought and remains so), and knows this being which self-consciousness involves (viz. thought) to be the complete and entire essence of everything. The new form and mode of experience that now arises is that of the Moral Life of the Spirit.[9]

The Marxist tradition attempted, in Marx's words, to "put Hegel back on his feet" by materializing the struggle between master and slave, between universal mastery and particularist work, by situating that conflict in the historical struggle to control the labor process and economic surplus. Central to the Marxist desire to achieve a society beyond politics was its uncritical appropriation of Hegel's totalistic conception of identity. Once the individual citizen of Hegel's universal, rational state had both negated and reaffirmed the particular identity of the bourgeois member of civil society as integral to the identity of the universal citizen, then the history of conflict between the universal state and its particular members would come to an end, as would history. But as George Lichtheim argues, there is no coherent ideological politics to be derived from Hegel's conception of history.[10] Readers interested in emphasizing his affirmation of civil society conceive Hegel to be a proponent of a neutral, liberal state governing a relatively autonomous civil society.[11] Bernard Yack, for example, offers a persuasive interpretation critical of Kojève's attempt to appropriate Hegel for Marxism. Yack is overtly sympathetic to Hegel's idealism. Thus, he affirms Hegel's conception of philosophical self-knowledge as a passive rather than active one, in which human beings comprehend their historical development as a self-knowledge that no longer needs to operate on the material plane. Yack argues that Hegel's conception of knowledge as reconciliation with the material world of modernity precludes his engaging in the willful hubris of a Nietzsche or Marx who wishes to remake nature in the image of humanity.[12] Unlike Marx who attempts to transform the world, Hegel only claims to comprehend it. The transformative project of history ends with Hegel's conscious recounting of it. Such a recollection can only occur in the spiritual realm of the pursuit of Science (knowledge).[13]

But the Hegelian dialectic of history can and has been appropriated by Marxists as integral to a more activist, materialist project. The manner in which Marx materialized Hegel's reflective end-of-history is faithfully projected by Alexander Kojève's reading of *The Philosophy of Mind.* Kojève attempts to link the philosophical course of *The Phenomenology* with the historical pattern of Hegel's philosophy of history. Marx put Hegel "back on his feet" by concretizing his end-of-history as the transcendence of a "prehuman" history in which individuals are dominated by social institutions that their actions help create—through the submission of slaves to masters—but that they do not control. In Kojève's Marxian reading of Hegel, the contradictions of society are transcended by the conscious mediation of self-governing human beings. Once the action of each is known to be the action of all, history ends and only death can create particular empirical existences.[14] The individual action that creates a product ends, in Kojève's analysis, when humans have completely satisfied their need for self-recognition.[15] In Hegel this self-recognition is achieved in a universal state that transcends all conflict through its totalizing bureaucracy. In Marx the bureaucracy withers away, and the agent of total harmony of universal and particular is the mutual interaction of species-beings who simultaneously embody both the particular individuality and the universality of humanity.

Marxism's most dangerous uncritical appropriation of Hegel, however, was his reading of Hegel's historicist teleology of freedom as relativizing, if not justifying, immoral acts committed in epochs prior to the realm of freedom. Marx democratized Hegel's conception of "the world historical individual" by assigning to the proletariat the final historical task of rationalizing society. For Hegel the agent of social transformation is not a class but a "world historical individual" who, embodying "the Truth of their age" and "the necessary, directly sequent step in progress," becomes obsessed with transforming the present. If such an individual acts in ways deemed by the conventions of his or her times to be immoral, or at best amoral, these "particular acts of passion" are rendered irrelevant by the contribution of those acts to the "cunning of reason that . . . sets the passions to work for itself"[16] and channels the passions of great souls toward transformative historical ends: "A World-historical individual is not so unwise as to indulge a variety of wishes to divide his regards. He is devoted to the One Aim [historical progress], regardless of all else. It is even possible that such men may treat other great, even sacred interests, inconsiderately; conduct which is indeed obnoxious to moral reprehension. But so might a form trample down many an innocent flower—crush to pieces many an object in its path."[17]

The reams of paper devoted to the contemporary Marxism and morality debate may be *prima facie* evidence that an implicit, moral commitment to freedom can be read into Marx. But, to appropriate the teleological amoral discourse of traditional Marxists, "it is no accident," given the Hegelian historicism of Marx, that many political activists—and theorists—in the Marxist tradition willingly condoned the injustices of their day, committed in the name of a future communism, as a necessary and rational, if perhaps lamentable, contribution to an emancipatory future. Hegel only was willing to analyze past suffering and cruelty as, sometimes, contributing to the progressive development of Spirit: "Regarding History as the slaughter-bench at which the happiness of peoples, the wisdom of States, and the virtue of individuals have been victimized . . . to what final aim these enormous sacrifices have been offered."[18] But Marxists too often justified the suffering they inflicted in the present as contributing to an alleged, future, progressive march of history. This uncritical appropriation of Hegel's "cunning of rea-

son," of the teleology of a self-comprehending, historical unfolding of freedom, crippled Marxism's moral sensibilities by engendering a historicist, ethical relativism. Alexander Kojève exemplified the dangers of a Hegelian-in-
spired Marxian amoralism. Kojève succinctly (but perhaps unconsciously)
reveals the relativist danger of interpreting the ability of human beings to
transform the world through work—the ability to make their species through
history—as a confirmation that all moral judgment is simply the rationalization of the winning side:

> Let us suppose, then, that a man assassinates his king for political reasons. He
> believes he is acting well. But the others treat him as a criminal, arrest him, and
> put him to death . . . But let us suppose that the assassin in question starts a
> victorious revolution. At once society treats the assassin as a hero. And in these
> conditions he actually is a hero, a model of virtue and good citizenship, a human
> ideal. Man can therefore transform a crime into virtue, a moral or anthropologi-
> cal error into a truth.[19]

Kojève's historicist relativizing of ethical judgment inspired Maurice Merleau-Ponty's provocative response, *Humanism and Terror*, to Arthur
Koestler's condemnation of the Stalin purge trials in *Darkness at Noon*. Regardless of whether Bukharin willingly condemned himself at the trial or not,
Merleau-Ponty held that history condemned Bukharin's advocacy of more
humane economic policies, as only Stalin's brutal policy of industrialization-
from-above enabled the defeat of Fascism. Of course, part of the defense of
a less brutal industrialization strategy must be a counterfactual, pseudo-em-
pirical one; a more moderate, mixed economic strategy probably would have
yielded better economic results, and certainly a nation and army less devas-
tated and divided on the eve of World War II. But even if that were not the
case, rapid industrialization certainly did not necessitate the killing of two-
thirds of the Communist Party's Central Committee and the forced collectivization and slaughter of millions of small landholders. Yet, in the eyes of
not only Merleau-Ponty but also millions of other leftists of his time, the
survival of Stalin's regime in World War II justified his brutal rule in the
1930s.[20] This unique brand of the Marxian ethics of the victor may seem
anachronistic to younger readers, given the recent collapse of Soviet power.
But the view that "the can" of Soviet achievements implied the moral
"ought" of its rulers' policies motivated the "world historical utilitarian"
justification of Soviet policies predominant among the Western left at least
until the 1956 Khrushchev revelations.

Another problematic influence of Hegel on radical thought lies in the appropriation of not only his historicist teleology of freedom but also his conception of the universal class and true, universal human interests. Marx, of
course, democratized Hegel's conception of the universal class from a small
civil service educated in the *Bildung* of the state to a universal proletariat
consciously organizing its social existence. But Marx also held onto Hegel's
belief that the social relations of a universal society would be characterized by

mutual recognition and reciprocation such that conflicts over the distribution of power and social roles would be transcended. Although Marx conceded that forms of institutional and social organization might still remain in more humane societies, he believed these practices would be spontaneously organized, not by the omniscience of Hegel's expert bureaucrats but by the everyday sociability of human beings who had transcended the tension between their particular and universal identities.

Marx transformed Hegel's vision of the end-of-history from that of a legal, rational state that treats all as equal citizens before the law into a "beginning of human history" in which humans would, for the first time, consciously control the institutions created by their efforts. But although Marx's vision of human freedom contains a more democratic impulse than does Hegel's, it reproduces Hegel's failure to affirm politics as the human practice that permanently mediates among distinct interests and diverse conceptions of the common good. Marx never used the term *end-of-history* but rather spoke of the end of a "prehuman history" characterized by social relations of domination and subordination. Though Marx's later writings abandon the neo-Hegelian, mystical ethos of *The Manuscripts* in which each individual shares in the particular pleasures of all members of the universal community, Marx's mature writing still shares the Hegelian project of ultimately transcending, rather than democratizing, the tension between the particular and the universal.

Less noted than the appropriation of Hegel's historicism is the Marxist appropriation, most notable in the work of Engels and Lenin, of Hegel's conception of a postpolitical bureaucracy. Such a communist postpolitical authority would administer "things, not people" by scientifically administering production ("things") in the objective interests of "all." No longer would capital "administer people" through its control over the labor process. Rather, without advancing any description of how work would be restructured, Marx, Engels, and Lenin all assumed that administration under socialism would objectively reflect policies that are in the interest of all. Subsequently, Leninist "scientific socialism" was unable to conceive of dissent as a reflection of legitimate social divisions. Rather, any dissent from the science of the party was seen to reflect the pollution of external counterrevolutionary influences or the psychological maladjustment of social deviants.

Of course, the proper role for impartial administration in a democratic society is a serious issue for democratic theory and practice. All democratic societies must seek to maintain fairness and avoid arbitrariness in the implementation of laws and regulations. Not only radical theorists but also early-twentieth-century, liberal schools of public administration found the concept of objective, scientific public managers attractive. Since the 1960s, however, there has been widespread recognition, even among public administration theorists, of the inherently political and discretionary nature of aspects of bureaucratic decision-making. Since then there has been considerable theoretical investigation—and some practical experimentation, particularly in the environmental arena—with more input and participation by grassroots citizens in the regulatory process.[21] Although an open institutionalization of public participation in supposedly "professional," but inherently political, administration is healthy, a democratic polity would still need to strive to achieve a more politically constructed variant of Hegel's concern for due process and administrative fairness. The rule of law requires that a democratic state implement laws and regulations in a fair manner that advances the public interest rather than the self-interest of the bureaucracy.

The antinomies of Hegelian thought have informed not only the classical radical tradition; they are increasingly influential among contemporary democratic theorists striving to develop a more pluralist and civil-society-oriented conception of democracy. Recent interpretations of Hegel by democratic theorists such as Shlomo Avineri, Stephen Smith, and (to a lesser extent) Charles Taylor praise his radical pluralism and validation of collective life in a civil society relatively autonomous from state interference.[22] But these theorists fail to place this alleged commitment to pluralism and an "autonomous" civil society within the context of Hegel's statism and his hostility to democratic politics. Thus, like Hegel, they fail to see that an effective radical democratic pluralism necessitates a political critique of undemocratic interests, as well as a defense of the political, rather than the solely bureaucratic, mediation of relations among democratically structured interests. Such a restructuring of undemocratic interests and mediation among democratic interests to produce ever-shifting public policies necessitates not only vibrant, relatively autonomous associational life in civil society. It also requires active public participation in the political and regulatory activities of the democratic state.

Contemporary communitarian thought relies heavily on Hegel's critique of the liberal atomized self and on his argument that identity is always situated by membership in particular moral communities.[23] But many communitarian theorists also inherit from Hegel a failure to differentiate between democratically and undemocratically constructed communities. Nor do Hegel or contemporary communitarians adequately envision the central role for a democratic politics in mediating among these distinct communities and in politically determining their relationship to the larger polity. Hegel opts for a statist inculcation of universal identity to overcome the centrifugal forces endemic to a pluralist society. Contemporary communitarianism unfortunately avoids dealing with the tension between particularity and universality by veering between the atavistic romanticism of Alasdair MacIntyre's monastic communities or the vague imprecations of national community of an Amitai Etzioni.[24]

In addition, contemporary theorists of civil society (both post-Marxist and non-Marxist), attempting to break with the economic reductionism and statist legacy of Marxism, often celebrate Hegel as the conceptual founder of a civil society of moral relations that are neither instrumental nor economic, nor universal and statist.[25] But as with the communitarians, these theorists at times forget that relations in civil society are structured on a terrain of unequal power relations and inegalitarian distribution of cultural, political, and economic resources. Such inequalities must be redressed by the actions of a democratic state if equality of citizenship in both political and associational life is to be achieved; that is, truly democratic life in both civil society and the state depends on the democratization of hierarchical institutions such as corporate power. Both communitarians and one-sided advocates of the autonomy of civil society share Hegel's critique of the instrumental nature of marketplace relations. But although Hegel wished to transcend politics by means of a universal civil service mediating among these interests and instilling in each of them a sense of universal purpose, contemporary celebrants of civil society often abandon any democratic interrogation of the existing structure of interests. Such an interrogation can only occur if society sustains a vigorous political life that moves beyond simply preserving the freedom of existing interests in a civil society to criticizing the undemocratic power relationships that often constitute them.

THE HEGELIAN STATE: MEDIATION, NOT DEMOCRATIC PARTICIPATION

In both his early and later work, Hegel joined Rousseau in describing modern civil society as a conflictual world of particular interests. But, as Hegel argued in the *Philosophy of Right*, those particular interests could promote human beings' self-recognition as members of a unified state if properly "mediated" (*vermitteln*) by a complex structure of intermediate corporate bodies, which have a status both in civil society and the state. As Steven B. Smith has argued, Hegel rejected Rousseau's suspicion of particular interests, contending that the liberal right to mutual respect could only be realized concretely through membership in the intermediate organizations of civil society.[26]

While rejecting Rousseau's solidaristic elimination of particularism, Hegel simultaneously opposed classical liberalism's conception of the nightwatchman, minimalist state guaranteeing the free play of particular interests in civil society. The unintended consequences of the "invisible hand," in Hegel's analysis, could never achieve the common good. Only state regulation of civil society by a bureaucracy educated in the culture of the common good would ensure that the classes and communities in which citizens established their particular identities reconciled their specific interests with those of the universal state.

This identification of modern citizens with the common good would not be as immediate, or unmediated, as citizens' identification with the ancient polis. But through daily participation in the governance of "the external state," the corporate bodies of civil society, and through limited, indirect participation in political affairs, the modern citizen would come to recognize, in the words of Shlomo Avineri, that "what appears as something alien and external—political power—is nothing else than the externalization of his own will."[27]

Hegel presumed, however, that most citizens best exercised their individual freedom not through political participation but through acquiring private property. Acutely aware of the centrifugal tendencies of the market, Hegel advocated participation in corporate bodies, such as guilds and professional and trade associations, as a way for citizens to derive broader social meaning from their particular economic and social pursuits. Stephen Smith describes Hegel as a "liberal corporatist" who believed in nonmarket corporate institutions as the central arena for the development of human moral identity. In Smith's analysis, Hegel's conception of politics avoided both "the excessive centralization from the state above or excessive atomization from the market below."[28] Such a reconstruction of Hegel as a "liberal corporatist" defender of a social pluralism rejecting both statism and marketplace liberalism ignores, however, Hegel's ultimate belief in the objective universal interests of the state. Although Hegel's intermediate corporate institutions preserve a veneer of participatory politics within civil society, the universal class's defense of the "universal" interests of the state ultimately precludes democratic participation in the affairs of the "real, rational state." Contemporary "participatory democrats" frequently celebrate localist participation and "community control" while ignoring the serious constraints the structure of national and, increasingly, international economic and social power places on choice at the local level. Hegel, however, is guilty of tipping the balance in the other direction by fostering a show of participation at the local level while retaining real power in the hands of the national executive bureaucracy.

Although Hegel does not advocate an authoritarian state that would repress or arbitrarily restructure the interests of civil society, the supreme mediating function of the state bureaucracy impedes the democratic evaluation and reconstruction of social interests. Bernard Yack asserts that the "mature" Hegel abandoned the radical project of a "total revolution" aimed at abolishing the heteronomy of social institutions. Hegel abandoned such a project because he recognized that human institutions inherently involve "contingencies of nature" and thus can never fully correspond to human aspirations. Individual freedom, in Yack's interpretation of Hegel, can never be realized in social community but only in the realm of thought. Thus Yack presents Hegel as a pragmatic alternative to Marx's hubristic and willful attempt to achieve freedom through real-world community.[29] Yet the Hegelian project of transcending the conflict between the universal and the particular through a philosophic teleology of self-comprehending reason is as postpolitical a vision as Marx's materialization of the Hegelian dialectic. Hegel's idealist, "dialectical" reconciliation with the institutional structures of nineteenth-century European constitutional monarchies places no more faith in democratic politics than does the Marxian project of transcending politics out of the belief that social roles will be spontaneously organized by communist citizens in accord with the "objective" demands of "true human freedom." Neither Hegel nor Marx understood that in a democratic society the dialectic between universal and particular, or in more prosaic terms, between the common good and particular interests, never ends.

In Hegel's view democratic politics cannot promote a universal ethic because democracy's demand for social equality threatens the structure of private property; and it is through the ownership of private property that citizens exercise their free will and develop their character. In the modern age, civil society has reached its "highest" stage of articulation, in which each citizen can realize his true freedom through the mutual recognition of contractual exchange. But Hegel is well aware that the price of contractual freedom is growing poverty and social inequality. These conflicts of propertied society can be mitigated, Hegel believes, not only through state-facilitated awareness of the interdependence of the division of labor, but also through corporatist institutions taking responsibility for their disadvantaged members. Grafted onto Hegel's acceptance of the rise of commercial society is a longing for the often-romanticized organic bonds and paternalist responsibility of feudalism. But the corporatist bodies of civil society which promote such social bonding should not facilitate the transformation of economic and social interests.[30] The democratic participation of the "masses," defined by Hegel as groups not already structured by membership in particular civic institutions, can only lead, in Hegel's analysis, to tyranny and the unstructured, abstract freedom of the French Revolution. The Hegelian state aims neither to recreate the Athenian polis nor to construct an activist, authoritarian state. In the social relations of modern private property, Hegel contends, human beings have discovered rational freedom. The Hegelian state regulates this civil society of freedom, aiming to mitigate its inevitable social conflicts. But it excludes from meaningful political participation citizens who might democratically transform the structure of interests and property in an emerging commercial capitalism.

MODERN PRIVATE PROPERTY:
THE HIGHEST FORM OF SOCIAL FREEDOM

Apart from his teleological conception of history, Hegel's greatest influence on the radical tradition lies in his critique of natural rights liberalism. Hegel rejected social contract liberalism's grounding of political obligation in a theory of the "rational pursuit" of desire—whether that desire was fear of death or the pursuit of happiness. He joined Kant and Rousseau in believing that the rational will, unencumbered by particular desire, must be the ultimate grounds of political obligation. In contrast to Kant and Rousseau, however, Hegel rejected the will as the ultimate creator of community. Rather, the existence of a free political will presupposed the historical development of a political community founded on the principle of mutual respect and equality before the law.[31] These principles could be realized only in a state guaranteeing personal ownership of property and freedom of contract. In his early writings, Hegel, in language foreshadowing that of Marx, criticized the industrial labor process for dehumanizing and impoverishing the working class. But he offered no concrete alternative to the alienation of labor, to mass poverty, or to the hierarchical power relations of the emerging corporate firm. Some contemporary radical Hegel scholars, such as Richard Dien Winfield, believe that there is an implicit critique of modern capitalism within Hegel's assertion that the actual (*Wirklichkeit*) should conform to the rational (*Vernunft*) of self-determining freedom. According to Winfield's reading of Hegel, truly free human beings would not subject themselves to the working and living conditions of capitalism. Instead business corporations would evolve into social institutions jointly governed by managers and employees.[32]

What these contemporary "left Hegelian" interpretations downplay is Hegel's insistence on the central role that private property, including control by the owners of the goods produced by their workers, plays in the social instantiation of freedom. Although Hegel lamented poverty, mass unemployment, and dehumanized labor as by-products of civil society, they were for him the unavoidable price society paid for the rational freedom of private property. Hegel maintained that the poor would be morally improved by public begging because it affirms their dignity, whereas state provision of jobs or income support negates the desirable freedom of the market and is a demeaning form of unearned alms.[33] Nonmarket social provision, for Hegel, violates the search of the rational will for self-definition through "free" contractual, propertied relations.

Hegel referred to Rousseau and Kant as his two great forerunners, for they too had attempted to found a regime grounded on human will and reason. But their proffered solutions were marred, according to Hegel, by their abstract nature and their failure to instantiate freedom in the concrete social relations of property rights and contract. Hegel saw the categorical imperative and the general will as purely "negative" concepts; although they critiqued social relations, they did not offer a concrete alternative conception of community. Hegel supported Rousseau's quest to found political obligation on the will rather than in the passions. But he castigated Rousseau for failing to specify the political and social structure in which the general will could be embodied and for his hostility to particular identities and interests. Hegel praised Rousseau's critique of Hobbesian and Lockeian social contract liberalism. Rousseau's critique held that the liberal social contract was flawed by its founding a regime on the passions and an alleged natural law rather than on the free rational will, "adducing the will as the principle of the state . . . adducing a principle which has thought both for its form and its content, a principle indeed which is thinking itself, and not a principle, like gregarious instinct, for instance, or divine authority, which has thought as its form only."[34] But Hegel also criticized Rousseau for failing to ground the general will in the "absolutely rational element in the will" rather than in an element empirically common to everyone's particular will.

Hegel's reading is unfair to Rousseau, who carefully distinguished between an objective, unifying "general will" and an arbitrary "common will" contingently embraced by an unhealthy majority.[35] But Hegel's opening criticism in *The Philosophy of Right*—that Rousseau's general will negates the existence of particular wills and particular institutions—is a telling one, because the concept of the general will would contribute to the left's homogenizing conception of universal citizenship. *The Philosophy of Right* is haunted by the French Revolution's degeneration into the "absolute freedom" of the Terror. Although it was the first revolution made in the name of reason and self-determination, it engendered, in Hegel's view, "the negative freedom" of "the fury of destruction"[36] because freedom conceived as "arbitrariness" attacks all "differences of talent and authority . . . and the institutions which [the revolutionaries] had made themselves since any institution whatever is antagonistic to the abstract self-consciousness of equality."[37] Universal freedom, in Hegel's view, could develop only in a modern society that preserved the particular social inequalities of its constituent interests, while simultaneously promoting their identity with a universal state that actualized rational social interdependence.

The opening of the *The Philosophy of Right* is a passionate defense of private property and contractual exchange as the site of determinate moments of freedom. Property is described as the institutional basis for free and rational social relations among human beings. In Hegel's view, freedom is neither a faculty given by nature nor a capacity of the self. Rather, it is a socially structured relationship among individuals wherein the self-determination of each is constitutively related to that of others through mutual recognition and self-respect. The "abstract liberty" of Kant, in Hegel's view, conceived freedom to be a faculty of choice, an autonomous act of choosing among ends existing independently of that will. Hegel, in contrast, asserted that the will should not be conceived of as radically distinct from the social relationships that constitute it. Kant's project was bound to fail, in Hegel's view, because the will cannot give itself an end that owes its *content* only to the will itself.[38] Hegel believed that Kant's moral maxims could only produce a sense of duty constraining individual behavior. They could not develop within the individual a notion of freedom as being constituted by social relationships among a multiplicity of wills. That is, Kant failed to comprehend that freedom could only be institutionalized through willed social relationships among human beings.

For Hegel, the social institution of private property best institutionalized these willed bonds among humanity: "Contract presupposes that the parties entering it recognize each other as persons and property owners. It is a relationship at the level of mind objective, and so contains and presupposes the moment of recognition. . . . Contract brings into existence the property whose external side, its side as an existent, is no longer a mere 'thing' but contains the moment of a will (and consequently the will of a second person also)."[39] Through the ownership and control of property, particular persons are rendered distinct by the specific objects in which their will achieves socially recognized objectification, that is, socially recognition by fellow citizens. Hegel, however, rejects social contract liberalism's conception of the state as being created by a social contract among the people. To guarantee contracts—the realm of freely chosen, "arbitrary exchange"—the state must have a prior existence as a rational objective necessity. The state is the guarantor of contract and thus it is absurd to believe that contract can establish the state. In contrast to feudalism, in modern society no one can make a private contract between himself and the state. All are universal subjects of the state:

> The rational end of man is life in the state, and if there is no state there, reason at once demands that one be founded. Permission to enter a state or leave it must be given by the state; this then is not a matter which depends on an individual's arbitrary will and therefore the state does not rest on contract, for contract presupposes arbitrariness. . . . The great advance of the state in modern times is that nowadays all the citizens have one and the same end, an absolute and permanent end; it is no longer open to individuals, as it was in the Middle Ages, to make private stipulation in connection with it.[40]

Thus, grounding the creation of a state on the rule of law is both a historical and logical prerequisite for the existence of contractual freedom. Although Hegel overemphasized the ethos of the universal state at the expense of the relative autonomy of particular communities, he understood, as some communitarians do not, that equal membership in a universal state that treats all citizens equally before the law is a prerequisite for a lawful, pluralist society.

Still, Hegel's belief in the critical role that property plays in the "supersession of the pure subjectivity of personality"[41] does not lead him to endorse an egalitarian conception of a propertied democracy. Each person must be a property owner in order to be a citizen; but the natural play of differential talents and diligence in the marketplace will inevitably produce substantive inequality. The inequalities generated by equality of opportunity in the market in no way interfere with the Hegelian conception of equality of citizenship: "The equality which might be set up, e.g., in connection with the distribution of goods would all the same soon be destroyed again because wealth depends on diligence. . . . Of course men are equal, but only qua persons, that is, with respect only to the source from which possession springs; the inference from this is that everyone must have property. . . . But this equality is something apart from the fixing of particular amounts, from the question of how much I owe."[42]

Although Hegel countenances considerable inequality, the existence of poverty confronts him with an ethical dilemma. If one does not possess any property, how can one be a free contracting citizen? Jeremy Waldron contends that to be consistent Hegel should have favored a property-owning democracy that would guarantee a minimum amount of property to each citizen.[43] But Hegel's commitment to marketplace civil society as the realm of freedom forestalled his consideration of economic redistribution. Aware of the threat that social inequality posed to social integration, Hegel presumed that state regulation of the corporations and the corporations' voluntary care for their indigent members would curtail the poverty and anomie that inevitably accompany marketplace freedom.

THE HEGELIAN STATE AND CIVIL SOCIETY: THE HIGHEST FORM OF REASON

Hegel is undoubtedly the first great communitarian critic of liberal conceptions of morality; thus, it should not be surprising that striking parallels exist between his critique of Kantian ethnics and those of Michael Sandel and Alasdair MacIntyre. Part Two of *The Philosophy of Right*, the section on Morality, contends that a Kantian ethics of "the pure unconditioned self-determination of the will as duty" can exist only in the abstract realm of conscience. To abolish the radical gap between the Kantian *ought* of the conscience and the *is* of social reality, moral obligations must be built into the fabric of an "objective ethical order" that replaces "good in the abstract" with "a stable content independently necessary and subsistent in exaltation above subjective opinion and caprice. These distinctions are absolutely valid laws and institutions."[44] Moral life in Hegel's ethical society is no longer an abstract duty constraining individual behavior, but rather a commitment on the part of the individual to a society that enjoins him or her to promote its structures and to live according to its precepts. *Sittlichkeit* or the "concrete ethics" of Part Three of *The Philosophy of Right* is no longer subject to the radical gap between a Kantian *ought* and the *is* of a nonrational reality. Moral obligations are built into the very fabric of the ongoing rational community of the rational, corporatist marketplace society to which the modern citizen belongs.[45] In this sense the moral individual is the creation of a moral community rather than the creator of it.

In one sense Hegel's assertion at the opening of Part Three of *The Philosophy of Right* seems unextraordinary in the context of contemporary moral and political theory. Hegel appears to assert straightforwardly that human beings constitute their moral identities through communal and cultural life, rather than through the abstract workings of conscience. The "objective spirit" of a society is its norms as expressed in everyday social practice. But in the rest of *The Philosophy of Right*, Hegel makes a more radical claim: namely, that the modern state is the embodiment of reason and therefore of ethical life. But why should this be the case? Hegel offers a considered response: the modern state is the first in which human beings freely express their will in the diverse institutional and communal settings of civil society. Only in the social complexity of modernity can human beings, through their participation in the state-regulated corporations of civil society, comprehend how their particular identities relate to the "truly concrete universal" of the modern state. In modernity, *Geist* or Spirit fulfills itself because human beings, for the first time, comprehend the cosmic spirit—the World—their wills have (unintentionally) created.

But here Hegel's defense runs up against the standard objections to moral realism and teleological ethics which also apply to Marx. Even if human beings have a transparent understanding of their social role in society, does that make such interdependence morally good or just? A neo-Hegelian response might state that in modernity human beings do not simply comprehend their social situation; they also consciously create it. Does Hegel's regime, however, conform to the criteria that its members freely and consciously create its institutions? Do all members share equally in creating the institutions they allegedly accept as legitimate? Hegel is well aware of the inequality between the buyer and seller of labor-power in a modern marketplace economy. Yet he appears to believe that each judges his situation to be rational and free. Hegel never considers whether political means exist for members of society to deliberate on whether or not they deem their society just; he never subjects his "rational state" to the criteria of democratic legitimation. Is deliberative life in the corporations and estates sufficiently robust that members of such institutions endorse their situation by their very participation?

Although Hegel never embraces democracy, he still might have considered whether the social norms of mutual recognition implied in his description of civil society and the state were violated by the social reality of his day. Ironically, though often viewed as an early practitioner of "immanent critique," Hegel never applies that method to the modern state. The historical teleology of both *The Philosophy of Mind* and *The Philosophy of Right* is ultimately a conservative one, which implies that emerging liberal constitutional monarchies necessarily embody the highest form of rationality and freedom. But why can't modernity morally improve on itself? And why won't such improvement involve the action of fighting and struggle which Hegel identifies with all previous historical epochs? The answer, implied in the quiescent tone of *The Philosophy of Right*, is that attempts to lessen the inequalities of modern marketplace society will threaten functioning, integrative institutional structures with the terror of the "negative freedom" of the abstract will.[46] Modernity has traveled as far as it can toward social equality; to go further would threaten society with the social leveling and abolition of stable institutional freedoms witnessed during the Terror. Although political theorists have long debated his attitudes toward social reform, it is best to take Hegel for his word in *The Philosophy of Right*: "Since philosophy is the exploration of the rational, it is for that very reason the apprehension of the present and the actual, not the erection of a beyond, supposed to exist, God knows where, or rather which exists, we can perfectly well say where, namely in the error of a one-sided, empty ratiocination."[47] Although minor ameliorative reforms are possible, the dialectic of freedom and domination, of master and slave has ended, because the arbitrary imposition of the will has been transcended by legal, rational, bureaucratic governance.

Tragedy can only be studied in modernity; it cannot exist—or be criticized—because Hegel believes rational modernity has incorporated all the competing "one-sided ethics" that expressed partial truths in the past.[48] There are no more heroes in modernity, for ethical struggle has ceased:

> The tragic destruction of figures whose ethical life is on the highest plane . . . come on the scene in opposition to one another together with equally justified but different ethical powers which have come into collision through misfortune, because the result is that then these figures acquire guilt through their opposition to an ethical law. Out of this situation there arises the right and wrong of both parties and therefore the true ethical Idea, which, purified and in triumph over this one-sidedness, is thereby reconciled in us. Accordingly . . . we are elevated not by the destruction of the best but by the triumph of the true. This it is which constitutes the true, purely ethical, interest of ancient tragedy . . . But the ethical Idea is actual and present in the world of social institutions without the misfortune of tragic clashes and the destruction of individuals overcome by this misfortune. And this Idea's (the highest) revelation of itself in its actuality . . . is what the external embodiment of ethical life, the state, purposes and effects, and what the ethical self-consciousness possesses, intuits, and knows in the state and what the thinking mind comprehends there.[49]

Thus, prior to his analysis of the ethical life of modernity in Part Three of *The Philosophy of Right*, Hegel declares that it fulfills the demands of the ethical Idea.

Bernard Yack praises this Hegelian reconciliation of reason with reality in the world of thought because it avoids the violence of "the longing for total revolution"—the ineluctable effort to transform social institutions to conform fully to the human will. Yack contends that those who reject this Hegelian reconciliation of mind with nature in the realm of thought "would have to argue either that nature, in itself, serves human purposes or that the power of the human will is so great that it can destroy the forces of nature rather than merely redirecting them and mitigating their effects."[50] Apart from orthodox Marxists and self-defined, postmodern Nietzscheans, few would argue with Yack's assertion that both Nietzsche's will-to-power and Marx's vision of full communism pose dangerous utopias that ignore the limited ability of human subjects to shape their individual or collective destiny exactly to their expressed wills. But the collapse of the brutal, willful, and ineluctable project of planned industrialization from above (something far different from Marx's theory of the teleological supersession of advanced capitalist democracy by communism), neither logically nor empirically proves that democratic transformation is either impossible or already accomplished. The casual observer need only witness the epic struggles about the nature of democracy within not only the former Soviet empire but also Brazil, South Korea, Mexico, and South Africa. The same objection may be made to Frances Fukuyama's conception of the contemporary end-of-history.[51] What is peculiarly absent from the writings of the mature Hegel—or Fukuyama—is any spirit of radical reform, the faith that human beings can democratically restructure social institutions and "redirect them" in an emancipatory direction. Such struggle is possible without holding to the belief that emancipation will ever be fully attained. Although *The Philosophy of Right* opens with a radical critique of liberalism's atomized conception of human nature and its failure to conceptualize a free and pluralist community as a prerequisite for rights, it concludes by endorsing a liberal,[52] corporatist state as the highest form of civilization. This is why it is puzzling that contemporary "left Hegelians" such as David MacGregor, Richard Dien Winfield, and Stephen Smith believe that Hegel's project can be reappropriated in the service of a radical democratic pluralism.

MODERN CIVIL SOCIETY: THE INTERDEPENDENCE OF THE MARKETPLACE

For Hegel, civil society is fragilely held together by the mutual interdependence of human social and economic needs. The state's major function is to sustain and create barriers, both within and above civil society, which limit the centrifugal force of self-interest which simultaneously motivates and threatens life in civil society. If left to its own internal regulation, civil society would be overwhelmed by the concurrent development of uncontrollable needs and unsatisfied wants.[53] This insatiable drive for self-subsistence led to the ethical corruption of the substantial but undifferentiated ethical life of the ancient polis. Plato, recognizing this threat, banned private property and the family—the constituents parts of civil society—from the life of the ruling elite of his model polis. Hegel's vision of the rational modern state conceptualized the universal of the good society being reconciled with the particular freedom of the members of civil society.[54] The ancient world could not fend off the principle of particularity, nor could it satisfy it materially. Hence the materialist decadence of Rome and the spiritual inwardness of Christianity reflects, for Hegel, the inability of the ancient world to strike a proper balance between particular material needs and the spiritual need for universal self-comprehension.[55]

The Smithian system of interdependent needs is only one determinate moment of Hegel's civil society. The administration of justice in civil society, which liberal theorists traditionally assign to the state but which Hegel cites as part of civil society, renders clear the principle of universality behind the pursuit of property, while the *Polizei* (or "public authorities")[56] and corporations integrate particular economic interests with the common interest. Hegel's initial description of the Smithian "system of needs" is an homage to the workings of the invisible hand. He explicitly takes issue with Rousseau's critique of the market as artificially and dangerously expanding human needs. Hegel praises the liberation beyond the simple needs of natural society produced by an advanced division of labor and market society. The working of the marketplace ensures that "each man in earning, producing, and enjoying on his own account is *eo ipso* producing and earning for the enjoyment of everyone else." The expansion of needs teaches human beings to appropriate a multiplicity of objects through creative labor, and the division of labor not only "makes necessary everywhere the dependence of men on one another and their reciprocal relation in the satisfaction of their other needs" but also "makes work more and more mechanical, until finally man is able to step aside and install machines in his place."[57] Only in the later sections on the corporations does Hegel fear that the social interdependence of the division of labor will not be transparently evident to citizens increasingly defined by their circumscribed economic roles. The corporations consciously aim to foster that sense of interdependence among employers and employees of diverse skills working in the same economic sector or industry.

Amid this portrayal of growing abundance and the potential transcendence of manual labor, strikingly akin to that envisioned by Marx in the *Grundrisse*, Hegel admits that citizens will share in these general resources according to their differential contributions of capital and skill. Skill, Hegel acknowledges, in a manner prefiguring the argument of John Rawls, depends on "accidental circumstances" such as "natural, bodily and mental characteristics, which were already in themselves dissimilar." Hegel does not deny that marketplace society accentuates these inequalities of skill and resources and constructs them into differences of "even . . . moral and intellectual attainment." But he warns that any attempts at a crude leveling of these inequalities would do violence to the particularity of modern society: "To oppose to this right a demand for equality is a folly of the Understanding [*Verstehen* as contrasted to *Vernunft*] which takes as real and rational its abstract equality and its ought to be."[58]

Hegel momentarily worries that the inequalities of civil society may render some men less than full citizens, a fear described at greater length in the section on poverty. But, in Hegel's analysis, the state poses limits only on extreme destitution; to do otherwise would interfere not only with the workings of the market but also with modern subjectivity. In describing the liberation of needs engendered by the transcendence of mere natural needs and appetites, Hegel notes that with luxury also comes increased poverty because the material to meet these new needs is "permanently barred to needy man because it consists of property . . . the embodiment of the free will of others, and hence from his point of view its recalcitrance is absolute." Although Hegel offers the vague hope that "this situation can be brought into a harmony . . . by a state which has powers over it," he explicitly rejects the "Platonic" solution of the abolition of private property, asserting that "to exclude particularity from [the] state . . . is of no help, since help on these lines would contravene the infinite right of the Idea to allow freedom to the particular."[59] Although some locate the origins of the modern welfare state in Hegel's support of the *Polizei*'s regulation of market forces and its construction of public works, Hegel staunchly refuses to countenance redistribution of income or wealth. To do so would threaten the sanctity of private property which lies at the core of Hegel's concept of the modern free subject.

CLASS AND CORPORATE IDENTITY AS INSTITUTIONS OF SOCIAL INTEGRATION

Hegel, however, was acutely aware that social solidarity could not be engendered solely through the interaction of atomized producers in the free market. The workings of the market, he held, needed to be mediated through institutions of class and corporate solidarity. With family identity eroded by participation in civic life, class solidarity emerges as the most important form of social identification. For Hegel the word *Klasse* does not simply signify an individual's functional role in the mode of production; it also conveys a way of life shared by those working in a specific branch of the economy.[60] Hegel feared that the functional role of class in the emerging industrial division of labor would displace its social meaning. This anxiety motivated his advocacy of state-regulated corporatist institutions that promote cultural solidarity among those working in a specific economic sector, regardless of, in the modern functional sense, their class position. Despite the conflicting, "crisscross movements of reciprocal production and exchange," Hegel hopes that members of a class will partake in a common culture of shared "needs, modes of satisfaction and . . . theoretical and practical education." Class membership is thus transformed from a narrow economic category into a social meaning: "The family is the first pre-condition of the state, but class divisions are the second. . . . Although private persons are self-seeking, they are compelled to direct their attention to others. Here then is the root which connects self-seeking to the universal."[61]

Thus Hegel employs the term *Klasse* in two distinct ways: at times rather anachronistically, to indicate a postfeudal conception of shared work in a common economic sector; at other times in its modern industrial sense of a shared functional position in the division of labor (e.g., workers, capitalists). This ambiguous usage reflects the tension in Hegel's work between his longing for organic social solidarity and his recognition of the atomizing tendencies of an emerging capitalist order. Hegel wrote at a time when nascent industrial capitalism had yet to strip many artisanal workers of ownership of the means of production. But he was prescient enough to fear that emerging industrial class divisions would emerge as a defining social cleavage, unless countered by corporatist institutions preserving some aura of the social solidarity of artisanal production.

Hegel recognized the profound conflict between his postfeudal ethic of class solidarity and the bourgeois ethos of individual freedom underpinning the class mobility of industrial capitalism. The primary function of the "administration of justice" in civil society is not to reinforce group identity, but to ensure that every individual is treated as identical under civil law: "A man counts as a man in virtue of his manhood alone, not because he is a Jew, Catholic, Protestant, German, Italian, etc." But this ethos, if carried to the extreme of "cosmopolitanism in opposition to the concrete life of the state," may lead the individual to abandon communal attachments, "settling upon particular social position as [a] restriction on his universal character."[62]

To serve an integrating social function, class must be viewed by citizens as a cultural phenomenon rather than an arbitrary, or strictly achieved, economic distinction. Civil society's cohesion depends on the mediated interrelationship of particularist, defined social groupings (*Klasse* in his postfeudal usage). Yet Hegel implicitly recognizes that a citizen achieves "membership" in a modern economic class through competition in the atomized marketplace (*Klasse* in the modern functional sense). This tension between the solidarity of a shared cultural enterprise and individual class mobility is evidenced in Hegel's description of the *esprit de corps* of a class and how it is constructed on the basis of contingent, individual endeavor:

> In this class-system the ethical frame of mind therefore is rectitude and *esprit de corps*, i.e., the disposition to make oneself a member of one of the moments of civil society by one's own act . . . to fend for oneself only through this process of mediating oneself with the universal, while in this way gaining recognition both in one's own eyes and in the eyes of others. Morality has its proper place in this sphere where the paramount thing is reflection on one's doings, and the quest of happiness and private wants, and where the contingency in satisfying these makes into a duty even a single and contingent act of assistance.[63]

Underlying his defense of a seemingly anachronistic, postfeudal corporate identity is Hegel's concern that modern class consciousness, produced by "the quest of happiness and private wants," may not be a sufficient vehicle for social integration. Hegel also fears that the particularist pursuits of the two major classes of economic life, agrarian and business, lead to a situation in which no specific group attends to the "business" of social integration. Subsequent to the expression of this fear, Hegel advances a conception of a third class, "the universal class," which has no productive function in economic life. The private interest of the "universal class" finds its "satisfaction in its work for the universal."[64] Unlike Marx's universal class that encompasses all working people, Hegel's is limited to salaried state officials whose sole job is to promote the common good of the vast majority of citizens who pursue their particular interests.

The main task of the universal class appears to be alleviating the social conflicts of the commercial order and pursuing the general interests of the state. Yet Hegel devotes scant attention to defining how such general interests are determined, other than to say they are the concerns of the administrative corps and indirect representatives of the two economic estates. The "dispassionate, upright and polite demeanor" of the civil servants is produced through "direct education in thought and conduct."[65] Pressure from the sovereign above and the corporations below, Hegel believes, will ensure that the bureaucracy does not develop into the ruling "aristocracy" that Marx was to warn against in his *Critique of Hegel's Philosophy of Right.*[66]

Hegel mentions only in passing his understanding of how the "universal class" develops its conception of the universal interest. The good of society as a whole does not result from mass, democratic deliberation; nor is it simply an administrative science, though this "mechanical" training is important. It appears that governing in the interests of society as a whole can only be learned through that activity itself. Only by running the affairs of state do civil servants learn to abandon the subjective interests of members of civil society.[67] But as Hegel admits, given proper education, a surfeit of middle-class citizens could demonstrate the "objective . . . knowledge and proof of ability" necessary to serve in the civil service.[68] One need not be a genius to be a civil servant. So why is participation in the "important affairs of state" limited to so few? Hegel's answer appears to be that most affairs of state can be reduced to arbitration among competing interests that can be accomplished by any representative dispassionate civil servant. And although good administrators and arbitrators are needed, too many mediators would spoil the regulation. But if "the important affairs of state" primarily involve practical political judgment, rather than the discerning of objective truths, and if defining the common good involves choosing among divergent conceptions of public policy rather than identifying an objective collective interest, then the Hegelian argument for curtailing political participation in favor of dispassionate judgment carries little weight. Undoubtedly a modern, diverse society will need certain forms of bureaucratic authority to ensure the fair administration of politically determined laws and regulations. But to ensure this fairness, such servants of the public will need to be subject to popular, democratic accountability.

Hegel insists that a proper bureaucracy mainly administrates. In language surprisingly close to Weber's definition of the "scientific administrator," whose person is separated from his office,[69] Hegel writes: "The nature of the executive function is that they are objective and that in their substance they have been explicitly fixed by previous decisions. . . . Between an individual and office there is no immediate natural link."[70] Unlike Hegel, however, Weber realized that political judgment involved a complex normative process that went beyond "neutral" civil servants discovering allegedly objective, universal truths. Weber recognizes that political judgment is an inherently value-laden process that cannot be carried out by bureaucratic executors of political decisions. Weber worried obsessively about how political meaning might be reintroduced into an increasingly bureaucratized society. Even if his qualified hope for charismatic, plebiscitary leadership, to be checked by parliamentary representation of interest groups, is less than fully democratic, it has the merit of being a more political conception of the state's role in interest-group mediation than is Hegel's faith in a value-free civil service as a leadership class.[71]

If any political deliberation is necessary, Hegel advocates indirect representation of the corporations, which ensures that only the most educated and talented sit in the legislature. Each corporation elects members to the business estate, while the civil service selects the members of the agrarian estate. Direct democratic suffrage is not employed to elect any members of the two legislative chambers. Hegel favors such indirect modes of election because his greatest fear is the terror that results from the unmediated, direct democratic rule of the French Revolution. The rational state must be a structured, corporate state, in which each individual's identity is shaped by membership in a state-regulated class or corporate group:

> The sovereignty of the people is one of the confused notions based on the wild idea of "the people." Taken without its monarch and the articulation of the whole . . . the people is a formless mass and no longer a state. It lacks every one of those determinate characteristics—sovereignty, government, judges, magistrates, class-divisions, etc.—which are to be found only in a whole which is inwardly organized. By the very emergence into a people's life of moments of this kind which have a bearing on an organization, on political life, a people ceases to be that indeterminate abstraction which, when represented in a quite general way, is called the "people."[72]

Hegel, however, fails to investigate the structure of power within the corporations. If their internal deliberative life is less than democratic, then there is no assurance that interests will be democratically represented in the legislative estates, which themselves only advise the universal class. Only the universal class, uncontaminated by the influence of particular interests, can discern the true interests of society. Although Marx's concept of the universal class may also have homogenized the divergent interests likely to persist in a democratic, egalitarian society, at least his concept of the universal class aspired to be truly universal in its membership.

THE WORKING CLASS AND THE POOR:
THE LIMITS OF HEGELIAN SOCIAL SOLIDARITY

Due to his concern that members of civil society be provided with a constituent identity intermediary between market and state, Hegel devotes considerable attention to the one social problem he self-admittedly failed to solve: poverty. For the poor, alone among modern citizens, have neither a class nor corporate identity. The theoretical and political difficulties posed by a group of individuals who do not possess a culturally established, collective identity may also be the reason why, as compared to the early writings of the *Jena Manuscripts*, Hegel devotes little attention to the working class in *The Philosophy of Right* (*die Arbeitenklasse* in the *Jena Manuscripts*).[73] In *The Philosophy of Right*, the working class initially appears as a part of the manufacturing section (*die Fabrickenstand*) of the business estate (*die Stande des Gewerbes*). The business estate consists of those involved in craftsmanship, mass-production or manufacturing, and commerce and exchange. In the *Jena Manuscripts* Hegel devotes lengthy sections to the plight of the nascent industrial working class and the emergence of class conflict, and he employs the class categories of modern industrial society more than the post-feudal categories of business and landed estates: "Factories, manufacturing works depend for their very existence on the misery of a class [*Klasse*]—the class of industrial workers. . . . Masses of the population are condemned to labor in factories, manufacturing works, mines, etc.; work which is totally stupefying, unhealthy, insecure and faculty-stunting."[74]

In *The Philosophy of Right* Hegel makes only one indirect reference to the emerging working class as a group distinct from the owners and managers of the manufacturing class (those who are depicted as controlling the labor of the working class of the *Jena Manuscripts*). In the section where he describes the growth of mass poverty as a correlative of the division of labor's production of material wealth, Hegel notes in passing: "The other side [of the growth of needs and wealth] is the subdivision and restriction of particular jobs. This results in the dependence of and distress of the *class* tied to work of that sort, and these again entail inability to feel and enjoy the broader freedoms and especially the intellectual benefits of civil society."[75]

Perhaps Hegel barely mentions the working class by name in *The Philosophy of Right* because he could not conceive of how to include it in the system of corporate representation. Why should workers hold an allegiance to a society and state in whose benefits and freedoms they can, Hegel admits, little enjoy? And why should they share a cultural allegiance with the owners and managers who dominate the manufacturing corporations? Perhaps the fact that there were relatively few industrial workers in Hegel's day led him to believe that their nonincorporation did not pose a threat to the legitimacy of the modern state. But this is an unlikely opinion of a social theorist who envisaged the rapid growth of mass production and predicted that the modern nation-state would engage in a conscious search for overseas markets to solve an emerging crisis of industrial overproduction.[76] Hegel clearly hoped that limited participation by the working class in a common corporate life alongside the owners and managers of the manufacturing class (*die Fabrikenstande*) would produce a shared corporate identity. His intense focus on the emerging phenomenon of mass poverty, however, indicates that he believed it posed a greater threat to the stability of the modern regime than did the suffering of the working class.

Hegel is widely recognized to have left the problem of poverty unsolved in *The Philosophy of Right*. But he also failed to indicate any way in which the working class might overcome its alienation. The social integration of workers would supposedly result from their participation in the life of a manufacturing class dominated by owners and managers. Some contemporary "left Hegelians," such as David MacGregor, believe that Hegel's theory of the corporation implies a conception of "social ownership" that would humanize industrial labor. MacGregor argues that, at a minimum, Hegel's *Polizei* prefigured the ameliorative social policies of the welfare state. Truly shared corporate membership, MacGregor argues, would necessitate co-determinant forms of management among owners, white-collar personnel, and workers.[77] But the textual evidence for Hegel as a forerunner of social democratic corporatism is absent from Hegel's mature writings. Hegel undoubtedly believed there to be an integral relationship between private property and freedom. And integral to Hegel's conception of ownership is the right to control the use of one's possessions. Although Hegel indirectly defended some minimal voice for workers within the corporations, he never advocated democratic control of economic institutions as a prerequisite of freedom.

As with Adam Smith, however, Hegel was well aware of the emotional and moral price of the freedom of the market. Although he opposed redistribution of wealth and income, his *Polizei* prefigures the role in advanced capitalist regimes of regulatory agencies and state macroeconomic and trade policy. Hegel explicitly states that "freedom of trade should not be such as to jeopardize the general good." But because Hegel believes the aim of government regulation is to allow the individual citizen "the right to work for his bread as he pleases," he rejects any *public* redistribution schemes, as opposed to any voluntary redistribution that private corporate solidarity might produce. To provide the poor with public welfare programs would be to violate the basic source of freedom in modern civil society—individual labor. Either public grants or alms from the wealthy would mean that "the needy would receive subsistence directly, not by means of their work and this would violate the principle of individual independence and self-respect in its individual members."[78]

Even if the government were to provide public jobs for the able-bodied poor, this would not eliminate the pervasiveness of poverty which, Hegel believes, is caused by overproduction. Hegel may have presaged many of the aspects of the modern regulatory state, but he did not envision Keynesian demand management. An adherent to classical political economy's belief in a chronic overproduction, underconsumption cycle, Hegel writes that "despite an excess of wealth civil society is not rich enough, i.e., its own resources are insufficient to check excessive poverty and the creation of a penurious rabble." Temporary poverty among a small group of people will not, Hegel hopes, threaten the fabric of civil society. The dignified poor still aspire to be full contributing members of civil society. But persistent poverty among a large number of people who reject the work ethic and yet demand subsistence from the state inevitably engenders "a rabble" (*Pobel*). "The rabble" poses a danger to the stability of civil society because they "join to poverty a disposition of mind, an inner indignation against the rich, against society, against the government, etc."[79] Hegel believes that achieving one's livelihood through selling one's labor on the market is essential to citizenship. Yet Hegel's adherence to the Malthusian assumptions of classical political economy leads him to regret that an unemployed "rabble" is likely to be a permanent condition of modernity. Hegel recognizes this problem but studiously avoids any further discussion of it. Undoubtedly he held to a radical, communal conception of human identity. But as his refusal to challenge the immutable rights of private property demonstrates, a radical ontology need not yield a radical democratic politics.

Though Hegel appears indignant at the rabble who claim "their rights," he cannot deny that poverty, being a "natural product" of the business cycle, capriciously excludes many from civil society: "The poor still have the needs common to civil society, and yet since society has withdrawn from them the natural means of acquisition and broken the bond of the family—in the wider sense of the clan—their poverty leaves them more or less deprived of all the advantages of society, of the opportunity of acquiring skill or education of any kind, as well as of the administration of justice, the public health services, and often even of the consolations of religion, and so forth."[80] Hegel wishes that the public authority could take responsibility for providing for the poor; but the only means he can discern for doing so would violate the work ethic central to the maintenance of civil society. Hence, his final words on the subject of poverty in *The Philosophy of Right* is that its persistence poses "one of the most disturbing problems which agitate modern society." The best interim solution Hegel could offer was the "Scottish solution"—public begging. In Hegel's analysis, beggars find social consolation by avoiding a loss of self-respect by "working" for their alms. But the fact that "the lower classes, the mass of the population, have been left more or less unorganized"[81] continues to vex Hegel throughout the rest of *The Philosophy of Right*.

Hegel understood that the classical liberal, "nightwatchman" state confuses the task of civil society, the pursuit of individual material desires, with the state's true role of promoting human community. The rational state must do more than simply ensure the laws of the market. It must promote communal identification, both within civil society and with the state's universal identity: "If the state is confused with civil society, and if its specific end is laid down as the security and protection of property and personal freedom then the interest of the individuals as such becomes the ultimate end of their association, and it follows that membership of the state is something optional. But the state's relation to the individual is quite different from this. Since the state is mind objectified, it is only as one of its members that the individual himself has objectivity, genuine individuality and an ethical life."[82] The poor pose a vexing challenge to Hegel because their fragile ties to the market cannot be institutionalized into a stable corporate identity. The poor also starkly reveal that an uncritical celebration of the associational life of civil society which ignores power differentials cannot guarantee the equal moral worth of all citizens.

The Corporation: Providing Private Business
with a Public Character

In *The Philosophy of Right* the corporation is the main institution for promoting communal identification with the state. Although Hegel admits that this postfeudal institution is fast fading throughout commercial Europe, he argues for its revitalization as the best means for combating the economic excesses of civil society. The corporations would strengthen the sense of common membership among marketplace competitors participating in the same economic sector. Hegel exempts both the agrarian class and the civil service from this corporate structure, because the agrarian class is allegedly communally rooted by its natural and familial orientation and the civil service has the universal explicitly as its ground and aim. The main function of the corporation is to provide those members of the "business class" who work in the same industry or trade with a sense of communal membership previously supplied by the extended family. Corporations can take numerous forms—trade associations, artisanal guilds, industry-wide interest groups. They look out for the collective interest of their members and provide for their general welfare and education. In particular they can provide for their poor members without stripping them of dignity: "Within the Corporation the help which poverty receives loses its accidental character and the humiliation wrongfully associated with it. The wealthy perform their duties to their fellow associates."[83]

At the same time that the corporation's bonds of solidarity combat one of the market's worst side effects, poverty, they also inhibit the very avarice that engenders poverty. As members of the corporation, entrepreneurs gain a sense of membership and security that curtails their need to establish their identity through ruthless marketplace competition. This normative regulatory function of the corporation is usually overlooked by Hegel scholars, who tend to describe the corporation as an arena for political participation. But it is the normative function of corporate membership, its providing members with a moral purpose and restricting the desire to achieve recognition through crass individualism, which Hegel describes at greatest length:

> When complaints are made about the luxury of the business classes and their passion for extravagance—which have as their concomitant the creation of a rabble of paupers—we must not forget that besides its other causes (e.g., increasing mechanization of labor) this phenomenon has an ethical ground . . . Unless he is a member of an authorized Corporation . . . an individual is without rank or dignity, his isolation reduces his business to mere self-seeking, and his livelihood and satisfaction become insecure. Consequently, he has to try to gain recognition, external proof of success in his business, and to these proofs no limits can be set. He cannot live in the manner of his class, for no class really exists for him, since in civil society it is only something common to particular

persons which really exists, i.e., to something legally constituted and recognized. Hence he cannot achieve for himself a way of life proper to his class and less idiosyncratic.[84]

The corporation makes explicit the interdependent, social content of a society based on needs which appears to the unaided human understanding as a society of competitive, atomized individuals. The identity derived from participation in the market corresponds to Hegel's description of the concept of *Verstehen* in *The Philosophy of Mind* —the "understanding" that only comprehends the particular identities of needs-based civil society. The corporate structuring of society, Hegel hopes, will produce a social identity corresponding to his concept of *Vernunft*. That is, "reason" will be the essence of a state whose members comprehend the universal, structural interdependence among the particular constitutive organizations of society.

To locate in Hegel's corporations a major arena for political participation is to exaggerate the deliberative import of what transpires within them. Matters of state, Hegel believes, are best left to experts and bureaucrats: "Under modern political conditions, the citizens have only a restricted share in the public business of the state, yet it is essential to provide men—ethical entities—with work of a public character over and above their private business. . . . We saw earlier . . . that in fending for himself a member of civil society is also working for others. But this unconscious compulsion is not enough; it is in the Corporation that it first changes into a known and thoughtful ethical mode of life."[85] Like the Rotarians, the corporations stress the public benefits that private enterprise brings to society.[86] They regulate the ethics of business conduct, but they do not determine state policy at either the national or local level. Their role in politics is confined to serving as sites for the selection of representatives to the legislative estates. "Selection" is the most appropriate term because citizens only indirectly elect representatives to the legislature. The business corporations elect some of the representatives of the legislative estates. But the civil service of the executive branch reserves the power to co-opt representatives to the estates from the corporations.[87]

Hegel describes the identity that most citizens have with the state in terms not far from those of an instrumental liberalism—citizens obey the state because of the protection the state provides their particular endeavors. Although the state may have a "higher universal orientation," it is "premised upon the preservation of the lower, less comprehensive spheres. My particular freedom should become identified with the universal end, or otherwise the state is left in the air." In peacetime, Hegel writes, the particular spheres of civil society "mind their own business" and contribute "to the support of the whole" through the operation of the invisible hand, aided by the social control mechanisms of the corporations. The corporations promote identification with the state; but they do not promote participation within it. If the corporations make clear to their members that the state is the grand facilitator of their particular endeavors, then the corporations will have fulfilled their primary task, instilling loyalty to the state: "This is the secret of the patriotism of the citizens in the sense they know the state . . . maintains their particular spheres of interest together with the title, authority of welfare of [the citizens]."[88]

Hegel rejects the invisible hand argument that the unregulated pursuit of individual interests naturally promotes the general interest.[89] As Hegel comprehends civil society to be a realm of both conflict and interdependence, he advocates the development of corporatist institutions in civil society which ameliorate market conflicts and strengthen consciousness of social interdependence. Hegel may have believed, as Steven Smith argues, that individual rights based on mutual self-respect can be realized only in the context of community.[90] But the communal life of the corporations neither provides an arena for substantive political participation nor for social relations of mutual respect.

Political theorists who contend that Hegel was the first philosopher to advocate a rich associational life in a civil society located between the bureaucratic state and the atomized market fail to investigate Hegel's specific description of the corporations. Such an investigation reveals the corporations to be primarily institutions of ideological exhortation. The corporations fail to give equal voice to their members in the shaping of their particular associational life or in the politics of the broader society. Hegel's ultimate vision is not one of democratic pluralism, but of an epiphenomenal pluralism that obfuscates the power relations within civil society. To prevent social conflict, Hegel proposes that any conflict promoted by these inequalities of wealth and power be mediated by corporations whose behavior is guided by an allegedly universal class of civil servants. Hegel rejected the central, though by no means exclusive, role that the play of interests must have in a democratic politics because of his premonition of the centrifugal tendencies inherent to social pluralism. Hegel partially shared the radical tradition's critique of the classical liberal belief that the free play of interests within civil society would result in a fair and stable society. But his greater concern for social stability meant he did not pursue a thoroughgoing critique of the undemocratic nature of power relations within civil society, particularly property relations. Such a critique remains a prerequisite for a radical democratic conception of political pluralism.

WHAT GOES ON IN THE HEGELIAN STATE: THE ADMINISTRATING AWAY OF POLITICS

Aside from the bureaucrats and the figurehead monarch—who dots the *i*s and crosses the *t*s of legislation in a manner similar to that of contemporary constitutional monarchs—who minds the Hegelian state? Hegel divides the modern state into the legislature, the executive, and the crown. He rejects Montesquieu's conception of the separation of powers, arguing that the different arms of the state must work together to produce a unified state policy.

Hegel argues that such a unity could not result if the different branches' "function is to oppose one another and as a result of this counterpoise to effect an equilibrium on the whole, but never a living unity." Most interpretations accept Hegel at his word that the legislature, divided into two chambers representing the business and agrarian estates respectively, is the realm for deliberation about the political direction of society as a whole, "the power to determine and establish the universal." An examination of the operations of Hegel's legislature, however, discloses its deliberative functions to be limited to setting the level of taxation, "the exaction of services from [private individuals]," and aiding the executive (the universal class) in regulating "the rights of communities, Corporations and organizations affecting the entire state." The legislative estates are not to deliberate about the constitutional structure of the state, let alone transform it. Instead, Hegel counsels almost a Burkeian conception of prescriptive virtue, arguing that "the constitution should not be regarded as something made, even though it has come into being in time. It must be treated rather as something existent in and by itself, as divine therefore, and constant, and so as exalted above the sphere of things that are made."[91]

The essential function of the legislature is to serve as a transmission belt for information to the bureaucracy from the two estates and the corporations. Hegel holds that the criteria of selection for members of the legislature should not be their representation of the interests of the various corporations, but the possession of a middle-class "political and administrative sense and temper" that can work "in common with the organized executive . . . they are a middle term preventing both the extreme isolation of the crown . . . and also the isolation of the particular interests of persons, societies and Corporations [from the bureaucracy]." The legislature serves as scouts for the universal class, providing the bureaucracy with "additional insight . . . into the activity of such [Corporate] officials as are not immediately under the eye of the higher functionaries of the state." They also serve to keep the bureaucracy in touch with mass opinion by "the anticipation of criticism from the Many," ensuring that the bureaucracy deals with these demands "only in accordance with the purest motives."[92] Instead of state policy resulting from a separation of power between a legislature that makes general laws and an executive that administers them in particular cases, Hegel describes a unified state in which the bureaucratic executive definitively regulates competing interests in civil society based on information provided by the legislative representatives of the two estates. Rather than a professional bureaucracy providing technical assistance to a sovereign legislature, the true locus of sovereign power in Hegel's state is in the bureaucracy of the executive branch.

Hegel does not hide his disdain for direct, popular sovereignty. He asserts that the bureaucrats of the executive branch will possess sounder political judgment than do legislative representatives because bureaucrats pursue solely universal interests, whereas representatives of the estates and corporations in the legislature pursue the interests of their narrow *Stande* or *Klasse*:

As for the conspicuously good will for the general welfare which the Estates are supposed to possess, it has been pointed out already . . . that to regard the will of the executive as bad, or as less good [than that of the ruled] is a presupposition characteristic of the rabble or of the negative outlook generally. This presupposition might at once be answered on its own ground by the counter-charge that the Estates start from isolated individuals, from a private point of view, from the particular interests, and so are inclined to devote their activities to these at the expense of the general interests, while *per contra* the other moments in the power of the state [the executive bureaucracy] explicitly take up the standpoint of the state from the start and devote themselves to the universal end.[93]

Hegel believes that instances of political opposition between the legislative estates and the executive will be extremely rare because the precommercial agrarian estate will "naturally" support the universal interests of society, as annunciated by the bureaucracy. As a stable, "natural class," insulated from the competition of the market and committed to traditional values of social deference, the agrarian estate will invariably side with the bureaucracy in any dispute it might have with the interest-ridden business estate.[94] The preeminent concern of the agrarian estate with working the land leads it to possess, in Hegel's terms, a healthy disdain for political life. Members of this estate care so little for politics that they do not demand competitive elections to the legislative estates, allowing the executive to select their representatives. Thus, for Hegel, political passivity by ordinary citizens is a virtue rather than a vice, despite the claims of those who wish to find in Hegel a vigorous defender of participation in civic life.

The countervailing power of the agrarian estate against the interest-ridden business estate is not the only means by which Hegel proposes to limit the political meddling of the legislature. He also proposes that the deliberations of the legislative estates be limited to "their mediating function" of providing advice to the bureaucracy: "In this way their opposition to the executive is reduced to a show. . . . if they were opposed, not merely superficially, but actually and in substance, then the state would be in the throes of destruction."[95] Hegel does not wish the legislative estates to deliberate over political issues, because such activity would bring interest-laden conflict into the harmonious state. He has faith that those in the business estate will agree to limit their role to providing information to the bureaucracy because the venal nature of the commercial class leads them to focus their energy on the private haggling of civil society and the pursuit of patronage positions within the legislature. Hegel believes that the executive can harmlessly satisfy this desire for patronage by doling out sinecures that have minimal political power but considerable social status. In two striking paragraphs Hegel openly derides the trivial affairs of the corporations and approvingly notes that their concern with patronage and economic aggrandizement will salutarily keep the minds of citizens off of the grand affairs of state. Hegel celebrates the alienation of the average citizen from politics and takes evident pleasure in describing the affairs of the corporation as exercises in inconsequential vanity. The governance of the corporations do not serve as local schools of democracy. Rather Hegel conceives them to be a useful distraction for the average citizen from larger political affairs best left to the civil service. Regarding the internal governance of the corporations, Hegel writes:

> The administration of a Corporation's business by its own officials is frequently clumsy because . . . they have a far less complete appreciation of the connection of those affairs with more remote conditions and the outlook of the state. . . . This sphere of private interest, however, may be regarded as the one . . . which affords a playground for personal knowledge, personal decisions and their execution, petty passions and conceits. This is more permissible, the more trivial, from the point of view of the more universal affairs of state, is the intrinsic worth of the business which in this way comes to ruin or is managed less well or more laboriously, etc. And further, it is all the more permissible, the more this laborious or foolish management of such trivial affairs stands in direct relation with the self-satisfaction and vanity derived therefrom.[96]

As long as the corporations relegate their activities to "the trivial playground" of private interest, they enable the universal class to devote its exclusive attention to the true interests of the state. Hegel's conception of indirect representation is not a precursor of modern "democratic corporatism" or functional representation, but an undisguised ideological apparatus for imparting a sense of universal import to the constituent classes of civil society's "trivial pursuit" of private gain.

Hegel evinces no greater faith in the political capacities of the legislative estates than he did in that of the corporations, even though part of the function of the estates is to aggregate the interests of the more particularist corporations. Members of the legislative estates, at least, fight over trivial state appointments, while corporation members only haggle over the private organization of commerce: "The Estates have to deal, not with the essential elements in the organism of the state, but only with rather specialized and trifling matters, while the passion which even these arouse spends itself in party cravings in connection with purely subjective interests such as appointments to the higher offices of state."[97] Hegel's writings on the deliberative roles of the corporations and legislative estates further demonstrates his pessimism as to the average citizens' capacity for democratic participation. The legislative estates provide crucial information to the bureaucracy about the mood within civil society, and the estates can also supposedly check any effort by the relatively autonomous bureaucracy to transform the basic constitutional laws. This function does not reflect Hegel's wish to empower the legislature to legislate, but rather his wish to ensure that the bureaucrats of the legal, rational state only arbitrate and mediate rather than attempt to restructure power relations in civil society. The structure of the estates purposely precludes their exercising direct political power. The estates reveal to their subsidiary corporations the functional role of the mediation of the bureaucracy in reconciling the interests of the various constituencies of civil society. The existence of the legislature also serves to distract the most active citizens from seeking political power by tempting them with the spoils of figurehead offices.

Hegel hereby prefigures another classic antinomy of future radical thought: the stark counterposition of centralized and decentralized forms of authority. Such a counterposition has often made it easy for radicals to defend regimes that supposedly allow for broad forms of local political participation while suppressing open political competition over national affairs. Hegel at least is honest about the aim of his conservative decentralization: to distract ordinary citizens from the major questions of the day. Democratic radicals, however, need to remember that there cannot be meaningful grassroots political participation if national affairs of state are not also open to democratic popular deliberation.[98]

Hegel's goal of building social solidarity through official codification and regulation of social differentiation is an immense project of social integration from above. Its main technique is bureaucratic management rather than political decision-making. No other modern philosopher, apart from Marx, more unsparingly explored the internal tension within modernity between universal and particular forms of identity. Yet Hegel's proffered solution to these tensions is a bureaucratic mediation of conflict which acquiesces in the given distribution of power in civil society. Hegel believed that making members of civil society more conscious of their mutual interdependence would mitigate civil society's war of all against all. But he proposed to achieve that social integration through citizens' participation in anachronistic corporatist structures whose real-world economic and social functions are strikingly amorphous, beyond the promotion of a vague ethos of social solidarity. A vibrant democratic politics, in Hegel's analysis, would only facilitate the playing out on the public stage of the latent conflicts in civil society. The alleged chaos and tyranny of the French Revolution's attempt at democratically restructuring civil society convinced Hegel that democracy could not mend a fractured civil society. Hegel preferred that the problems of civil society should be rendered manageable and containable by an enlightened universal class of civil (*not political*) servants. Social conflict should be bureaucratically regulated rather than freely deliberated over by a politically engaged citizenry.

But then is there any politics left in the Hegelian state? It is no accident that the major political undertaking of the Hegelian state is war. For war is the only act of state that transcends the particular interests and crass materialism of civil society: "War is the state of affairs which deals in earnest with the vanity of temporal goods and concerns. . . . This is what makes it the moment in which the ideality of the particular attains its right and is actualized."[99] The latter sentence precisely expresses the function that the Hegelian state serves. It is the ideal expression of the unity of interdependent, particular interests. War provides a naturally selfish bourgeoisie with a remedial civic education. In peacetime the state's aim is to prevent the war of all against all in civil society. But only in war is the true unity of these mediated particular interests realized. Thus Hegel joins such "republican" theorists as Cicero, Machiavelli, the founding fathers, and Hannah Arendt in celebrating the founding of states and their preservation through war as the highest form of politics. (Arendt, to be fair, is more a celebrant of founding than of war.) But in their celebration of grand political moments, republican theorists frequently disdain analyzing the "instrumental," interest-laden socioeconomic and cultural conflicts that characterize the day-to-day politics normally confronting ordinary citizens.

Hegel hoped that the vain pursuit of material goods would lead most citizens to be indifferent to politics, thus freeing the civil service to regulate social conflict dispassionately. Such bureaucratic management of civil society in the universal interest of all would, Hegel hoped, eliminate the desire of classes in civil society to transform society by political means. Lurking beneath Hegel's endorsement of the rule of a dispassionate civil service is his fear of the mass democratic upheaval of the French Revolution. Hegel did not ignore the possibility that his state bureaucracy might develop into an interest unto itself, as Marx predicted in the *Critique of Hegel's Philosophy of Right*. Hegel wished the legislative estates to curtail bureaucratic aggrandizement, and the bureaucracy to prevent the legislative estates from allowing class interests to determine state action (another charge of Marx's). Marx accepted the conception of crude forms of instrumental liberalism that politics can never rise above the pursuit of particular interests. Hegel tried to transcend politics by curtailing the political influence of interests through the bureaucratic mediation of conflict by his universal class of civil servants. Marx's universal class, in contrast, aimed to transcend politics by coming to power and abolishing the very particularity that, in his view, gives rise to politics in the first place. By socially controlling both nature and production, Marx believed that people would be set "free" to engage in the predominantly individual pursuits of their "species-being." Hegel, in distinction to Marx, correctly perceived the importance of particular identities and communal projects within civil society to the social development of freedom. He also correctly cautioned that the distance between ourselves and the projects in which we invest ourselves—the process of "objectification"—can never be fully overcome. But his fear of political anarchy precluded him from envisioning either a democratic political role for secondary associations within the political life of the state or the political possibility of internally democratizing the structure of interest groups.

Marx had a utopian faith that once the duality between civil society and the political state had been eliminated there would be no need for representation or mediation among social institutions truly governed by their members. Hegel realistically denied that the duality between state and civil society could ever be completely abolished. But rather than advancing a conception of the democratic political regulation of power relations in civil society,

Hegel defended a system of bureaucratic management of such conflict. The legislative estates would provide citizens with a semblance of representation, while essentially serving as a transmission belt linking particular interests to the workings of an omniscient ruling bureaucracy of experts. Hegel attempted to preclude transformative political possibilities through expert management of the social status quo. Marx, as will be examined in the next chapter, was oblivious to the permanence of the transformative potential of human interests in even "postrevolutionary" societies.

The Origins of Marx's Hostility to Politics

THE DEVALUATION OF RIGHTS AND JUSTICE

Marx's Explicit Rejection of
Moral Philosophy—The Root of His
Postrevolutionary Moral Agnosticism

Throughout his work Karl Marx chided utopian socialists for developing extensive blueprints of a future socialist society. In contrast he held that the primary role of the socialist theorist should be to analyze the laws of motion of capitalist society and the socialist society pregnant within capitalism. Marx's hostility to speculation about the postrevolutionary institutional and political organization of socialism is not, however, solely a product of his materialist opposition to idealist philosophy. It also derives from his faith that "full communism" would be a classless, conflict-free society that transcends scarcity and thus the need for political and juridical institutions. The free development of each would be the precondition for the free development of all through a vague and underspecified collective administration of the means of production by "the free association of producers." This vision of the elimination of tension between individual and collective choice ignores the inevitable persistence in even the most humane of societies of the social problem of aggregating individual preferences into a collective choice. Given that there is no one perfect solution to problems of social choice, it would be necessary to solve them politically in the most just of societies.[1]

Although in his journalistic work Marx acknowledged the role of religious and national identity in political conflict, his formal materialist schema recognized only class as the structural basis for social interests. Come the revolution and the abolition of class society, social interests would be abolished, as would the need for politics to adjudicate among them. In addition, his historical materialist critique of classical political economy's ahistorical, naturalized assumptions about the market led Marx to emphasize, in his own methodological reflections, a "scientific" and stageist conception of "historical materialism." Consequently Marx's insistence on his analysis of capital as a "science" led to his downplaying the role of politics in social change in his formal and analytical writings such as *Capital*, although many of his journalistic and historical writings implicitly recognize a relatively autonomous, causal historical role for politics.[2]

In light of the human rights violations committed by regimes acting in

Marx's name, radical democrats need to move beyond Marx's postrevolutionary agnosticism and outline a democratic conception of postcapitalist politics, justice, and freedom. This is not to argue that Marx's vision of communism directly prefigures the authoritarian statism and repressive industrialization policies of twentieth-century Communist regimes, but his rejection of an explicit political and ethical theory of socialism severely weakened the ability of socialists critical of authoritarian communism to claim his mantle. This chapter examines both the intellectual resources and barriers within the Marxist tradition for a moral vision of radical democracy. The greatest barrier to discovering an unambiguous normative vision of democracy and freedom within Marx remains his self-conception as a "scientific socialist," a materialist neo-Hegelian delineating the laws of motion of historical development while eschewing allegedly hollow moral pronouncements. When human beings live a truly emancipatory life, possible only under the advanced material conditions of full communism, they will, in Marx's view, need no superfluous moral guidelines to codify their already-humane existence.

Yet existing alongside this self-conceived materialist Marx is the work of an implicit moral theorist who condemns capitalism for violating human freedom and who envisions a society in which social institutions are democratically constructed and social goods are distributed according to human needs. Not even in his analysis of the radical democracy of the Paris Commune, however, does Marx adequately recognize the role of social pluralism, checks and balances on state power, and institutionalized civil and political rights in the life of a democratic society.[3] This failure of recognition derives not solely from the prohibitions of the materialist Marx against normative speculation. Even in his implicitly normative writings on communist society, Marx fails to comprehend the centrality of political deliberation and conflict to the achievement of individual autonomy through communal life—the great challenge of all democratic projects. He is blinded to the role of democratic institutions and norms by an Enlightenment-influenced faith in the technological possibility of completely transcending scarcity, his belief that human beings share a comprehensive set of true universal interests, and by his rigid conception of alienation which opposed all mediating institutions as distancing individuals from spontaneous human relations. Marx brings to its greatest height that tension in Enlightenment thought, most pointedly analyzed by Roberto Ungar, between its commitment to a deterministic science of society, on the one hand, and to the transcendent value of human freedom on the other.[4]

Simplistic ideological critiques of Marx often accuse him of being a leveling egalitarian. Yet his utopian commitment to the flowering of individuality and his rejection of a homogenizing egalitarianism ironically contribute to his rejection of moral principles as inevitably treating human beings unfairly. By subjecting unique individuals to universal principles, Marx believes moral norms invariably ignore relevant differences among individuals. This conception that moral norms unfairly subject unique individuals to homogenizing standards precludes Marx from systematically theorizing about those normative principles essential to a democratic society.

Contrary to Marx's spontaneist conception of social organization under communism, neither human needs nor the practices of self-governing institutions are transparently given *a priori*. Rather, they must be democratically discovered through institutional practices that respect the rights of diverse individuals and communities. Otherwise, how would a communist society determine distribution according to needs? Such a principle of distribution involves an implicit theory of justice which states that "true human needs" have greater claims on social resources than do superfluous human wants[5] But by what procedures does society determine what are true human needs? How should communist society adjudicate among distinct, and potentially competing, interests of individual and community, workplace and macroeconomy, region and nation (or international society/state)?

Marx advances the naively utopian assumption that full communism will completely transcend scarcity; thus, under communism true human interests will spontaneously be in accord. The assumption of postscarcity allows Marx to be oblivious to the role of democratic institutions in resolving social disputes now "solved" undemocratically by the inequalities of power of the capitalist market and state. Yet the inherent scarcity of time and the complexity of modern social institutions inevitably means that the transcendence of one form of scarcity will engender other scarce goods. Although efficiency is obviously a socially constructed norm, it is hard to imagine a society that fully transcends the trade-off between its own conception of efficiency and popular participation. Market mechanisms, for example, may provide producers with increased information about consumer demand, but they cannot produce perfect information about externalities or future demand. Participation may increase democratic input but may also lead to relative scarcities of information and expertise. Democratic political institutions provide the only means for adjudicating among these conflicting interpretations of interests and norms.[6]

MARX'S SELF-UNDERSTANDING: THE SCIENTIFIC AMORAL ANALYST OF THE LAWS OF MOTION OF CAPITAL

Marx's conscious desire to transcend moral philosophy is the key epistemological underpinning to his expressed agnosticism regarding the institutional structures and moral practices of a postrevolutionary society. As a materialist appropriator of Hegel's historicism, Marx shared Hegel's disdain for Kant's alleged attempt to construct an abstract moral argument for what ought to be.[7] Human practices, according to Marx, are developed within specific historical circumstances; to judge them apart from these circumstances is to engage in irrelevant moralizing. Rather, Marx conceived his work to be a scientific, materialist analysis of the future socialist society developing within increasingly interdependent, social, capitalist forces of production. Marx acknowledges that those who employ moral language claim to make impartial and universal judgments. In reality, however, Marx believes that moral language only cloaks the partial interests of its advocates. During a brief revolutionary conjuncture, a rising revolutionary class may effectively promote the interests of all subordinate classes. But once the revolutionary class's hegemonic rule is established, the morality of the "general interest" serves only to obfuscate the particular dominance of the nonexistent ruling class.[8]

Marx's epistemology precluded the separation of facts and values, thereby contributing to his reluctance to make a distinct, *explicit* moral argument for socialism. Although Marx praised communism for producing the first society in which human beings autonomously create and control their social relationships, he appears to conceive of autonomy and freedom as nonmoral goods. That is, for Marx, the capacity for freedom is a fact about human desires and capacities which naturally motivate human beings, in a manner similar to the desire for good health. It is the objective good of human autonomy rather than a subjective moral good, such as honor or duty, that motivates human resistance to domination.[9]

Alan Gilbert has ambitiously attempted to reconstruct Marx as a moral realist deeply committed to the enhancement of human freedom. Gilbert admits, however, that Marx's implicit moral realist project was seriously hampered by his surface commitment to a meta-ethical relativism. Gilbert contends that a neo-Kantian fallacy accounts for the belief of some contemporary moral theorists that moral realism poses an inherent barrier to coherent moral reasoning due to its tenet that moral norms reflect particular nonmoral facts. This fallacy equates all moral deliberation with a "quasi-Kantian" noumenal conception of justice as the reflection of the free will of rational beings unencumbered by heteronomous, material constraints. In Gilbert's analysis, Marx moves ambiguously between a primary meta-ethical relativism and occasional but recurring moral realist patterns of analyses which are more in accord with his implicit moral commitments. Gilbert attempts to reconstruct Marx as a "moral realist" whose conception of justice derives from reflection on the natural, "objective" characteristics of human beings, such as their demonstrated capacity for moral personality.[10] But Gilbert admits that this reading of Marx stands in stark contrast with Marx's explicit statements that moral norms are not objective or universal, but rather historically relative to the functional needs of a given mode of production.

If reading Marx as a moral realist poses the best grounds for rescuing the moral theorist in Marx, Allen Wood's interpretation of Marx as a neo-Hegelian who viewed morality as a system of regulatory norms operating within a specific social organism, better captures Marx's expressed self-conception as a meta-ethical relativist and historical materialist.[11] This self-conception precluded Marx from advancing his implicit norms of autonomy and freedom as criteria for evaluating subsequent socialist societies. According to

Wood, Marx believed that in a stable, "healthy" social order, one capable of reproducing itself, moral norms are in accord with the functional needs of that system and with the interests of its ruling class. When Marx self-consciously employs the term *justice*, it is as a systems-relative concept. What is just or unjust depends on the coherence of those acts or opinions to the regulatory needs of the given mode of production. And in a mode of production in which no classes existed, there would be no need for falsely universal theories of justice to rationalize the nonexistent domination of a (nonexistent) ruling class.

According to Marx's materialist depiction of human motivation, human beings are creatures of historically and class-determined needs and purposes rather than bearers of transhistorical normative values. Thus Marx writes in *The German Ideology* that when a "communist materialist" stands in front of "a crowd of scrofulous, overworked and consumptive starvelings," he sees "the necessity, and at the same time the condition, of a transformation both of industry and of the social structure."[12] A typical bourgeois idealist philosopher, Feuerbach in this case, would lament the situation but fail to see either the necessity or possibility of social transformation. Marx does admit in *The Communist Manifesto*—perhaps referring to his own historical role—that although most of the bourgeois intelligentsia rationalize capitalist domination, in times of revolutionary crisis a minority of the intelligentsia will throw in their lot with the working class. These members of the intelligentsia are motivated by an understanding of the system "broader" than that of the more materially driven, economically active members of the bourgeoisie.[13] This broader understanding might well include a different moral evaluation of capitalism than that held by other members of the intelligentsia. Yet Marx writes as if the only motivation for the switch is that prescient intellectuals follow their own interest in siding with the inevitably victorious universal class.

Marx the historical materialist deems that the civil rights of freedom and equality facilitate the fundamental economic process of free exchange and contract characteristic of the capitalist mode of production. This process works to the advantage of capital and to the disadvantage of labor because labor-power unfortunately produces more value than it is worth, economically speaking. The reason is that the historically and culturally determined subsistence wage, the social cost of reproducing labor-power, represents the full value of the worker's labor-power as a commodity. Thus the worker is not robbed or treated unjustly by his employer if his labor-power produces more value in commodities than the value of his wage: "The value which its use creates during one day is double what the capitalist pays for that use; this circumstance is a piece of good luck for the buyer, but by no means an injustice towards the seller."[14] Not only is the extraction of surplus value not an injustice, but capitalism could not exist without it. For without the profits created by surplus value, capitalists simply would not and could not invest.

Only when a disharmony or antagonism develops between the forces of production and the existing relations of production does Marx believe that effective demands for emancipation, and a resulting change in the moral and juridical order, can be made. In late capitalism an increasingly social mode of production is fettered by the individualist, contractual relations of production that had successfully regulated the social organism in its earlier stages of existence. Only by developing cooperative, social relations of production consonant with the increasingly social forces of production can society avoid the recurrent economic crises endemic to capitalism. Capitalism, in Marx's materialist analysis, will not be abolished because it is unjust, but because it is no longer a rational, efficient mode of production which can satisfy the true interests of the working class. And communism will be the first society to transcend the narrow constraints of judicial and moral conceptions of the good society, because distribution will be determined strictly by expressed need, rather than by moral claims of desert or merit.[15]

MARX AS IMPLICIT MORAL THEORIST: CAPITALISM'S THWARTING OF HUMAN FREEDOM

Yet coexisting throughout Marx's work with this self-conceived "scientific," amoral analysis of capitalism is the work of a nonsystematic, implicit moral theorist who frequently condemns capitalism in conventional moral terms. Thus, Gilbert's project of reconstructing Marx as a moral realist is not groundless, provided one acknowledges how the meta-ethical relativism of Marx's historical materialism works against this reconstruction. There are two souls to Marx, one scientistic, the other humanistic. The ethical Marx has difficulty subordinating all his moral indignation to the logic and cunning of history. Marx's description of the dehumanization of the worker under capitalism and his image of the worker as a "wage-slave," enslaved by a capital that he creates but does not control, is depicted not in morally neutral, "scientific" terms but in highly emotive, descriptive language that in the very process of describing condemns. Marx's use of emotive language is most evident in Chapter 10 of Volume 1 of *Capital*, the famous chapter on "The Working Day." His description of capitalists whose "insatiable hunger for surplus labor . . . oversteps not only the *moral*, but even the merely physical maximum bounds of the working day" (emphasis added)[16] can only be described as a moral condemnation of capitalism. Although labor may be paid a just wage according to the laws of exchange of capitalism, Marx frequently in *Capital* condemns capitalism as resting on the "theft" of surplus labor from the worker, who is paid less for the value of his or her labor-power than the value of the products that labor-power produces. He refers to the surplus product as "the tribute annually exacted from the working class by the capitalist class" and contends that "even if the [capitalist] uses a portion of that tribute to purchase the additional labor-power at its full price, so that equivalent is exchanged for equivalent, the whole thing still remains the age-old activity of the conqueror, who buys commodities from the conquered with the money he has stolen from them."[17]

Thus, alongside Marx's "scientific" conception of justice as a system-specific juridical concept is an implicit moral conception of a humane society in which individuals consciously create and control their social relationships. This overt condemnation of capitalism has engendered a cottage-industry debate in contemporary moral philosophy as to whether Marx repudiated capitalism as morally unjust. No participant in the debate denies that Marx condemned capitalism once it had accomplished its historically progressive task of economic development. But these analysts differ as to whether Marx criticized capitalism on the grounds of a nonrelative, moral conception of justice[18] or on the basis of a nonmoral, historicized conception of freedom, achievable only after the final crisis of capitalism.[19] It may be possible, however, that Marx held capitalism to be both just and unjust, in two distinct senses of the term. While explicitly contending that capitalism was just according to its own juridical and moral norms, Marx might consistently also hold that capitalism is unjust according to the alternative moral norms of a truly humane society, communism. G. A. Cohen contends that by the criteria of capitalist laws of exchange Marx understood capitalism to be just, while according to an implicit natural or nonrelativist conception of justice Marx condemned capitalism as a system of wage-slavery based on theft: "Now since . . . Marx did not think that by capitalist criteria the capitalist steals, and since he did think he steals, he must have meant that he steals in some appropriately non-relativist sense. And since to steal is, in general, wrongly to take what rightly belongs to another, to steal is to commit an injustice, and a system which is 'based on theft' is based on injustice."[20]

Steven Lukes insightfully argues that Marx's seemingly inconsistent views on the justice of capitalism are best explained by recognizing that Marx engaged in a "multi-perspectival" analysis of the issue, even if only semi-coherently.[21] Marx, in Lukes's first perspective, frequently analyzes the issue of capitalism and justice from the perspective of the functioning, dominant laws of capitalist exchange. Under these laws, paying the laborer only the value of his labor-power, his daily subsistence, is certainly not an injustice. Allen Wood and Robert C. Tucker interpret this position to be Marx's sole perspective on capitalism and justice.[22]

But much of *Capital*, Lukes correctly recognizes, is devoted to exposing the ideological workings of the free market as obfuscating the real relations of domination in capitalist production. This second perspective of an immanent critique of capitalist relations of production enables Marx to see how capitalism can be described as both just and unjust from two distinct points of view. Thus, capitalism is just from the perspective of capitalist exchange, but unjust from the perspective of an immanent critique of the material relations of capitalist production.[23] In the passages from *Capital* that criticize the bourgeois conception of freedom of exchange in the market as an ideological concept because its rhetoric of "free exchange" obscures the workers' domination by capital in the production process, the emotive condemnation of capitalism as an unjust system of wage-slavery is strikingly evident. In Chapter 6 of *Capital*, Volume 1, "The Sale and Purchase of Labor Power," Marx demystifies the alleged freedom of the realm of exchange by taking the reader "behind the scenes" of the realm of production where he exposes the true relationships of domination. Capitalist ideology, Marx holds, celebrates the realm of exchange, the market, as the "very Eden of the innate rights of man." But in the reality of production, the supposedly free wage-laborer brings "his own hide to market and now has nothing else to expect but—a tanning" from the capitalist who dominates him.[24]

In Lukes's schema, Marx's third perspective on whether capitalism is just criticizes capitalism for being unjust from the viewpoint of first-stage communism. Capitalist distribution fails to fulfill the rhetorical claims of capitalist political economy that it pays the wage-laborer the full value of his labor (his or her marginal product). Capitalist exploitation derives from the reality of the laborer being paid less for his or her labor-power than the total value of the goods which that labor-power produces. Only under first-stage communism's distributive principle of "to each according to their contribution" is the worker paid in true proportion to his or her productivity.[25] Hence Ziyad Husami's "third perspective" interpretation of Marx as criticizing capitalism for being distributively unjust.[26]

Lukes contends that Marx's "fourth perspective," which neither judges capitalism to be just or unjust but condemns it for being incapable, as compared to full communism, of transcending narrow distributive criteria of justice, best approximates Marx's self-conception as a "scientific socialist" whose analysis transcended considerations of bourgeois justice. Marx holds that the contributory conception of distributive justice under the first stage of communism substantively fulfills the rhetorical claims of capitalist justice. But he also claims that from the "higher" perspective of a postscarcity full communism such a normative, distributive principle thwarts human freedom by utilizing a common standard, labor productivity, by which to judge unique individuals. Such a distributional procedure necessarily produces unequal rewards. In his defense of distribution according to needs, Marx implies that any standard of justice which applies a common standard, such as productivity or hours worked, to unique individuals denies their true individuality. Thus, in a truly human society, the goods of human actualization and creativity, which Richard Miller and Allen Wood claim are nonmoral, would transcend the narrow horizons of bourgeois justice.

Thus Miller and Wood contend that Marx conceived of communism as the first truly free society that transcends the homogenizing standards of justice by realizing the unique freedom of the individual, though as Jon Elster astutely points out, reward according to need is also a distributive conception of justice which necessitates evaluative institutionalization—unless one assumes that all wants under communism are valid needs that can be materially satisfied under conditions of complete abundance.[27] Although Miller and Wood describe freedom as a "nonmoral good" that is desirable in and of itself, just like pleasure or happiness, they reject a utilitarian conception of communism as the maximization of the nonmoral good of freedom. Utilitarianism, in their respective analyses, is simply another flawed, transhistorical, "moral" conception of justice. Such a conception, in Miller's and Wood's analyses, fails to comprehend that the maximization of the nonmoral good of freedom will not come about through the adoption of utilitarianism as a "transhistorical" moral philosophy, but only by means of the material development of a communist mode of production.[28] As implicit "scientific socialists," Miller and Wood contend that all theories of justice are specific to a mode of production. In their view, Marx believes that the "nonmoral goods" of freedom become realizable only when the empirical prerequisites for a free mode of production have developed. Thus Miller believes Marx's theory of communism cannot be termed a moral theory because factual possibilities rather than moral injunctions determine whether social change is both feasible and desirable. Miller does acknowledge that Marx advances a "humane and decent" social theory, but somehow, in Miller's analysis, such a theory remains nonmoral.[29]

Although Marx in his "fourth perspective" mode explicitly states that full communism transcends moral considerations, he obviously considers it to be a humane and desirable society. Nor does he—or Wood or Miller—offer an adequate explanation as to why freedom is a desirable "good" (whether moral or nonmoral) or why the content of freedom is any less societal-relative than that of justice. Are not bourgeois conceptions of freedom in the market—"negative freedom"—distinct in content from the "positive freedom" of self-actualization envisioned under communism? Simply put, why is a Marxist conception of freedom desirable? Must not Marx's vision of communist freedom ultimately have a normative content if we are to believe that Marx considered communism to be a desirable society rather than simply an achievable or inevitable state of affairs? Marx believed communism to be a desirable society because it promotes human beings' capacity to be autonomous choosers, a capacity he deemed integral to the fulfillment of human potentiality.

Alan Gilbert contends that this endorsement of communism as fulfilling human beings' capacity for freedom contradicts Wood and Miller's conception of Marx as a nonmoral materialist. Rather, Gilbert argues that Marx is most usefully philosophically reconstructed to be a "moral realist" who criticized capitalism for failing to fulfill humanity's *objective* moral interests in human autonomy.[30] The desire for freedom, in Gilbert's analysis, is neither a subjective, ideological interest nor an empirical, teleological culmination of historical development. Rather, freedom is an objective human need—just like nourishment or health. The objectivity of this human desire for freedom is demonstrated by the struggle, across historical epochs, of human beings for freedom. Thus, communism is a desirable society because it promotes the objective interests that human beings have in freedom.

It is beyond the scope of this study to evaluate the claim of "moral realism" that objective ethical knowledge conforms to real, "objective" properties of human well-being.[31] Gilbert does admit that Marx's explicit "meta-ethical relativism" renders Marx's views on morality, at best, ambiguous. But this acknowledgment fails to recognize sufficiently how Marx's historicist ethical relativism precluded him from rendering specific normative evaluations of past events which would be in accord with his alleged moral realist intuitions. Gilbert holds that Marx's admiration for Spartacus demonstrates that he solidarized with all revolts against domination, no matter how futile they might be due to the absence of the material prerequisites for freedom. But Marx's willingness to subordinate his moral intuitions to the imperatives of historical development led him to such morally ambiguous positions as endorsing British imperialism in India as historically "progressive" because it displaced economically stagnant "Asiatic despotism" with the capitalist prerequisites for development toward socialism.[32] Not that this meta-ethical relativism fully captures Marx's actual behavior; one finds it hard to imagine Marx going down to the docks of Liverpool to cheer off, as harbingers of freedom, British troops departing for India. Yet Marx's inability to unambiguously defend Indian resistance to British imperialism initiated a tragically debilitating Marxist tradition of subordinating moral intuitions against human suffering to the teleological needs of economic development. As Leszek Kolakowski's early writings contend, any attempt to develop a consistent socialist ethics must separate sociological analyses of what is materially achievable from the act of ethical judgment.[33]

Moral desirability certainly does not guarantee historical achievement, as "ought" unfortunately does not logically entail "can." But many Marxists engaged in the immoral practice of justifying the "can" of historical development, such as authoritarian communism, because they allegedly promoted the teleological "ought" of the development of the material prerequisites for socialism. Thus Marxists have often condemned contemporary (or past) human beings to be the cannon fodder for the alleged benefits of future generations. Not that present generations do not, on occasion, consciously choose to suffer for the benefit of their offspring—such is the motivation for much of the resistance to injustice. But to be judged as humane choices, these sacrifices must be voluntary. And, as John Dewey eloquently argued in his debate with Leon Trotsky on socialism and morality, the benefits of such sacrifices must be realizable within a proximate "end-in-view." To justify present suffering by its alleged contribution to benefits that can only be known by distant generations is to preclude reasoned judgment of whether sacrifice is justifiable. If there is no statute of limitations on the time horizon for the alleged benefits, then any barbarism in the name of a far-off good can be defended.[34]

Although Marx cannot be fairly judged a consistent "moral realist," the interest in "moral realism" on the part of Marxist-influenced contemporary political philosophers has facilitated recent investigations into the moral underpinnings of a radical democratic society.[35] The desire of classical Marxists, from Kautsky to Lenin, to avoid the "ideological, moral point of view" reinforced Marx's initial, tragic failure to outline the moral standards that a socialist or communist society should uphold. Miller's and Wood's conception of communism as instantiating the nonmoral good of freedom further reproduces the tendency of Marxist traditionalists to side with Marx's self-conception as a scientific, moral agnostic who delineated communism's teleological capacity to transcend justice. Miller and Wood still hold that socialists should abandon the fruitless, liberal practice of ahistorically delineating desirable "oughts." Rather, socialists should set tasks for humanity that can and will be achieved by historical development. But who can believe today that communist emancipation is teleologically immanent, even in advanced capitalist democracies? In the absence of an explicit description of the institutional structure and political norms of a free society, how can Marxists evaluate whether an alleged communist society has achieved human freedom or whether a "transitional reform" within democratic capitalism promotes the socialist aim of increasing economic, social, and political democracy? Marx's moral agnosticism severely inhibited the ability of Marxists to condemn authoritarian communist societies as violating socialist—or simply human—morality.

But are there any resources within Marx for establishing normative guideposts for a socialist or communist future? Marx repeatedly offers an Enlightenment vision of a "planned society" in which the "associated producers" would "rationally" control the mode of production. Marx's seeming association of all market transactions with alienation from one's product and fellow workers hindered his outlining a realistic matrix of workers' ownership, market coordination, and democratic state regulation that would promote democratic control of the economy.[36] But there remains a normative element within Marx's vision of communism which implies a commitment to democratic self-government. Thus, British factory legislation regulating wages and hours is portrayed by Marx as a precursor of a human, democratically controlled economy and not simply as a "mere reform."[37] Unfortunately, Marx's vision of emancipation is usually phrased in the libertarian and individualist discourse of the free development of the individual. Outside of the writings on the Commune, Marx rarely uses the language of democratic self-government, except for the vague phrase "free association of producers,"[38] which fails to explain how producers are to deal with other relevant publics, such as consumers or citizens who are not participants in the workforce.[39]

Marx, however, historicized this normative vision of freedom by contending that it could serve as a relevant yardstick of judgment only if the material preconditions for emancipation existed. Marxism never developed an ethical topography to show how societies lacking the material and political prerequisites for socialism might develop in a humane direction. This lacuna is strikingly demonstrated by the paucity of radical thought as to how former authoritarian planned economies in Eastern Europe and the Third World might make the transition to democratic polities and mixed forms of production. Will Lenin and Bukharin's writings on the New Economic Program (NEP) of the early 1920s remain the first and last Marxist-inspired thoughts on a mixed economy? NEP undoubtedly was a more humane vision of economic development than the forced-draft industrialization of Stalinism. But although NEP favored economic pluralism, it rejected all forms of political pluralism, prefiguring China's current effort to institute a mixed capitalist economy under the domination of an authoritarian Communist Party.

Marx at times acknowledged that although the state would wither away, collective "administration" would not. But Marx failed to provide clear textual arguments for opposing the rule of a "vanguard" claiming to rule in the name of an "interest-free" collective harmony. He could not do so because he believed that in a classless society free of interests "administration" would be transparent and spontaneous. Even today, a democratic Marxist theorist such as Andrew Levine can defend the withering away of the state as a coherent, achievable ideal because, he claims, the abolition of classes would ensure that no particular interests would try to capture the administrative apparatus. As a "consensus on ends exists," Levine writes, "now we just need to administer things."[40] But how would a socialist society know whether a "consensus on ends exists" if not through a democratic political process involving institutions that we would recognize to be a form of state authority? Would not this "administration of things" engender democratic conflicts among equal citizens about how to live our lives in common? Levine contends that democratic participation would psychologically transform individuals by increasing their commitment to the common good. But would a democratic socialist common good be an objective consensus on a comprehensive set of social priorities? More feasibly, the common good would approach a less comprehensive, shared commitment to determining social priorities through democratic contestation among equal citizens and divergent, non-class-based interests, constructed around ethnicity, region, workplace, gender, moral values, etc.

Marx's materialist moral agnosticism provided no intellectual insight into the conundrums confronting communists who achieved state power in societies that had yet to develop a capitalist mode of production or democratic institutions. Nor did it provide ethical signposts for those fighting for socialism in societies that had achieved the abundance that Marx deemed a material prerequisite for communism. The credulous perfectionism of Marx's totalistic vision of harmony so contradicted the complexities of the real world that this unreal vision justified nightmarish attempts to force society toward a distant, alleged communist perfection.[41] The few serious Marxist attempts at ethically defending real-world Communist regimes, most notably Leon Trotsky's *Their Morals and Ours* and Maurice Merleau-Ponty's *Humanism and Terror*,[42] suffer from this perfectionist defense of the "means" of murdering hundreds of thousands of "counterrevolutionaries." Merleau-Ponty's argument involves a provocative historicist wager: if Bukharin's more moderate industrialization strategy had won out over Stalin's, the Soviet Union would not have defeated Nazi Germany.[43] Thus, the end of defeating Nazi Germany justified the party purges and the killing of millions of peasants during forced Soviet collectivization.[44] Such inhuman means could be justified because they allegedly contributed to what John Dewey correctly termed the "distant end-in-view" of full communism.[45]

Revolutionary agnosticism about the real communist present has not been an honest moral option since 1917. The costs in human lives of the purges and forced collectivization were certainly widely known in the West by the late 1930s, thanks more to the efforts of Trotskyists than to those of American liberals, who were mostly naively impressed by alleged "full employment" in the Soviet Union of the depression era. Certainly such agnosticism could no longer ground a viable politics in post-World War II democratic capitalist regimes, with nearly half the world's population ruled by authoritarian regimes that claimed to be communist. Hence the Italian Communist Party (since 1992 the Italian Party of the Democratic Left), the only mass-based Communist party in the West to survive with some vigor into the 1990s, broke with Stalinism by 1956. It is tragic how many Marxists abjured thoroughgoing criticisms of "real existing socialism" until these regimes were overthrown by the very workers in whose name they claimed to govern.

It is just as ironic that many democratic Marxists are shocked today that the working classes of Eastern Europe initially wanted little to do with any "*s*" word ideology—be it an authentic democratic socialism or social democracy—that reminded them of the official ideology they had just overthrown. This is most true of the Soviet Union, where the official dogmatization of Marxism had hegemony for the longest time. The "enemy of my enemy is my friend" is an emotion that often guided Western anti-imperialists' tolerance of left authoritarian regimes in the Third World that were unjustly besieged by the United States. So should one be surprised that Thatcherites and Reaganites would, initially, be viewed by postcommunist survivors as the true friends of ex-communist societies?[46] To retrieve the democratic elements of Marx from the injustice committed in his name demands a forthright return by radical activists and theorists to ethical analysis of the role of democratic politics and human rights in postcapitalist societies. The evidence that many working people in Eastern Europe are now turning to only partially democratized ex-communist, nominally socialist parties to respond to the harshness of IMF-style economic reforms makes the project of radical democratic renewal not simply a theoretical issue.

A doctrinaire Marxist might object that this imprecation is just another exhortation for hollow moralistic defenses of a particularist ideology (e.g., misguided "bourgeois reformism").[47] But, as demonstrated above, even "scientific socialists" engage in a form of moral argument when they justify means that they admit are "bad" but "necessitated" by good ends. This is the "world-historical utilitarian"[48] structure of the Marxist moral argument defending unpleasant but "necessary" means to achieve the good end of a communist future ("you can't make an omelette without breaking some eggs"). Even the harshest forms of "realpolitik," left or right, claim that only good ends can justify bad means. Those suspicious of "realpolitik," who believe that its practitioners are immoral and solely out for power as an end-in-itself, may prefer to interpret "world-historical utilitarian" arguments as yet another hypocritical case of vice paying homage to virtue. That is, few immoral politicians announce that they are not acting in the best interests of the entire community; of course, how racistly or homophobically that community is defined is a critical question. The most famous defender of "realpolitik," Machiavelli, is perhaps most fruitfully read as a moral utilitarian who argued that only plausibly achievable, good ends can justify the last resort of absolutely necessary bad means. Machiavelli consistently argued that any unnecessary violence—even if not a barrier to success—was unjust. Essentially Machiavelli developed a secularized version of just war theory and applied it to domestic politics as well.[49] Real-world Marxists of all stripes have always implicitly or explicitly engaged in moral argument, as nonperverse human beings have a need to justify their actions, particularly violence against other persons, as necessary and beneficial to the community in the long run. This is not to deny that immoralists define the human community more narrowly than democrats deem just, because the immoralists dehumanize other human beings. And individuals who claim that their violent acts promote a just end that is so distant and improbable that such consequentialist claims must be judged to be highly unlikely, must also be judged to be immoral. Kantian, utilitarian, or moral realist theory can provide moral guidance for radical democratic movements; one's epistemological justification for one's moral judgment does not vouchsafe or condemn its validity. That is, philosophic epistemologies or ontologies do not, in a mechanistic causal fashion, determine ethical behavior. But the historicism and perfectionism of Marx did preclude the development of a dominant Marxist moral tradition in accord with either the pragmatist, contextualized ethics advanced by Dewey in *Their Morals and Ours* or the Kantian ethical socialism of the early writings of Kolakowski in *Towards a Marxist Humanism*.

MARX'S CRITIQUE OF RIGHTS AND HIS HOSTILITY TO POLITICS

Marx's materialist critique of moral language is not the only intellectual source of his refusal to overtly condemn capitalism for violating human rights. Because Marx believed that the concept of rights primarily functions as an ideological justification for private property, he denied that rights could serve as an effective weapon against the inequities of capitalism. This functionalist interpretation of rights as defending rampant individualism and thus precluding community and fostering domination is central to the Marxist hostility to rights.[50] Individual rights, in Marx's view, do not unite humans but rather reflect and promote the economic *bellum omnium contra omnes* of civil society. The essence of bourgeois liberty is, in Marx's analysis, "the right of self-interest. This individual freedom and its application as well constitutes the basis of civil society. It lets every man find in other men not the realization but rather the limitation of his own freedom."[51] The equal right to property yields a society of unequal possessors who view their fellows as a threat to the exercise of their free will.

For Marx, this bourgeois concept of freedom fulfilled its revolutionary role in the early stages of capitalism by separating the realms of political authority and property which had been conjoined under feudalism. Under feudalism a human being's civil status determines his legal, political status. In such a society there is no talk of human rights, of rights that individuals are entitled to merely by being human, regardless of one's particular occupation or social status. By destroying the estates, guilds, corporations, and privileges that separate people from the community, the bourgeois revolution "abolishes the political character of civil society," thus making "the political state the business of all."[52] By dividing political authority from property rights, the bourgeois revolution liberates one's political side.

But the liberation of the communal, political side of women and men remains only a revolution in theory. For the bourgeois revolution also throws off the political fetters that had restrained the egoistic spirit of civil society and the marketplace. Because the bourgeois revolution does not subject the constituent elements of civil society ("needs, labor, private interests and private right") to revolutionary criticism, the particularism of civil society emerges as the true underpinning of the supposedly universal state. The bourgeois revolution culminates in the dominance of capitalist civil society over the falsely universal state.[53]

It is rather ironic that in contrast to Hegel's classical conception of the state as the realm of true rationality and community, Marx's predominant conception of the "normal" capitalist state coincides with the liberal conception of the state as preserving the free play of interests in civil society. Of course, Marx, unlike classical liberalism, believed such free interplay led to capitalist domination. In Marx's analysis, any attempt to impose the classical, universal state on civil society would result in terror. Marx deems terror to be the result of a subjectivist attempt by a newly revolutionary bourgeois state, emancipated and separated from civil society, to reimpose itself on civil society by crushing its particular interests. The Jacobins' fervent faith that political will alone could bring about social transformation engendered, in Marx's analysis, their brutal effort to impose the anachronistic classical polis—which subsumed the economic beneath the political—on modern marketplace society. Robespierre's efforts to abolish religion and private property are not just Sisyphean, in that without the material preconditions for such an abolition, religion and private property are later restored with a vengeance; but the terror is also uselessly violent: "At those times when the state is most aware of itself political life seeks to stifle its own prerequisites, civil society and its elements—and to establish itself as the genuine and harmonious species-life of man. But it can only achieve this end by setting itself in violent contradiction with its own conditions of existence, by declaring a permanent revolution. Thus the political drama is bound to end with the restoration of religion, private property, and all the elements of civil society just as war ends with peace."[54] In the absence of a mass movement transforming social relations from below, attempts by a state to impose social change from above will result in a nightmare of repression. This critique of the limits of political revolution led Marx to advance an alternative conception of a "social revolution" which transformed power relations within civil society, as well as the state. This alternative vision may have contributed to Marx, in his theoretical writings, downplaying the rights of freedom of speech and conscience which he defends in his political writings on the Commune. His desire to move beyond political revolution may have led him to assume that social revolutions would simply incorporate existing "bourgeois" democratic rights.[55] Nevertheless his theoretical writings on rights clearly state that a truly human society would transcend the need for human rights.

In Marx's view the bonds of affection in a fraternal and sororal society need not be codified in a doctrine of rights. A legal system, for Marx, necessarily stands in an external, alien relationship to human beings. Law merely codifies norms that exist prior to law and that are essential for the smooth functioning of that society. But were those needs truly inner human needs, it would be unnecessary to codify and enforce them in a humane society. Hence, the existence of a legal system is a sign that the social needs of human beings are not yet internalized in the spontaneous practices of their daily lives.

Absent a social revolution in civil society, the bourgeois state inevitably remains an alien structure ruling above society in the name of an illusory community. Marx's rejection of statist transformation from above might serve as the textual basis for a Marxian critique of the economic developmentalist project of authoritarian communist regimes. Unfortunately, in the history of world socialism, a voluntarist rejection of the constraints of material development came to be identified with the Leninist will to power, whereas a sensitivity to the limits that material circumstance place on political and economic possibilities came to be identified by Marxian revolutionaries with the stodgy, evolutionary determinism of Kautskyian social democracy. Revolutionary communists astutely recognized that social democratic caution about the absence of material conditions for socialism neither addressed the immediate suffering of peasants and a nascent working class in less-developed nations, nor did it speak to the corrupt nature of ruling *comprador* bourgeoisies and bureaucracies.

Thus classical Marxism's historicist stageism did not offer a socialist alternative to the unjust status quo of either conservative agrarian oligarchic domination or inegalitarian capitalist modernization. Yet although revolutionary communists argued for the political imperative of an immediate communist seizure of power in noncapitalist societies, they failed to develop any coherent postrevolutionary strategy for the humane development of societies not possessing the political and economic prerequisites for Marx's vision of communism. Scant thought exists on equitable, democratic, mixed development strategies within the weakened world left, despite nearly fifty years of postcolonial experience demonstrating that statist, command economies cannot yield effective, equitable development.[56] In short, the teleological nature of Marx's economic schema contributed to the paucity of creative thought on the socialist left about transitional political and economic strategies for moving noncapitalist societies in a more egalitarian, if not immediately socialist, direction.

Marx's utopian faith in the internal identification of men and women with a socialist society historically limited the socialist movement's insight into the nature of authority under socialism. Marx, of course, believed that under communism the creative powers of women and men would be subject to the conscious direction of society. He hesitates to call this authority the state, because for him the state represents a false universality, a false democracy where administrators control the polity on behalf of the particular interests of the ruling class. Those who defend Marx as having a coherent conception of postrevolutionary politics point to his writings on the Paris Commune and *The Communist Manifesto* to argue that in the first stage of communism Marx did not believe the state would wither away but would rather be radically decentralized and democratized. In the introduction to *The Civil War in France*, Engels alleges that Marx's notion of the "dictatorship of the proletariat" was that of a radical democracy in which the bureaucracy, judiciary, and police are subject to the control of responsible, democratically elected "agents of society."[57] Here Marx's aim seems less to destroy every function of the modern state as we know it, than to employ radical democratic measures such as universal suffrage, the recall, the election of judges, and the combining of legislative and executive power. (Despite the economistic commitment to equality for women evident in Engels' *Origin of the Family, Private Property and the State*, nowhere, to this author's knowledge, did Marx explicitly call for women's suffrage.) These proposed reforms aimed to ensure that the state will be truly controlled by society's members: "The few but important functions which still would remain for a central government were not to be suppressed, as has been intentionally misstated, but were to be discharged by communal, and therefore strictly responsible, agents . . . while the merely repressive organs of the old government power were to be wrested from an authority usurping pre-eminence over society itself and restored to the responsible agents of society."[58] This vision of the state as the servant of civil society rather than an independent force controlling and subduing it informs Marx's brief comment on the state under socialism in *The Critique of the Gotha Programme*. Here the language is strikingly Lockeian in tone, as society clearly controls the acts of the state: "Freedom consists in converting the state from an organ superimposed upon society into one completely subordinate to it."[59] The democratic state serves the interests of a democratic society.[60]

From a radical democratic perspective, the tragic lacuna in Marx's thought is not so much that he failed to adumbrate a detailed plan for democratic socialist government, but that he paid scant attention to the rights of particular communities, workplaces, and individuals in relationship to a socialist central "authority." Marx insightfully criticizes narrow liberal conceptions of rights which subordinate personal rights to property rights. But he failed to recognize that not all liberal theories of rights subordinate the rights of the individual to the rights of corporate property. What Marx surely did not comprehend is that any pluralist democracy would need an operative conception of rights to adjudicate among the claims of diverse individuals and social interests, even if they might be functionally organized around social roles other than those of class.[61] Marx's own insight into the illusory nature of the universal capitalist state could function as a powerful critique of a socialist state that obliterates social pluralism by imposing its own false universality on a diverse population. Although Marx envisions human individuals fulfilling their individuality through the "free association of producers," he never discusses the role such associations might have in relationship to the broader democratic society and state (and vice versa). To adjudicate among those social roles, a legal and constitutional system of rights and responsibilities would be needed.

Authority in the name of the entire working class, standing above all interests, only serves the particular interests of those who control the apparatus of "authority." The traditional socialist belief in a "rational plan" that can authoritatively adjust, and thereby control, all interests requires a faith that all interests can be reduced to a common, fungible currency. Is it liberating to trade the homogenization of the "commodity-values" of capitalism for the "use-values" of state socialism? Homogenizing a diverse society and culture inevitably involves repression. In order to ensure a lively, democratic interplay between the central authority and the particular institutions of local government, unions and democratic management, neighborhoods, etc., a democratic socialist society would need both a constitutional and ethical understanding of the rights and responsibilities of particular institutions and individuals and of the politically determined balance among the institutions of the state, civil society, and the market.

A SOCIALIST NORMATIVE PROJECT? THE SUBSTANTIVE FULFILLMENT OF THE RHETORICAL CLAIMS OF DEMOCRATIC CAPITALISM

Although Marx refuses openly to describe the socialist future in terms of the substantiation of bourgeois rights, in his guise as an implicit moral theorist he frequently mocks bourgeois society for contradicting, in practice, the rhetorical claims of its universal ideals. If bourgeois ideas were simply bourgeois, that is, only suited to the interests of the bourgeoisie, then it would not be false consciousness to assume that capitalism in practice lived up to these principles. Much of Marx's political writings imply that capitalism could not exist if it truly fulfilled its rhetorical claims of liberty, equality, and fraternity. The aim of communism in these philosophical and political writings appears to be to expand and substantiate the rights rhetorically proclaimed by bourgeois society.[62] If Marx had consistently embraced this goal of an immanent critique of democratic capitalism then perhaps the subsequent world Communist movement would have been less dismissive of "mere bourgeois civil liberties."

In *On the Jewish Question*, Marx contends that bourgeois equality before the law tolerates a social inequality that in turn erodes the original principle of legal equality.[63] In *The Eighteenth Brumaire of Louis Napoleon*, Marx embraces the political tactic of exposing the hypocritical nature of the bourgeoisie's alleged commitment to democracy: "This parliamentary regime lives by discussion; how shall it forbid discussion? . . . It leaves everything to the decision of majorities; how shall the great majorities outside parliament not want to decide? When you play the fiddle at the top of the state what else is to be expected but that those down below dance?"[64] The bourgeoisie are victims of illusion because their narrow self-interest precludes them from comprehending the revolutionary potential of their own democratic principles. These principles possess a revolutionary potential because they cannot be fully achieved within the narrow confines of bourgeois civil society.

In *The Critique of the Gotha Programme*, Marx terms bourgeois democracy "vulgar democracy," implying that bourgeois practice violates democracy's lofty aims. Contrary to the traditional Leninist disdain for "mere bourgeois democracy," Marx consistently evidenced his preference for bourgeois democracy over authoritarian capitalist regimes. Marx argued that the German socialist movement should struggle for a liberal, "vulgar democracy" against the Prusso-German empire because such a liberal democratic regime affords the working class greater freedom for political organizing. Marx criticized LaSalle for failing to distinguish between bourgeois democracy and Bismarck's authoritarian regime. Lasalle, by countenancing support of Bismarck's regime for its development of social welfare programs, Marx contended, was engaged in the ludicrous project "of demanding things which have meaning only in a democratic republic from a state which is nothing but a police-guarded military despotism."[65] Unfortunately, Marx defends the bourgeois republic predominantly on the instrumental grounds of its value for proletarian political organizing. Marx never unambiguously held that bourgeois democracy is preferable to an authoritarian regime because it affords women and men a greater degree of freedom than does despotism. Rather, Marx implied that bourgeois democracy's major positive attribute was that it afforded the working class a better terrain on which to struggle against capitalism.

Believing that ideals such as justice and equality are manifestations of alienated social relations, Marx tragically refused to unequivocally turn "bourgeois" ideals against their class authors by forthrightly endorsing the substantive institutionalization of political, civil, and social rights as the goal of the socialist movement. Not surprisingly, Marxist movements that evolved toward treating democratic values *as ends in themselves* first had to tragically learn how a strictly instrumental view of "bourgeois" rights eviscerates the struggle against authoritarianism.[66]

Although the equal worth of civil and political liberties may be curtailed by social inequality, even in their limited form these liberties are best conceived by radical democrats as ends-in-themselves. Radical democrats need not concur with Isaiah Berlin that "freedom from" government interference is the only true form of liberty. Conceptions of freedom that speak of those goods necessary for individuals to have the "freedom to" develop their capacities do not, as Berlin held, necessarily entail an authoritarian conception of true human interests. But radical democrats should give lexical priority to the civil and political liberties of "freedom from," while striving to expand the social rights of "freedom to."[67] In societies without a codified degree of "freedom from" state interference in the form of legally guaranteed civil liberties, claims of "freedom to" health care, education, etc., often serve as thinly veiled justifications for authoritarian rule. And there is no definitive empirical evidence that the repression of civil liberties promotes greater equity in social provision. If anything the evidence tends the other way, because possibilities for democratic mobilization are a powerful barrier to class and status privileges for allegedly "revolutionary" ruling elites.

Perhaps as an indirect legacy of Marx's failure to speculate about the *particular rights* of groups and institutions *within civil society* under socialism or first-stage communism (where Marx admits that state authority would persist), both social democrats and communists have focused inordinately on the issue of political power at the level of the state rather than on the democratization of civil society. Social democrats have sought democratic control of the bourgeois state in order to use its machinery to improve the livelihood of the working class. Communist vanguards have endeavored to seize state power in order to use it to transform society. Both historic movements, however, largely ignored Marx's teaching, particularly evident in *On the Jewish Question*, that for a true social revolution to transpire, the nature of power within the institutions of civil society, particularly the workplace, must be transformed. Marx, of course, failed to spell out how the power relations in social institutions would be democratized. Vague as his futurology may have been, we can retrieve and emphasize one critical aspect of Marx's vision— human freedom cannot exist in a society in which the structure of civil society remains hierarchical and in which interests in civil society are undemocratically structured.

The politics of a democratic socialist society would focus on both the democratization of institutions within civil society and also building a democratic relationship among those institutions and between them and the state. Once the romance with the "never existing capitalism" of the unfettered market ends in Eastern Europe, it is likely that the transition from authoritarian communism to democracy will also focus on democratically determining the (ever-changing) proper relation between state, civil society, and the market. Democratic socialism, if it is to have any humane promise, must allow all individuals to participate in defining the multiple institutions that affect their daily lives. Such a process means a flowering of politics and of potential, though less brutal, conflict. Socialist statecraft would aim to adjudicate such conflicts and to establish the combination of democratic planning, market coordination, and decentralized community and workplace control that would maximize political participation. That postrevolutionary politics has rarely been conceived within the radical tradition as a humane but difficult art, contributed to the triumph of an antipolitical, socialist vision of postrevolutionary harmony. Any final arbiter aiming to eliminate all conflict, be it an omnipotent party or state bureaucracy, will inevitably visit repression on those who dissent from an *a priori* postulated harmony.

JUSTICE AND COMMUNISM: THE NEED FOR RULES IN A RADICAL DEMOCRATIC SOCIETY

The concept of justice presupposes people pressing competing claims and justifying them by universal rules or standards. In Marx's brief writings on communism, the final stage of full communism is depicted as transcending "the narrow horizon of bourgeois rights" because the abolition of material scarcity would eliminate competing material claims: "from each according to their ability, to each according to their needs." Marx did not contend that the realm of necessity would be completely eliminated under communism. Rather, necessary production would be organized in a rational, cooperative manner that would leave workers ample "free time," the true realm of freedom. Marx, however, consistently maintained that true communism required the complete development of the productive forces and the elimination of scarcity.[68] Marx, however, had little to say about how society would politically determine what production is "necessary" and how to organize it. Nor does distribution according to needs eliminate the necessity of politically evaluating what expressed desires are truly needs.

Marx failed to recognize that many material goods are valued because of their scarce, positional location. Because this value is tied to spatial location or relative scarcity, it cannot be transcended by an increase in material production. In fact, material abundance can threaten the value of positional goods, such as an isolated wilderness cabin, a courtside seat at the municipally owned basketball team's games, a sailing boat on a relatively uncrowded lake. All these goods become less desirable or less possible to possess if they become more readily available. But even if we bracket this failure to consider positional goods, Marx defines justice too narrowly, solely in terms of the distribution of material goods. As Michael Walzer has eloquently argued, justice also consists of the standards men and women establish in all fields of human endeavor in order to distribute rewards, power, recognition, and status. Just standards consist in treating equals equally and unequals unequally, in proportion to their relevant differences.[69] Defining these "relevant differences" is often the most difficult task in constructing norms of justice.

In *The Economic and Philosophical Manuscripts*, Marx makes a more radical claim than the simple assertion that when basic needs are satisfied the competition for material goods is mitigated: Under the postscarcity conditions of true communism, there would exist no need for authoritative social institutions that would distribute social roles according to "relevant differences." As G. A. Cohen has described it, Marx's vision of communism is of a "postinstitutional" society.[70] But is a society with no permanent institutional structure feasible? Can human beings continuously create social relationships without any institutional guidance; and how would social memory be preserved in such societies? Institutions exist not only to promote norms for efficient and desired behavior but also to facilitate social learning diachronically. Would a society constantly in flux, devoid of any institutionalization of past practices, be desirable? The above questions are relevant not only to Marx but also to the "antinecessitarian" radical democratic theory of Roberto Ungar, who celebrates the permanent transformative possibilities of radical democracy.[71] But in any viable democracy, certain institutional principles of the basic social order—such as civil liberties, freedom of association, competitive political parties—must be part of the permanent social structure. Constitutional limits, whether formal or informal, on institutional change are as central to democracies as are the possibilities of democratically altering institutions not deemed permanently essential to the democratic order.[72]

Perhaps Marx could envision a society beyond the need for a theory of material distributive justice because the species-being of the early Marx transcends egoistic need. The consumer mentality that views work as a means toward the ends of material fulfillment would disappear, Marx argued, because the very process of life—work—becomes human beings' true need. With life-work as its own reward, *homo faber* no longer needs individual recognition or reward. In addition to his or her own self-realization in communal work, human beings' other all-consuming needs are for fellowship and the sensual perception, if not consumption, of human creations. Under communism both wealth and poverty take on a human rather than economic meaning: "It is apparent how the rich man and wide human need appear in place of economic wealth and poverty. The rich man is simultaneously one who needs a totality of human manifestation of life and in whom his own realization exists as inner necessity, as need."[73] Human fellowship, unlike wealth, cannot be distributed according to distributive rules. It can only develop spontaneously.

Although individuals under communism would have unique personalities, as "social beings" they are fully conscious of the totality of human activity in the community. In Marx's early, most utopian writings, he contends that the human senses will be radically socialized under communism. Human beings no longer appropriate nature in the "stupid and one-sided" manner of private property "that an object is ours only if we have it." Instead, with the socialization of production, the "senses" of human beings are also socialized; they perceive all objects as the subjective product of a unified humanity. Communist men and women are so sensitized to the experience of their fellows that they appear to appropriate others' sensual experience as if it were their own: "The senses and satisfaction of other men have become my own. . . . Though man is therefore a particular individual—and precisely this particularity makes him an individual, an active individual, an actual individual communal being—he is equally the totality, the ideal totality, the subjective existence of society explicitly thought and experienced."[74]

This vision of the communalization of the senses represents a metaphysical mystification, akin to Hegel's transcendence of the universal and the particular, which the mature Marx abandons. Yet the vision of a social being who experiences the spontaneous cooperation of communism and therefore has no need for imposed standards of justice persists in a less metaphysical fashion in the mature Marx's critique of justice. Justice, for Marx the moral agnostic, is simply another theory of rights needed only by human beings who view others as external competitors. A social being who conceives others to be a moment of his or her own social being needs no rules to teach him or her how to cooperate. In *The Economic and Philosophical Manuscripts*, a young, romantic Marx offers an excessively utopian vision of fraternity and sorority, in which men and women are brothers and sisters to such an extent that their subjective experiences are shared. Although the mature Marx never fully returned to this beatific vision of intense community, the search for an intense fraternity and sorority, for the bonds of sympathy among people who conceive themselves to be equal members of a close-knit, homogeneous community has informed radical thought to this day. A longing for an overly intense solidarity has hindered the development of either a socialist or communitarian theory of justice which offers equitable and relevant standards for evaluating and adjudicating the particular moral claims of distinct individuals and communities who share the broader but more minimal norms of a solidaristic but also pluralistic democratic polity.

An underdeveloped communism, where the forces of production have yet to develop fully (referred to as "crude communism" in *The Manuscripts* and as "primitive communism" in *The German Ideology*), is characterized by envy and greed because people still possess the competitive, individualist consciousness of the bourgeois society they have only recently left. In *The German Ideology* Marx describes a "primitive communism" that collectivizes an underdeveloped economy and creates a world in which the state becomes "the universal capitalist." Primitive communist human beings are so dominated by the bourgeois desire to consume and so envious of their neighbors that a *modus vivendi* can be produced only by ensuring that all will consume an equal, preconceived minimum.[75] This vision of a communist society, emerging from the womb of a less-than-fully economically developed society, is strikingly akin to the traditional conservative criticism of communism as a crude leveling of humanity. Of course, part of Marx's motivation for writing these passages was to warn against premature efforts to achieve communism where the material and social prerequisites did not yet exist.[76] In primitive or crude communism, human beings so fear that their fellows may demonstrate some personal talent that would improve their relative standing in the community that crude communism "abstracts" from human "talent by force" and negates individual personality. It destroys the entire world of culture and civilization, returning humanity to a life of poverty, because only in destitution are all truly the same. Envy and the desire to level, in Marx's view, constitute a cultural legacy of a bourgeois society which has yet to be transcended.[77]

In crude or primitive communism, envy warps all desires. Human beings wish to consume privately; but in order to ensure that no one receives more than his or her equal share, private consumption must take place in a communal manner. Thus, marriage, the paradigm of exclusive private property, is transformed into "the community of women," the model of "universal private property." Man's obsession with receiving his own personal due, a legacy of bourgeois society, leads him to deny the personality of all women so that they may be possessed as the "handmaid of communal lust."[78] The drive for personal recognition, for a "just" reward, ultimately destroys human community. Contrary to the stereotype of his day, that Marx advocated "free love" and a "community of women," he endorses individuated romantic relationships as the embodiment of personal mutual respect in a fully communist community. Primitive communism's structural fault is that it does not generate the economic surplus necessary for overcoming the division of labor. In *The German Ideology*, Marx writes that a collectivization of poverty—the attempt to construct communism in an underdeveloped society—would simply lead to "the same old crap in new forms."[79] Man is still a wage-laborer, obsessed with deriving an equality of wages from the community as "universal capitalist."

The description of communism "just as it emerges from capitalist society" in *The Critique of the Gotha Programme* is not as materially harsh as that of the crude and primitive communism described in *The Manuscripts* and *The German Ideology*. The *Gotha Programme* describes the only first stage of communism which Marx describes as desirable, but he does so in a stageist manner that would have led an orthodox Marxist to oppose attempts at building communism in one underdeveloped, isolated revolutionary state.[80] Marx makes quite clear that this more humane first-stage communism of *The Critique of the Gotha Programme* is possible only after the full economic and political development of an industrial, capitalist democracy. The "birthmarks" of this first-stage communism reflect the continued existence of the division of labor and of a community of wage-laborers who demand back from society in consumption an exact proportion of the labor values they have contributed to social production (diminished by the proceeds necessary to cover depreciation of social capital and social insurance). This first-stage communism, Marx holds, fulfills in both principle and practice the bourgeois right of just and equal exchange. Bourgeois right asserts that a given amount of labor in one form, production, should be exchanged for an equal amount of labor in another form, consumption or wages. Under first-stage communism all humans are workers, society is the only capitalist, and bourgeois justice rules supreme and consistently.

In realizing bourgeois rights in principle, first-stage communism, in Marx's view, exposes the very limitations of all systems of justice. All theories of justice advance relevant criteria by which to judge individuals. Because these criteria, however, can only judge partial aspects of human character, Marx contends that rules of justice inevitably establish a hierarchy among people while ignoring their totality as human beings. In first-stage communism, the maxim of justice "from each according to his ability, to each according to his contribution" measured by an equal standard of labor—either by labor's intensity or duration—favors those who by nature of superior physical or mental endowment can labor longer or more intensely. Equal bourgeois right inevitably produces inequality because it "tacitly recognizes unequal individual endowment and thus productive capacity as natural privilege." Therefore, among individuals who possess unequal productive capacities, "this equal right is an unequal right for unequal labor . . . *a right of inequality in its content, like every right. Right by its very nature can consist only in the application of an equal standard; but unequal individuals (and they would not be different individuals if they were not unequal) are measurable only by an equal standard in so far as they are brought under an equal point of view, are taken from one definite side only."[81]

Marx contends that under the merit criteria of first-stage communism the palpably "unjust" situation could arise where a married worker with several children might be paid the same wage as an unmarried laborer with no dependents who contributed an equal amount of labor. He argues that "to avoid all these defects, right instead of being equal would have to be unequal."[82] One might expect Marx to argue that a first-stage communist (or socialist) system of justice based solely on distribution according to output is inadequate and should be supplemented by principles of justice founded on need. Need criteria presuppose the desirability of some universal standard condition, for example, an income adequate to family size, that if not achieved through market distribution should be met through public forms of distribution. Not to have any distribution according to need would impose an undeserved hardship on the party whose basic needs have not been met through the wage-labor market. Special disabilities, such as a large family or sickness, involve special needs and call for special treatment if the standard condition of treatment is to be met. If family income in an emerging socialist society still affects the life opportunities of children, a needs-based principle of justice, supplementary to a productivity-based wage structure, might call for a minimum per capita family income.

Perhaps Marx did not openly advocate a distributional theory of need to rectify a labor-based theory of justice which rigidly applies uniform standards of productivity to diverse individuals, because such a theory of need would necessitate political deliberation to establish such needs-based criteria. Marx does admit that some form of state or social authority would persist under first-stage communism. But the only roles he specifies for such a state is the repression of any violent counterrevolutionaries and the increase of production through a vague notion of "rational planning" and incentive-based distribution.

Marx implies that a postscarcity "full communist" society can dispense with criteria of distributive justice and fulfill all needs without any role for allocative institutions. The maxim "from each according to his ability, to each according to his needs" which full communist society "inscribes on its banners" describes an achieved, *a posteriori* social reality rather than any principle to guide social distribution. In the postscarcity "full communist" future, needs will no longer be determined *a priori* by a political authority. Marx seems to believe that under second-stage communism human needs will be self-limiting because, in his view, the truest human need is for creative labor. The one truly human need appears to be to live in a society of mutual cooperation. "After labor has become not only a means of life but life's prime want,"[83] society can dispense with judging whether individuals are contributing according to their ability. Work will be strictly self-motivated. Marx never considers the potential problem expensive "needs" might pose for a communist society, such as an individual's need to travel widely or compete in the People's America's Cup international sailing competition. Marx was not anticonsumerist; he realized that needs were multiplied and expanded by economic development. In fact, he frequently praises capitalism for creating consumers, producers, and recreators who are "many-sided" or "universal individuals." Thus Marx's faith in the productive capacity of communist society to satisfy all human needs is rather puzzling, in light of his recognition that not just capitalism but all complex cultures have a capacity to expand human wants with astounding rapidity.

Marx's assumptions about communist production are highly controversial because they assume *the total elimination* of not only material scarcity and the division of labor but also the limitations of time and the costs of gaining knowledge and expertise. Such intractable realities argue that any plausible socialist futurology needs to relax the assumption that all scarcities can be overcome, which in turn assumes that the division of labor can be radically democratized but never fully eliminated, and that every consumer demand cannot be readily met.[84] Once these assumptions are made, we are faced with the necessity of establishing distributional criteria in even the most advanced democratic societies. For example, one group of socialist citizens might contend for a universal, free distributional system of "basic needs" and the use of discretionary income for "luxury" items. They might also favor merit selection in certain technical jobs and a period of compulsory, universal service to accomplish those dull, taxing tasks that cannot be fully automated. That is, who will pick up the trash after the revolution will remain a perennial question. Other socialist citizens might challenge the specific merit criteria for certain tasks or claim that bureaucratic or meritocratic rule in certain social arenas violates socialism's commitment to democratic participation. Marx, however, provides us with no guidance as to what political principles should govern allocational choices in positional goods, jobs involving a high degree of skill and lengthy training, political office, etc., either under socialism (first-stage communism) or *nearly* total communism.

Marx's paucity of thought about how a more democratic division of labor might be organized under communism ultimately reflects an Enlightenment faith in the technical, noncontroversial nature of automating necessary labor. It also reflects a monolithic conception of the remaining "free labor time" as involving self-sufficient aesthetic and scientific pursuits. In his most utopian conception of "full communism," Marx contends that communist society "so regulates the general production and thus makes it possible for me to do one thing today and another tomorrow, to hunt in the morning, fish in the afternoon, rear cattle in the evening, criticize after dinner, just as I have a mind, without ever becoming a hunter, a fisherman, a herdsman, or a critic."[85] Even this most famous citation of his belief that full communism will abolish the division of labor reveals that Marx had an inkling that communist society would still have to make decisions about how to "regulate the general production." Yet nowhere does Marx tell us by what decision-making and institutional mechanisms society "so regulates the general production." Nor does he suggest who should do the regulating: workers at the site of production, democratically elected managers, political representatives, etc.? Doesn't such regulation necessitate political decisions about societal priorities? Marx must have also been aware that each activity he cites in the famous quotation is preindustrial and a form of individual rather than collective labor. Each activity can be attempted without lengthy training, though our critical critic might write for the *People's Weekly Reader* rather than the *People's New York Review of Books*. And even to attempt surgery, computer software design, or tool- and dye-making requires lengthy apprenticeship. Even university professors would admit that developing into a skilled teacher involves a lengthy, self-reflective process.

There is further textual evidence that the mature Marx did not believe in the possibility of *completely eradicating* the division of labor. In his later writings in the *Grundrisse* and *Capital*, Marx no longer talks of the total elimination of the division of labor but rather of radically diminishing the time devoted to "necessary production." Curtailing necessary labor-time will provide individuals more free time to devote themselves to fulfilling their manifold scientific and aesthetic interests. Individual material needs expand under communism, but so does the productive capacity to satisfy them. Through cooperative regulation of production, the division of labor between mental and physical labor is eroded, though the scientific and aesthetic labor of "free labor time" appears to be intrinsically more rewarding than the tasks of necessary production. Descriptions of the distinction between necessary and free labor are scattered throughout the *Grundrisse* and Volume 1 of *Capital*, but the argument is most succinctly advanced in Volume 3 of *Capital*:

> In fact, the realm of freedom actually begins only where labor which is determined by necessity and mundane consideration ceases; thus in the very nature of things it lies beyond the sphere of actual material production. . . . Freedom in this field can only consist in socialized man, the associated producers, rationally regulating their interchange with Nature, bringing it under their common control. . . . But it nonetheless remains a realm of necessity. Beyond it begins that development of human energy which is an end in itself, the true realm of freedom, which, however, can blossom forth only with the realm of necessity as its basis. The shortening of the working day is its prerequisite.[86]

In Marx's vision of communism, true freedom arrives through conscious planning. Marx, however, never explicitly recognizes planning to be a political question, perhaps because of his Enlightenment belief in the "technical" nature of "science," a faith that manifests itself more acutely in the work of Engels and Lenin. Marx acknowledges that necessary labor, the wrestling with nature to provide physical necessities, is never eliminated. Such labor, however, can be rendered less onerous, Marx asserts, if the community cooperatively designs working conditions suitable to intelligent human beings. But planning *involves choice*—the establishment of standards and priorities. On the macro level, a democratic socialist polity would have to determine democratically the proper sphere for particular activities. What productive activities are best coordinated by market choice or by imperative planning? Would the main role of state economic policy be utilizing fiscal and monetary policy to regulate a predominantly market-socialist society of mixed forms of ownership: workers coops, small private firms, municipal and state-owned firms? Which firms, if any, should be owned by the state—natural monopolies such as utilities, large finance banks? And should these state industries be run by workers' control or by boards that include consumer and government, as well as worker and manager representatives? A democratic socialist polity might decide that markets best aggregate consumer demand and allocate labor but do not adequately register demand for public goods, such as education and job training, or do not adequately fund risky, long-term, massive capital investment in, for example, telecommunications, public transportation, and other social infrastructure. Should national economic goals aim to shorten the necessary working day or continue to expand production for basic human needs (housing, food, health) or provide surplus capital to less developed regions and nations? If economic decision making is to be democratized—and thus politicized—then a polity's collective sense of social priorities will be reflected in the politics of economic and social policy.

It is not only society's conception of justice, in the Aristotelian sense of an all-embracing virtue reflected in a proper ordering of a society's activities, which is embodied in public policy. Democratic planning also involves evaluating the nature of "human needs." In his brief remarks on "false needs" in the *Economic and Philosophical Manuscripts*, Marx argues that capitalism promotes inhuman needs because profit-seeking entrepreneurs are indifferent to the quality of the needs they serve. Socialist producers, on the contrary, consider the human significance of their products because they do not ask the question, "Can I sell it?" but the question, "Do we truly need it?" The capitalist appeals to whatever momentary, "unhealthy" appetite may be stimulated in the individual consumer.[87]

Whether or not "true human needs" can be objectively discerned, as contemporary moral realists claim, Marx believes that his description of the "true human needs" realized under communism goes beyond "ideal-regarding" conceptions of what true human needs *ought* to be. Marx contends that human beings, through the historical process of securing conscious control over the means of production, will for the first time actualize "true human needs"—the need for associational life, creative production, and aesthetic consumption. Marx's faith is that rational discussion among consumer-producers, minus the mediation of the capitalist who stirs up "inhuman needs," will establish a set of needs that can objectively be called truly human. But will Marx's conception of the true human need for creative labor, particularly aesthetic and scientific pursuits, be automatically endorsed by a communist society? Would not such a view of the good life have to be politically advocated—and would it not be possible that a communist society might reject it in favor of a more leisure-oriented, materialist, or athletic conception of the good life?

Bracketing the question of whether his faith in the intrinsic attraction of creative production would be endorsed by free socialist citizens, Marx tacitly admits that socialist producer-consumers inevitably make choices as to what constitutes the best life. Yet in believing that there would result one set of true human needs, Marx fails to recognize that this democratic, collective establishment of social needs would result from a political process. As Benjamin Barber has eloquently argued, political deliberation, even under the most egalitarian of power relations, never results in one "true," *a priori*, predictable result.[88] Just as individuals choose how best to apportion their labor time, so the socialist community as a whole must debate how to apportion social production time.

Any mode of social cooperation involves the satisfaction by specific individuals and communities of the expectations of others. John Rawls contends that we are rationally committed to act justly by our very status as persons engaged with others in endeavors designed to promote common or complementary interests.[89] We cannot rationally expect the cooperation of others if we ourselves do not provide an equal return for benefits received. In a socialist community, where the common interest is supposedly more evident than under capitalism, a person or group that failed to live up to these standards of moral reciprocity would be subject to moral censure, if not to economic or criminal sanctions. The paucity of democratic socialist thought on moral responsibility and economic incentives, as well as on issues of crime and punishment, under socialism manifests the antipolitical utopian nature of most socialist futurology.

Purposive work, by its very nature, implies evaluative standards of competence. A worker-owned or worker-managed auto plant would depend on the timely delivery of machine tools built to proper specification by another worker-owned or worker-managed machine tool plant. Work might be distributed in the socialist auto plant so that workers assembled entire cars in teams instead of performing a single, tedious task on an assembly line. The workers might contribute to the design of the vehicles they construct. But poorly built or designed cars would lower the public's image of socialist auto workers. Within the firm we would expect that certain individuals would gain respect for their innovative designs or their skilled mechanical abilities. Ineffective workers might have to be retrained or shifted to a task for which they were better suited or motivated. One could readily conceive of similar examples for, say, computer software design, if readers find the auto industry insufficiently postindustrial in nature.

Jon Elster argues that self-realizing work must be mentally challenging and that there are two basic and distinct ways in which socialist citizens might engage in such communal labor. The first involves self-realization through deliberation with others in the politics of both the polity and the workplace. For most citizens, however, this deliberation would involve a limited voice in setting policy goals to be carried out by political representatives, civil servants, and managers. Thus, the second form of self-realization, creative production with others in the workplace, Elster holds, would be essential to the average citizen's development of mental and physical capacities.[90]

Elster ties this belief in self-realizing labor to a noninstrumental argument for a market socialist system of worker-owned firms in which firms run the risk of bankruptcy. Elster is well aware of the efficiency arguments in favor of market socialism, a system of predominantly worker-owned firms coordinating their behavior by means of a socially regulated market: greater efficiency, clearer economic incentives and lines of responsibility, and the virtue of limiting central planning to establishing basic fiscal, monetary, and investment-incentive policies.[91] Elster, however, places greater emphasis on a moral, noninstrumental argument for market socialism. Socialist creativity and solidarity, he holds, is best achieved through the challenge of particular communally owned projects in which both individuals and the collective face the possibility of success and failure. The risks of the market ensure that we are not just playing at participation and cooperation; rather, they guarantee that our decisions have real consequences. In Elster's words, "The threat of bankruptcy, like the threat of war, concentrates the mind wonderfully."[92]

In attempting to render Marx's conception of individual self-realization through communal participation plausible, Elster argues that the successful fulfillment of one's ambitions will not be guaranteed in the most just of societies. A democratic socialist society cannot guarantee that "the free development of each will be the precondition for the free development of all." Rather, Elster advocates a society of decentralized firms competing in a market system, cushioned, of course, by the redistributive effects of strong public provision, unemployment compensation, and active industrial and labor market policies. As an alternative but less mellifluous slogan for this complex vision of democratic socialism, Elster suggests "the free and partial self-realization of some as a result of the attempted self-realization of all, justified by the fact that the benefits of success also accrue to those who fail in the attempt."[93]

The above parable of the role of standards and evaluation in socialist communal projects need not be read to hold that the identity of individuals under socialism would be solely defined as auto worker, computer software designer, or high-tech engineer. Job mobility and retraining should increase under socialism; adult education programs might be widespread; our average socialist auto worker, after his or her three hours of necessary labor time at the auto plant, might also be an accomplished violinist or local political leader. Although socialist fraternity and sorority might not reach the utopian heights outlined in the *Manuscripts*, socialist citizens, it is hoped, would recognize their fellows as equal moral agents, with plans and aspirations worthy of a consideration equal to that given their own. If socialist citizens respect each other as responsible moral agents, they would hold each other responsible for inadequacy of effort, if not always for inadequacy of performance. Recognizing the diversity of human beings, socialist society might avoid giving individuals tasks unsuited to either their natural or cultivated abilities. Nevertheless, a job well done would still be admired and respected if socialist citizens are to treat each other as responsible members of a democratic community.

A Prolegomena for a Socialist Theory of Justice and Politics: Equal Potential for Individual Development

Why then did Marx fail to address the just standards and expectations inherent to any society engaged in purposive, cooperative tasks, even a socialist one? One answer can be divined from Marx's Enlightenment faith in scientific progress and the transcendence of scarcity—and, therefore, of choice. Marx contended that machine production would abolish both wage-labor and the division of labor. In the *Grundrisse* Marx praises science and machinery for providing the material basis for a society that has outgrown the need to measure individual labor time and to reward workers according to the labor value they contribute: "The theft of alien labour time, on which the present wealth is based, appears a miserable foundation in face of this new one, created by large-scale industry itself."[94] Under automation, workers are no longer able to calculate the individual value of their productive input. The bulk of productive power derives from the collective knowledge of humanity embodied in technology and a complex division of labor. Marx implies in the *Grundrisse* that capitalist cybernetics prefigures the transcendence of the labor theory of value of capitalist political economy.

Marx, however, never adequately confronts the implications of automation and cybernetics for the quality of work in an industrial or postindustrial society. Under capitalism, machine production simplifies each particular task to such an extent that it "deprives the work of all interest": "The special skill of each individual machine-operator, who has now been deprived of all significance, vanishes as an infinitesimal quantity in the face of the science, the gigantic natural forces, and the mass of social labor embodied in the system of machinery, which, together with those three forces, constitutes the power of the 'master.'"[95] Capitalist industry also prefigures the erosion of the division of labor by necessitating the variation of work for each individual worker. Its recurrent "catastrophes" and "crises" force the laborer to develop varied skills as he or she is shunted from job to job by the anarchy of the market:

> Large scale industry, through its very catastrophes, makes the recognition of variation of labor and hence of the fitness of the worker for the maximum number of different kinds of labor into a question of life and death. This possibility of varying labor must become a general law of social production, and the existing relations must be adapted to permit its realization in practice. . . . the partially developed individual, who is merely the bearer of one specialized social function, must be replaced by the totally developed individual, for whom the different social functions are different modes of activity he takes up in turn.[96]

Marx appears not to recognize that what he celebrates as the end of the division of labor is, according to his own description, nothing more than the rotation of the worker through tasks that are individually tedious.[97] Nowhere in *Capital* or the *Grundrisse* does Marx envision an enrichment of the basic tasks of factory production: "Labor does not seem any more to be an essential part of the process of production. The human is restricted to watching and supervising the production process."[98] A variety of tasks, however, cannot be the spice of life if each particular task is tedious. Perhaps when Marx contends that "freedom will come to the realm of necessity" through cooperative management, he envisions the redesigning of the labor process. But Daniel Bell is unfortunately correct when he argues that Marx had little to say about how concretely to alter the organization of work, the fundamental cause of alienation.[99]

If what Marx terms the "conductor's" role of management is all that changes in socialist factories, the "conductor" being transformed from corporate owners and managers to worker-owners or worker-elected managers, then when socialist citizens are "playing" rather than "conducting," they are bound to be frustrated:

> All directly social or communal labor on a large scale requires, to a greater or lesser degree, a directing authority, in order to secure the harmonious cooperation of the activities of individuals, and to perform the general functions that have their origin in the motion of the total productive organism, as distinguished from the motion of its separate organs. A single violin player is his own conductor; an orchestra requires a separate one. The work of directing, superintending and adjusting becomes one of the functions of capital, from the moment that the labor under capital's control becomes co-operative. As a specific function of capital, the directing function acquires its own special characteristics.[100]

Though Marx believed that the "conducting" role of management should be carried out under communism by the "free association of producers," nowhere does he specify how this might be institutionally accomplished. And even if the "conducting" of management were to be rendered cooperative, this does not necessarily address the issue of job enrichment. Even if job rotation is democratically established, if each "piece" one plays remains elementary, then the players will be bored even if each shares in the conducting process and changes instruments frequently.

Nor would rotation of tasks necessarily be the *sine qua non* of a just distribution of work. Marx realized that artistic accomplishment required considerable practice. In this vein one might best fulfill oneself by developing one's exceptional talent as a master carpenter, while neglecting one's average skills as an accountant, social worker, educator, computer software designer, or pipe-fitter. It would also be naive to believe that all socialist citizens would equally enjoy or be equally competent at management tasks, or if one prefers a less hierarchial-sounding term, facilitation of task-coordination. Some workers may excel in management not only because they are imaginative and well-organized but also because of their sensitivity to the desires of the less articulate. If management were to be elected democratically, it is hoped that all workers would vote in management council elections and would participate in their shopfloor section meetings. But not all would choose to run for the industry management council or national representative bodies. Schemes for selecting a minority of council seats by rotation might be used to expose all workers to management tasks and to discover those with previously undetected management skills. But if a socialist society values efficiency to a politically determined degree, certain tasks will continue to be selected on criteria of technical competence rather than the criteria of need or equality. How rank-and-file workers, and even elected managers, will maintain ultimate control over these technical workers is a critical issue in workplace democracy. Without widespread technical education and access to independent technical advisers, the rank and file might well be dominated by a new technocracy. This is one reason why the belief that workplace democracy precludes the need for free trade unions may be problematic. Even if management is democratically elected, it may not always serve the interests of its electorate. Just as pressure groups influence elected representatives, so might democratic trade unions lobby elected managers and technical workers within the context of a worker-owned firm.

Marx had little to say about job distribution because he believed that the advent of machine production would radically curtail the necessary workday, allowing ample time for individuated, desired pursuits. Efficient necessary labor would provide the material base for the more rewarding pursuits of "the realm of freedom." Marx's paradigm for "free labor" is aesthetic and scientific labor. In the *Grundrisse* Marx writes: "The counterpart of this reduction in necessary labor time is that all members of society can develop their education in arts, sciences, etc., thanks to the free time and means available to all. . . . Free time . . . is practice, experimental science, materially creative and self-objectifying knowledge."[101] Aesthetic and scientific production transcend narrow economic questions of distributive justice because individual consumption of a work of art or scientific discovery does not diminish another consumer's pleasure. A work of art or scientific theory cannot be privately owned and locked away in a cooperative society.

But it is rather ironic that the communist Marx emphasizes aesthetic and scientific pursuits as the paradigm of "free labor"; for aesthetic and scientific endeavors have not traditionally been pursued in an interdependent, cooperative fashion, though they are socially learned crafts and scientific researchers often work in teams. Although Marx claims in *The Manuscripts* that scientific activity remains a social activity because "the language I use and even my own existence is a social product," he admits that science is "an activity I can seldom pursue in direct community with others."[102] Is Marx, the theorist of human community, suggesting that men and women would fulfill themselves in communist society by engaging in a few hours of daily, communal, mundane industrial labor in order then to retreat into the enriching privacy of their studio or laboratory?

In a relatively unknown part of the *Grundrisse*, Marx concedes that evaluative standards of work would continue under communism. And such standards inevitably involve questions of justice. Free labor is difficult, Marx holds, because the worker strives to fulfill certain standards and objectives. In a remark that today would be judged by many to be both sexist and derogatory toward service workers, Marx argues that free labor cannot "be made merely a joke, or amusement, as Fourier naively expressed it in shop-girl terms. Really free labor, the composing of music for example, is at the same time damned serious and demands the greatest effort."[103] Although aesthetic and scientific standards may be societal-relative, they have a critical impact on the moral life of a community by affecting the expectations, aspirations, and rewards of creative beings. As species-beings, communist individuals would seek recognition for their efforts in the eyes of others. They may be pleased by their own artistic production, without having to gain the praise of others. But their own personal standards will depend on their socially acquired sense of judgment. Communist society cannot ensure that scientific experiments will not sometimes fail, nor that some people will not have less vocation for study or artistic creation than others.

In trying to reconstruct within Marx a nascent socialist theory of justice, it is most profitable to turn to his writings on money in the *Economic and Philosophical Manuscripts*. The central point of his critique of the role of money under capitalism as "the pimp between man's need and the object" is that in a truly human society satisfactions would correspond to the real abilities of the person and dissatisfactions to real incapacities. Communist citizens receive what they truly deserve and can use, because the power of money no longer transforms "real imperfections and chimeras—essential powers which are really important, which exist only in the imagination of the individual—into real powers and faculties."[104] In contrast to life under capitalism, where wealth often mediates between the possession of a talent and its realization, what "I am capable of" under socialism should be determined solely by one's individual ability and effort. A socialist citizen who excels in one field will not be able to use money to compensate for his or her inadequacies in another realm of human activity. Once exchange value is relegated to, at most, a means of determining relative costs of production and not of evaluating all human capacities, justice becomes the true exchange of qualities for their proper equivalents: "Assume man to be man and his relationship to the world to be a human one: then you can exchange love only for love, trust for trust, etc."[105]

But what of the socialist who wishes to enjoy art but is not particularly aesthetically sensitive, or the socialist who desires to influence his or her fellows but is not particularly persuasive, or the lover who does not evoke love in return? After the revolution Marx himself admits that there still will be unrequited love. The pain encountered by people whose aspirations are not fulfilled under socialism is, Marx says, "true human suffering" because they can never console themselves with the thought that their disappointment is undeserved. When money is no longer a "pimp," when economic power is no longer fungible into other forms of power, we must look to ourselves for the source of our success or failure or blame misfortune or chance, rather than structural injustice.

When Marx writes in the *Manuscripts* that "suffering apprehended humanly, is an enjoyment of self in man,"[106] he tacitly admits that the communist goal of abolishing the tension between objectification and self-confirmation is a chimera. Marx contends that in contrast to capitalist society, where alien powers often stifle the exercise of a human being's true capacities ("If I have the vocation for study, but no money for it, I have no vocation for study"[107]), under socialism human beings have the opportunity to develop fully their individuality. Only by putting their capacities to the test, by taking the risk of failure and suffering, will human beings discover their true individuality. Marx tacitly acknowledges that a risk-free society, a society without failure or frustration, would not only be boring; it would be contrary to a human being's sociable and creative nature. The risk-taking conception of socialism advanced here is more akin to John Stuart Mill's conception of a just regime encouraging its citizens to develop themselves through the pursuit of excellence than it is to the utopian transcendence of the distinction between individual and community of *The Manuscripts*.

The risk-taking conception of socialist society is more in line with the perspective of "true human suffering" which runs as an alternative leitmotiv in *The Manuscripts* to the dominant, neo-Hegelian theme of the transcendence of the particular and the universal. According to this leitmotiv, under communism, for the first time, "true human suffering," in contrast to previous "inhuman" suffering, will exist. Such a suffering may be termed human, rather than inhuman, because it is not imposed from without by alien institutions over which the individual has no control, but instead results from the failure of free human beings to fulfill their aspirations. Suffering is often the price paid for attempts at self-development. As Jon Elster notes, "The only way for the individual to find the limits of his ability is, often, to come up against them."[108] Under communism this suffering would be truly individual rather than imposed on the individual from without by undemocratic institutional constraints.[109] Bernard Yack is partly correct that Marx's conception of "species-being" strives in a utopian manner to obliterate the distinction between humanity and nature, because nonalienated human beings would completely control their "natural" surroundings. But in the same *Manuscripts* that Yack references, Marx's concept of "true human suffering" recognizes that human beings cannot always fully control the outcomes of their creative efforts, even in a humane society.[110]

Although one can read from Marx's critique of money and his conception of "true human suffering" a nascent theory of communist justice as equal opportunity for self-development, any society attempting to flesh out such a moral point of view would have to render some complex political judgments. As Steven Lukes has pointed out, Marx provides no guidance as to whether his commitment to equal self-development implies an equal opportunity for each individual to develop his or her talents or a guarantee of the equal actual fulfillment of each individual's potential.[111] The latter conception approaches a radical conception of equality of results—equal fulfillment of nascent abilities—rather than the former conception of substantive equality of opportunity, through the abolition of institutional or material barriers to attempting to develop one's capacities. A socialist society might decide to devote extra social resources to those with special needs or with talents whose development requires inordinate resources. But would it choose to devote, for example, an extended amount of surgical training to a medical student who has less than the average manual dexterity deemed necessary to be a decent surgeon? Could a democratic socialist citizen expect society to devote a large amount of resources to an avocation of, say, motor car racing, when providing our socialist Mario Andretti with a yearly model change to remain race-competitive might tax the time and effort of our most skilled socialist auto designers and mechanics? How many citizen Andrettis could society fund?[112] The balance between these two conceptions of equal individual development can only be determined politically. Part of this judgment would involve evaluating how the devotion of exceptional resources to people with special needs affects the overall good of society. A political choice between a quasi-Kantian respect for persons as ends-in-themselves versus a more utilitarian conception of maximizing aggregate social welfare can only be transcended in theory by a dogmatic adherence to the concept of postscarcity communism. Such choices could not be avoided by any feasible democratic socialist society.

G. A. Cohen's writings on the potentially conflictual relationship between the ethical socialist commitments to self-ownership of labor and to collective ownership of capital further demonstrates how a socialist society's understanding of the nature of individual talent and effort is a quintessential political question for which there is no one right, nonpolitical answer. Cohen's two seminal articles on "Self-Ownership, World-Ownership and Equality" aim to retain for a democratic socialist theory of justice the intuitive moral appeal of self-ownership—the vision of individual autonomy over ourselves and the creations of our labor.[113] But Cohen frankly admits that self-ownership, Marx's vision of nonalienated labor, stands in tension with Marx's critique of an exploitation caused by the private ownership of a socially created capital. If control over capital is completely socialized, then either a majority or an individual, in the case of consensus decision-making, would have veto power over whether a given individual develops their preferred talents. For without external resources, there can be no development of one's creative capacities.[114] On the other hand, if a democratic socialist society opts for a liberal, "starting-gate theory" of equality of opportunity by distributing social capital in equal per-capita individual lots, then market transactions will inevitably produce significant inequalities by rewarding those who possess scarce talents or scarce goods.[115] In Cohen's analysis there exists no viable intermediate socialist "constitution" that would uphold both the vision of self-owned labor and world-owned capital and fulfill both socialist aims of relative equality of condition and individual autonomy in the workplace. The likelihood that a workers' syndicalism or people's capitalism would lead to prosperous firms or individuals hiring the labor of those who no longer own substantial capital (as happened with prosperous, worker-owned firms in market-socialist, former Yugoslavia) makes Cohen hesitate to embrace uncritically the "starting-gate theory" of socialist equal opportunity in the market. But he also is acutely aware of how pure public ownership of capital and comprehensive national planning preclude real autonomy for particular firms and individual abilities and talents.[116] As a second-best alternative, Cohen opts for a market socialist "starting gate theory," with the proviso that the desire to maintain relative economic equality will necessitate "some (not necessarily drastic) limitation of people's rights in their own power, or to the fruit of their exercise . . . to maintain (even roughly) equality of condition."[117] That is, progressive taxation is not theft in Cohen's analysis, but a reasonable political measure to facilitate redistributing some, but not all, of the rewards the market confers on those firms and/or individuals who possess scarce talents or abilities.

Ian Shapiro offers an even more explicit defense of the role for politics in adjudicating questions of distributive justice in an egalitarian and democratic society. His essay "Resources, Capacities and Ownership: The Workmanship Idea and Distributive Justice" focuses on the tension in the radical tradition between "the workmanship ideal," which holds that human beings should own and control the products of their laboring selves, and the conception of capital as a socially created good.[118] Along with Cohen, Shapiro points out the potential contradiction within Marx between his view that the modern division of labor renders illegitimate the private, individual appropriation of a socially created capital, and his vision of a postalienated society in which individuals control their own labor. But Shapiro wants to force radical democrats to address more than the tension between self-ownership and world-ownership. He implies that radical theorists have yet to grapple with the radically socialized view of human talents central to the theories of justice of both John Rawls and Ronald Dworkin. These theorists are canonically described as contemporary liberal, rights-based theorists. Initially, they were sometimes denounced by traditional Marxists as advancing a theory of justice which is overly concerned with distribution and individual rights and insufficiently concerned with democratic control over production. Certainly Rawls and Dworkin are agnostic about the form of ownership of capital that would best promote their egalitarian theories of justice. But their mutual belief that talents and abilities should be rewarded as if they were socially, rather than individually, owned advances a radical, nonliberal conception of the social ownership of individual talents and abilities.[119] Rawls and Dworkin argue that talents and abilities have no inherent claims on distributive justice because the morally arbitrary factors of genetic luck and socialization critically affect the development of these capacities. Rawls contends that this understanding means that the distribution of primary goods, those goods that supposedly enable all individuals to pursue any particular plan of the good life, should not be determined by the market or other alleged metrics of labor contribution.[120] Dworkin's distributive scheme renders talents and abilities irrelevant to distribution by arguing that material distribution should be determined by the results of a hypothetical auction in which people originally endowed with equal external resources ensure themselves against possible handicaps, disabilities, or talents that are in overabundant supply.[121]

Shapiro shares Rawls's and Dworkin's critique of Nozick's libertarian view that an unregulated market justly distributes goods. These critics of Nozick's market libertarianism recognize that markets do not objectively reward talent, effort, or ability but rather in a morally arbitrary way set prices based on the assets one brings to the market and the contingent, relative scarcity of one's skills and abilities at a given moment. But Shapiro believes that this dismissal of the justice of market reward does not adequately speak to the widespread intuition that productive contribution should play some role in just distribution.[122] Despite explicitly rejecting this intuition, Rawls and Dworkin implicitly acknowledge its pull through distributive provisos that violate a strict conception of the social ownership of talents and abilities. Dworkin claims that although "physical and mental powers" should not affect resource distribution, people's "tastes and ambitions" can be rewarded because any adequate theory of justice needs to be "ambition sensitive."[123] Rawls, in a similar vein, says that although the distribution of primary goods should not be influenced by talents and abilities, how well an individual uses those goods is an irrelevant consideration for the theory of justice.[124] That is, Rawls believes a proper theory of justice should ignore how different preferences, tastes, and abilities yield different qualities of life among people who have the same primary goods (i.e., income, wealth, opportunity).

Shapiro's astute retort is that if a society treats the distribution of talents and abilities as being constructed by a complex interaction of nurture and nature that should be treated as morally arbitrary, it should treat the socially constructed distribution of preferences and ambitions in the same way.[125] In other words, why should distributive schemes be neutral about talents and abilities but reward those who have those "tastes and ambitions" that arbitrarily fit well with the present structure of society? Does Rawls believe that people with tastes for goods that happen to be relatively scarce (i.e., expensive) should have less opportunity to fulfill their desires than should others with less expensive tastes? There is no true answer to this question. As Elster indicates, society may have to set political limits on the amount of resources devoted to any individual's pursuit of self-realization.[126] Rawls avoids addressing the above query, perhaps because it shows that a society's operative sense of justice inherently involves political judgments about which there is no one Archimedean truth.

The reason for the inconsistency of both Rawls and Dworkin on rewarding talents and abilities is that they are caught between two moral intuitions that can yield no one theory to "correctly" balance them. First, democrats recognize that the possession and development of human talents is, in many ways, a question of luck and the fortuitous circumstances of a nurturing environment. But, on the other hand, if a plausible conception of personal identity and responsibility is to survive, a just society would hold people responsible for their actions. Shapiro notes that Dworkin and Rawls fail to abandon completely the "workmanship ideal" by holding "people responsible only for choices they make in life, not for things over which they have no control."[127] But this response to the intuition fails to recognize that our choices or preferences are often shaped by our awareness of capacities over which we allegedly have no control. For example, a rational eighteen-year-old male or female who is relatively short of stature, average of speed, and not a particularly good outside shot probably long ago has given up his or her childhood ambition of playing varsity college basketball.

Short of a postscarcity society in which goods fell like manna from heaven, a just society would need to make deliberative judgments as to the structure of political and economic authority, the division of labor, and distributive rewards for effort and talent. An attractive radical democratic society might decide to incorporate aspects of the workmanship ethic by using some market-based incentives to distribute goods and opportunities to both worker-owned firms and workers within the firm. That society might also choose to limit the resulting economic and social inequalities by means of a strong social safety net and quality public provision of goods that the society democratically desires to decommodify and provide publicly (e.g., health, education, job training, child care). Such a society might also strive to increase avenues for political participation, but with that deliberation furthering the pursuit of concrete social activity. Jon Elster points out that, contrary to the spirit of a Hannah Arendt or Benjamin Barber, there is no intrinsic value to public talk; to be valuable such talk must enhance the capacity of ordinary citizens to solve concrete social, cultural, and economic problems.[128]

The reason why the conditional *might* is used above in referring to the distributive practices of a socialist society is that these questions can only be settled by political deliberation. Pushed to its extreme, the work ethic could yield a society of competitive individuals and cutthroat competition among "people's capitalist" firms. Yet, if the ethic of collective ownership of productive resources is pushed too far, particular groups and individuals would not control the specific resources needed to pursue their particular conception of the good life. There exists no one proper moral balance between the radical democratic ethos of "the workmanship ideal" and the ethos of communal ownership of capital. Rather, the proper balance, as Shapiro forcefully argues, can only be decided politically. Thus, a plausible and attractive radical democratic theory of justice would ultimately rest on the actual deliberative judgments of a democratic community.[129]

Perhaps Marx failed to construct an adequate socialist theory of justice because he expected both too much and too little from social relations in a communist society—too much in that his early writings' vision of each individual so intensely sharing in the experiences of others violates the less-than-fully intersubjective nature of distinct human personalities; perhaps too little in that the richly developed individual of *The Grundrisse* appears to be almost completely autonomous and asocial. He or she finds intrinsic reward in individual creative labor, and personal satisfaction and development appears to be independent of the judgment of others. In the communist society described in *The Economic Manuscripts*, the supreme human need is the need for the other person. Conflict disappears in a world of mutualism and complete harmony. Marx's depiction of aesthetic creation reflects this mutualist vision. The fulfillment of the producer, the artist, depends on the developed human sensitivity of the audience. Artistic creation appears to be devoid of egoism, for it involves neither a setting apart of the product to the exclusion of others nor competition with others. Obviously, Marx ignores many artists' reputations in prior societies as being inordinately egotistical and obsessed with the admiration of others. But he fails to observe that even in this most mutualistic of pursuits there remains a potential for conflict. Audience and artist may not share the same aesthetic values, socialist critics may not always be fair in their judgments, socialist artists will not always gain recognition from their fellows.

Neither the paradigm of communist production as aesthetic creation advanced by *The Grundrisse* nor the paradigm, developed in *The Economic Manuscripts*, of human mutuality as the romantic relationship between man and woman eliminates all problems of conflicting standards, expectations, and desires. Romantic love, like artistic creation, is not always a social relationship shared by the community; it is often privatizing. Even if the personal is ultimately political in that the behavior and expectations we bring to relationships are socially constructed, we do not always choose to share these particularist relationships with the community as a whole. A romantic relationship can, at times, set a couple apart from society in a world seemingly of their own, even if the rewards of that particular sphere may liberate the couple for more fruitful independent and cooperative participation in society. Though a sexually fulfilling relationship between lovers may "indicate the extent to which man's natural behavior has become human,"[130] romantic love can only facilitate sexual harmony, not ensure it (and vice versa). A long-standing love relationship is usually not characterized by youthful romantic enthusiasm, but by a quiet trust and respect, often produced by trying periods of conflict in which both partners make acknowledged compromises. Love, however, can fade when one partner feels that his or her concessions and adjustments have not been reciprocated. Even the mutuality of love does not always escape the couple's informal normative evaluations of its fairness and justice. Such norms can often be highly restrictive, and the love and trust in the close family often cohabits with conflict, jealousy, and even, at times, hatred and sexual oppression. The burdens and rewards of romance and family life should be freely accepted only as long as there exist emotional benefits for all parties concerned. As movements against the battering of women and children correctly argue, a society that construes all aspects of family life as personal and free from state and social regulation renders the mistreated and powerless individuals within the family extremely vulnerable.

Thus, the mutuality of socialist society cannot rest on an abstract, reified ethos of fraternal and sororal mutuality where one's own projects become indistinguishable from all others' projects. In a complex, advanced or postindustrial society, social harmony can only be developed through a democratic political mediation among conflicting interests. If particular workplace collectives, ethnic groups, trade unions, neighborhoods, etc. are not granted a codified degree of limited autonomy, individuals will not have a protected arena in which to pursue their specific desires and enterprises. Conversely, without limits to decentralized autonomy there can be no effective coordination and cooperation among the diverse interests cohabiting a radical democratic commonwealth. Nor could there be any assurance that undemocratic and oppressive social relationships would be prohibited. Sketching out the very scope and limits of such rights and spheres of autonomy might well prove to be the essence of socialist politics. Such a quest may render socialist politics more dynamic and conflictual than politics under capitalism, even if each conflict may be less intense. For as the economist Abba Lerner once wrote, "An economic transaction is a political problem already solved," at least according to capitalist ideology. In the state-regulated, mixed economies of contemporary capitalism, the relative economic power of interests in the marketplace too often determines the outcome of conflict, both economic and political. If political, economic, and social relationships are to be further democratized, then our lives in common will be subject to more—rather than less—political deliberation.

A democratic distribution of resources and power under socialism would hopefully render the distribution of social power more equitable than it is under democratic capitalism. A more egalitarian distribution of power might lessen both the stakes and the intensity of any given political conflict. Still, for citizens to believe that their society is just, they would have to feel that their particular individual and group endeavors are protected by the state and will not be sacrificed to an abstract common interest over which they have no effective say. On the other hand, for a socialist society to benefit all, its citizens must realize that there are democratically determined limits to their own rights. The women and men of a radical democracy may not be capable of empathizing with the plight of every one of their fellow citizens. Nor will they vicariously thrill to each of their fellows' accomplishments. But they will derive greater rewards from both their own and their fellows' activities if a spirit of sympathy, tolerance, and diversity exists. This sense of justice and tolerance will be less affectively warm than the metaphysical bonds of fraternity lyrically described in *The Economic Manuscripts*. But the spirit of democratic justice and tolerance would permit a more diverse, dynamic community. To promote such a possibility, radical democrats must outline a theory of politics and a theory of justice relevant to the serious choices bound to face a polity more egalitarian than our own. If human freedom is to be defended and enriched, then politics must not cease "after the revolution."

Lenin (and Marx) on the
Sciences of Consciousness and Production

THE ABOLITION OF POLITICAL JUDGMENT

SCIENTIFIC SOCIALISM AND THE TRANSCENDENCE
OF POLITICAL DELIBERATION

Because Lenin has been canonized, both by his critics and followers, as a supreme political tactician, it would appear counterintuitive to think that he shared the radical tradition's desire to transcend politics. Even such an orthodox Marxist as Trotsky—not given to great-men theories of history—cited Lenin's skills as a political tactician as the crucial cause of the success of the October revolution.[1] And the primacy Lenin gave to the maintenance of Bolshevik political power facilitated his pragmatic abandonment of orthodoxy on such issues as building socialism in a less developed nation, and the transition from war communism to the New Economic Policy. Yet he ultimately conceived of communism as a postpolitical enterprise, and this conception meant that his pragmatic day-to-day political decisions never moved the Russian Revolution in democratic pluralist directions. For Lenin firmly believed in the vanguard party's ability to discern the true interests of the proletariat. This concept of homogenous, objective revolutionary interests, combined with his scientistic conception of socialist planning as the implementation of objective, technical laws, provided the theoretical bases for the Communist tradition's hostility to postrevolutionary social and political pluralism.

Lenin devoted most of his prerevolutionary writing to questions of political organization, focusing on how to construct a revolutionary party under conditions of Tsarist autocracy. His only work on postrevolutionary society, *State and Revolution*, has been analyzed, by scholars of different ideological persuasions, as a utopian conception of democracy, where political power would be directly exercised through workplace councils or soviets. Even Adam Ulam, a conservative scholar of Soviet history, finds the participatory rhetoric of *State and Revolution* so in tension with Lenin's hierarchical views on prerevolutionary party organization that he deems "the unfortunate pamphlet . . . almost a straight-forward profession of anarchism," aimed at appealing to mass populist sentiments.[2]

Read in a cursory manner, *State and Revolution* appears to be an exegesis of the radical democracy outlined in Marx's writings on the Paris Commune.

A close reading of Lenin's text, however, reveals a vision of a postrevolutionary society even less political than Marx's. Under first-stage communism, as Lenin envisioned it, all can participate in the administration of socialism because political choice has been rationalized out of society. Scientific modes of administration developed by capitalism enable the party to say confidently, "Even every cook we'll teach to run the state."[3]

Jurgen Habermas contends that the Marxist "science" of history contains two fundamentally opposed conceptions: a "productivist" tendency whose primary logic is the teleological development of the productive forces, and an emancipatory critique stressing the abolition of alienation through the conscious self-organization of social institutions.[4] Lenin's "scientific" Marxism accentuated the productivist side of Marx by celebrating the Taylorist rationalization of advanced capitalist production which sees "things produced in the factory and not social relations."[5] It is this conception of Marxism which constitutes the leitmotiv of factory discipline and the "administration of things" running throughout *State and Revolution*. It is a vision that denigrates the subjective aspect of revolutionary activity, ignoring the role of political and moral deliberation in the building of alternative political, cultural, and moral practices.

Two provocative, contemporary interpretations of *State and Revolution*, A. J. Polan's *Lenin and the End of Politics*[6] and David Lovell's *From Marx to Lenin*,[7] also point to Lenin's embracing of the "scientistic" side of Marxism as a cause of the absence of a role for political life in the soviets of *State and Revolution*. Administration, in Lenin's interpretation of Marx, can be performed by anyone because it is transparently and technically dictated by the requirements of advanced industrial production. There is no need for politics even in the first stage of communism because the elimination of capitalist ideology allows "science" to rule. As Lowell puts it, "Why should a society conforming to general scientific laws which can be elaborated independent of the masses need to consult the people?"[8] Polan takes Lenin to task for substituting "the *techne* of science and bureaucracy," of instrumental efficiency, for the "prudent *phronesis* of politics."[9]

Although my interpretation draws on the work of Lowell and Polan, it takes issue with them on one critical interpretative question: their contention that there is little if any relationship between Lenin's "voluntarist" conception of prerevolutionary political organization and his postrevolutionary views on the withering away of political life. On the contrary, a close reading of Lenin's writings on politics reveals a direct lineage between his conception of the vanguard party and his vision of postrevolutionary society. Both the vanguard party and postrevolutionary society are to be organized in accord with the objective, scientifically discerned interests of the working class. Defenders of a democratic Lenin often insist that the exigencies of political repression in Tsarist Russia forced Lenin to construct a party on paramilitary lines. But such repression did not necessitate Lenin's conviction that the working class, through its daily political struggles, could *never* achieve revo-

lutionary consciousness. This belief led him to endorse vanguard party organization even under conditions of liberal democracy. The conception that
true class consciousness could be embodied by only one, "correct" revolutionary leadership played an integral role in the "scientistic" view of politics
implicit in *State and Revolution*. For if there is only one objectively true
political line in the uncertainty of a prerevolutionary situation, then there
certainly need be no political conflict nor disagreement in a postrevolutionary society.[10]

Ralph Miliband notes the striking near-absence of any mention of the
revolutionary party in *State and Revolution*. But as pointed out below, its
one appearance in the text is extremely telling, because it starkly outlines
the party's guiding hand in the construction of postrevolutionary socialism.
Miliband criticizes *State and Revolution* for remaining silent as to how the
political will of the proletariat will be ascertained and implemented under
socialism. He believes that Lenin's conception that the technicians and experts will run society according to the unified will of "the armed workers"
is too simple and unmediated to be deemed credible.[11] It is credible—
though neither democratic nor attractive—if one accepts the implicit assumption in *State and Revolution* that the party is the natural expression of
the single, undivided, revolutionary proletarian will. This faith in the party's
guidance, combined with Lenin's belief in the apolitical, technical knowledge of scientists and engineers and the capitalist state's rationality, "the
highest technical equipment . . . for accounting and control,"[12] facilitates the
creation of a socialism that "make[s] all workers employees of one huge syndicate, 'the whole state.'. . ."[13] Despite Lenin's rhetoric of "the smashing of
the state," *State and Revolution* outlines the seizure by the working class of
the *unaltered*, efficient capitalist bureaucratic apparatus. The state as the repressive apparatus of the bourgeoisie is not, as Lenin sometimes writes,
"smashed"; rather, it is transformed into the repressive apparatus of the
armed workers.

Thus, Karl Kautsky demonstrated great prescience in his 1918 polemic
The Dictatorship of the Proletariat when he termed the Soviet regime a form
of "state capitalism."[14] Although "state capitalism" does not accurately describe a Soviet regime that never aimed primarily to maximize profit on state-
controlled capital, the term insightfully recognizes that Lenin never intended
a radical democratization of the hierarchical management structures characteristic of capitalism. Lenin's grim, productivist vision is grounded in what
Rosa Luxemburg described in a perhaps excessively psychosexual metaphor
as Lenin's belief in "the authentic proletarian's voluptuous pleasure in abandoning himself to the clutch of firm leadership and pitiless discipline."[15] The
role of the technocracy and "proletarian discipline" renders *State and Revolution* more than just an exegesis of Marx's ambiguously democratic text,
The Civil Wars in France. It represents a significant transmogrification of
Marx's sketch of a decentralized and representative, though insufficiently

pluralist, state. Only a clearer understanding of Lenin's views on proletarian consciousness and the vanguard party, however, can enable the reader to penetrate beneath *State and Revolution*'s surface argument in favor of the soviets as a form of direct workers' democracy.

LENIN AND MARX ON PROLETARIAN CONSCIOUSNESS: CAN THE WORKING CLASS LIBERATE ITSELF?

Beginning with Marx's famous distinction between "the class-in-itself" and "the class-for-itself," Marxist theorists have frequently distinguished between the objective situation of a class, its structural position in the mode of production, and its subjective comprehension of this situation, its "class consciousness." But within the Marxist tradition there have been divergent views as to how objective class position affects the development of class consciousness. Even in *The Communist Manifesto* there exist the seeds of a tension between "structuralist" and "cultural" interpretations of class consciousness. On one hand, Marx asserts that the structural nature of capitalist production, the social nature of large-scale factory production, facilitates the development of collective consciousness; on the other, Marx contends that only through prolonged political struggles will the working class develop true self-consciousness. Marx never reconciled these "objective" and "subjective" strands in his analysis of working-class consciousness, and to this day Marxists tend to emphasize one or the other side of the equation. When explaining the origins of class solidarity (or its weakness), "structuralist" theorists (e.g., Louis Althusser or Nicos Poulantzas in his early works) stress the long-term causal influence of "objective" conditions, whether it be the positive influence of highly concentrated mass production or the fragmenting tendencies of decentralized, post-Fordist production. Marxists who emphasize the subjective element in the development of class consciousness (e.g., Antonio Gramsci, E. P. Thompson, Gareth Stedman Jones, Stuart Hall) stress the influence of specific cultural and historical traditions, whether those be initial collective action for the suffrage rather than control of the means of production, or cultural divisions within the working class forged by racism, ethnicity, or religion.

Lenin firmly believed that to any question of revolutionary strategy there existed only one scientifically true answer: "The modern use of the term 'freedom of criticism' contains the same inherent falsehood. . . . Those who are really convinced that they have made progress in science would not demand freedom for the new views to continue side by side with the old, but the substitution of the new views for the old."[16] This belief in "Marxism as a science"—a methodology that enabled the revolutionary to determine the "objective" interests of the working class—is critical to Lenin's conception of the vanguard party. It leads Lenin to conceive political debate as irrelevant to the governance of a postrevolutionary society. His "scientism," however, has roots in the more "structuralist" side of Marx's own work. An examination of Marx's writings on class consciousness may help clarify both the theoretical lineage between Marx and Lenin and Lenin's "deviations."[17]

In his early writings Marx examines how human community can be realized outside the illusory realm of the political state. It is through this quest to bridge the gap between man as bourgeois and man as "*citoyen*," and not in his later study of political economy, that Marx first discovers the proletariat. The proletariat cannot end its suffering through bourgeois politics, because it possesses no property and has no particular interests to defend through the state. For the young Marx, the virtue of the proletariat is precisely its lack of particular attributes. Lacking property, a nation, a grievance that can be readily ameliorated, the human needs of the proletariat transcend the capacity of bourgeois society. The solution to its suffering can come only through a social revolution that would obviate the need for political power by creating, for the first time, a real human community.

Marx soon realized, however, that the proletariat as depicted in the *Introduction to a Contribution to the Critique of Hegel's Philosophy of Right* could hardly be a candidate for the role of the universal class. How could the most oppressed and dehumanized of women and men be destined to transform society in the most radical way? Thus, in his subsequent writings Marx no longer dwells on the proletariat's "total loss of humanity" as its revolutionary virtue. Rather, he emphasizes the long political struggle necessary both to overthrow the bourgeoisie *and* to self-transform the proletariat. At times Marx romanticizes the effects of proletarian self-organization: "The most striking results of this practical development are to be seen when French socialist workers meet together. . . . The brotherhood of man is no empty phrase but a reality."[18] But Marx also emphasizes the difficult, long-term project of transcending the alienation of the working class. In his 1850 attack on the Blanquist insurrectionists in the Communist League, Marx condemned millenarian politics: "We say to the workers: you have fifteen, twenty, fifty years of civil war to go through, in order to alter the existing circumstances, and to train yourselves for the exercise of political power."[19]

In Marx's analysis a self-conscious class forms itself only insofar as it carries out a common political struggle against another class. Only through common political struggle against a common class enemy could functionally divided workers achieve class solidarity. The workers' "common association," Marx believed, eventually became an end-in-itself: "In face of the unity of the capitalists the maintenance of the combination becomes more important than upholding the level of wages." The mass of working-class individuals, "the class-in-itself," only becomes a self-conscious, "class-for-itself" when its particular economic struggles are transformed into a national, political conflict: "Economic conditions had in the first place transformed this mass of the people into workers. The domination of capital created the common situation and common interests of this class. Thus, this mass is already a class in relation to capital, but not yet a class for itself. In the struggle of which we have indicated a few phases, this mass united and forms into a class for itself. The interests which it defends become class interests. But the struggle between classes is a political struggle."[20]

Whereas Lenin asserted that trade unions possessed no revolutionary potential, Marx considered both trade unions and working-class political parties to be potential revolutionary vehicles. Although Marx believed independent working-class political parties to be the fullest expression of class consciousness, he also valued trade unions, not only as organizations of working-class self-defense, but also because, on occasion, they matured into consciously political institutions. Marx wrote in *The Communist Manifesto* that "this organization of the proletarians into a class, and consequently into a political party"[21] signaled the maturation of the working class. Yet in his "Instructions to the Delegates of the 1866 Geneva Congress of the First International," Marx spoke of the indispensable role of radical trade unions in the movement to overturn capitalism: "If the trade unions are required for the guerilla fights between capital and labor, they are still more important as organized agencies for superseding the very system of wage labor and capital rule."[22] Whether class consciousness was expressed by trade union or political party activity, Marx analyzed it as a subjective creation of the working class.

There are passages, in Marx, however, that prefigure Lenin's belief that the "objective" material location of the working class in the capitalist mode of production engenders "objective" class interests. In the famous passage in *The Eighteenth Brumaire* metaphorically describing small peasants as a "sack of potatoes," Marx depicts their social isolation as the critical barrier to expressing their common interests as a coherent class (as a "class-for-themselves").[23] In contrast, Marx held that the social nature of industrial production and mass communication facilitates the transformation of specific working-class grievances (e.g., shop floor issues) into the collective activity of trade unions and political parties.[24] The formation of *class consciousness* coincides with the rise of comprehensive *class organizations* (trade unions and political parties), and these two processes mutually reinforce each other.

Marx's analysis of class organization as central to the development of class consciousness emphasizes the "subjective" development of class consciousness while downplaying Marx's analysis of the "objective" or materialist basis of class consciousness. Underlying Marx's view of how individuals form a self-conscious "class-for-itself," however, is an implicit belief that, in the long run, the formation of class consciousness is influenced by objective class interests structured by the mode of production. The economic structure of capitalism, in which surplus value is extracted from the producers by the owners of capital, produces an objective interest on the part of the proletariat in eliminating capital's control of the social surplus. At times Marx comes close to identifying these objective, structural interests with an objective or "true" proletarian consciousness. In *The Holy Family* Marx's description of the structural determination of the proletariat's "aims" has a striking affinity to Lenin's conception of "true consciousness": "The proletariat does not go through the hard but hardening school of labor in vain. It is not a question of what this or that proletarian or even the whole proletariat momentarily *imagines* to be the aim. It is a question of what the proletariat is and what it consequently is historically compelled to do. Its aim and historical action is prescribed, irrevocably and obviously, in its own situation in life as well as the entire organization of contemporary civil society."[25]

But Marx refrains in this passage from equating the structurally determined objective interests of the proletariat with the actual "consciousness" of the proletariat. The proletariat must still, Marx continues, become "conscious of its historic task" and "develop that consciousness into complete clarity by itself."[26] Whether the proletariat will meet this historic challenge sometimes appears to remain an open question for Marx. Nowhere did he assert that structural class *locations* determine an objective consciousness that revolutionaries can voluntarily impute to be that of the working class; rather, those locations critically influence the actual development of class consciousness:

> But with the development of industry the proletariat not only increases in number; it becomes concentrated in greater masses, its strength grows and it feels that strength more. . . . Now and then the workers are victorious, but only for a time. The real fruit of their battle lies, not in the immediate result, but in the ever-expanding union of the workers. This union is helped on by the improved means of communication that are created by modern industry. . . . [These] centralize the numerous local struggles, all of the same character, into one national struggle between classes. But every class struggle is a political struggle. . . . This organization of the proletarians into a class, and consequently into a political party, is continually being upset by the competition between the workers themselves. But it ever rises up again, stronger, firmer, mightier.[27]

Yet if a materialist analysis of capitalism determines a structure of objective class interests, even if they are not inexorably embraced by the proletariat, then a conception of "true" or "objective class consciousness" is not such a radical departure from Marx's more cautious position. Marx's teleological conception of history, working class consciousness "ever rises up again, stronger, firmer, mightier," is obviously in tension with his expressed belief that only the working class can emancipate itself. That is, what if it doesn't take on its historically assigned revolutionary duty? Perhaps Marx never openly confronted this question, because although there were ebbs and flows in the growth of the working-class movement during his time, working-class political self-organization in industrial Europe during Marx's era trended secularly upward. Not surprisingly, the vanguard reinterpretation of Marx emerged early in the twentieth century after mass working-class parties had achieved significant reforms within European capitalism but had neither overthrown capitalism nor prevented World War I. Lenin could not openly abandon faith in the revolutionary capacity of the mass working class, because that would have been too blatant a revision of Marx. Thus Lenin openly condemned only a stratum of the Western and Central European working class, the revisionist leadership of the labor aristocracy who had been bought off by capitalist concessions and the fruits of imperialism. But Lenin also knew full well that "this labor aristocracy" had greater support from the mass working class than did more revolutionary activists. Thus, implicitly, Lenin offered the first revolutionary vote of no confidence in the mass European social democratic movement.

Marx, in contrast, rejected the position that communists should establish a vanguard party *separate* from mass working-class parties. Marx prefigured Lenin's belief that communists possess a more advanced understanding of working class interests than do reformist political activists. In the *Manifesto* he described the communists as "the most advanced and resolute section of the working class parties" and states that they have the advantage of "clearly understanding the line of march . . . of the proletarian movement."[28] But in his polemics against Blanqui and other advocates of conspiracy tactics, Marx opposed those communists who believed they were justified in forcibly imposing their views on the working class. Marx urged parties in which he exercised influence not to establish themselves as an independent vanguard but to participate in mainstream working-class political activity. Marx believed that the experience of the working class would, over time, lead it to voluntarily embrace communist politics. He openly proclaimed that his theories represented the most advanced aspects of proletarian thought. But he never claimed that these theories actually constituted "the true consciousness" of the working class. This would be the case only if a mass proletarian movement subscribed to them.

In his advocacy of communism, Marx faced the dilemma of all political visionaries who seek confirmation by a constituency who presently do not share the visionary's conception of that group's "true interests." Even as nonviolent a radical as Martin Luther King advanced tactics of direct action and civil disobedience which were initially rejected by established African-American leaders in the South as excessively risky. Marx did not have a "want-regarding" notion of interests; he rejected the notion that the true interests of a group are defined by the group's current wants or desires. He openly distinguished between the present desires of the working class and its long-term, "objective" interests, which the communists advanced *within the present movement*: "The communists fight for the attainment of the immediate aims, for the enforcement of the momentary interests of the working class, but in the movement of the present they also represent and take care of the future of the movement."[29]

Marx implicitly held an "ideal regarding" conception of working class interests which might be schematically outlined as follows: "Policy *y* is in the proletariat's "true interest," even if they presently adhere to alternative policy *x*, if through active participation in the mass proletarian movement, revolutionaries (who in the present may possess a more sophisticated analysis of the dynamics of capitalism) can eventually convince the mass party that policy *y* is preferable." But to preclude a vanguardist reconstruction, Marx would have had to add the caveat "*if and only if*" the mass party, in a relatively open society, eventually subscribes to policy *y* "*in advance of its implementation*." The Leninist version of this schema contends that because of the ideological domination of the bourgeoisie and "the false consciousness" of an alienated, divided, and reform-oriented proletariat, the majority of the proletariat can never, in a prerevolutionary society, comprehend their true interests. The Leninist conception of the interests the working class would subscribe to *under optimal conditions* can be depicted as follows: "Policy *y* is in the interests of the proletariat, if after that policy is implemented (in spite of the organized, open prior adherence of the majority of the proletariat to alternative policy *x* and open opposition to policy *y*) the proletariat *eventually* retrospectively supports that policy and its consequences."

A revolutionary party's comprehension of the laws of capitalist motion serves as the criteria of verification for Leninist "true consciousness"; the proletariat's "empirical," present consciousness is irrelevant to the test of whether "true consciousness" has been discerned by the revolutionary party. Both theoretically and historically, Leninism failed to put a statute of limitations on the "eventuality" of the working class voluntarily embracing vanguard policies it initially may have opposed. This failure radically increased the antidemocratic potential of this conception of revolutionary consciousness and enabled an entirely new generation, formed by the dominant ideology, or silenced by the terror, of a communist regime allegedly to verify the party's wisdom. The traditional escape clause for "democratic Leninists" is that the repressive conditions of Tsarist Russia precluded a democratic working-class political life that could have accurately ascertained working class self-consciousness. But even a democrat who accepted that interpretation, Rosa Luxemburg, contended that the day after the revolutionary seizure of power the democratic opinions of the citizenry must be openly ascertained and respected.[30] But in Lenin's conception the actual, "empirical" consciousness of the working class, even after the vanguard's seizure of power, has no moral claim over the party that acts in its name.

Marx never discussed how a revolutionary movement should react if over a prolonged period the mass working class ignores its imprecations, perhaps because he exercised considerable influence within mass working-class movements. But his faith that over the long term capitalism's material structuring of interests would profoundly influence the "aims" of the proletarian movement left Marx open to a Leninist reading. To appropriate the language of contemporary postmodern political theory, Marx never considered the possibility that, even in the long run, the working class might not adopt a conception of "true class consciousness" that could be "read off" by a revolutionary observer from the "objective," structural class position within the mode of production. Marx never investigated the problematic that such a disjuncture between political consciousness and the material preconditions for socialism might pose for his theory of class consciousness. Such a disjuncture occurred in Russia in 1917 when a vanguard party seized state power in a predominantly peasant, preindustrial society. The political consciousness of one organized political wing of the small, radicalized urban proletariat had outstripped the material development of Russian society.

By stressing the materialist Marx and downplaying his emphasis on the centrality of the subjective consciousness of mass political movements to democratic revolutionary transformation, the Bolsheviks developed their antidemocratic conception of "imputed" consciousness. Ironically their materialist, determinist view of class consciousness engendered an extremely voluntarist conception of political power. The party, through subjective will, could impose on a recalcitrant civil society the alleged objective interests of the working class. Yet Russian society was far from being the advanced capitalist society that the Bolshevik revolutionaries as Marxists should have used to discern the true interests of the proletariat. Ignoring Marx's warnings in *On the Jewish Question* against the "terror" of a state trying to prematurely transform civil society from above, Lenin's heirs would utilize state power to collectivize a civil society in which the material preconditions for socialism did not exist.[31]

What Is to Be Done? The Substitution of Party Consciousness for Working-Class Consciousness

What Is to Be Done? Lenin's major treatise on the ideological and organizational tasks of Russian social democracy, is best read as both a contextual critique of the rise of "economism" in Russia and a theoretical statement of the relationship between ideology, political organization, and political consciousness. The work is also a critique of reformism's inordinate focus on immediate working-class economic gains at the expense of long-run socialist transformation. *What Is to Be Done* has traditionally been interpreted as a straightforward manual on revolutionary organization under conditions of autocratic repression. But in the work Lenin also advances a theoretical account of working-class consciousness and the role of the modern division of labor in promoting efficiency in both revolutionary parties and social institutions in democratic capitalist societies. Lenin's obsession with efficiency and the division of labor in all forms of social organization has rarely been examined, although it had profound implications for his conception of both party-building and communism. This celebration of efficiency foreshadows the Taylorist vision of communism in *State and Revolution*. And Lenin recommends a party based on expertise, full-time commitment, and hierarchical organization not only for communists who need to operate under clandestine conditions but also for socialists operating openly in bourgeois democratic societies.

In his debate with "economistic" tendencies in the Russian Social Democratic Party, which argued that the party should concentrate its energies within the trade unions, Lenin stressed the need for socialists to play a leading role in the broad democratic movement against Russian autocracy. He believed that the "economists" inordinately privileged the short-term economic demands of the trade union movement, ignoring the twin tasks of building a broad democratic movement against the autocracy and an independent revolutionary socialist organization. In 1902 Lenin still adhered to the classic Russian Marxist conception that the first stage of the Russian revolution would be liberal democratic, with the aim of creating a bourgeois democratic regime that the working class could then oppose. But contrary to Marxist orthodoxy, Lenin believed that the peasantry, rather than the bourgeoisie, would be the primary ally of the nascent working-class movement. As Neil Harding's comprehensive two-volume work on Lenin's thought demonstrates, Lenin's strategic orientation was heavily informed by his theoretical work.[32] Lenin opposed those in the Social Democratic party who would subsequently become Mensheviks, who favored allying with the bourgeoisie against the autocracy. Lenin favored an alliance with the peasantry because of his reading of Marx's analysis of the betrayal of the French and German working class by the bourgeoisie in the 1848 revolutions against the autocracy. Lenin advocated a primary alliance with the peasantry against the aristocracy because his theoretical work in the 1890s, *The Development of Capitalism in Russia*, convinced him that capitalist market forces were penetrating the countryside and setting a peasantry increasingly besieged by market pressures against a commercialized, landed aristocracy.[33] Lenin rejected granting exclusive primacy to the working-class movement as a revolutionary agent within an autocratic, overwhelmingly peasant nation: "The Social Democrat's ideal should not be the trade-union secretary, but the tribune of the people who is able to react to every manifestation of tyranny and oppression . . . no matter what stratum or class of the people it affects."[34]

Lenin's contention that trade union struggles alone could not generate revolutionary consciousness represented a heretical break with the Marxist tradition, more so than did his oft-noted assertion that socialist theory must be brought to the working class by intellectuals. Marx evinced a faith that workers would come to recognize, *through their own experience* such as the struggle to shorten the workday, the need for a political party that could not only transform state policy but ultimately contend for state power. In striking contrast to Marx, Lenin contended that neither the immediate struggles of the working class nor their collective reflection on those struggles could generate socialist consciousness: "Taken by themselves the strikes were simply trade union struggles, not yet Social Democratic struggles. They marked the awakening antagonisms between workers and employers; but the workers were not, and could not be, conscious of the irreconcilable antagonism of their interests as to the whole of the modern political and social system, i.e., theirs was not yet Social-Democratic consciousness."[35] In Lenin's analysis a hermetic barrier separates the struggle for immediate economic reforms from the formation of revolutionary consciousness. Lenin believed that economic concessions to the working class could, in the absence of intervention by a revolutionary party, lead to the co-optation of the working class: "'Economic' concessions . . . are, of course, the cheapest and most advantageous from the government's point of view, because by these means it [the government] hopes to win the confidence of the working masses."[36] Thus it is necessary to maintain a vanguard party separate from—though integrally involved with—the daily struggles of the working class.

Perhaps Lenin feared that the small working class in Russia might develop into a privileged stratum, divorced from the broader struggle against the autocracy. More likely, his disdain for the "revisionist" relegation of the class struggle to "narrow trade unionism and to a 'realistic' struggle for petty, gradual reforms"[37] made him keenly aware that working-class struggle alone might not engender a revolutionary socialist politics. For Lenin, unlike any previous Marxist, the commitment to socialism necessitated an attitude of, at best, critical support for the day-to-day economic struggles of the working class. Not only were professional party cadre to lead a life separate from that of the ordinary worker, but the rank-and-file social democratic worker would be distinguished from the ordinary worker by his political disdain for bread-and-butter issues: "The Social Democratic worker, the revolutionary worker . . . will indignantly reject all this talk about struggle for demands promising palpable results, etc., because he will understand that this is only a variation of the old song about adding a kopek to the ruble."[38]

Thus, as early as 1902 Lenin had become the first Marxist theorist to fear that the working class, if left to its own devices, might "sell out." Fourteen years before he analyzed the bounty imperialism might yield for a stratum of workers in the advanced nations in *Imperialism: The Highest Stage of Capitalism*,[39] Lenin believed that the working class could be bought off by the fruits of capitalist development. Marx never anticipated this possibility, faithfully assuming that the struggle for immediate reforms would over time lead the working class to struggle against the system: "Out of the separate economic movements of the workers there grows up everywhere a political movement, that is to say, a movement of the class, with the object of enforcing its interests in a general form, in a form possessing general, socially coercive force."[40]

Lenin never contended that the Bolsheviks should avoid participation in trade union struggles.[41] But from 1902 on Lenin urged communists to work within the unions, "no matter how reactionary," to combat mere "trade union consciousness."[42] Trade union activity was a "spontaneous element" in working-class life that, although representing class "consciousness in an embryonic form," had to be nurtured and transformed by the party before it could develop into revolutionary consciousness.[43] Only after arguing that trade union struggles cannot spontaneously generate revolutionary class consciousness does Lenin assert the critical role of intellectuals in developing the theory of socialism: "The history of all countries shows that the working class, exclusively by its own effort, is able to develop only trade-union consciousness. . . . The theory of socialism, however, grew out of the philosophical, historical and economic theories elaborated by educated representatives of the propertied classes, by intellectuals."[44]

Though this may be the best-known passage from *What Is to Be Done?* it represents what was then a standard sociology of knowledge among Marxists of all persuasions. Few could deny that socialist intellectuals played a crucial role in all socialist movements. Where Lenin breaks new ground as a socialist theorist, however, is in his assertion that *only one vanguard revolutionary party with the correct revolutionary theory can bring socialist consciousness to the working class*: "Without revolutionary theory there can be no revolutionary movement. . . . The role of vanguard fighter can be fulfilled only by a party that is guided by the most advanced theory."[45] The centrality of the socialist political party in the struggle for socialism is also integral to most early-twentieth-century socialist theory. But Lenin's conception of a single "correct" revolutionary theory developed independently of the mass working-class movement, and, embodied in a single party, represented an innovation of profound import. Marx's political writings took for granted the existence of multiple working-class parties in capitalist societies, and he recognized that they existed in the Paris Commune, where the party that sided with Marx in the First International made up the minority of socialist representatives. Marx consistently argued that communists should not form their own separate, vanguard party: "The Communists do not form a separate party opposed to other working class parties. . . . They do not set up any sectarian principles of their own, by which to shape and mould the proletarian movement."[46]

Kautsky, whom Lenin quotes at length to affirm his contention that revolutionary class consciousness must be imported from outside the workers' movement, concurred that bourgeois intellectuals developed the "science" that the Social Democratic Party brought to the working class. Kautsky's conception of "scientific socialism" reinforced Lenin's belief that politics was a realm of choice between objectively "correct" and "incorrect," "proletarian" and "bourgeois" positions. It is worth quoting Kautsky to reveal how his mechanistic Marxism profoundly influenced Lenin's conceptualization of economics, technology, and consciousness as "sciences" whose practices were radically divorced from those of moral deliberation: "The vehicle of the science is not the proletariat but the bourgeois intelligentsia. . . . Thus, socialist consciousness is something introduced into the proletarian class struggle from without and not something that arose within it spontaneously. . . . The task of Social Democracy is to imbue the proletariat [literally saturate the proletariat] with the consciousness of the position and the consciousness of its task. There would be no need for this if consciousness arose of itself from the class struggle."[47]

Lenin, however, goes well beyond Kautsky's mechanistic, materialist Second International orthodoxy by asserting that a working class not infused with scientific socialist consciousness is "objectively bourgeois." Kautsky never claimed that working-class political activity not guided by the proper revolutionary socialist party served "objectively" to shore up capitalism. Trade union activity, for Lenin, is not simply nonrevolutionary in its nature, a thesis with which Marx or Kautsky might concur; such activity, in Lenin's view, positively reinforces bourgeois dominance. Neither Kautsky nor Marx ever hinted at Lenin's position, which asserts the primacy of revolutionary theory, and the vanguard party embodying it, over a mass working-class practice that, if left to its own self-development, is "objectively" bourgeois: "There can be no talk of an independent ideology formulated by the working masses themselves in the process of their movement; the only choice is— either bourgeois or socialist ideology. . . . Working class trade unionist politics is precisely working class bourgeois politics."[48]

This reading of Lenin, that the vanguard party embodies objective revolutionary-class consciousness even if its beliefs are rejected by the mass working-class movement, is theoeretically posed most starkly in George Lukacs's writings on class consciousness. Lukacs's theory of class consciousness was dismissed by the Comintern in 1923 as "metaphysical nonsense" because of its explicit roots in a Hegelian teleology of conscious self-recognition rather than in a structural, strictly materialist conception of consciousness. But, in its neo-Hegelian form, it depicts Lenin's theory of class consciousness in a philosophically rigorous manner, imputing to structural class positions in the capitalist economy an "ideal" class consciousness that the proletariat would achieve *under optimal historical conditions.* As Lukacs wrote in *History and Class Consciousness,* this imputed consciousness "objectively" exists whether or not any individual proletarian *actually* adheres to it:

> By relating consciousness to the whole of society it becomes possible to infer the thoughts and feelings which men would have in a particular situation if they were able to assess both it and the interests arising from it in their impact on immediate action and on the whole structure of society. That is to say, it would be possible to infer the thoughts and feelings appropriate to their objective situation. . . . Class consciousness consists in fact of the appropriate and rational reactions "imputed" to a particular typical position in the process of production. This consciousness is, therefore, neither the sum nor the average of what is thought or felt by the single individuals who make up the class. And yet the historically significant actions of the class as a whole are determined in the last resort by this consciousness and not by the thought of the individual—and these actions can be understood only by reference to this consciousness.[49]

This metaphysical, neo-Hegelian rendering of Lenin's reinterpretation of Marx contends that, in the final instance, structural economic position determines an "ideal" class consciousness that would be recognized and embraced by a "rational" worker. Which "rational" agent expresses that consciousness, whether it be a mass party, a vanguard party, or a demagogue, is strictly a contingent factor.[50] This subordination of actual "subjective" class consciousness to an "objective," structurally determined revolutionary consciousness resulted in a radical reorientation of socialist revolutionaries toward the actual practices of the working class. Lukacs's conception that "true class consciousness" is embodied in the structure of capitalism justifies any party, or even an isolated intellectual, claiming to comprehend the laws of capitalist development, asserting that this party or individual embodies the "true consciousness" of the working class. Whether or not members of the working class share this consciousness is morally irrelevant, although mere "empirical" mass consciousness may affect the revolutionary party's ability to garner the necessary political strength to seize power. Lukacs recognized that this imputed class consciousness might not become the actual consciousness of the proletariat; nor would the party representing this imputed consciousness necessarily be strong enough to seize state power. Certain, however, that the crisis tendency within capitalism would eventually lead to economic collapse, Lukacs posited that if the revolutionary vanguard did not achieve state power, capitalism would inevitably lead to "the mutual ruin of the contending classes." Lukacs's essay "History and Class Consciousness" is haunted by this vision of social collapse engendered by the failure of the mass working class to embrace revolutionary socialism. Despairing of the political immaturity of the working class amid the chaos of the post-World War I collapse of the Austro-Hungarian empire and the failure of the Hungarian soviet uprising of 1918, Lukacs discovered in the Bolshevik triumph a potential road to power for "true class consciousness" despite the "opportunism" of the mass working-class movement of Western and Central Europe of his day.

WHAT IS TO BE DONE? AND THE DIVISION OF LABOR: THE PARTY AS SCIENTIFIC ORGANIZATION

The argument in *What Is to Be Done?* for a professional vanguard party, governed by the principles of democratic centralism, initially raised less controversy within the social democratic movement than did the polemic's critique of trade union consciousness.[51] Few European social democrats of his day denied Lenin's contention that a fully democratic political organization could not be built in a repressive society. As Rosa Luxemburg noted, however, Lenin too readily transformed unfortunate necessities into unqualified virtues.[52] Despite the disclaimer that "here, and further on, of course, I refer only to absolutist Russia,"[53] it became apparent in subsequent writings that Lenin believed that centralized leadership by people of talent, combined with a rigid division of organizational labor, would benefit revolutionary parties whether they operated under repressive or "bourgeois" democratic conditions. That autocratic Russia made this a necessity, rather than simply an advisable course, was not a situation Lenin regretted. Though he only officially advocated democratic centralist organization for all communist parties when the twenty-one principles of the Comintern were enunciated in 1921, in *What Is to Be Done?* Lenin enthusiastically expressed his faith in expertise and leadership from above as a necessary response to the underdeveloped consciousness of the masses *everywhere.*

Lenin's belief in the necessity of a specially trained revolutionary vanguard did not lead him to adopt an elitist attitude toward all members of the working class. He believed that talented workers—"working class intellectuals"—could become professional revolutionaries as effective as those drawn from the intelligentsia. But he also contended that any effective political organization, no matter how massive or democratic, would have to be led by a relatively permanent leadership of talent. Lenin stood Michels on his head, making a virtue of the oligarchical leadership of German Social Democracy which Michels was later to lament, while accepting its alleged necessity:

> Take the Germans. It will not be denied, I hope, that theirs is a mass organization, that in Germany everything proceeds from the masses, that the working class movement there has learned to walk. Yet observe how these millions value their "dozen" tried political leaders, how firmly they cling to them. . . . Political thinking is sufficiently developed among the Germans, and they have accumulated sufficient political experience to understand that without the "dozen" tried and talented leaders (and talented men are not born by the hundreds), professionally trained, schooled by long experience, and working in perfect harmony, no class in modern society can wage a determined struggle.[54]

In the conclusion of the section of *What Is to Be Done?* on "'Conspiratorial' Organization and 'Democratism,'" Lenin makes clear that the imperatives of leadership, division of labor, and expertise pertain to *all* modern social organizations, not just to revolutionary organizations in repressive societies.[55] Lenin concludes with an exegesis of Beatrice and Sidney Webbs's work on English trade unions. He cites the Webbs to criticize the "primitive democratic" position that offices be held by rotation. Only after the painful experience of incompetent administration and bankrupt strike and benefit funds did the British working class realize the need within their own unions for representative democracy, full-time staffers, and the hiring of "experts."[56]

Lenin also explicates at length Kautsky's critique of German "primitive democracy," a theory that contended that the party should abandon its reliance on professional journalists, parliamentarians, and staff. Lenin seconds Kautsky's criticism of those who favor total participatory democracy, excoriating those false democrats who "'striving for effect' extol direct legislation by the whole people completely failing to understand that this idea can be applied only relatively in modern society."[57] A reasoned defender of representative democracy could agree with much of Lenin's argument and also criticize him for later neglecting his own defense of representative institutions when he uncritically extols the direct democracy of the soviets in *State and Revolution.* Socially complex institutions, as Lenin claims, necessitate certain roles for expertise and some division of tasks. Yet Lenin's near-frenetic defense of leadership and expertise eliminates any concern with democratic checks from below and efforts to make *the purposive goals* of the experts, if not their techniques, accessible and open to public debate. As Rosa Luxemburg stressed repeatedly in her criticisms of Lenin's democratic centralism, the concept expresses a fear of democratic spontaneity, a fear that without proper control from above the movement will fail. Luxemburg, in her 1904 polemic against Lenin's conception of democratic centralism, accused Lenin of joining the tradition of egoistic, conspiratorial Russian revolutionaries: "In Lenin's overanxious desire to establish the guardianship of an omniscient and omnipotent Central Committee in order to protect so promising and vigorous a labor movement against any misstep, we recognize the symptoms of the same subjectivism that has already played more than one trick on socialist thinking in Russia."[58]

It would be a misreading of the historical record to describe Lenin as both the logical and historical precursor of Stalin. Though the pre-Stalin Bolshevik Party certainly is responsible for the brutal repression of thousands of unarmed opponents (bracketing the question of conduct in an armed civil war against armed domestic opponents and tens of thousands of foreign invaders), it is unlikely that Lenin, had he lived, would have engaged in the physical extermination of tens of thousands of opponents within his own party or of millions of peasants by initiating an outright civil war in the countryside. NEP represented a belated but programmatic and ideological compromise with the realities of peasant Russia, although Lenin, prefiguring the contemporary Chinese market "reforms," made no concessions in the direction of political pluralism and representation for peasants and other social strata. Lenin's obsession in his dying years with the bureaucratic rigidification of the party indicated his fears of what was to come. But Lenin's entire political and theoretical orientation provided no basis for him to recognize the imperative need for internal party democracy, institutionalized civil liberties, and democratic political authority over both the party and state bureaucracy. That is, Lenin's lifework left no legacy of either moral or institutional barriers against the rise of Stalin.

THE REPRESSIVE STATE VERSUS THE TRANSITIONAL STATE IN MARX: THE OPENING TOWARD LENIN'S ADMINISTRATION WITHOUT POLITICS

Defenders of a democratic Marx traditionally cite his writings on the Paris Commune as definitive evidence that his vision of a postrevolutionary socialist or first-stage communist society was unequivocally that of a grassroots, radical political democracy. Given that *State and Revolution* rests heavily on an exegesis of Marx's *The Civil War in France*, if Marx's vision of postrevolutionary politics is that of the vibrant public life of the Commune, what are the implications for Lenin's work? Is Lenin, at a minimum, the author of a visionary plan for a society governed by democratic workers' councils (soviets), an author who either had no intention of implementing that vision or tragically was prevented from doing so by historical exigencies? Or could Marx's writings on the Commune both eulogize the memory of the slaughtered Communards' short-lived representative democracy as well as reveal his own ambiguous credentials as a democratic theorist?

Marx's emotional defense of the Commune captures the vitality of its brief democratic life. And his conception of a first-stage communist state that plans both production and distribution provides an opening for a vision of postrevolutionary politics. But Marx fails to take advantage of that theoretical opening because his reductionist analysis of politics as class conflict assumed that in a classless society there would be no politics but just "the administration of things." And his faith that in a classless society undistorted human interests would be so universally shared led him to believe that political institutions would not be needed to mediate differences of opinion and interests. Social governance would occur under first-stage communism, but somehow without being politics. Thus Marx provides no challenge for Lenin to develop a postrevolutionary theory of politics. Lenin moved beyond Marx's ambiguities on the role of politics in a postrevolutionary society by providing a clearer picture of how social decisions would be made in the soviets of first-stage communism. The "administration of things" would occur according to the laws of science and technology and the rationality of the bureaucratic apparatus developed by late capitalism and appropriated by the armed workers in their seizure of the capitalist state.

It is through the prism of his conception of the role of the state in capitalist society that Marx theorizes the role of the state in a postcapitalist society. The post-World War II profusion of Marxist conceptions of the capitalist state reflects Marx's failure to develop a systematic theory of the state, a failure that would have profound implications for his conception of the state after capitalism. Schematically put, Marx's work advances two basic images of the state, neither of which is rigorously systematized. The predominant image is that of the "servile" state—the state as the servant of the dominant class, enforcing its class dominance over other classes, by force if necessary. In this view the state is class-ridden, instrumentally enforcing the interests of the dominant class in civil society. A second image of the "dominant" state, however, emerges from Marx's political writings. This state has a certain "relative autonomy" from social interests ("relative" in that the state's ultimate existence still depends on the continued growth of the capitalist mode of production). The "dominant state" performs numerous functions—from promoting class cohesion within a divided ruling class, granting concessions to subordinate classes, and fracturing the interests of the working class to occasionally pursuing its own bureaucratic self-interest. In this image society can, at times, be judged to be state-ridden, with the state developing, as Marx termed it in *The Eighteenth Brumaire*, into a "parasitic excrescence upon society."[59]

Marx utilizes the image of the dominant state ruling above civil society to analyze societies characterized by class stalemate—societies in which the ruling class is too weak to rule without the force of the state apparatus and the rising class is not yet strong enough to assert its ascendancy. For Marx, the state is only truly democratic when it is converted "from an organ superimposed upon society into one completely subordinate to it."[60] Marx was acutely aware of the dangerous potential of a dominant, "sorcerer's apprentice" state,[61] which goes beyond reflecting the dominance of the hegemonic class and comes to dominate society as a whole. The "sorcerer's apprentice" state resulting from a stalemate between contending classes is vividly described in *The Eighteenth Brumaire*. But the possibility of a relatively autonomous state bureaucracy serving its own particular interests at the expense of all other social classes is first developed in Marx's early philosophical writings, *On the Jewish Question* and *The Introduction to the Critique of Hegel's Philosophy of Right*, both of which analyze the division in the bourgeois era between civil society and the state.

In *The Introduction to the Critique*, Marx portrays the Hegelian "universal state" as utilizing its privileged position to serve its own particular interests: "In bureaucracy the identity of the state's interest and particular private purpose is established in such a way that the state's interest becomes a particular private purposes opposed to other private purposes."[62] In *On the Jewish Question*, Marx wrote in a similar vein, "At those times when the state is most aware of itself political life seeks to stifle its own prerequisites, civil society and its elements."[63] Even in *The German Ideology*, where Marx first describes the state as an instrument of class repression, he still contends that the state must pretend to act in the interests of society as a whole. Despite Althusser's claim that *The German Ideology* represents a complete break with his early writings, Marx still sounds the theme of the state's pretense to universality as being a manifestation of alienated human capacities for community, a theme central to his "prematerialist writings":[64]

> This crystallization of social activity, the consolidation of what we ourselves produce into an objective power above us, growing out of control, thwarting our expectations, bringing to naught our calculations is one of the chief factors in historical development up until now. And out of this very contradiction between the interest of the individual and that of the community the latter takes on an independent form as the State, divorced from the real interests of individual and community, and at the same time as an illusory communal life.[65]

Marx contended that the state could only achieve its democratic potential when a working class movement employs state power to create the material basis for a society that would be truly self-governing. That is, the state plays a central role in the construction of socialism (or first-stage communism). As described in *The Communist Manifesto*, the construction of socialism is a *gradual* political and economic process. The first stage involves the proletariat winning "the battle for democracy," apparently by parliamentary means.

Once the proletariat has won state power, it implements reforms that incrementally encroach on the prerogatives of capital. The transitional demands in *The Manifesto* include the abolition of inheritance and the private ownership of land, and the confiscation of the property of all emigrants and rebels. But other private enterprises would only gradually pass into the hands of the state. The transitional working-class democracy aims to "wrest by degrees all capital from the bourgeoisie, to centralize all instruments of production in the hands of the State, i.e., of the proletariat organized as a ruling class, and to increase the total forces of production as rapidly as possible."[66] In this image of the transition to socialism, the state plays a positive role of social reconstruction, going well beyond the repression of the bourgeoisie. But nowhere does Marx explicitly describe how this process of economic reorganization will be politically structured.

Marx's ambivalence toward political power, however, is evident even in *The Manifesto*, the text in which he comes closest to endorsing a role for postrevolutionary politics, though only under first-stage communism. Once socialized production is achieved, Marx argues, social governance moves from the sphere of politics to the realm of "public power." He describes this public power as a form of social administration or governance. He refuses to describe it explicitly as a form of political power, for he restrictively defines politics as class conflict. Marx never describes what this nonpolitical governance or administration would involve. Once the anarchy of capitalist production has been eliminated by the social organization of production, all social conflict appears to wither away: "When in the course of development class distinctions have disappeared, and all production has been concentrated in the hands of a vast association of the whole nation, *the public power will lose its political character. Political power, properly so called, is merely the organized power of one class for oppressing another.*[67] (emphasis added)

Once the proletariat has expropriated the bourgeoisie, the working class has abolished the conditions for its own class supremacy. In "place of the old bourgeois society with its classes and class antagonisms we shall have an association, in which the free development of each is the condition for the free development of all."[68] Marx is unclear as to when this withering away of politics occurs. In first-stage communism there is a tension between the repressive functions of the state and the transitional, socially constructive functions involved in "building up the forces of production." Marx never describes how the proletariat would democratically govern such a transitional socialist society. But the Paris Commune, which Engels termed "the dictatorship of the proletariat," is often taken to be Marx's model of a postcapitalist, functioning radical democracy of artisan, petty bourgeois, and working-class representatives.[69] After the slaughter of the Communards, Marx did eulogize the Commune "as the political form discovered under which to work out the economic emancipation of labor."[70] Beforehand, however, he warned the Parisian workers and artisans that they lacked the strength to defeat both the French republican army and that army's new-found allies in the victorious Prussian army. The best that the Commune could achieve, he argued, was to bargain for as democratic a form of bourgeois republic as possible to replace the defeated regime of Louis Bonaparte.

Marx's letter to Nieuwenhuis in 1881 (eleven years after the Commune) demonstrates that Marx did not view the Commune as a dictatorship of the proletariat, a *form* of working-class, socialist power: "The majority of the Commune was in no ways socialist and also could not have been."[71] The majority of the Commune's eighty-six deputies were not Marxists, but Blanquists and Proudhonists. Only twenty-five of its eighty-six members were workers and an almost equal twenty-one deputies represented conservative, bourgeois parties. The Commune failed even to nationalize the Bank of France which, Marx believed, could have served as a bargaining chip in negotiations for a peaceful compromise with the Thiers's Third Republic. Marx's celebration of the Commune treats it for it what it actually was—a short-lived, radical, but nonsocialist, pluralist democracy.

Marx's writings on the Commune are often cited by those contending that *the form of government* that Marx identified with socialism was a form of "direct democracy." The Commune did replace a professional police and standing army with an armed public militia. Municipal councilors and judges were elected and subject to recall. The municipal council combined executive and legislative functions, with all public service done at working-class wages. Yet the Commune was also a representative form of democracy, based on the same jurisdictional boundaries as previous republican municipal governments of Paris. Representation was by territory and not by workplace—it was not a workers' council or soviet form of government. It did not expropriate bourgeois property and even promised to pay compensation to the communalized property of entrepreneurs who had fled Paris. Workers cooperatively ran some abandoned firms. But the Commune's greatest legislative inroad on the rights of private property was its ending of nightwork in bakeries.[72]

Thus, the Commune was at most a radical form of democracy, closer to the spirit of nineteenth-century artisanal radicalism than industrial working-class socialism. Yet *The Civil War in France* provides ambiguous evidence that Marx desired a representative political democracy *as the form of state* for the transition to socialism. Despite the Commune's petty bourgeois and artisanal support, as well as its working-class core constituency, Marx described it in *The Civil Wars in France* (significantly, his only *public* writing on the Commune and thus the most polemical in intent) as "the struggle of the producing against the appropriating class, the political form discovered under which to work out the economic emancipation of labor."[73] After the slaughter of 20,000 Communards in one week by the triumphant troops of the future Third Republic, Marx authored a laudatory epitaph for the Commune, ascribing to it more socialist aims than he privately believed it had: "[the] intention to abolish . . . class property. It aimed at the expropriation of the expropriators. . . . United co-operative societies are to regulate national production upon a common plan."[74]

One cannot with convincing textual evidence assert that the essence of Marx's conception of "the dictatorship of the proletariat" is reflected in the flowering of politics which Marx described in the Commune. In other writings on communism, Marx stresses that the capitalist state would ultimately be transcended not by a radical political democracy but by a stateless society spontaneously working out its nonalienated harmony. The Hegelian impulse to transcend the division between particularity and universality governs Marx's vision of a "social administration" transcending politics. In *The Manifesto* and *The Critique of the Gotha Program*, Marx admits that during first-stage communism, when the forces of production still need to be developed and when the possibility of counterrevolutionary activity remains, then a workers' state or "dictatorship of the proletariat" will be necessary. But Marx never describes a public space in which political debate and difference could flourish in that postcapitalist state. Rather, prefiguring Lenin's even more technocratic conception of the first-stage communist state, Marx's silence on the role for politics implies that organizing production and repressing the bourgeoisie will be readily discernable tasks agreed on by all class-conscious workers in a first-stage communist society.

In a society organized in accord with universal human interests, there will exist neither classes nor class domination and therefore, by Marx's definition, no politics and no state. This underlying search for the universal may account for why Marx makes no mention of political conflict in his published eulogy of the Commune, even though twenty-one of the eighty-six representatives were from conservative parties and profound political divisions existed between the centralist, insurrectionist Blanquists and the anarcho-syndicalist Proudhonists. In Marx's conception of postrevolutionary organization, the issues of how firms should be organized and what purposes they should serve do not appear to be matters for political discussion. In a metaphor that comes close to reducing postcapitalist politics to the act of choosing the best technocratic manager, Marx reduces political choice in a postcommunist society to public selection of the right person for the right job. As the goals of repressing counterrevolutionaries and developing the forces of production according to laws of science appear to be solely questions of technical competence, politics can be reduced from a process of collective deliberation to the "correct" choice of the properly skilled administrator. And such a choice could be made as skillfully by a random representative individual as by a deliberative public: "Universal suffrage was to serve the people, constituted in the Communes, as individual suffrage serves every other employer in the search for the workmen and managers in his business. . . . *Companies, like individuals, in matters of real business generally know how to put the right man in the right place, and, if they for once make a mistake, to redress it promptly.*"[75] (emphasis added.)

In a classless society there appears to be for Marx no *functional* difference between the results of collective or individual deliberation. People pick representatives based not on political programs and priorities, but on whom they would trust to do a job whose purposes they agree on without dispute. Voting becomes a simple matter because all share the same goal—the advancement of the collective will. Recall allows quick redress if the voters make a mistake by choosing an incompetent administrator. The voters can fire elected officials in the same way a manager fires an incompetent employee. In addition, paying all public servants a working person's wage prevents the emergence of a separate caste of self-interested bureaucrats. The implicit operative assumption that the goals of socialist planning would be reached easily and by consensus is rendered more explicit in the famous section on the fetishism of commodities in the first chapter of *Capital*. Here Marx opines that the goals of a communist society will be as transparent— and as easily adhered to—as Robinson Crusoe's plans for a day of work on his island. Although no person may be an island, in a socialist society planning a society's future appears in Marx to be as transparent and simple as planning the life of one individual's day in a society where he or she is the only member.[76]

Perhaps because Marx could not conceive of significant political and social divisions within a classless society, he tragically failed to specify what limits on democratic freedoms a "proletarian dictatorship" might legitimately apply against the recently expropriated bourgeoisie. Would all members of the bourgeoisie be denied political rights? Or would they retain full civil liberties and the right to meaningful labor, with liberty being denied only to those who engaged in illegal, armed acts of resistance to the democratically elected proletarian government.[77] An analogy might be made between this conception of how "the democratic dictatorship of the proletariat" treats the opposition and how Lincoln's Civil War government treated supporters of the South. But what would be the rights of those who favored the transition to socialism but opposed the policies by which the regime was allegedly carrying it out? Would they be deemed "objectively bourgeois" opponents of the regime with their civil liberties denied?

Given the use of the term "dictatorship" in nineteenth-century political discourse, one could reasonably surmise that Marx only intended that this temporary state would have the equivalent repressive powers of a bourgeois democratic regime during a "state of siege" or "martial law," when certain civil liberties are temporarily limited in order to defend the future of democracy against armed, undemocratic opponents.[78] But despite this effort to put Marx's use of the unfortunate term in historical context, when explicitly challenged Marx did not offer a considered answer to the question of what limits would be placed on a transitional state's capacity for repression. This inadequate performance occurs in his self-constructed fictional debate with Bakunin in Marx's marginal notes or "conspectus" of Bakunin's *Statehood and Anarchy*. Here Marx endorses some form of state coercion with respect to bourgeois property rights as necessary to constructing socialist relations of production. But when challenged by Bakunin's work to outline the democratic rights of either the bourgeoisie or the proletariat in a postrevolutionary society, Marx remains conspicuously silent. In his notes on Bakunin, Marx initially appears to endorse representative democracy as the proper means of social governance in a postrevolutionary society: "Can it really be that in a trade union, for example, the entire union forms its executive committee? Can it be that there will disappear from the factory all division of labor and difference of functions stemming from it? And in the Bakunist arrangement 'from bottom to top' will everyone be at the 'top'? In that case there will be no 'bottom.' Will all the members of the township in equal measure supervise the general affairs of the 'district'? In that even there will be no distinction between township and district [*sic*]."[79] Marx contends that decentralized, representative government will enhance political participation, with *representative* government from the level of the township up involving as many as "40 million Germans" in the process of self-rule.

But when challenged by Bakunin to define how the workers' representatives can democratically "rule" working people without "dominating" them, Marx dodges the question. Instead of defending constitutionally guarantees of civil liberties and the need for a democratic representation of interests and points of view, Marx retorts that as *class distinctions* no longer exist neither will political government. Marx again employs the image of government as business, the administration of things. All that the working class need do through participation is choose their most trusted administrators. There appears to be no need for debate over what decisions these administrators should make. But business, as Marx well knew, can be run autocratically. He provides absolutely no answer to Bakunin's prescient fear that "the so-called people's state will be nothing other than the quite despotic administration of the masses of the people by a new and very non-numerous aristocracy of real and supposed learned ones. The people is not learned, so it will be entirely freed from the cares of governing, wholly incorporated into the governed herd."[80]

Marx assumes that "administrative and technical" personnel have no power in a classless society. But this is simply assuming away Bakunin's fear that all officeholders have the potential power to dominate. Marx, however, cavalierly assumes that no new ruling group is possible in a "classless society" because political rule, by Marx's crude definition-by-assertion, always reflects class interest. The administration of things cannot involve domination nor choice among competing conceptions of how to organize society, because a postclass society will be organized according to the allegedly objective, technical needs of an advanced industrial society: "The character of elections depends not on these designations [political] but on the economic foundations, on the economic ties of the voters amongst one another and from the moment these functions cease being political 1/ no governmental functions any longer exist; 2/ the distribution of general functions takes on a business character and involves no domination; and 3/ elections completely lose their present political character."[81] But can an election be meaningful if it is not political, if it is not about the democratic allocation of social power and the ability to make policy? If the position holds no power and permits no discretionary choice, why have an election at all—why not simply rotate the office or choose applicants on their technical or administrative, rather than political, capacities?

In responding to Bakunin's objections, Marx inadvertently demonstrates how little he thought about the possible social forms of power "administrators" under socialism might exercise. Marx asserts that the proof that worker administrators would not dominate the working class is that the managers of workers' cooperatives never abuse their power: "If Herr Bakunin knew even one thing about the situation of the manager of a workers' cooperative factory, all his hallucinations about domination would go to the devil. He would have to ask himself what form the functions of administration can assume on the basis of such a worker state, if it pleases him to call it that."[82] But Marx himself never describes the democratic forms those functions would assume. Obviously, managers of state-owned firms or administrative agencies can and have dominated workers based on management's greater expertise, control over investment and finances, or power over personnel questions. If there exist no constitutionally enforced measures for managerial recall nor the provision of funding for independent expert consultants for the workers, then the rank and file can readily be subordinated to the power and/or superior knowledge of state managers, even if they have a formal say in selecting them. Anyone who has worked in a production cooperative or volunteered in a consumer food coop knows that tensions frequently exist between the rank-and-file members and the managers they elect. In fact, most food coops, if they are successful, grow to the point of considering full-time staff and managers rather than strictly volunteer member labor. Marx's failure to consider differential power relationships based on knowledge, experience, and expertise marks another embarrassingly naive performance in his "conspectus" on postrevolutionary power.

In the transition from capitalism to communism described in *The Communist Manifesto*, there is a potential political role for the transitional state. Marx states that such a state must allocate social roles and assign responsibility and rewards according to the "bourgeois right" of "from each according to their ability to each according to their contribution." But in the transition described by Engels and Lenin as "the administration of things, not people," this tenuous opening for a political role in policy making withers away immediately; the proletarian state's apparently sole function is to repress the remnants of the bourgeoisie, while the socialist forces of production develop according to the laws of motion of industrial production. The political role of the state disappears as soon as the bourgeoisie are completely repressed. Lenin's vision of the apolitical, purely technical nature of the socialist production process draws heavily on Engels's *Socialism, Utopian and*

Scientific. There Engels contends that as soon as the "proletariat seizes political power and turns the means of production into state property" the state begins to wither away. In Engels's view the development of the forces of production is governed by material laws that become transparent to all. This means that there is one "correct" answer to the amount of social surplus that should be allocated to diverse social endeavors (e.g., education). Engels writes:

> As soon as class rule, and the individual struggle for existence based upon our present anarchy in production with the collisions and excesses arising from these, are removed, nothing more remains to be repressed, and a special repressive force, a state, is no longer necessary. . . . State interference in social relations becomes, in one domain after another, superfluous and then dies out of itself; *the government of persons is replaced by the administration of things, and by the conduct of processes of production. The state is not "abolished." It dies out.*[83] (emphasis added)

In his attempt to render concrete Marx's search for the harmonious, universal society, Lenin emphasizes in *State and Revolution* the scientistic view of postrevolutionary society first advanced by Engels. Engels's and Lenin's scientism ultimately would cripple the socialist movement's ability to conceptualize a democratic role for politics after the revolution. Marx's eulogy of the radical representative democracy of the Commune[84] and his description of the first-stage communist state's role in governing the economy provides a narrow opening for those who wish to read Marx as a committed, postrevolutionary democrat. But his reductionist equation of politics with class conflict and his assumption that the interests of working people would be homogeneous precluded him from developing a democratic conception of postrevolutionary politics which might have been mobilized against the even more technocratic, scientistic conception of postrevolutionary society advanced by Engels and Lenin.

Lenin's *State and Revolution*: Scientific Administration and the Withering Away of Politics

Lenin's *State and Revolution* aimed to combat mainstream social democracy's "servility" to the imperialist state in its final act of carnage, World War I: "Socialism in words, chauvinism in deeds is characterized by a base, servile adaptation of the 'leaders of socialism' to the interests not only of 'their' national bourgeoisie, but also of 'their' state."[85] Lenin's insistence in *State and Revolution* that a socialist revolution would have to "smash the power of the bourgeois state" represented a significant break in his thinking. Until the winter of 1916–17, Lenin adhered to the orthodox view of the Second International, drawn from *The Communist Manifesto*, that the first stage of the socialist revolution would involve the proletariat seizing the bourgeois state and using it to construct the material prerequisites for socialism. In *State and Revolution* Lenin significantly distances himself from both Marx's and Engels's belief in the value of working-class electoral efforts and the institutionalization of radical reforms within bourgeois democracies. He also advances a technocratic conception of immediate postrevolutionary administration which denudes both the soviets and Marx's transitional, first-stage communist government of any democratic political life. Thus, rather than a utopian tract in favor of direct democracy at the shop floor level, *State and Revolution*, when read in the context of Lenin's overall theoretical orientation, is the culmination of his technocratic and bureaucratic conception of socialism.

In the winter of 1916–17, Lenin, in exile in Switzerland, turned his attention to analyzing the accretion of capitalist state power during wartime. The contemporary writings on the capitalist state of the Dutch-born German socialist Anton Pannekoek (later a founder of "council communism") and the young Bolshevik theoretician Nikolai Bukharin heavily influenced this endeavor.[86] Both viewed the capitalist state apparatus through the lens of Marx's conception of the relatively autonomous, parasitic capitalist state. They also argued that the emerging militarist state apparatus posed a fundamental threat to both democracy and working-class power. Pannekoek developed a nascent theory of corporatism, contending that class compromise was gradually incorporating European working-class organizations into the bourgeois state apparatus. He was also one of the first Marxists to describe the state bureaucracy in advanced capitalism as a class, separate from the bourgeoisie, with distinct interests: "The political bureaucracy is a class in its own right, with its own interests, which it attempts to realize even at the expense of the bourgeoisie."[87]

In *Imperialism and the World Economy* (1915), Bukharin argued that the West had entered a new era of state capitalism in which the state played a dominant role in coordinating both domestic economic activity and economic competition against other imperialist states.[88] In a subsequent article, "Toward a Theory of the Imperialist State," written with the help of Pannekoek for an emigré journal that Lenin edited, Bukharin held that social democratic parliamentary activism no longer posed a threat to bourgeois rule. In order to smash the power of the bourgeois state machine, he wrote, the working class "must outgrow the framework of the state and burst it from within as they organize their own state power."[89] Initially Lenin rejected Bukharin's disdain for working-class parliamentary activity, terming the article "quite incomplete, not thought out, useless."[90] In opposition to Bukharin, Lenin favorably cited Kautsky's prewar position that "socialists are in favor of using the present state and its institutions in the struggle for the emancipation of the working class, maintaining also that the state should be used for a specific form of transition from capitalism to socialism . . . the dictatorship of the proletariat, which is also a state."[91]

To further his polemic with Pannekoek and Bukharin, in the summer of 1916 Lenin re-read Marx on the Eighteenth Brumaire, the Commune, and the Gotha Program. This reading introduced into his work the first explicit awareness of Marx's "sorcerer's apprentice" image of the relatively autonomous state. Lenin's readings highlighted Marx's vague but frequent statements during periods of conservative and authoritarian rule in France and Germany in the 1850s and 1870s, respectively, that the bourgeois state apparatus would have to be "smashed" if working-class democracy were to be achieved. In January of 1917, almost two months before the February revolution and the reestablishment of soviets in Russia, Lenin for the first time identified the soviets of 1905 with the Commune state of Marx and outlined his theory of "dual power." He wrote of the necessity of "the replacement of the old ("ready made") state machine and of parliaments by soviets of workers' deputies and their mandated delegates."[92] This represented Lenin's first recognition that soviets might function, beyond the airing of workplace grievances, as some form of governing political institution that could supplant the "bourgeois" parliament. Lenin's subsequent increased hostility toward all forms of parliamentarism would initiate the flawed Marxist tradition of counterposing direct democracy to representative democracy. And Lenin's opposition to political pluralism within the soviets—by 1919 all other political parties were banned in Russia and by 1921 all factions within the Communist Party were abolished—meant that the soviets would never develop into democratic political institutions.

Lenin's seeming conversion to the "democratic" vision of the Commune in *State and Revolution* has been exaggerated by "left communists" who claim Lenin as one of their own. Harding claims that Lenin adhered to the vision of the Commune state for the first six months of revolutionary power.[93] Others defend the "democratic" Lenin until he banned factions within the Bolshevik party in March 1921 or subsequently crushed the Kronstadt revolt.[94] The evidence against this view of Lenin as a temporary convert to "council communism" is not simply the rapid establishment, on the taking of state power, of one-man management in industry, and the suppression of independent factory committees and trade unions.[95] It is the text of *State and Revolution* itself.

Although *State and Revolution* frequently calls for the "smashing of the bourgeois state" and the empowering of "the democratic state of the soviets," its substantive description of working-class power is even more apolitical and productivist than Marx's in *The Civil Wars in France*. The "armed workers" smash the state by 1) throwing the bourgeois bureaucrats out of office; 2) replacing them with elected working-class delegates, subject to mandate and immediate recall, who carry out the supposedly "simple accounting and checking" that administration involves; and 3) hiring the skilled technicians, scientists, and agronomists who will work under the supervision of rotating working-class "bosses" in the same manner that they served their capitalist masters. But nowhere in the text does Lenin outline the institutional mechanisms or procedures for deciding what policies should be "administered" or how experts should be selected to serve the working class. Nor does he attempt to square the circle between his implicit admission of the need for national political authority and his seeming desire to devolve all power to the factory-level soviets. In Lenin's view, neither "accounting or checking" (i.e., administration), allegedly rendered transparent by the science of management inherited from capitalism, nor the supervision of experts, who apparently gain no class or political power due to their knowledge, engenders political divisions among the unified "armed workers."

Citing Marx's letter to Kugelman of April 1871, Lenin insisted that what distinguishes Marx's politics from other variants of socialism was his insistence on the postrevolutionary "dictatorship of the proletariat" and "the smashing of the state."[96] But Lenin failed to see the irony that what he envisioned as the post-"smashed" form of revolutionary administration for "new workers' state" was simply "the armed workers" appropriating *intact* the state and planning apparatus that imperialist, finance capitalism had developed. Lenin argued that finance capital had socialized capitalist production to its fullest extent, while simultaneously destroying its progressive potential on the shoals of imperialist competition and war. The social planning and communications apparatus of the banks, cartels, and trusts created the functional prerequisites for the average worker to administer production. Simultaneously, the imperialist bloodbath caused by finance capitalism would, in Lenin's opinion, engender an international proletarian revolution enabling the working class to seize and "smash" the capitalist state apparatus. But although Lenin describes how the armed workers seize the bourgeois and corporate administrative machinery, he never outlines how they transform, let alone "smash," the internal practices of those entities.

Lenin failed to comprehend that if the *structure* of the capitalist bureaucracy remains intact, even if its personnel changes, then its previous ability to escape democratic political control may persist under socialism. How could Lenin believe that the very mechanisms that capital had devised to protect its own narrow interests could be transferred into organizations of revolutionary popular self-administration simply by workers' "seizing them?" If abuses of power are avoided by rotating the administrative overseers of the technical experts, the concomitant risk arises that these rotated functionaries may never gain sufficient competence to supervise the permanent technocracy. Lenin's obsession with the metaphor of "smashing" hindered his reflections on how the "smashed" state apparatus should be reconstructed. In truth Lenin never truly describes the "smashing of the state"; rather, the capitalist state, in its current functional structure, is simply "seized" by the armed workers and administered in the interests of the working class.

The text indicates that Lenin believed postcapitalist authority relations would operate according to the same logic of hierarchical efficiency as they did under capitalism. These relationships of authority, however, would produce policies in the objective interests of the newly ruling working class. Once the workers replace the bourgeoisie as the heads of the hiring hall, the new, supposedly nonbureaucratic "mechanism" operates according to the same "scientific" logic of the old bureaucratic "machine":

> Capitalist culture has created large-scale production, factories, railways, the postal service, telephones, etc., and on this basis the great majority of functions of the old "state power" have become so simplified and can be reduced to such simple operations of registration, filing and checking that they will be quite within the reach of every literate person. . . . A witty German Social-Democrat of the seventies of the last century called the post-office an example of the social-ist system. This is very true. At present the post-office is a business organized on the lines of a state capitalist monopoly. . . . But the mechanism of social man-agement is already at hand. Overthrow the capitalists, crush with the iron hand of the armed workers the resistance of these exploiters, *break the bureaucratic machine of the modern state—and you have before you a mechanism of the highest technical equipment, freed of "parasites," capable of being set into motion by the united workers themselves who hire their own technicians, bookkeepers,* and pay them, all, as indeed every "state" official, with the usual workers' wages.[97] (em-phasis added)

Lenin focused obsessively on two elements of the bourgeois state: its re-pressive apparatus and its bureaucracy. Early in *State and Revolution*, he asked, "What does this [state] power mainly consist of?" Lenin's answer is not a sophisticated structuralist or instrumentalist account of the state as a mechanism for enforcing class domination, creating social legitimacy through public provision, or coordinating disparate individual capitalist in-terests. Rather, Lenin's conception of the state is surprisingly Weberian in nature, but with a peculiar Marxian twist: The state is *uniquely* distinguished by its monopoly of the legitimate use of force (Weber) *and* this force is *exclu-sively* mobilized to enforce class rule (Marx). The essence of the capitalist state is, simply put, "special bodies of armed men who have at their disposal prisons, etc. A standing army and police are the chief instruments of state power."[98] Lenin explicitly rejected alternative theories of the state which fo-cused on its role in mediating and coordinating the multiplicity of interests and institutions of complex societies. Although Marx explicitly discussed in *The German Ideology* the need for the state to coordinate a complex division of labor and to establish a collective, if class-biased, public good mediating among competing capitalist interests created by a complex division of labor, Lenin explicitly condemns this view, conceiving of class domination as the sole defining function of the modern state: "To the question, whence arose the need for special bodies of armed men, standing above society and becom-ing separated from it (police and standing army), the Western European and Russian philistines are inclined to answer with a few phrases borrowed from Spencer or Mikhailovsky, by reference to the complexity of social life, the differentiation of functions, and so forth."[99]

Lenin held to a more constricted account of the possibilities of state autonomy than did Marx. If the state apparatus threatened to develop policies independent of the expressed interests of the capitalist class, Lenin believed the bourgeoisie would immediately mobilize its wealth to bribe the bureaucracy back into its service. If "the special bodies of armed men" is the most utilized phrase in *State and Revolution*, "bureaucratic placemen" runs a close second. Lenin used a partial quote from Engels, lifted out of the context of a defense of non-insurrectionary tactical alternatives to armed insurrection, to assert that universal suffrage is strictly a means of bourgeois domination. The suffrage, Lenin quotes, is but "an index of the maturity of the working class; it cannot, and never will, be anything else but that in the modern state."[100] Electoral campaigns are a useful vehicle for developing revolutionary working-class consciousness; but parliamentary means can never secure reforms that unambiguously benefit the interests of the working class. This advances a radically different analysis of working-class gains in parliament than did Marx's analysis of the British parliament's Ten Hours Bill.

In both *The Eighteenth Brumaire* and *The Class Struggles in France*, Marx describes the bourgeoisie's profound ambivalence about the democratic republic as its natural form of governance. Marx never developed a systematic theory to explain why in "normal times" the bourgeoisie exhibit an elective affinity for constitutional, parliamentary rule. His work implies that the democratic republic (or "vulgar democracy," as he terms it in *The Critique of the Gotha Program*) grants the bourgeoisie the greatest degree of political maneuverability vis-à-vis the state bureaucracy because the bourgeoisie can use its ideological legitimacy and economic power in civil society to mobilize popular opinion and to pressure elected officials. An authoritarian state bureaucracy, independent of the pressures of a class-biased but formally democratic politics, can gain a greater degree of insulation from bourgeois influence. Normally confident in its economic and social power, the bourgeoisie can afford to have a democratic state "mediate" among the fractional interests of capital as well as incorporate and fragment the working class through moderate social reforms. But Marx also believes that "bourgeois democracy" is potentially too democratic to remain stably "bourgeois." A growing working class threatens to use the franchise to fundamentally transform economic power relations. Marx fears that the bourgeoisie, when threatened by the power of this suffrage, will opt for authoritarian solutions that preserve its economic power at the expense of curtailing its political independence. In *The Eighteenth Brumaire* Marx describes how a "man on horseback" and a well-fed independent bureaucracy rule in place of a self-abdicating bourgeoisie that abandons political rule in return for the authoritarian regime maintaining bourgeois economic power.

Lenin rejects Marx's conception of parliamentary democracy as a significant, although limited, weapon in the political arsenal of the working class. In a crudely venal and instrumental conception of power, Lenin invokes the bribing of ministers as the major means by which the bourgeoisie preserves its hegemony. The representatives and bureaucracies of the democratic state appear not to worry about gaining noncoerced support from a mass electorate. Rather, they are owned and controlled by the capitalist class. For Lenin the democratic republic is the most secure form of capitalist rule because its democratic claims are completely a sham: "The omnipotence of wealth is thus more secure in a democratic republic, since it does not depend on the poor political shell of capitalism. A democratic republic is the best possible political shell for capitalism. . . . Once capital has gained control (through the Palchinskys, Chernovs, Tseretelis and Co.) . . . no change, either of persons, or institutions, or parties in the bourgeois republic can shake it."[101]

In contrast to Marx, who located the potential for socialism in both capitalism's increasingly social forces of production and in the growing political power of democratic working-class parties, Lenin located his teleology of socialist development almost exclusively in the inexorable centralization and concentration of capitalist production. The vision of the "administration of things" serves as a recurrent shorthand in the works of both Engels and Lenin for the governing of society according to the "scientific" norms of modern industrial production. The postrevolutionary state is needed only for its repressive capacities; the "toiling classes need the state only to overcome the resistance of the exploiters."[102] There is no need for a state to mediate politically the already scientifically determined direction of postrevolutionary economic and social development.

Lenin downplayed Marx's conception of the "dictatorship of the proletariat" as the transitional state organizing the social transformation from capitalism to communism. He rarely repeats Marx's distinction between a first-stage communism in which there seemingly is still a role for the state and for political deliberation and the second-stage communism of postscarcity abundance. This absence of the distinction partly explains why *State and Revolution* appears to advance a strikingly antistatist conception of communism. In the introduction to the work, Lenin claims that *The Eighteenth Brumaire* represents a great step beyond *The Manifesto* because it recognizes that "all revolutions which have taken place up to the present have helped to perfect the state machinery, whereas it must be shattered, broken to pieces."[103] The proletarian state as the organizer of the economic transition from capitalism to socialism withers away in the initial discussions of socialist society in *State and Revolution*. Once the bourgeoisie is expropriated, there is not even a need for further repression. Thus the people's democracy and the proletarian state disappear almost immediately upon the seizure of power. In his section on first-stage communism, Lenin quotes approvingly from *The Poverty of Philosophy*, Marx's most striking passage on the withering away of politics and the state after the revolution: "In the course of its development the working class will replace the old bourgeois society by an association which excludes classes and their antagonism and there will no longer be any real political power, for political power is precisely the official expression of the class antagonism within bourgeois society."[104]

Lenin and the Transitional Socialist State: The Persistent Flight from Politics to Administration

Lenin obviously had read *The Manifesto* and could not completely ignore Marx's conception of the socialist state in the first-stage transition to communism. Here, as argued in the previous chapter, is the realm where Marx's analysis of postrevolutionary politics might have flourished, where society might for the first time democratically determine the allocation of social roles and of socially necessary labor.[105] Lenin in one passage suggests the political possibilities of first-stage communism, describing it as "the bourgeois state without the bourgeoisie" characterized by "the equal right of all to determine the structure and administration of the state."[106] In another passage he also acknowledges the role of the proletarian state as the guiding force in a lengthy transition from capitalism to communism: "The proletariat needs state power both for the purpose of crushing the resistance of the exploiters and for the purpose of guiding the great mass of the population—the peasantry, the petty-bourgeoisie, the semi-proletarians—in the work of organizing Socialist economy."[107] Yet although everyone supposedly has an equal say in the construction of the postrevolutionary society, nowhere in *State and Revolution* is there a description of the role of politics in the construction of a socialist society.

Most commentators account for the striking paucity of references to the party in *State and Revolution* as evidence of its utopian advocacy of direct democracy. But they fail to note that the one substantive discussion of the party occurs precisely in the section where Lenin discusses the transition from capitalism to socialism. Lenin admits that in conditions of scarcity decisions must be made regarding the allocation of labor and the definition of social roles. And in the transition to a classless society, other classes, beside the repressed bourgeoisie, must be negotiated with, led, and ruled. And so presumably must those members of the proletariat who do not possess true class consciousness. In the *lone passage* in *State and Revolution* that describes a society sociologically resembling Russia, in which the peasantry, petite bourgeoisie, and semiproletarians constituted 90 percent of the population, the vanguard party unequivocally surfaces to guide the other exploited classes and "degenerate" workers on the path to socialism. Although Lenin does not mention the Bolshevik party by name, he clearly implies that there is one and only one vanguard workers' party capable of leading the masses in the tasks of socialist construction: "By educating a workers' party, Marxism educates the vanguard of the proletariat, capable of assuming power and of *leading the whole people to Socialism*, of directing and organizing the new order, of being teacher, guide and leader of all the toiling and exploited in the task of building up their social life without the bourgeoisie and against the bourgeoisie."[108] Although directing and organizing the new order involves the obvious exercise of political power carried out by a party ruling the proletarian state, nowhere in *State and Revolution* does Lenin discuss how the party should be internally structured, relate to other interests and parties, or guarantee minority opinion within its ranks. If the party's only function is to determine a scientifically discernible proletarian will and to organize a scientifically determined mode of production, then internal party politics can also wither away into science.

Although the concluding sentence of Chapter 2 of *State and Revolution* states that "the transition from capitalism to Communism will certainly bring a great variety and abundance of political forms, but the essence will inevitably be only one: the dictatorship of the proletariat,"[109] Lenin never discusses these possible political forms. As with his earlier description of the capitalist state, the predominant role of the socialist state is class repression. Lenin terms the Commune state of first-stage communism "something which is no longer really the state in the accepted sense of the word" because as the "organ of suppression" the state is for the first time constituted by the majority, the armed workers: "'a special force' for suppression is no longer necessary. In this sense the state begins to wither away."[110] On the basis of this description, the uninformed reader would never imagine that the representative municipal council of the Paris Commune contained members from numerous political parties, including several that were explicitly procapitalist.

Lenin concurred with Marx that administration and authority would continue under socialism. Just as the entire working class participates, or at least sanctions, state repression of the bourgeoisie, so do all participate, or at least passively concur in, state administration. This universal participation, through rotation of administrative posts, is rendered feasible only because of Lenin's radical distinction between technical and administrative functions. Administration, for Lenin, consists in keeping track of the workings of the technical and productive apparatus. The metaphors of "accounting, checking, registering and filing" obsessively reappear in his descriptions of administration. Administration does *not*, in Lenin's view, involve discretionary judgment, choices about the social goals the state or social institutions ought to pursue, which are determined by the needs of industrial production. Parallel to Lenin's faith in Taylorism in production is his faith in "scientific" administration. The administrators merely check that the technical workers are doing their work properly. If they are not, "the armed workers" can easily choose someone else to do the job. Thus, just as state repression as the task of a ruling class minority is eliminated by socialism, so too is administration as a specialized task exercised in the interest of a minoritarian privileged class: "Such a beginning, on the basis of large-scale production, of itself leads to the gradual 'withering away' of all bureaucracy . . . an order in which the more and more simplified functions of control and accounting will be performed by each in turn, will then become a habit and will finally die out as special functions of a special stratum of the population."[111]

Although Lenin appears to endorse the withering away of hierarchical forms of administration, his belief in the "scientific" and complex nature of industrial production engenders his unambiguous support of hierarchy and expertise in the technical organization of production. Industrial production necessitates both an imperative command structure and technical expertise. The armed workers "check" on these experts and hire and fire them, but the workers cannot function without them: "The question of control and accounting must not be confused with the question of the scientifically educated staff of engineers, agronomists and so on. These gentlemen work today, obeying the capitalists, they will work even better tomorrow, obeying the armed workers." Not only are technical specialists needed, but so are managers. Lenin has no use for "utopians and anarchists" who believe authority should disappear immediately after the revolution. The socialist revolution must work with human nature as it is under capitalism: "We want the Socialist revolution with human nature as it is now, with human nature that cannot do without subordination, control and 'managers.' "[112]

Lenin's first description of this distinction between managers and the average worker betrays some uneasiness on his part, perhaps because he realizes the hierarchical implications of empowering "managers" in an alleged "workers' democracy." Lenin hopes that while managers will possess a disproportionate amount of technical knowledge, they will simply be "carrying out" the instructions of the workers. Their functional role, however, is described as equivalent to that of managers under capitalism. Their technical skills enable them to guide production. While they can be hired and fired by the workers, Lenin insists that "disciplined workers" will comprehend the need for technically knowledgeable managers to guide them: "We organize large-scale production, starting from what capitalism has already created; we workers ourselves, relying on our experience as workers, establishing a strict, an iron discipline, supported by the state power of the armed workers, shall reduce the role of the state officials to that of simply carrying out our instructions as responsible, moderately paid 'managers' (of course with technical knowledge of all sorts, types and degrees)."[113]

But if bureaucrats and technocrats increasingly gain autonomy from parliamentary representatives under capitalism, could not these same bureaucrats and technocrats also strive for autonomy from their alleged worker-supervisors under socialism? In order to ensure that skilled technical workers apolitically serve the interests of the working class, the vanguard party must attentively supervise their work. If political power is exercised on behalf of the unified will of the working class then, Lenin believed, an independent bureaucracy could not develop that would exercise power on behalf of its own interests. But Lenin never explains how the working class will ensure that its vanguard representatives do not end up ruling in ways that advance their own particular interests in power, prestige, and privilege.

Can Lenin's concern with working-class administrative control over the technical strata be read as an effort to reassert democratic political control over social organization? To achieve this end, Lenin holds, the separation of powers between legislative and executive functions must be eliminated. This is a plausible political position defended by many participatory democrats, though obviously one open to question. Weber held that executive functions were sufficiently complex, both in their technical and coordinating aspects, that they had to be done by specialists. To promote democratic control of these specialists, Weber favored presidential and parliamentary determination of the political ends of the bureaucracy, as well as careful parliamentary oversight of the bureaucracy. But Weber believed that there was an inherent tension between the bureaucratic skills of achieving a set aim (*zweckrationalität*) and the moral and political vocation of choosing among competing moral values (*wertrationalität*). Public policy, in Weber's view, should be determined by complex *political* negotiations between different interests and value orientations.[114]

Erik Olin Wright's essay on "Bureaucracy and the State" in his *Class, Crisis and the State* attempts to synthesize Lenin's and Weber's positions. Wright claims that Lenin's attentiveness to "social contradictions" enables him to perceive how capitalism promotes a hypertrophy of the bureaucratic apparatus. But Wright also astutely notes that Lenin's faith in the ability of the working class to administer democratically a postrevolutionary society is predicated on a "favorable productivist attitude towards the technical side of the bureaucratic apparatus."[115] Lenin believed that a certain degree of subordination is inherent to the productive process. By failing to develop both democratic life in the soviets and a multiparty, representative political system Lenin, Wright contends, could not discover the means by which the working class could develop the political capabilities to control the bureaucracy.

Weber, on the other hand, Wright asserts, had a weak sense of "social contradictions," downplaying the effect of capitalism in inflating the independent power of both corporate and state bureaucracies. But Weber's acute sense of "organizational contradictions" enabled him to see the imperative need for political control over bureaucracies in all modern societies. To achieve Weber's goal of greater democratic control over the bureaucracy, however, Wright believes the solution must go beyond Weber's advocacy of strengthened parliamentary leadership. For the power of capitalist interests in civil society renders parliaments increasingly impotent and strengthens the political power of administrative and executive agencies. Capital exercises substantial influence over public agencies through those agencies' reliance on the private sector for the provision of bureaucratic training and information.[116] Synthesizing the sensitivity of Lenin to "social contradictions" (i.e., class power) with that of Weber to "organizational contradictions" (i.e., bureaucratic power) would, in Wright's opinion, accord both politics and bureaucracy their proper role in a democratic socialist society.[117]

The viability of Wright's Weber-Lenin synthesis, however, depends on Lenin's worldview enabling its adherents to take seriously the role of democratic political authority in a postrevolutionary society. The inherent flaw in Weber's analysis is its inability to distinguish between the technological imperatives of bureaucracy and its class or political determinants. In Wright's analysis Weber fails to comprehend how capital bureaucratizes politics and then exercises power over the bureaucracy. Weber, in Wright's opinion, is overly pessimistic about the possibilities of democratic control over bureaucracies. Both Weber and Wright appear to accept the "scientistic" conception of technical expertise which holds that once the aims of a technocracy are democratically determined the implementation will be value-neutral. An analysis that recognized the political aspects of technological or bureaucratic decision-making would need to abandon the remnants of Marxian reductionism in Wright's conception that class domination is the predominant cause of an autonomous, nonresponsive bureaucracy. A key problem in democratic theory and practice, which both Robert Dahl and Michael Harrington highlight in their later works, is how to achieve democratic oversight over technical and scientific expertise. Technology and science are not strictly technological or scientific; they embody social values about the way humans work, create, and relate to the environment. Thus, any radical democracy would have to fund both worker and citizen advocacy groups and enable them to hire their own experts in order to monitor the actions of high-level technicians, managers, and administrators.[118]

Whenever the necessity for politics surfaces in his descriptions of the social organization of communist society, Lenin hastily retreats to the language of the "administration of things."[119] For example, Lenin's assurance that some form of representative institutions would persist under socialism, even after the elimination of parliamentarianism, at first seems to unambiguously embrace the continuation of politics after the revolution: "Without representative institutions we cannot imagine democracy, not even proletarian democracy; but we can and must think of democracy without parliamentarism, if criticism of bourgeois society is not mere empty words for us."[120] But not once in *State and Revolution* does he describe how those representative but nonparliamentary institutions might function. There is no discussion of representation in either the party *or the soviets*. Nor does Lenin grapple with how the soviets, a workplace-based institution, inherently exclude those outside the formal workforce from democratic deliberation (i.e., the retired, full-time homemakers, students, the unemployed, etc.). His only description of voting is Marx's passage from the Commune which equates universal suffrage with the individual suffrage of a businessman choosing his workers and employers. As analyzed previously, this vision of communist suffrage implies there is one "correct" choice to be made—and that objective, technical truth can be discerned as readily by one skilled manager as by a mass electorate. As in Marx, suffrage and representation play no role in mediating among distinct wills and conceptions of the good. Lenin cannot conceive of political divisions existing in a universal, socialist society: "Universal suffrage was to serve the people, constituted in Communes, as individual suffrage serves every other employer in the search for the workmen and managers in his business."[121]

The reader might expect a further description of the role of the suffrage and politics under socialism in *State and Revolution*, Chapter 5, "The Economic Base of the Withering Away of the State." The chapter opens with a gloss from Marx's *Critique of the Gotha Program*, where Marx explicitly discusses the nature of postrevolutionary politics and the socialist state: "What transformation will the state undergo in a Communist society? In other words, what social functions analogous to the present functions of the state will then still survive? . . . Between capitalist and Communist society lies the period of the revolutionary transformation of the former into the latter. To this corresponds a political transition period in which the state can be no other than the revolutionary dictatorship of the proletariat."[122] Rather than fleshing out the nature of this political transition period, Lenin devotes the rest of the section to condemning bourgeois democracy for devaluing the worth of the suffrage for the working class and poor. Lenin decries poverty's depoliticization of the proletariat, capitalist domination of the press, and suffrage qualifications as "restrictions [which] exclude and squeeze out the poor from politics and from an active share in democracy."[123] But when he discusses the true democracy of the dictatorship of the proletariat, he focuses exclusively on the repressive role of the state under socialism. The state is highlighted as the force that denies freedom to the bourgeoisie. Aside from rhetorical claims that the dictatorship of the proletariat expands democracy, there is absolutely no discussion of the state or politics as institutions that increase the substantive political participation denied to workers under capitalist democracy:

> Together with an immense expansion of democracy which for the first time becomes democracy for the poor, democracy for the people, and not democracy for the rich folk, the dictatorship of the proletariat produces a series of restrictions of liberty in the case of oppressors, the exploiters, the capitalists. We must crush them in order to free humanity from wage-slavery; their resistance must be broken by force; it is clear that where there is suppression there is also violence, there is no liberty, no democracy.[124]

Lenin's belief in the "simple" nature of the state machinery of first-stage communism as a repressive force of "armed workers" stands in stark contrast with his striking candor about the epochal nature of the transition from first-stage communism to full communism. Full communism, Lenin explains, necessitates a stupendous increase in the forces of production, eliminating both the division between mental and physical labor and the compulsory nature of work. This radical transformation of human social relations is such a distant possibility that Lenin proclaims, "It has never entered the head of any Socialist to 'promise' that the highest phase of Communism will arrive. . . . The great Socialists, in *foreseeing* its arrival, presupposed both a productivity of labor unlike the present and a person not like the present man in the street, capable of spoiling, without reflection, like the seminary students in Pomyalovsky's book, the stores of social wealth, and of demanding the impossible."[125]

Lenin accurately summarizes Marx's view in *The Critique of the Gotha Program* that the principle of distribution under first-stage communism would be *the bourgeois right* "from each according to their ability, to each according to their contribution." The authority that carries out this allocation of labor and consumption is the state: "For a certain time not only bourgeois rights, but even the bourgeois state remains under Communism, without the bourgeoisie."[126] Again, Lenin comes face-to-face with the potential continuation of the state under socialism and the necessity of postrevolutionary political life. After discussing the repressive use of the "bourgeois state without the bourgeoisie" against the bourgeoisie, he continues that this "workers' democracy" also "signifies the formal recognition of the equality of all citizens, the equal right of all to determine the structure and administration of the state." Lenin contends that the imperative question of the day is "the expropriation of the capitalists, the conversion of all citizens into workers and employees of one huge 'syndicate,' the whole state—and the complete subordination of the whole of the work of this syndicate to the really democratic state of the Soviets of Workers' and Soldiers' Deputies."[127]

But Lenin avoids any discussion of the politics of the soviets and once again conflates politics with scientific administration. The formal political rights of workers under socialism devolve into the right to participate in the administration of industry. The planning apparatus of socialist production allegedly allows everyone to participate equally in decision making. But there is no need for any consideration of how power, social roles, and social status will be politically allocated, because the way to organize socialist production is scientifically prefigured by the technically advanced, highly efficient nature of late capitalist production. Lenin's conception of universal working-class participation in socialist administration of industry is almost as limited in its deliberative impact as he conceives the universal suffrage of capitalist representative democracy to be. In a telling description of universal participation in the governance of the first-stage communist state, Lenin refers to universal participation in administration, but not in political life within the state:

> If every one really takes part in the administration of the state, capitalism cannot retain its hold. In its turn capitalism, as it develops, itself creates prerequisites for "every one" to be able really to take part in the administration of the state. Among such prerequisites are: universal literacy . . . the "training and disciplining" of millions of workers by the huge, complex and socialized apparatus of the post-office, the railways, the big factories, large-scale commerce, banking, etc., etc. With such economic prerequisites it is perfectly possible, immediately, within twenty-four hours after the overthrow of the capitalists and bureaucrats, to replace them, in the control of production and distribution, in the business of control of labor and products, by the armed workers, by the whole people in arms.[128]

Lenin devotes the final section of *State and Revolution* to a polemic against the critics of "primitive democracy." This attack is directed at social democrats who claim that some division of labor would persist in a socialist economy between the political establishment of social priorities and their administrative accomplishment. The critics of "primitive democracy" believed in the necessity of expertise, division of labor, and political supervision of the bureaucracy in any complex society, including a socialist one. Lenin's opposition to this viewpoint seems paradoxical, given his celebration of technical expertise in *State and Revolution* and his earlier, sharp critique of "primitive democracy" in *What Is to Be Done?* There Lenin applauds Kautsky's and the Webbs's critique of those socialists who are utopian proponents of direct democracy and who reject the functional specialization and representative institutions necessitated by a complex division-of-labor. In *State and Revolution* he attacks these very same writings that he cited with approval fifteen years earlier. Lenin claims that Kautsky defended the working class's ability to seize state power but abandoned revolutionary Marxism when he denied the necessity of destroying the state capitalist machine.

Beyond this tactical dispute lies Lenin's hostility to Kautsky's insistence that bureaucracy and representative forms of politics would persist under any feasible form of democratic socialism. Kautsky believed that under socialism there would be varied forms of economic enterprise: "bureaucratic" (i.e., state administered), trade union, cooperative, and private. Lenin, however, contended that Kautsky's outline of socialist society envisaged the same bureaucratic hierarchy of state capitalism. Lenin vigorously condemned as undemocratic the division of power between representatives and bureaucrats which Kautsky proposes in his description of railway delegates supervising the bureaucratic experts who help run the railways. In Kautsky's analysis, "there are, for instance, such enterprises as cannot do without a bureaucratic organization: such are the railways. Here delegates form something in the nature of a parliament, and this parliament determines the conditions of work, and superintends the management of the bureaucratic apparatus. Other enterprises may be transferred to the labor unions, and still others may be organized on a cooperative basis."[129]

Lenin vehemently rejects Kautsky's association of the delegates with "parliament" and the experts with a "bureaucracy." In Lenin's conception of industrial soviets, the delegates must be elected, subject to recall, and engaged in administrative work—they will not be mere "talkshop" parliamentarians. As all workers can and should participate in the functions of control and superintendence, everyone serves as "'bureaucrats,' for a time, and no one, therefore can become a bureaucrat."[130] And, because the experts will be paid workers' wages and be supervised by ordinary workers, they will not have the same status and power as capitalist managers and experts have. Lenin, however, fails to deal with Kautsky's central claim that to make the trains run on time some degree of expertise and management will be necessary. The workers, in Kautsky's account, can democratically elect and recall management, but they cannot eliminate the functional role of management coordination as they might in less technical and smaller-scale, collective forms of production. Kautsky's frank admission of the persistence of the division of labor under socialism makes it easier for him to discuss openly the role of politics after the revolution. Kautsky assumes that politically determining the basic goals of an enterprise is a process related to, but distinct from, the technical and managerial tasks of accomplishing those goals. Obviously, a critique of this division of labor between representatives setting goals and bureaucrats fulfilling the goals might inquire whether in such a system technical and bureaucratic strata will inevitably usurp substantive political power. But to admit the possibility of such a tension—and the necessity of confronting it—is to admit the necessity of politics after the revolution.

In *State and Revolution* Lenin is not an authentic advocate of participatory or "primitive democracy," because he privileges scientific experts in the postrevolutionary society. But the withering away of politics is predicated on the viability of a form of "primitive democracy"—the possibility of everyone participating in administrative governance. Although Lenin claims to favor representative democracy under socialism, he cannot envision the pluralist social structure that creates the need for representative and democratic politics. If the vanguard party can comprehend the objective interests of the working class and the technological imperatives of advanced industrial production, it can fully represent the interests of all individuals. Thus the need for representative politics disappears. Participation in life of the state is reduced to the functions of "registration, filing, and checking." These tasks, in Lenin's view, involve no use of political or deliberative reason.

Lenin repeatedly asserts that "a revolution must not consist in a new class ruling, governing with the help of the old state machinery but in this class smashing this machinery, and ruling, governing by means of new machinery."[131] But Lenin never asks whether the new state machinery of socialism is structurally different from that of the old capitalist bureaucracy. This failure is exemplified by his attack on Kautsky's "superstitious reverence for ministries" as institutions of economic administration. Lenin asks, "Why can they not be replaced, say, by commissions of specialists working under sovereign all-powerful Soviets of Workers' and Soldiers' Deputies?"[132] In one of the few substantive descriptions of the workings of the soviets in *State and Revolution*, Lenin is so ambiguous that it is hard to discern the difference between his own position and that of Kautsky. Would not the soviet representatives supervising the specialists constitute a type of political administration—a political ministry governing the industry in question? Would not the soviets elect representatives to supervise the specialists with a major qualification being that the representatives possess sufficient background knowledge to supervise the specialists effectively? That is, to achieve a "workers' democracy," would not the soviets have to engage in representative, democratic politics—electing representatives, appointing oversight committees, appointing specialists, etc.?

The exigencies of maintaining revolutionary socialist power in a predominantly peasant nation made democratic government a highly unlikely outcome of the Bolshevik revolution. To facilitate democratization, the Bolsheviks would have had to abandon their role as a vanguard party and negotiate a majority coalition with peasant and other working-class parties. The Bolsheviks' abolition of the Constituent Assembly in January 1918 indicated they had no intention of doing so.[133] Lenin's faith that the vanguard party embodied an "objective," unified, revolutionary working-class consciousness renders implausible any counterfactual scenarios of a pluralist, democratic Lenin or Bolshevik party. His utter failure in *State and Revolution* to describe the political workings of the soviets also denies him the mantle of a seminal theorist of council democracy.

Lenin failed to comprehend that neither methods of production nor comprehensive conceptions of human interests can have the status of objective, foundational or scientific truths in a democratic culture. These are political questions open to democratic contestation, not "technical" questions having one objective answer. Even if such scientific answers might not be logically precluded, a democracy could never achieve universal agreement on such answers. Lenin also failed to realize that his quest to develop a Hegelian-like bureaucratic stratum that would rule in the general interest of the working class, although transcending any particular interests on the part of that bureaucracy, would prove exceedingly difficult in postrevolutionary Russia. Only institutionalized democratic practices can check the inexorable tendencies of bureaucrats or experts to advance their own particular conception of the social good, or even more readily, their own particular desires for economic and political power.

The last years of Lenin's life were consumed by a constant struggle against the inexorable growth of the powers of the state and party bureaucracy. Lenin failed to comprehend that only a vibrant democratic political culture involving numerous sites of political power can curtail the imperious growth of a centralized bureaucracy. Lenin opposed the bureaucratization of Soviet social life; but he never developed an adequate political analysis of this postrevolutionary growth of bureaucratic power. Lenin believed the cause was cultural, not political—the backwardness of the Russian workers and peasants. They had to rely on Tsarist and bourgeois *spetsy* (specialists) because they were not able to read and add, let alone construct administrative flowcharts.

Some of the cultural prerequisites for a democratic, accountable bureaucratic administration may have been absent in postrevolutionary Russia. This absence was intensified by the civil war's destruction of a large portion of the politically active members of the working class. But Lenin's own theoretical orientation severely enfeebled the party's ability to respond to bureaucratization. His last effort to curtail the bureaucracy was the creation of a cadre of allegedly virtuous party inspectors whose sole job was to combat bureaucratic excess (the *Rabkrin*, or Workers' and Peasants' Inspectorate). Of course, the *Rabkrin* rapidly degenerated into another layer of self-interested bureaucrats.

Lenin's faith in both technology and the unitary will of the proletariat vitiated any projection of a role for politics after the revolution. In the absence of postrevolutionary politics and social pluralism, it was inevitable that society would be ruled bureaucratically from above. On his deathbed, Lenin feared precisely that outcome. But he did not realize that its roots lay not only in the peculiar history of Russia but also in his own political vision. Nor could he realize that after his death Leninist ideology would hinder its more democratically inclined adherents from developing those democratic political institutions that might have overcome the ossification of repressive communist regimes.

Hannah Arendt's Politics of "Action"

THE ELUSIVE SEARCH FOR POLITICAL SUBSTANCE

ARENDT AND THE POLITICS OF "ACTION"—POLITICS AS THEATER

There exists one school of contemporary political thought which shares the radical tradition's hostility to liberal interest-group politics but which claims to break with the radical tradition by asserting the "virtue" of the political. The stated goal of these theorists of the contemporary "communitarian" and "civic republican" schools is not to transcend politics but to revitalize it by making political discourse central to the self-education of a moral community. These political theorists (Hannah Arendt, Alasdair MacIntyre, J.G.A. Pocock, Michael Sandel, Benjamin Barber, and Sheldon Wolin among others[1]) often praise the politics of the ancient *polis* as a model of public discourse in which citizens publicly reflected over the highest human aims. For these theorists, a political arena sheltered from the instrumental pursuit of material well-being enables human beings to deliberate, as equal citizens, over the nature of the common good. Only the separation of the public arena from the pursuit of material interests can make political equals of those whose natural endowments render them unequal in the marketplace.

Communitarians, such as Sandel and MacIntyre, long for communities of shared virtues which would promote the moral development of its citizenry. Although it is truer of MacIntyre than Sandel, both authors' vision of this moral community warns against the threat that excessive individual and group pluralism may pose to a free and diverse democratic society. Wolin, Barber, and Pocock might loosely be grouped as "civic republicans," because all are influenced by Machiavelli's conception of politics and thus better comprehend the centrality of conflict and divergent interests to politics than do the communitarians. Wolin fits less neatly into this categorization, since he takes explicit issue with Arendt for ignoring the structural barriers to equal political power posed by socioeconomic inequalities. And for a generation, he has been a central figure in the search for a more participatory, democratic politics free from class and other forms of domination. But Wolin's hostility to the instrumental, economistic nature of the "welfare/warfare" state of capitalist democracies leads him, at times, to join Arendt in equating the possibility of democratic discourse with the elimination of material and economic concerns from politics.[2]

The promise-making among free citizens, which both communitarians and civic republican theorists desire, has become a rare activity, according to

Hannah Arendt, in a mass consumer society where reason is instrumentally subordinated to the pursuit of material wealth. Modern politics, in Arendt's analysis, is no longer the realm of freedom but a subverted servant of the utilitarian, consumptionist goals of property owners, producers, and bureaucrats. Action—the realm of speech and physical courage—has been supplanted by the conformist behavior of mass society, while bureaucracy ("the rule of no-man") has supplanted political decision-making. "Public man" has fallen and modern citizens are left to search for meaning in the inner subjectivity of the isolated individual.[3]

There are evident distinctions to be drawn between Hannah Arendt and contemporary communitarian theorists, particularly as Arendt normatively desires a conflictual, agonal view of political discourse. But Arendt's attack on "modern society" and the conformist, apolitical life of "the masses" under the bureaucratic state reappears as a significant motif in subsequent communitarian and republican thought. MacIntyre, in contrast to Arendt, does not fixate on the political as the sole site of virtue, viewing more favorably the Aristotelian conception of virtues embodied in the structured social roles of various nonpolitical "practices."[4] Sandel's work thus far has focused primarily on a critique of the deontological assumptions of rights-based liberalism, while leaving open his own particular vision of "the politics of the good."[5] But all these theorists share Arendt's critique of modern representative democracy's limited avenues for political participation and her desire to eliminate the influence of socioeconomic interests on political deliberation because such materialism inevitably drives politics in an "instrumental," utilitarian direction.

Arendt's thought will be examined in some detail because it illustrates a larger difficulty the communitarian and civic republican schools have in advancing a realistic vision of political life. Rather than offering an institutional description of how political conflict might be democratized, the communitarian vision of politics is limited to a community exclusively engaged in political discourses about the nature of the good life. The creation of "community" appears to be the only substantive goal of politics. But "community" or "politics" cannot be a political end-in-itself because these communities can be either virtuous or evil and politics can be both just and unjust.[6] Unlike most communitarians, Arendt was wary of defining politics as a discourse about moral virtue—she derided this as "metadiscourse" and vociferously contended that politics can only be about opinions, not truths. But although clearly engaged with issues confronting the Zionist movement, the civil rights movement, the 1956 Hungarian uprising, and the peace movement, her hostility to the instrumental nature of politics ultimately moves her implicit understanding of politics in the direction of a communal "metadiscourse" about the good, rather than about the complex interrelationship of the "good" and "mere" life.[7] Arendt thus contributed to one of the greatest weaknesses of much of contemporary political theory: its radical separation of normative argument from concrete inquiry about the specific political and socioeconomic institutional practices that would instantiate such norms.

Although continually asserting the need for *common* values and institutions, Arendt and "communitarian" theorists such as MacIntyre and Sandel fail to advance any substantive moral or political criteria for choosing among *competing* values and institutions. Also, to the extent to which communitarian theorists join Arendt in wishing to banish the "social question" (the issues raised by differentials in political and socioeconomic power) from political deliberation, the communitarian vision becomes as anticonflictual—and therefore as antipolitical—as both the liberal and radical traditions it derides. Discourse about the "good life" will not transform the "mere life" of citizens if it avoids the nitty-gritty of political argument and conflict among competing social, economic, and state interests. "Disinterested" political theory cannot advance a theory of politics relevant to a world characterized by social interests and political conflicts over how to restructure them.

Arendt's stress on individual diversity—or, in her phrase, "the plurality of human beings"—leads her to reject Rousseau's conception of a universal general will and Hegel's and Marx's teleological reconciliation of freedom with necessity. In this sense her analysis points toward a criticism of liberalism that is also acutely aware of the antipolitical and antilibertarian tendencies of the radical tradition. In Arendt's view the outcome of political struggle will never be certain: the "plurality" of the human species renders the results of their social interaction inherently unpredictable. In politics, Arendt contends, human beings should neither be judged solely by their motivations nor by the consequences of their action. Motives are affairs of the heart which can only be publicly revealed by terror. And because no one can know in advance the endless chain of consequences set off by an individual act, one can only be held responsible for consequences that a reasonable person should have been able to anticipate in advance (which are certainly not all consequences). Political judgment is best exercised in relationship to the "principles" according to which individuals act, their codes of conduct—the pursuit of honor, virtue, distinction, or excellence.[8]

Arendt argues that true political freedom results in mutual promise-making, which is institutionalized in constitutions. A free society cannot be constituted by a monolithic general will that violates the plural nature of humanity. Although rejecting the radical attack on individuality, Arendt believes that social pluralism—economic and social interests—must be removed from the political arena if political freedom is to be reconstituted. Conflicts over the "social question" (socioeconomic distribution), in Arendt's view, destroyed the promise of political freedom of modern revolutions, save the American.[9] The fortuitous economic circumstance of prerevolutionary America meant that the "social question" did not emerge to prevent the establishment of constitutional liberties to protect against the rise of an om-

nipotent state. Although poverty existed, America's newness and relative af-
fluence precluded the existence of widespread "social misery."[10] But even the
American Revolution, the only "successful" modern revolution, failed to establish institutions that would facilitate "the public happiness" of participatory politics. In Europe the passions released by social "pity's " concern
for misery destroyed any potential for the constitution of political freedom.
The politics of human compassion produced ideological parties bent on serving the interests of the masses, thereby reducing politics to an instrumental
concern for social well-being.[11]

In Arendt's opinion, only by delegating "the social question" to the realm
of administrative and technical expertise can a political realm be constructed
in which "interest-free" discourse—the pursuit of "public happiness"—will
reign. In this desire to expel social interests from political deliberation,
Arendt unconsciously embraces the radical tradition's desire to transcend
social pluralism. Arendt criticizes Kant's "practical reason" for conceiving
moral actors as isolated, free-willing agents divorced from the phenomenal world. Although she rejects this originally "Cartesian" distinction between Being and Appearance, accepting the phenomenal world to be the
only *real* world, she retains the Kantian notion that "free" political deliberation should largely be divorced from considerations of both desires and consequences.[12] This radical divorce of politics from considerations of both interests and outcomes yields, as Benjamin Schwartz has perceptively termed
it, a "religion of politics" in which a metapolitical discourse of "glory and
memorable speeches" about community replaces baser political discourse
about conflicts among interests.[13]

As George Kateb has observed, war and constitution making appear to be
the primary vehicles for Arendtian politics.[14] Arendt laments that the rise of
the secular world strips humanity of its classical concern for immortality. The
classical striving for immortality, through glorious deeds in the founding—
or defense—of regimes, is the highest political "principle." Political accomplishment, in Arendt's view, is located in the quality of the performance, not
in the end product. Politics for Arendt is an art of performance; the polis
serves as a public theater where one's virtuosity can be judged by one's fellow
citizens freed from the necessities of labor and work: "This is the realm where
freedom is a worldly reality, tangible in words which can be heard, in deeds
which can be seen, and in events which are talked about, remembered and
turned into stories before they are finally incorporated into the great story-
book of human history."[15]

Modern liberalism, according to Arendt, banishes freedom from political
life by relegating it to the innocuous realm of "opinions," while subordinating political "action" to the pursuit of material interests and mortality: "For
politics, according to [the liberal philosophy] must be concerned almost exclusively with the maintenance of life and the safeguarding of its interests."[16]
Freedom as action is epitomized for Arendt by Machiavelli's concept of
virtù, the excellence by which the individual responds to his or her fortuitous

opportunities in the public arena.[17] Virtuous politics must disdain mere life and strive for remembrance and immortality. Arendt's contempt for modernity's preference for worldly and bodily concerns underpins her controversial judgment that the Jewish faith, being the most "this-worldly" of religions, hindered the Jewish people's development of both a historical sensibility and a concern for a politics of public virtue.[18]

In order for there to be politics as theater—citizens performing before an audience of peers—the theater must be set apart from nature to provide a space in which human survival and human interests are not at stake.[19] In a society characterized by scarcity, this can only be accomplished by limiting the rights of citizenship to an elite sheltered from the realm of necessity. Arendt's conception of the golden age of Periclean politics rests on a self-admitted elitism. Only inequality in society can produce equality among citizens in the polis. The Periclean citizen, as Peter Fuss reminds us, "left household administration to his wife, cultivation of his fields to slaves, the conduct of commercial affairs to foreigners, and sailed forth into the polis to act and speak in the company of his true peers. Here alone he could breath the air of freedom—free from 'private concerns'—those governed by standards of utility as well as those under the sway of necessity."[20] The Athenian citizen's mistrust of expertise and professionalism and his willingness to assume the burden of adjudicating and administrating public affairs stands in stark contrast with Arendt's attitude toward modern bureaucracy. Modern expertise and professionalism, in Arendt's opinion, can "solve" the social question and remove it from the realm of politics. But if the bureaucracy interferes with "politics," the realm of speechmaking, then it is guilty of the tyrannical "no-rule" of the bureaucracies of modern mass society.

Arendt fails to recognize that establishing a proper division of labor between the legislature and bureaucracy is ultimately a political question. And her disdain for representative government precludes her seriously analyzing the feasible roles for direct and representative democratic institutions in a complex industrial society. Nor does Arendt acknowledge that distinct, executive powers existed in even her favorite of participatory institutions: the magistrates of the New England townships, the officers of the polis (usually large landholders), and the executive bodies of the revolutionary councils. Arendt can maintain a permanent disdain for representative government only by ignoring the conditions for its emergence—the inability of every virtuous citizen to make a full-time occupation of politics.

For politics to be truly a theater, the community as a whole must subsidize it. Arendt fails to comprehend that such a subsidy immediately drags material and distributional questions back into the realm of politics. Politics as theater also cannot avoid the question of how the community structures political participation. Would everyone devote equal time to "acting" and "spectating?" Would only an elite perform? Would some prefer only to be critics, reserving a veto power over the actors through representative forms of government? Would the remainder of the community be relegated to the status of slaves, building the theater and tending to the needs of its actors but never judging their performance? In *On Revolution* Arendt implies that even in a federation of councils where politics nominally is open to all, only a self-selected few with a predilection for politics would participate. The majority would go on with their daily material pursuits, uninterested in the speeches occurring in the councils about the nature of politics.[21] Arendt makes clear that she is only endorsing a self-constituted elite in a society of ever-shifting public spaces from which no citizen is theoretically excluded. Like most other theorists of participatory democracy, Arendt devotes insufficient consideration to the status of those who are less taken by the virtues or self-realizing value of politics. As Michael Walzer has written, the best radical democrats can hope for is that greater opportunities for participation—in both formal political institutions and workplace and community settings—would increase the number of people who find that their lives are enriched through political participation. But a radical democracy must also be concerned with making sure that those who do not become inveterate "politicos" are still heard and that their interests and opinions are equally represented. That is, a radical democracy must be concerned with "the rights of the apathetic."[22] Anyone who has been involved in a democratic activist organization knows that a successful movement has to balance the interests and opinions of its most active members with those of the broader, less active group that the activist core claims to represent.

Although Arendt astutely rejects the Hegelian and Marxian view that freedom ultimately is in accord with necessity, her effort at defining an alternative radical philosophy of political action is severely disabled by her refusal to examine the relationship between political action and the transformation of social interests. As a result Arendt ends up divorcing her conception of politics from considerations of cultural or economic domination. Arendt's proposed politics of agonal struggle, though divorced from social reality, can only be comprehended in light of her analysis of the depoliticization of modern mass society. For it is modern "society"—the public emergence of "labor" from the privacy of the household—that obliterates the public realm. Only by transcending the interest-based construction of modernity does Arendt believe politics can be reborn.[23] Like Rousseau, Hegel, and Marx before her, Arendt declares war on private and social interests. But she does so in the name of politics. Whether there is any substantive content to her "interest-less" politics of virtue remains to be examined.

MODERN SOCIETY AS THE ENEMY OF POLITICS

Hannah Arendt's vision of politics cannot be comprehended apart from her own attempt to develop a phenomenology of human activity in *The Human Condition*. *The Human Condition* delineates a hierarchical ordering of three basic human activities: labor, work, and action. The book is haunted by the vision of a consumer society about to be freed by technological innovation from the burdens of labor. The vision disturbs Arendt because she fears that this "society of laborers about to be liberated from labor [knows] nothing about the higher and more meaningful activities for which freedom would deserve to be won."[24] "Labor" held the lowest position in the classical order of human activity because it only reproduced the biological conditions of human life. The *telos* of labor is simply to assure the means for the survival of the species. Human beings labor in order to consume and consume in order to labor in a never-ending cycle tied to the natural existence of *animal laborans*—the human being as a laboring animal.

"Work" distinguishes humans from other animals by creating an "artificial" world of things distinct from nature. Whereas the laborer remains a servant of nature, the worker fabricates a world of human-made objects which distinguishes him from his natural surroundings. The work of fabrication proceeds under the guidance of a "model" visible to the mind's eye. Thus work, for Arendt, is dominated by the rationality of means-ends calculation. During the work process every human activity is judged in terms of its usefulness for this preconceived end. But although the utilitarian world of work creates human-made objects that situate human beings within the cosmos, this utilitarian creation of "use objects" can never provide meaning to human life. It can never answer Lessing's query of the utilitarians, "What is the use of use?" In Arendt's view, "Homo faber is as incapable of understanding meaning . . . as the *animal laborans* is incapable of understanding instrumentality."[25] If the laboring human is a slave to bodily needs, *homo faber* is subordinate to the demands of his or her craft, to the model of the object.[26]

"Action," in contrast to labor and work, is the highest form of human activity because it alone "goes on directly between men without the intermediary of things or matter [and] corresponds to the human condition of plurality, to the fact that men, not Man, live on the earth and inhabit the world."[27] Human plurality, the basic condition of both action and speech, has the twofold character of equality and distinction. In order to understand one another, human beings must in some sense be equal. But if they were not also distinct and thereby unequal in attributes, they would need neither speech nor action to make themselves understood.[28] In Arendt's consciously pre-Socratic model, freedom lies in the exercise of citizenship among equals in a public space—the polis—devoted not to the production of material necessities but "to the shining brightness we once called glory."[29] Arendt defines her notion of freedom as pre-Socratic because, in her analysis, even Plato and Aristotle eventually abandoned the uncertainty of the freedom of politics as "praxis," for the model of the ruler as a craftsman creating a regime according to a preconceived plan.[30] The consequences of action are inherently unpredictable because it occurs in a web of conflicting wills and intentions, in which "one small act can change the entire constellation of human relationships."[31] This unpredictability of action, Arendt contends, is "related to the revelatory character of action and speech, in which one discloses one's self without ever either knowing himself or being able to calculate before hand whom he reveals."[32]

Political action must occur in company with others and for the sake of all because one can only reveal oneself to others and never to oneself. The "isonomy" of the polis is not an equality of condition but a structure of discourse that renders human beings equal when they act as citizens. No one rules in the polis, because the power of human beings promising together is what maintains the political life of the polis. What that power is used for and whom that power benefits are questions that Arendt leaves aside in her politics without ends. Arendt's semantic move of redefining "power" as "promise-making among equals" does not eliminate the historical reality that elites have often exercised control over subordinate groups in order to achieve instrumental ends. This relationship has been historically defined as "power," regardless of how normatively attractive Arendt's linguistic redefinition of power may be. Even a more egalitarian polity, in which citizens, by means of democratic "promise-making," had a more equal voice in the setting of social priorities, would still confront the "instrumental" question of how to organize socioeconomic and cultural institutions.

Action, according to Arendt, reveals the answer to the question of "who one is" not by conforming to standardized modes of human behavior, which judge motives and intentions, but by the criteria of "greatness . . . or the specific meaning of each deed [which] can lie only in the performance itself and neither in its motivation nor its achievement."[33] Arendt claims that Aristotle still had this sense of the "agonal" distinction of the polis when he said that politics "is the work of man." The human virtues are not qualities to be achieved but rather the actuality of one's way of life, or code of conduct.[34]

Arendt's description of the golden age of the Periclean polis as an arena for the demonstration of extraordinary deeds and the winning of "immortal fame," however, denudes politics of any content other than individual performance. Given that labor and work are conceptually opposed to the "free" nature of political action, there is little left to Arendt's conception of political action, as George Kateb has argued, other than speaking and writing.[35] If politics is synonymous with a conversation among equals, then to participate politically, one needs to be a direct participant. The centrality of speechifying to Arendt's politics motivates her hostility to any form of political representation. Although theorists of participatory democracy sometimes point to Arendt's desire for a face-to-face politics of equals as inspirational, such a reading of Arendt as a radical democrat fails to comprehend that her hostility to the role of "interests" in politics precludes her from engaging in a radical critique of existing social interests.

Arendt begrudgingly admits that there needs to be "a worldly objective reality" about which words and deeds, action and speaking refer.[36] But when human beings consciously endeavor to transform this "worldly objective reality," in Arendt's opinion, they conflate the free nature of political action with the instrumental nature of work. Thus, Arendt relegates all attempts at social reform to the realm of expertise and administration. The only activity that appears to rescue Arendtian politics from a peculiar metadiscourse of great speeches on the nature of politics are the projects of creating and defending regimes. But Arendtian politics deals only with the form of regimes, not with the content of their policies ("outputs"). Having stripped politics of any concern with interests or "life processes," the realms of work and labor, Arendtian politics is reduced to the grand politics of constitution making, war, the spontaneous creation of revolutionary councils, and collective civil disobedience to defend true constitutional principles.

Several commentators dismiss Arendt's description of classical politics and her prescriptive conception of politics as speech making as historically inaccurate and normatively vacuous. As Benjamin Schwartz points out, although Arendt believes politics properly defined has nothing to do with "rulership," much of the Athenian agenda was taken up with the ruling of noncitizens, slaves, and imperial subjects.[37] As the work of the distinguished ancient historian Moses I. Finley demonstrates, acute class conflict was endemic to the politics of Greek city-states. And, as Sheldon Wolin points out, the Solonic land reforms aimed at "expanding the meaning of equality to give socioeconomic content to isonomy."[38]

Arendt idiosyncratically redefines power as being constituted by voluntary promises among citizens. According to her definition, power cannot be constituted by force or violence. But as Jurgen Habermas has incisively noted, such voluntarily constituted "power" can still be mobilized by competing political and class interests. In addition, if educational and economic resources are distributed unequally, then some citizens may not be fully equal and autonomous agents when engaged in promise-making.[39] Even if one questions whether "true human interests" or "communicative competence" can ever be objectively determined, one cannot divorce access to educational and economic resources from the ability to discern one's subjectively best, if never objectively true, interest. Though Arendt, by a purely definitional move, wishes to divorce the coercion of violence from the power of promise-making, the historical record renders her conception of power at best a normative goal whose achievement would necessitate radically egalitarian socioeconomic and political reforms.[40]

But historical or empirical objections to Arendt's perspective perhaps misconstrue the nature of Arendt's normative project. As Judith Shklar argued, Arendt's history is "monumental" in nature, drawing a manichean distinction between the purely political as the realm of excellence and "Society" as the realm of evil.[41] For Arendt, the course of human history has been a declension from the isonomy of the pre-Socratic polis, where politics was a virtuous end-in-itself, to a perverted politics serving allegedly higher ends, which are in reality debased and instrumental ones. According to Arendt, subsequent political theorists' exasperation with the frailty of human affairs, "with the unpredictability of action's outcome, the irreversibility of its process and the anonymity of its authors,"[42] has rendered all post-Socratic political theory a quest for the "solidity of quiet and order."[43] Starting with Plato, political theory, Arendt believes, substitutes "making" for "acting" in order to give human affairs the solidity of work and fabrication.

Post-Socratic political theory and philosophy, in Arendt's analysis, both strive to create fixed states that can be codified and preserved by rules and law. The philosopher-king aims to achieve (to "make" or "fabricate") the idea of the good; the philosopher aims to create the idea of the beautiful. Political theory strives to escape the true politics of equal promise-making by introducing the concept of rule: "the notion that men can lawfully and politically live together only when some are entitled to command and others are forced to obey."[44] The rulers are those who know how to order the political community, while the actors are those who do not know but who obediently carry out the directives of their rulers. Thus the voice of the actors is excluded from the arena of politics. My analysis in this book of the radical tradition's hostility to politics has certain affinities with Arendt's perspective. But I would hope that my work is truer to the real nature of politics, which inherently involves a complex interrelationship between ideal and material interests. The democratic and egalitarian implication of Arendt's critique of a "post-Socratic" conception of politics, however, is eviscerated by her proposed technocratic solution to the "social question" of economic inequality. One might facetiously describe her proposed solution to the social question as standing her conception of virtuous, "agonal" politics on its head: those who know how to do ("to make or fabricate") engage in the "mere administration" of socioeconomic and material life, whereas those who know how "to act" discuss the nature of politics and the good life in an arena sealed off from the messy concerns of social and economic policy—and everyday life.

In Arendt's monumental history, the post-Socratic substitution of "making" for "acting" (of ruling for promising) degrades politics into a means to obtain allegedly higher spiritual, material, or cultural ends. In the political philosophy of antiquity, the political rule of the gentlemen serves the end of protecting the philosopher from the many. In the Middle Ages political rule is subordinated to the end of the salvation of souls. And in the modern age political rule is subordinated to the end of productivity and progress of "society."[45]

Arendt contends that the mastering of the necessities of life in the private household served as a precondition for the freedom of the public polis. In modern society, however, she laments that issues of daily maintenance formerly assigned to the household dominate public concern. The nation-state epitomizes the political form of modern society in which the social realm predominates. And the social realm is neither public nor private, neither revelatory nor intimate: "We see the body of peoples and political communities in this image of a family whose everyday affairs have to be taken care of by a gigantic, nation-wide administration of housekeeping."[46] The decline of the political is symbolized by the emergence of an intellectual field that would have been an oxymoron in pre-Socratic times, "political economy." Economics—what had been defined by the ancient theorists as a nonpolitical household affair—emerges as a "collective" political concern under the guise of society. Society, in Arendt's view, destroys both the isonomy of the public realm and the intimacy of the private realm. Private property is the space, according to Arendt, where "man" could shelter himself with his family and achieve a degree of stability, is transformed into the mobile property of wealth. Society submerges both the private and the public realm into the social, leaving the inner subjectivity of the individual as the only form of intimacy.[47]

Thus, in Arendt's view, Marx's assertion that the political realm has been subordinated to civil society is not an innovative discovery, but rather the explication of the basic assumptions of all modern political economy: "That politics is nothing but a function of society, that action, speech and thought are primarily superstructures upon social interest is not a discovery of Karl Marx, but on the contrary is among the axiomatic assumptions Marx accepted uncritically from the political economists of the modern age."[48] The economists of classical liberalism introduced the "communistic fiction" of a "harmony of interest" coordinated by the invisible hand. Using language reminiscent of de Tocqueville, Arendt describes at length the despotism of "conformism, behaviorism and automatism" that emerges from the masses crowded together in modern society. "Society" takes on a life of its own, demanding that its members behave as if they belong to one enormous family that has one opinion and one interest. Economics is the quintessential behavioral science because "men had become social beings and unanimously followed certain patterns of behavior, so that those who did not keep the rules could be considered to be asocial or abnormal."[49] Arendt contends that well before the emergence of communist regimes, the rise of the behavioral sciences promoted the withering away of the state into societies characterized by pure administration and the potentially tyrannical rule of "no-man"—bureaucracy: "the most social form of government."[50]

Arendt allegorically conceives of the rise of society as the triumph of *animal laborans* over *homo faber* (of "labor" over "work"). Work has the merit of producing objects whose value can be judged by the public in the market. Arendt views Marx as "a philosopher of labor" because she interprets his critique of exchange value and defense of use value as a criticism of the public esteem accorded to work(s).[51] Marx, Arendt contends, searches futilely to quantify in labor-power the absolute value of goods. Values, according to Arendt's phenomenology, can only be relative. Automation transforms the work of the artisan into a process of labor. Modern technology, by channeling natural forces into the world of human artifice, destroys the distinction between humanly created objects and nature. Machines no longer serve the world and its objects; rather, the automatic motion of their processes begin to rule, thereby destroying the independence of the world and objects.[52]

Human beings become slaves to automated labor and to natural processes; they lose their capacities as human artificers of a world of objects of their own conscious making.

Although Arendt retains one crucial aspect of the Kantian categorical imperative, that each person is a universal subject worthy of equal dignity and respect, in *The Human Condition* she rejects Kant's dictum that no human being must ever become a means to an end—that every human being is an end in him- or herself—because it yields what she idiosyncratically terms "an anthropocentric utilitarianism," which privileges one's happiness and devalues the usefulness of one's products. That is, the categorical imperative devalues nature and human interaction with it. Arendt traces this treating of humans as ends-in-themselves to the elevation of Cartesian, scientific introspection to an omnipotent device to conquer nature, which triumphs over faculties directed toward building worldly things. Making human beings the lord of all things devalues the world and nature. Every object becomes consumable and everyone is enslaved to labor. Weber's iron cage is finally realized. By making human happiness the ultimate standard, all values have been relativized and devalued. In the ancient world, political activity had been inspired by the aspiration for worldly immortality. In modern society politics sinks to the level of activity subject to the necessity of people's consuming desires.[53]

Marx's goal of emancipating human beings from labor turns out not to be a utopian vision but an accurate description, Arendt argues, of the nightmare of modern society. Necessary labor has been transcended by the productive power of scientific automation. Class distinctions wither away in mass society as government is replaced by the administration of things. The transcendence of necessary labor does not usher in the realm of freedom because the laborer has been stripped of the ability both to act and to craft.[54] The major "crisis" facing modern society is how to create enough demand for meaningless leisure activities to entertain *animal laborans* and to maintain levels of production and profit. Marx, in Arendt's opinion, refused to realize that the degradation of humanity by society might well be permanent: "Marx's utopian assumption derives from a mechanistic philosophy which assumes that labor power can never be lost, so that if it is not exhausted in drudgery it will automatically nourish higher activities."[55] But the spare time of *animal laborans* is spent in nothing but consumption and the satisfaction of craven appetites. Neither the artisan nor the person of action, in the Arendtian parable of history, ever demanded to be happy. The universal demand for happiness and the pervasiveness of unhappiness are manifestations of a society of laborers who live a futile existence because they never realize themselves in any permanent object.[56]

With the rise of automation, the laborer loses his or her individuality, becoming a functional participant in an industrial process. Only scientists "act" in modern society. But they act "into nature," by designing new "natural processes," rather than creating a web of human relationships.[57] Arendt concludes *The Human Condition* with a stark vision of humanity stripped of its capacity both to act and to create. In the few societies where negative constitutional freedoms still exist, thought remains a possible outlet for the few.[58] Even though Arendt condemns Rousseau's flight into the intimate, she joins him on his solitary walk of philosophical inquiry, distancing herself from the corruption of mass society. This may not be a completely balanced treatment of Arendt, because her writings on the civil rights and peace movement, the Eichmann trial, and the Hungarian uprising demonstrates, more so than does the more abstract work of most contemporary political philosophers, that she was an engaged public intellectual.[59] But Arendt certainly believed that the chances for truly "political" activity in a mass, consumer society— whether the United States or the Soviet Union—were extremely rare. And because her political commentary disproportionately centered on matters relating to war and peace, civil disobedience, and the workers' councils of the Hungarian uprising, she can hardly be said to have written widely on "instrumental" issues of social and economic policy, a big chunk of political life. As her writings on the council movements demonstrates, she believed that the creation of public political space under conditions of modern bureaucratic society would be extremely rare and fleeting. Arendt's remaining hope is that the reality of human natality would enable thought to one day again produce a brief outbreak of meaningful action. Those rare possibilities for meaningful political action in modernity are the subjects of her investigations in *On Revolution*.

THE FAILED REVOLUTION:
THE WORKERS' REVOLT AGAINST SOCIETY

On Revolution is not so much a study of revolutions as an examination of the possibilities for political promise-making among equals in modern society. The American founding fathers are the heroes of the work because they alone utilized political power—the "we can" of mutual promise-making—to construct an "abiding structure of shared public principles." This document, the U.S. Constitution, is a prerequisite for the restoration of the "public happiness" of political life.[60] A "monumental" creation of human artifice, the Constitution has preserved the negative freedoms of "civil liberties" for almost two centuries. But because it did not institutionalize a realm of direct political participation for the pursuit of the "public happiness," the private "pursuit of happiness" fostered a representative democracy in the United States ruled by bureaucrats, experts, and professional politicians. The vast majority of citizens pursue their happiness through insular, material concerns. Although *On Revolution* is predominantly a monumental narrative of how the obsession of modern revolutionaries with "the social question" of economic equality disables them from institutionalizing even the limited, negative constitutional freedoms of the United States, the work is also a parable of how the condition of human natality engenders the fleeting recurrence of spontaneous efforts at republican government in the form of "revolutionary councils."

Arendt foreshadows this theme toward the end of her earlier work, *The Human Condition*, where she describes working-class political resistance to incorporation into "society" as an alternative form of liberation to Marx's utopia of the transcendence of necessary labor. Although Arendt continually terms Marx "the philosopher of labor," his vision of free labor is much closer to Arendt's favorable description of work as the creative artificer of "permanent objects." Under Marx's communism, human beings would rationally organize and plan necessary production so that the realm of necessity would allow for considerable freedom. Truly free labor, beyond the realm of necessary labor, would approximate the craftsmanship of Arendt's work. Here human beings would struggle not with necessity but with their own human capacities, aiming to achieve the aesthetic creations Marx associated with true human freedom.[61] Arendt derides this "free labor" as individualistic "hobbies."[62] But Marx likened it to the individual effort of the sculptor and musician.[63] He believed that individual freedom could only be achieved through both the rational *collective* organization of necessary production and the freedom of the *individual* realization of creative, emancipated labor. Whether Marx's dualistic vision of communism as the simultaneous achievement of collective and individual autonomy is plausible remains a matter for conjecture. But Arendt undoubtedly misrepresented Marx's conception of free human labor—not because she was incapable of reading Marx closely, but because she had no faith that human freedom could be achieved in *either* the realm of labor or that of work. Arendt believed that both Marx's vision of meaningful labor and her vision of work would never be able to withstand the inexorable scientific "processes" coming to dominate both the mode of production and the human producers.[64]

In *The Human Condition* Arendt implies that the working class's last chance for emancipation was its *political* revolt against incorporation into modern "society." In Arendt's analysis, the rise of wage-labor "frees" the laborer from the specialization of craft production, which in turn allows the laborer to be dominated by the "division of labor." This "emancipation of labor" precedes the political "emancipation of the laborer," the incorporation of the working class into "society's" political system of representation.[65] Arendt believes that the periodic emergence of workers' councils across Europe in the late-nineteenth and early-twentieth centuries represented a conscious political revolt by the working class against the incorporation of its "interests" into the system of interest-group liberalism. Arendt locates the primary virtue of the council movement in its alleged disinterest in economic affairs, workplace management, and party politics. Arendt's description, however, departs freely from the actual historical record, as council movements often arose around issues of workplace control. But according to Arendt, the council movements' sole aim was to create a new public space for face-to-face political discourse. Thus the movement was joined by citizens outside the working class, who formed councils in their neighborhoods, universities, and workplaces.[66]

The council movement is also praised by Arendt for resisting, though unsuccessfully, domination by the various reformist and revolutionary working-class political parties. The councils, she claims, realized that political representation by a party would end the freedom of direct democracy. In Arendt's analysis, the demise of the working-class movement for freedom is caused by the amelioration of working-class economic suffering and by working-class incorporation into the formal, representative political system. Class society is transformed into mass society by the elimination of gross social injustice. The replacement, for most working people, of the insecurity of daily or weekly pay with a guaranteed annual wage means, in Arendt's view, that the worker today no longer stands outside society.[67] Workers form just another interest group; they have become jobholders like everyone else. Thus, the proletariat can no longer represent the interests of the people as a whole; they are no longer a universal class. The incorporation of the working class into the welfare state may have improved its material lot. But it also meant the end of resistance to the antipolitical materialist logic of society.[68]

This hostility to the welfare state is shared by many communitarian theorists and even radical democrats such as Sheldon Wolin, who also holds to the communitarian and Arendtian belief that making politics a servant to economic and social welfare overly "instrumentalizes" the political. The public sector, in this view, is not an arena for political reform or creative democratization and decentralization but an inherently paternalist, interest-regarding bureaucracy that depoliticizes the very constituencies that win "political" rights within it. In this analysis, resistance from within the bureaucratic welfare state appears impossible; even the most insurgent of political movements must accept its logic. Resistance from without is possible by only those few who reject its bureaucratic paternalism.[69]

In this discussion in *The Human Condition* of the working class's inability to sustain a political revolution against economic society, Arendt notes that Marx and Lenin momentarily transcended the destructive revolutionary obsession with "the social question" when they urged the oppressed to seek power and freedom rather than material gain. Marx's embrace of the Paris Commune reflects, in Arendt's interpretation, a return to the focus of his early writings on political emancipation. All his other writings after *The Communist Manifesto*, Arendt argues, defined the plight of the working class in strictly economic terms. In their search for a society transcending scarcity, Marx's later writings abandon the political vision of his early works.[70] In her discussion of working-class revolt, Arendt again exhibits a fervent desire to eliminate economic issues from politics. She hopes that the "social issue" will be finally solved by politically neutral, technical means, by procedures somewhat akin to Lenin's scientific "administration of things." Arendt, in fact, praises Lenin's statement shortly after the 1917 revolution that communism equals "electrification plus soviets." She applauds such a technocratic vision of socialism because, she claims, for a fleeting moment a revolutionary leader recognized that the social question could be solved technically rather than politically. But Lenin, in her view, subsequently and tragically politicized the social question by insisting that only the Bolshevik party, rather than neutral experts, could modernize the Soviet Union. By politicizing the social question, Lenin precluded the possibility of political liberty resulting from an apolitical, technical solution to the social question.[71] In Arendt's worldview experts do not rule but only solve technical questions that ought not to be politicized. But is a politically "neutral" technocracy any less of an anti-democratic utopian vision than that of "one-party democracy"? Has ruling been abolished? Or is Arendt unconsciously proposing the rule of a new bureaucratic elite that, in addition to its quasi-Leninist faith in technical expertise, strikingly also recalls Hegel's interest-free universal class of dispassionate civil servants?

ON REVOLUTION: THE VIRTUES AND LIMITS OF LIBERAL CONSTITUTIONALISM

Arendt contends that when revolutionary leaders supplant the noble political passion for distinction with social compassion for the poor, these revolutionaries inevitably embrace a conception of the general will which eliminates the differences between people integral to politics and freedom. The specification in the Declaration of the Rights of Man of positive rights "inherent to man's nature" reduces politics to the satisfaction of material necessity.[72] Meaningful freedom, Arendt claims in On Revolution, cannot be derived from abstract claims to positive social goods, but only from the existence of a body politic that facilitates mutual promise-making. If revolutionaries attempt to provide society with the "rights of life and nature" instead of "the rights of freedom and citizenship," then there will be no future for political liberty.[73] The numerous liberal constitutions of the French Revolution are reduced to meaningless "pieces of paper," their meaning destroyed by the masses' hunger for liberation from material oppression.[74] The demise of freedom in every revolution beginning with the French derives from the fact "that this passion for public or political freedom can so easily be mistaken for the perhaps much more vehement, but politically essentially sterile, passionate hatred of masters, the longing of the oppressed for liberation" from material want.[75]

In Arendt's view the genius of the American Revolution consisted in its location of sovereignty outside the body politic within the law—the Constitution. The people remain the source of power, but the Constitution is the site of sovereignty, of authority. The French Revolution's deification of the general will was the inevitable consequence of attempting to derive both power and authority from the sovereignty of the people. The American revolutionaries concurred with Montesquieu that laws were inherently artificial, conventional, and man-made. Their sovereign authority and "unquestioned respect" could only be derived from an absolute, superhuman source. In America that absolute authority was to become enshrined in "the self-evident truths" of the founding itself. Instead of resting sovereignty in the people, the American Revolution rested it in the founding, in the Constitution itself. In Arendt's view, in the United States power is situated in the legislature, the representative of the people, but sovereign authority is situated in the Constitution and the Supreme Court.[76]

Arendt is acutely aware that both the Exodus story and Virgil's *Aeneid* teach that freedom does not automatically follow liberation from oppression.[77] Postliberation authority, the "obedience [to law] in which men retain their freedom,"[78] historically has proved to be particularly elusive. The founders could solve the problem of legitimacy in America because the revolution fortuitously avoided confronting the social question. The American Revolution represents the only modern revolution in which social compassion did not play a significant role.[79] As Arendt notes without any overt lamentation, 400,000 black slaves were excluded from the freedom achieved by 1,850,000 whites, thus demonstrating the American Revolution's abjuring of any aspirations to be a social revolution.[80] A preexisting political elite led the American Revolution, inspired by the belief that colonial rule denied them full political freedom. This elite, Arendt writes, was blessed with the love of "distinction" which is necessary for the culture of politics. In John Adams's opinion, the desire to stand out on the political stage rather than the desire for social equality motivated the revolutionary elite: "The passion for distinction . . . the desire not only to equal or resemble but to excel . . . next to self-preservation will forever be the great spring of human actions."[81] Numerous commentators note that Arendt ignored the social conflicts of the American Revolution, such as the confrontations between the centralizing Federalists and decentralizing Anti-Federalists and the struggles over primogeniture, entail, and the suffrage that continued in the revolution's aftermath.[82] But few take issue with Arendt's refusal to characterize the American Revolution as a social revolution. Its "genius," in her analysis, was that it was a political revolution made by an elite. Its good fortune was that it was made in a new land of "relative plenty and little social misery."

Though its fortuitous circumstances had much to do with its relative success, the American Revolution, Arendt believes, offered certain lessons for a Europe consumed by the social question. The political theorist from whom to learn is Montesquieu; the theorist to reject is Rousseau. Montesquieu, according to Arendt, is fundamentally concerned with "the constitution of political freedom." Believing that power and freedom belong together, Montesquieu rested political power on the "I can" of promising among citizens, rather than on the undifferentiated "I will" of the homogenous sovereign people. As a theorist of federalism, Montesquieu believed that power could be divided, checked, and separated without losing its efficacy.[83] In contrast to the French, the American revolutionaries did not believe that rights could be derived from nature. Rights, according to American revolutionary doctrine, could be derived only from legitimately constituted authority.[84] Hence the Bill of Rights *proceeds* from the Constitution rather than *precedes* it. For Arendt, the American Revolution was the first to recognize that resting sovereignty exclusively in the people is a recipe for tyranny.

Like de Tocqueville before her, Arendt also is pessimistic about transporting American lessons to Europe. Only the peculiar experience of colonization permitted the American people to build up a tradition of "political societies"—of local government—that preceded the formation of colonies, states, and finally the national government. America did not face the "chief perplexity" of continental revolutions: having to find an "absolute" from which to derive authority for law and political power. The delegates to the Constitutional Convention derived their authority from existing districts, counties, and townships that had already participated in the drafting of state constitutions. Only a preexisting federal system, difficult to graft onto the nation-states of Europe, can avoid the crisis of legitimacy engendered by the vicious circle between Sièyes's "*pouvoir constituant*" and "*pouvoir constitué*," the theoretical source of the legitimacy crisis of the European nation-state. In Sièyes's theory of the nation-state, the will of the nation, the "*pouvoir constituant*," rests in a perpetual "state of nature" above the conventional laws of the "*pouvoir constitué*."[85] But in Arendt's analysis, grounding the nation-state on the will of the sovereign people leaves the regime hostage to fickle changes in that will. The will of a people, like that of a person, can be easily manipulated and changed by the enemies of freedom. Thus, the European nation-state could never achieve the stability of the American republic.[86]

America could forge a constitutional republic and avoid the potential majority tyranny of continental democracies because political power existed not only prior to the revolution, but also "in a sense prior to the colonization of the continent."[87] The Mayflower Compact and other "political societies" that established political power under the nominal rule of England taught Americans that political power and rights could be established without the possession or claim of sovereignty.[88] That is, the Federal republic was discovered through experience. According to Arendt, the colonists' theory of political legitimacy did not rely on the social contract theory of Hobbes or Locke, but rather on the Puritan conception of the covenant of Israel.[89] This covenant among the people established society and government simultaneously, rather than, as in the Lockeian contract, creating a society by equal contract which then decides by majority rule what type of government will best preserve that society.

The American Revolution never developed a political theory of the social covenant because, according to Arendt, ever since the Periclean age political thought had parted company with political action. Fortuitous experience, not theory or learning, taught the Founders that power, but not sovereignty, could reside in the people. The American revolution failed to distinguish theoretically between its origins in the "mutual promise" of the covenant and an emergent postrevolutionary doctrine of passive consent to the rule of a sovereign state, whose power fortunately was limited by a constitutional bill of rights. Government, in Arendt's analysis, consists of both power and authority. The colonists' attachment to the Crown and royal charters served as authority during the colonial period. In the postrevolutionary period of the Articles of Confederation, a brief crisis of authority emerged, only to be solved by the establishment and subsequent veneration of the Constitution.[90]

But the founders failed to comprehend theoretically the nature of power and public freedom. Thus the American Revolution quickly abandoned the "pursuit of public happiness" for the private "pursuit of happiness." Government came to be viewed as a means to promote the happiness of society, not as a sphere of happiness itself. The American public philosophy shifted rapidly from a focus on the Constitution's creation of a realm for public excellence to the Bill of Rights' imposition of those constitutional restraints on government necessary to secure individual rights.[91]

The "sad fact" for Arendt is that the blessings of "limited government," the pursuit of civil rights instead of political freedom, has only been guaranteed by one revolution. No revolution has yet secured the public happiness of direct political participation. The Constitution itself focused exclusively on representative institutions, ignoring the rich American tradition of direct, local political participation. Jefferson knew well that although the revolution "had given freedom to the people, it had failed to provide a space where this freedom could be exercised."[92] Although Arendt states that "the question whether the end of American government should be prosperity or freedom" has never been answered, she ultimately believes that even in this country "freedom and power have parted company."[93] The republican tradition's most promising experiment, in Arendt's view, in the end only produced the freedom of limited government. Thus the American Revolution, the one revolution whose avoidance of the social question would have enabled it to take up the challenge of creating power out of political participation, did not assume that challenge. The American republic associated government with a necessary evil and fatefully equated "power with violence . . . [and] the political with government."[94] For Arendt, constitutionally limited government is preferable to the despotism of the unlimited sovereignty of the European nation-state. The possibility of achieving public happiness, however, faded with the institutionalization of American representative democracy.

THE MYTH OF THE COUNCIL: PARTICIPATORY POLITICS WITHOUT SUBSTANCE

Arendt, however, does not conclude her parable of revolutions by defending U.S. representative constitutional government as humanity's highest political achievement. Though the masses force politics to become the servant of society, humanity's natality and capacity for freedom also makes possible a periodic course of republican revival. Occasionally, federations of revolutionary councils spontaneously arise from the people themselves. It is the people who spontaneously form the forty-eight sections of the French Revolution's

Paris Commune and transform them into a municipal revolutionary government. And they do so again in 1871. *On Revolution*'s final chapter is a saga
of the struggle of the popular associations, political clubs, and councils of the
republican tradition against the bureaucratic, parliamentary party system that
continually crushes them. The *sansculottes*, who in the opening of the book
are blamed for making the social question central to the French Revolution,
are celebrated at the end of the work for defending their *sociétés revolutionnaires* against Jacobin centralism. (Arendt appears oblivious to her contradic-
tory portrayal of the *sansculottes* within the same work.)

Jefferson's repeating of Cato's invocation: "Divide the counties into
wards" anticipates the councils, soviets, *Räte* and *sociétés revolutionnaires*
that "spring up as spontaneous organs of the people" in every revolution,
"not only *outside of all revolutionary parties* but entirely unexpected by
them and their leaders."[95] Arendt contends that these councils are ignored
both by the revolutionary tradition and by historians because they are viewed
only as temporary organs of dual power that fade away once the revolutionaries seize the state.[96] Arendt argues that the councils deserve to be treated as
an entirely new form of government. Not surprisingly she never addresses
the question of how these localist councils would achieve greater regional or
national coordination of policies or whether or not there would be a need for
representative, parliamentary institutions, as well as councils, in a participatory democracy. The councils defy the nation-state tradition of party politics
which asserts, in Arendt's analysis, that power and violence go together. According to Arendt, the power of the soviets rests strictly on the action of the
people. Violence plays no role in their establishment nor maintenance. This
is not to say that Arendt's critique of a "dictating violence" is an absolutist
defense of pacifism on her part. In fact, she states that the revolutionary
republican abhorrence of violence is one of the reasons why the councils are
so easily crushed.[97]

Arendt claims that political parties play no role in the establishment of the
councils. Rather, as soon as the councils emerge, the parties try to control
them for their own instrumental purposes. Although it is true that the Jacobins and Bolsheviks ultimately repressed all the clubs and soviets that they did
not control, Arendt is historically inaccurate in her disassociation of party
politics and ideological struggle from the origins of the councils. Certainly
both Jacobin activists in the French Revolution and Bolshevik, Menshevik,
and Social Revolutionary party activists played a leading role in establishing
revolutionary councils. Nor is her radical disjunction between direct and representative democracy an accurate history of the struggle between democratic councils and authoritarian parties. The most celebrated example of
council government, the Paris Commune, elected its *representatives* along
party and district lines, while subjecting them to mandate and recall. The
"representative" and party-based Constituent Assembly of postrevolutionary
Russia more democratically reflected the diversity of the Russian people than
did the disproportionately urban soviets in which the peasant parties played

a much weaker role. Thus the Bolsheviks claim that the soviets more accurately represented the opinions of the postrevolutionary masses than did the Constituent Assembly was not only inaccurate; it also was spurious, because the Bolsheviks by 1919 had crushed all non-Bolshevik activity within the workers' soviets.

Throughout her work Arendt manifests a deep hostility to political parties. All modern parties, Arendt believes, rapidly degenerate into Michelian oligarchies. They are interested only in implementing their programs. They demand the execution of their programs, but they eschew political "action" and reasoned debate. Arendt believes that *both* one-party and multi-party systems become oligarchic and eventually totalitarian. Only the two-party system of Great Britain and the United States avoids such a fate because they recognize the opposition party as an institution of government.[98] But the best that the two-party system can achieve is the protection of constitutional liberties. The two parties can only represent interests; they cannot engage in meaningful political deliberation: "The only thing which can be represented and delegated is interest, or the welfare of the constituents, but neither their action nor their opinions."[99] The passive voter lobbies through interest groups in an attempt to "blackmail" the government into fulfilling their material needs. Interest groups only "represent" their predetermined needs. They do not engage in open discourse, creating the power that arises out of joint action and joint deliberation. Modern representative government degenerates into an oligarchy of professional political ward-healers. The government is pseudo-democratic in that popular welfare is its goal; but the privilege of public happiness rests only with the oligarchy of representatives.[100]

Nowhere in her writings does Arendt envision the revitalization of democratic life *within* political parties as a means to escape the political passivity of representative democracy. Even in a direct democracy, in the absence of vibrant internal party life or organized political caucuses or groups within institutions, how would dialogue among diverse groups and opinions be constituted and how would perceived interests be both aggregated and reconstituted? Would political deliberation only go on in the plenary sessions of the councils? Would there be no secondary political associations in a radical democratic republic, promoting political dialogue across workplace and neighborhood councils?

Arendt associates representative party politics with the rise of the welfare state. She condemns the welfare state with equal vigor as being contrary to the spirit of politics. Arendt's words strike the contemporary reader as akin to Sandel's, Wolin's, and MacIntyre's critique of the instrumental and anticommunal nature of the national welfare state: "The defenders of this system, which actually is the system of the welfare state, if they are liberal and of democratic convictions, must deny the very existence of public happiness and public freedom; they must insist that politics is a burden and that its end is itself not political."[101] Although both the communitarian and participatory-democratic critique of the bureaucratic paternalism of the welfare state expresses a profound *partial* truth, a serious radical democrat cannot glibly call for the welfare state's abolition. This is true not simply because mass democratic movements have fought to achieve the social rights that the welfare state institutionalizes. Movements can, of course, sometimes fight the wrong battles or realize that prior gains bring with them new problems. But social provision of adequate levels of health, education, and welfare are necessary if citizenship is to be meaningful to all, regardless of their socioeconomic status. Obviously the welfare state can be restructured in ways that move the regime toward becoming more of a civil society of shared caring rather than a bureaucratic welfare state. Welfare programs can be decentralized; various schemes can and have been advanced for the democratization of social provision, as well as for the introduction of greater mechanisms of choice and accountability. The rigid public/private distinction that governs most thinking about the welfare state could be transcended, for example, by community-administered health clinics and cooperative workplace-sited daycare centers that are run neither by the state nor private business. These are concrete sites for the construction of relatively autonomous institutions of civil society which obey neither a statist nor an instrumental-economistic logic. But no matter how society democratizes social provision, if this society is to be a relatively egalitarian one, then a democratic state would have to assure adequate funding and minimal standards of provision within these civil institutions.[102] Of course, a democratic citizen has the right to argue against the belief that the state should guarantee certain social rights. But few communitarians are willing to express, at least openly, such an antistatist, economic libertarian position.

As noted earlier, Arendt continually vacillates between attacking the welfare state and recommending that all issues of social welfare be treated by experts outside the realm of politics. For a brief moment toward the end of *On Revolution*, Arendt seems to realize that if all the questions that the welfare state deals with were solved by experts in "the realm of the administration of things" there might not be anything left to deliberate about within the political sphere. If what provisions the welfare state should provide, how it should be structured, and how it should be financed are all questions for the experts, then what issues of the public sphere are left to political deliberation? As Arendt herself notes:

> [if] all political questions in the welfare state are ultimately problems of administration, to be handled and decided by experts, in which case even the representatives of the people hardly possess an authentic area of action but are administrative officers, whose business, though in the public interest is not essentially different from the business of private management . . . then, to be sure, the councils would have to be considered as atavistic institutions without any relevance in the realm of human affairs. . . . In a society under the sway of

abundance, conflicting group interests need no longer be settled at one another's expense, and the principle of opposition is valid only as long as there exist authentic choices which transcend the objective and demonstrably valid opinions of experts. When government has really become administration, the party system can only result in incompetence and wastefulness. . . .[103]

Arendt, unlike Marx and Lenin, is worried by this image of scientific management eliminating the need for politics. But like the revolutionary theorists she critiques as antipolitical, Arendt fails to see that the ways we structure both production and social provision are inherently political issues. That is, Arendt need not worry about the allegedly inexorable withering away of politics in abundant, materialist societies. Her recognition of the plurality of both individual and group identity in modern (or postmodern) industrial societies should have enabled Arendt to comprehend that the allocation of social roles in a free society could never be a strictly scientific matter.

But Arendt insists on drawing a radical distinction between politics and economics. Although admitting that council governments are often rendered politically vulnerable because they do not adequately attend to either economic or government administration,[104] she insists that to be true to their purely political purposes the councils must not engage in economic management: "In the form of workers' councils, they have again and again tried to take over the management of the factories, and all these attempts have ended in dismal failure. 'The wish of the working class,' we are told, 'has been fulfilled. The factories will be managed by the councils of the workers.' This so-called wish of the working class sounds much more like an attempt of the revolutionary party to counteract the councils' political aspirations, to drive their members away from the political realm and back into the factories."[105]

Arendt constructs a myth of council life which contends that political discussion took up all of their time, while questions of economic and workplace management were of marginal concern. Although this may have been true in the most explosive political periods of council organization— Hungary, October 1956; Gdansk, August 1980—it is simply false to assert that economic management was not a central concern of many workplace councils. The best counterexample to Arendt is the case of the post-World War I German *Räte*. Although the majority of workers supported workers' participation in factory management through workers' councils, a strong majority also opposed the revolutionary socialists' efforts to overthrow a parliamentary social democratic regime. The majority of socialist workers supported the perspective that the nation-state would best be run by parliamentary parties, whereas the workers' councils should not be mere talk shops but concern themselves with actual economic and production policy on the shop floor.[106] Although a role for the *Räte* in industrial management was enshrined in the Weimar constitution, this goal was not fully achieved due to the remaining powerful prerogatives of private owners and managers and the rightward drift in German politics and public policy over the course of the 1920s.

Arendt congratulates the political maturity of those workers' councils that eschewed the role of economic management, "whereas the workers' wish to run the factories themselves was a sign of the understandable, but politically irrelevant desire of individuals to rise into positions which up to then had been open only to the middle classes."[107] Arendt insists that political criteria are improper for choosing talented managers. By exorcising the social question from politics, she loses all interest in the possibility of democratizing social organization. Political and managerial talents may well be somewhat distinct, but this does not preclude democratic participation in discerning both enterprise goals and managerial talent. Any committed democrat believes that organizations that have binding power over the actions of their members should be governed by those members. Whether or not members of an interdependent workforce would choose to elect managers would be the democratic prerogative of those workers. But the workers of a democratic polity must have partial sovereignty, along with consumers and the polity as a whole, over the policy goals and management of their collective enterprise.[108]

Arendt, however, believes that social organizations must be governed by rules of efficiency which inherently conflict with principles of participation: "The [political man] is supposed to know how to deal with men in a field of human relations, whose principle is freedom, and the other must know how to manage things and people in a sphere of life whose principle is necessity."[109] Councils should not manage the economy because they would improperly bring an element of action (i.e., political participation) into the "administration of things." In Arendt's opinion the party apparatus is an admirable organization for running an economy because it is oligarchic and thereby well suited to functions of command and control.[110] The experience of command economies, however, demonstrates just the contrary. Oligarchic parties are disastrous managers of economies. The absence of participation and decentralized sources of information (both market and nonmarket) characteristic of party/state centralized economic control leads to massive inefficiency. Arendt's disdain for political economy, what she derisively terms "macrohousework," is accompanied by an absence of knowledge about that subject. Most communitarian theorists have demonstrated a similar inability to analyze the complex relationships between political economy, civil society, and the state. A democratically determined mix of political participation, democratically monitored management, and market coordination would characterize the social governance of production in any plausible radical democratic society.

Anyone attempting to ground a radical democratic theory of politics in Arendt's work must also be wary of her social elitism. While explaining that the local councils would discover their purpose through experimentation,

Arendt notes that only a self-selected elite of people who care about the political would participate in such a process. Council membership would consist of a political elite who spring from the people but who are neither nominated from above nor supported from below.[111] That is, they represent no one except themselves. But if the councils are to make decisions that affect those who do not care to go to meetings, should not the nonattenders be consulted? Would not the agendas of the meetings need to be known and advertised in advance, so the widest possible self-selected audience might attend? And if that agenda is to be representative of the interests of the broader workplace or community that the council ostensibly governs, would not some representative agenda-setting committee be necessary? That is, as Norberto Bobbio has argued, a direct democratic institution of any but the smallest size will inevitably utilize representative forms of decision making if that institution is to ascertain the array of interests and opinions within the self-governing community.[112] If the councils are to have significant political power and remain democratic, then Arendt's (and other "participatory democrats' ") polar opposition of representative to direct democratic forms of rule is not feasible.

Arendt describes a utopian federal system of councils that would be pyramidal in structure. By resting authority among politically active peers at each level of the pyramid, the federal council system would, according to Arendt, reconcile equality and authority. Each council would freely choose who would represent it at the next highest level of political jurisdiction. They would be those who most love politics: "The joys of public happiness and the responsibilities for public business would then become the share of those few from all walks of life who have a taste for public freedom and cannot be 'happy' without it. Politically, they are the best, and it is the task of good government and the sign of a well-ordered republic to assure them of their rightful place in the public realm."[113] But Arendt moves far afield from the republican tradition's defense of the intrinsic value of political involvement in her unqualified defense of rule by an elite that emerges naturally from the people. Arendt is not overtly rejecting the democratic principle of equality, in that any member of the polity may become active, at any time, in the myriad islands of democratic associational life. But Arendt's implied opposition to affirmative efforts to introduce the broadest range of individuals to politics—or at least to make sure that a democratic polity is not dominated by those who live for politics—undercuts her credibility as a democratic theorist. Only a mentality of crude egalitarianism, Arendt argues, "tends to deny the obvious inability and conspicuous lack of interest of large parts of the population in political matters as such."[114] Thus Arendt's "aristocratic" councils abandon the most attractive aspects of the republican tradition, the view advanced by theorists ranging from de Tocqueville to Mill, that the diversification of opportunities for political participation would hopefully enhance both the political capacities *and* the level of political interest of the average citizen. Who is to say that those who initially gravitate to political activism are more suited for the political life than those who have yet to experience it—or that those not drawn to politics as a vocation should not have their opinions and interests equally represented?

Arendt quite cavalierly mentions that a pyramidal republic of councils might eliminate the need for universal suffrage. But in the absence of a universal guarantee of access to the political system, the initial self-selected participants could restrict future access. There would be no constitutional guarantees to check the self-selected elite. Or even if cultural or constitutional traditions did preserve the possibility that anyone could at any time join the political elite, might not the social and cultural practices of that elite be intimidating, exclusivist, or self-reproducing? Arendt's own description of this self-selected but democratically open elite indicates how its practices might not be that attractive to noninitiates: "To be sure, such an 'aristocratic' form of government would spell the end of general suffrage as we understand it today; for only those who as voluntary members of an 'elementary republic' have demonstrated that they care for more than their private happiness and are concerned about the state of the world would have the right to be heard in the conduct of the business of the republic."[115] Arendt argues that a principle of self-exclusion is not derogatory toward those who exclude themselves from political deliberation. Such a self-exclusion, Arendt contends, would give substance to a critically important negative liberty, the freedom from politics.[116] But in a truly democratic society, the choice to exit or enter politics must always be open to every citizen. The elitism of Arendtian republicanism assumes that the self-selected political elite will always properly look after the general interests of society and avoid constructing barriers to entry into political life for those not yet active. Arendt does not worry about representing the interests of those who do not attend the council meetings. In fact, to do so, she believes, would degrade the peer equality of those who choose to join the political elite. With the virtuous deciding, the rights of the nonvirtuous citizens need not be considered. This social elitism toward the "masses" and the society of passive consumers not only ignores the right of the less active to political consideration; it also abandons a democratic republican commitment to exposing the presently apathetic to the possible benefits of political participation. No one should be forced to participate. But in a democratic republic, all citizens should be exposed to the potential rewards of participation.

Arendt's critique of the absence of public space for political deliberation in modern representative democracies proved to be strikingly prescient. As early as the late 1950s, she perceived that the relationship between representative and voter in Western democracies was being transformed into that of seller and buyer. But alleviating this situation necessitates the democratization of political party life as well as a vitalization of council life in neighborhoods and workplaces. Each of these institutions would have to deliberate on substantive issues deemed appropriate to their jurisdiction by political society as a whole.[117] A national representative assembly might set the broadest social priorities. The existence of internally democratic political parties would facilitate the articulation of shared interests among divergent social groups, as well as the development of alternative conceptions of national priorities. On the other hand, in order to engage in meaningful deliberation, local councils would have to control certain socioeconomic resources and the implementation of national priorities at the local level.

Arendt's wish for the political economy to be managed by experts and for councils to engage in only "disinterested" discussion denudes political deliberation of any substantive content. About what are political decisions to be made? Or is politics not about decision making but just a mere talk shop? In a roundtable discussion, Mary McCarthy, a sympathetic friend of Arendt, once challenged her to delineate the substance of modern political deliberation. McCarthy rhetorically asked: "If all questions of economics, human welfare, busing, anything that touches the social sphere are to be excluded from the political scene, then I am left with war and speeches. But the speeches can't be just speeches. They have to be speeches about something."[118] Arendt's answer was that people always have affairs "worthy to be talked about in public."[119] In medieval times, she claimed, people talked (politically?) in churches about the existence of God. Today juries deliberate about guilt or innocence, town meetings decide where to build a new bridge. Any subject matter "which we cannot figure out with certainty," Arendt claims, is appropriate to the political sphere. But no amount of speeches or discussion, she believes, can solve the urban or housing crisis of the contemporary United States. These are critical social problems "which can be really figured out" and which should be settled "in the sphere Engels called the administration of things."[120]

Despite her worship of "the religion of politics," in the final analysis Arendt shares the radical impulse to remove matters of social conflict from the realm of public deliberation. Although she desires agonal discourse about the nature of the good life, any concrete social problem appears to be amenable to Engels's (and later Lenin's) faith that in a society of abundance scientific expertise can solve all social problems. This deep-seated desire to exclude conflict from the public arena may have subliminally arisen from Arendt's understandable visceral abhorrence of the brutal, ideological, and racist politics of her native post-World War I Germany. Leaving aside the social-psychological origins of this abhorrence of conflict on the part of an otherwise public intellectual, this aversion to strident political conflict underpinned Arendt's argument that the issue of school integration should be removed from the political agenda. For Arendt, the problem of race relations was such a volatile "social question" that it could be solved only by experts operating outside the political process.[121] Racism threatened to tear the nation's fabric apart just as the "social question" demolished revolutionary France. Though the issues of school integration and equal access to education involve bitter political controversy down to this day, they can be confronted only through politics. Not to do so would be to abandon political argument about the function of public and private education in a democratic society and the role that racial inequality plays in subverting the promise of U.S. democracy. If to affirm the republican tradition of political participation is to remove the "social question" from the political sphere, then Arendt's republican vision may well be as anticonflictual—and therefore as antipolitical—as both the liberal and radical tradition it derides.

Arendt's romanticism of the *polis* transfixes on a "high politics" of "glory and memorable speeches" about the final ends of the political community. These speeches, however, appear to have little in common with the lives of ordinary people and the substance of conventional politics in liberal democratic societies. War and constitution-making appear to be the only forms of Arendtian "politics," as if founding and perishing and striving for immortality were the only true political concerns.

Arendt claims that true politics lies unambiguously in the realm of freedom. But although politics may be one of humankind's most creative endeavors, it transpires in a realm of necessity involving clashes among particular individuals, interests, and parties over the distribution of not only social goods but also social roles. Politics involves not only mediating clashes about particular policies or distribution patterns, but also maintaining a democratic dialogue among divergent conceptions of "the common good"—both those shared political rules of the game and those social resources deemed by the polity to be essential for full membership. Arendt and, subsequently, the communitarians have highlighted how the overly instrumental and bureaucratic nature of interest-group liberalism can eviscerate the coherence of a political community. But the construction in a pluralist political community of an evolving, operative consensus over the nature of democratic public life cannot occur solely through metapolitical discourse. Such a shared political community is constructed through concrete political contestation about specific public policies and social priorities. That is, to draw a radical dichotomy between the theory of politics and its practice is to ignore the reality that political community is constructed by a complex dialectic of ideal and material interests.

Conclusion

REDRESSING THE RADICAL TRADITION'S ANTIPOLITICAL LEGACY—TOWARD A RADICAL DEMOCRATIC PLURALIST POLITICS

THE ELECTIVE AFFINITIES OF
DIVERSE RADICAL THEORETICAL PROJECTS

The desire of radical political theorists to eliminate social conflict prevented them from envisioning a democratic conception of politics. Their project aimed to transcend the preconditions of politics—a plurality of social groups, particular communal identities, and divergent social interests. In their search for a harmonious society, they wished to eradicate, or, in Hegel's case, regulate through bureaucratic management, the particular communities and social interests through which people develop themselves. The radical critique of rights-based liberalism—that rights promote a divisive social war of all against all—accurately describes a potential function of private property rights in societies where concentrated ownership of corporate property gives power to owners and managers over the labor of others. But this insight does not eliminate the necessity of legal and social guarantees for the relative autonomy of particular individuals and secondary associations in any egalitarian democratic society—no matter how, relatively speaking, "harmonious" or "nonexploitative" its social relations may be.

The argument of this book may strike some readers as being akin to that advanced by Jacob Talmon in *The Origins of Totalitarian Democracy*, where he claims that the radical Jacobin tradition culminates in Marx, a theorist whose philosophic approach lies at the heart of modern totalitarianism.[1] Obviously my work is more sympathetic than was Talmon's to Rousseau's critique of competitive marketplace societies and to Marx's vision of collective self-determination. Nor do I accept Talmon's view that implicit in Rousseau's concept of the general will are the practices of a powerful, modern technocratic state subjecting its atomized population to ideological indoctrination. Rousseau is too suspicious of concentrated state power and of political and social mobilization to be the unequivocal philosophical founder of modern totalitarianism. Contrary to totalitarian ideology, Rousseau believed that citizens, in civil society, should lead as self-sufficient lives as possible. An omnipotent, activist state is absent from his description of the periodic general assemblies and government by expert magistrates. Nor can Hegel don

Talmon's mantle as the founder of the modern totalitarian state bureaucracy, for Hegel favored a greater role for associational life in civil society than did classic totalitarian regimes. Marx's ultimate vision of the withering away of the state, and perhaps all social authority, is too much a postscarcity anarchist vision to equate it with modern authoritarian Communist regimes.

Talmon's belief in a direct lineage between the founding radical theorists and modern totalitarianism is too reductionist. Nonetheless, these theorists' conception of "universal" societies contributed to the absence in the radical tradition of an explicit defense of the unique worth of associational and political life. If diversity, pluralism, and politics had been treated as goods-in-themselves by the classical radical tradition, this might have provided an ethical prophylactic against twentieth-century radicalism's flirtation with, and often explicit defense of, antipluralist, authoritarian regimes. Talmon's work, however, ascribes to the political theorist an inordinate ability to affect the course of history. History never runs directly along the paths outlined by political philosophers. Historical subjects confront both circumstances and choices that no analyst can envision in advance. Undoubtedly Marx did not advocate—in fact he warned against—attempting to build communism in less developed, predominantly agrarian, nondemocratic societies. Nor did every radical theorist examined here explicitly argue for the authoritarian abolition of democratic politics. Yet each of them longed to transcend the conflicts arising from modern social differentiation.

I have attempted to recognize the unique intellectual project of each thinker and grant each one his or her respective, "particular" consideration. Rousseau's search to create common bonds of obligation among social equals is distinct from Hegel's central focus on the state bureaucracy's corporatist promotion of particular interests' identification with the universal state. Hegel countenances the diversity of social identities within civil society more favorably than did either Rousseau or Marx. But Hegel is too readily celebrated by many contemporary communitarian theorists as a defender of the social construction of individual identity through participation in the communally cooperative activities of autonomous groups within civil society.[2] That is part of Hegel's stance. But Hegel also held that society could only achieve the harmony of the "reason of state" if the social interests of civil society are properly organized by a universal state bureaucracy. Hegel's statism cannot be ignored or wished away, because it relegated all significant political issues to the state bureaucracy.

The corporatist aims of Hegel's mature writings, however, are not equivalent to Marx's project of abolishing the domination of capital over labor or to Marx's quest for a socially transparent "human society" in which the free development of each would be the precondition for the free development of all. Here the state withers away. In reality, the authoritarian states of "real existing socialism," rather than withering away, strove to eliminate autonomous organization in civil society. By a Hegelian "cunning of reason" not envisioned by twentieth-century Communists, their smothering of initiative in civil society decisively contributed to the economic inefficiency and political collapse of Communist regimes. Some would contend that the authoritarian statism of "real existing socialist" regimes occurred because communism only came to power in societies characterized by material scarcity. But it would be prudent to assume that any society, no matter how affluent, can achieve the abolition of political conflict only if a repressive state suppresses all conflict. Despite the relevant differences, there remains an evident elective affinity between Lenin's faith in a vanguard ruling according to the "sciences" of technology and class consciousness, Marx and Engels's concept of the noncontroversial "administration of things," Hegel's universal bureaucracy utilizing the "reason of state" to integrate diverse social groups, Rousseau's virtuous "government magistrates" applying the general will to specific cases, and even Arendt's technocrats eliminating the "social question" from political discourse.

This common impulse in the radical tradition to abolish social conflict weaves its way through distinct concerns on the part of each theorist about the inequality and injustices of liberalism. Although recognizing the affinity these distinct theoretical projects share in their ambivalence toward social pluralism— their longing for social unity and their impulse to transcend politics— I have attempted to respect the spirit of pluralism by not creating a Procrustean unity among these theorists' distinct concerns and social analyses.

Toward a Radical Democratic Pluralist Politics: A Critique of Overly Solidaristic Communitarianism and Excessively Particular Postmodernism

Fully developing a prescriptive argument on behalf of radical democracy is a project beyond the scope of this concluding chapter. Here I can only frame the issues a contemporary radical democratic political theory and practice should address in light of both the legacy of the radical tradition and its current historical crisis. The focus of this prescriptive argument is the development of a radical democratic pluralist politics of citizenship which transcends the false dichotomies of universality versus particularity, solidarity versus difference, and economism versus the primacy of the political. The argument aims to move beyond a critique of the classical radical tradition to analyze both the politics of communitarian solidarity and the politics of postmodern "difference," because they represent the major contemporary theoretical efforts claiming to advance a radical democratic conception of politics. These political efforts explicitly reject both the alleged instrumental nature of liberalism and the antipolitical, reductionist elements of the Marxist and socialist tradition. To foreshadow my argument, I contend that any realistic radical democratic politics must incorporate elements of both the liberal and socialist traditions if it is to avoid either an overly solidaristic, universalist conception of community or an excessive, fragmenting celebration of particularism. In a telegraphic, somewhat polemical form, I hope to offer a radical liberal antidote to excessive universalism and a democratic, pluralist, socialist antidote to the false polarization between universal and particular of a "politics of difference."

The alleged antinomy between universality and particularity advanced at either extreme by communitarianism and the politics of difference is not only theoretically questionable; it also fails to grasp a key problematic in the tenuous practical project of democratic politics—building community through the shared participation of diverse groups in public life. Unity and particularity cannot be radically counterposed in a democratic, pluralist polity; rather, democratic solidarity can be achieved only through a shared public life among particular groups and interests. The excessively solidaristic project of virtuous communitarianism harks back to a restrictive, pseudo-Aristotelian conception of the good which denies the plurality of modern conceptions of the good life.[3] On the other hand, the postmodern celebration of fragmented, particular identities denies the reality that human emancipation can only occur in a democratic context in which diverse groups recognize the just claims of other constituencies. The flourishing of difference on a terrain of structural inequality will only reduce the opportunity for communities with fewer economic, cultural, and political resources to develop the potential of their members.

Communitarian theorists offer a radical break with liberal conceptions of identity, and another break with the radical tradition by asserting the virtue of politics, sometimes even asserting that politics is the only truly "free" human activity. These scholars uphold political deliberation, the defining of a virtuous community, as a model for the revitalization of contemporary political life. But does this loosely knit school of contemporary political thought offer a viable, postliberal conception of democratic pluralist politics? Is it theoretically adequate to the task and does it grasp the political and policy barriers to the reconstruction of a democratic political community?

Hannah Arendt was among the first contemporary theorists to uphold the politics of the ancients against the interest-oriented bureaucratic nature of modern society. Whether acknowledged or not, Arendt had a profound impact on subsequent communitarian thought. Both Arendt and the communitarians desire that considerations of economic and social policy be removed from political debate in order for the political arena to be freed from allegedly instrumental, utilitarian concerns. Their inability, however, to analyze how the distribution of socioeconomic power profoundly influences political power renders their conception of "interest-free" politics distinctly apolitical.

Communitarians, particularly Michael Sandel and Alasdair MacIntyre, in their sketchy outlines of a normatively desirable politics share Arendt's search for a "politics" of community which transcends conflict over questions of socioeconomic distribution and power. They too are hostile to the welfare state and to any discussion of democratic political control of socioeconomic institutions. This is also somewhat true of Benjamin Barber's conception of strong democracy, which warns against democratic deliberation succumbing to the instrumental concerns of economic policy making. (This is how Barber justifies distancing himself from the democratic socialist tradition.)[4] Strikingly absent from both Barber's and the communitarians' analyses is any grappling with how political economy—the structure of a capitalist or state socialist economy—thwarts the possibility of democratic politics by engendering huge disparities in power among competing societal and state interests. In their preference for small, tightly bonded communities, communitarians fail to discuss the national government policies and international forms of social movement cooperation and institution-building needed to control those undemocratically structured private institutions, such as transnational corporations, which frequently thwart community control. Moreover, in the absence of significant economic redistribution, community empowerment often yields community control of poverty. The disdain of communitarians for representative democracy leaves them with nothing to say about the institutional mechanisms for mediating tensions among the diverse *communities* bound to exist in any democratic industrial society. Nor can they tell us what specific form of politics and policies might successful construct a modern, pluralist sense of national community.

Both Arendt and the communitarians generally eschew the national political arena as a locus for the resurgence of republican political virtue. Alasdair MacIntyre in *After Virtue* writes that "the construction of local forms of community within which civility and the intellectual and moral life can be sustained" may provide the ray of light by which to fend off "the new dark ages" of statist, technocratic-bureaucratic rationality.[5] Arendt's work also has a decentralist, populist side, celebrating the participatory nature of the local "elementary republics" of the Commune, the soviets, and the Hungarian workers' councils. But alongside this populist strain exists an aristocratic impulse contending that only those few who demonstrate their talents in the local republics would be worthy participants in the political life of the national republic.

Communitarian critics of the impersonality of mass society often share with radical democrats a belief that participation in intermediate forms of community (e.g., neighborhood planning boards, schoolboards, workplace councils) may be central to the development of motivated, self-governing citizens. But communitarians rarely occupy themselves with the concrete political dilemma of what centralized state functions would have to be altered or devolved if local participation is to be enhanced. Also absent from most communitarian analyses is any conception of the role of economic power in structuring inequalities in political and social power which thwart possibilities for meaningful democratic participation.

Though continually asserting the need for *common* values, communitarian theorists advance no substantive moral criteria for choosing among *compet-*

ing values and institutions. They express sympathy for communities that "in defense of their way of life" wish to ban pornographic bookstores or prevent industries from moving out. But would they also defend a community's right to "defend its way of life" by excluding African-Americans? Communitarians often appeal to traditional community values as if such values were inherently rational, thus unconsciously mirroring Hegel's attitude toward the modern state. But if traditions at times "root" people, they can at times shackle them. To avoid a conventionalist defense of all self-defined communities, egalitarian communitarian theorists must advance a concept of human potential and of the political and socioeconomic structures that best realize that potential. They cannot avoid politics by worshiping "disinterested" political theory.

The emergence of mass social movements organized around identities of race, gender, sexual preference, and ethnicity has made democratic theorists increasingly sensitive to the distinct conceptions of community and morality that various ethnic, racial, and social groups hold in modern societies.[6] In the absence of guaranteed rights for particular communities, the communitarian search for a "politics of the common good" could lead to an authoritarian imposition of one idea of the good on all arenas of life. The communitarian longing for a premodern view of one universal conception of the good life offers no feasible alternative to liberalism's failure to generate a compelling theory of community.[7] What may promote a sense of community among diverse citizens and communities within a democratic state is the common commitment of citizens to the limited but substantive political ends of a democratic society. The central end of a pluralist democratic state may be precisely those shared constitutional and political practices by which distinct communities work out, mediate, and come to live with their differences.

If communitarian theorists are to be able to reject intolerant conceptions of community, then they must incorporate a theory of rights into their allegedly "post" or "nonliberal" conceptions of virtuous communities. One may accept the communitarian critique that a theory of rights cannot be adequately defended by a metaphysical conception of human beings as "unencumbered selves," who discern universal moral principles by distancing themselves from their particular social identities and moral outlooks. This critique of a specific method for defending rights does not, however, prove that rights serve as an inherent barrier to community. If democratic, communitarians' conception of the good places a primacy on the self-development of each individual, then would not the vision of the good society include a conception of the political, educational, and social opportunities that each individual must have if they are to be full citizens? If so, common political discourse would call these entitlements civil, political, and social "rights." Might it not be both necessary and desirable for democratic communitarians to derive a conception of rights from their conception of the good, particularly if that good society is to resemble a political and social democracy?

Thus, rather than depending for its defense on a metaphysical conception of human beings as "unencumbered selves," the value of rights can be derived from a "situated" conception of "reflective" selves who are members of a democratic community. Because these communities value equally the public voice of each of their members, they are committed to institutional guarantees against discrimination and repression. Membership in a vibrant democratic community promotes such a moral commitment to guaranteeing the possibility of participation. As Will Kymlicka has argued, this democratic self is not so "radically situated" that it cannot discern the need for "rights" to guarantee the ability of individuals to "self-reflexively" evaluate their political and moral beliefs.[8] Amy Gutmann has described how procedural constraints on democratic majorities need not be derived from a narrow conception of liberal individualism but can stem from a democratic commitment to guarantees of individual political participation.[9]

Communitarian critics of Rawlsian social-contract liberalism have failed to make a convincing case that ontological disagreements about the nature of the self necessitate political differences. Pressed by the insights of communitarian critics, John Rawls admits that his notion of the liberal self is embedded in a conception of a liberal democratic community. In the Dewey lectures and subsequent articles, Rawls describes the original position as a heuristic device for explicating notions of impartiality and plural conceptions of the good held by citizens embedded in liberal democratic cultures.[10] In fact, certain analysts have argued that this attempt to explicate the embeddedness of his theory of justice in a liberal democratic culture has led his major response to his critics, *Political Justice*, to abandon *A Theory of Justice's* serious concern with redistribution of economic and social goods and opportunities.[11] Communitarians may still feel that Rawls's conception of the self is inadequate; but they have yet to offer a concrete political alternative to the politics of either traditional social-welfare liberalism or a more radical democratic socialism. Vague incantations of "community" are no more a coherent political vision than Arendt's conception of politics as "disinterested" speeches about the good life.

Both Arendt and the communitarians offer a compelling critique of the instrumental and bureaucratic nature of the political culture of mass liberal societies. But their complete dismissal of representative democracy, the welfare state, and political control of the economy leaves them with nothing to say about how to democratize institutional practices. Until their critique moves from the realm of detached political theory into the seamy world of institutional politics, the influence of both Arendtian and communitarian critics of liberalism will rarely exist outside the academy. The Clinton administration itself has taken up these vague, communitarian themes of "the politics of meaning" and "community" in part because it is politically unable to take on dominant socioeconomic interests, such as the health insurance industry. In the name of a self-defeating "pragmatism," the Clinton administration compromises with powerful interests in advance, rather than first vigorously combatting them and then, if necessary, compromising. Witness the administration's designing of an initial health-care plan that aimed to appeal to big business and the large health insurance companies, only to have those vested interests desert the plan at the first opportunity. Clinton's striking unwillingness to take head-on the ideological shibboleths of the Reagan-Bush era that Americans are taxed too heavily and that our national defense is "weak" has precluded his government from advancing those progressive tax reforms and defense cuts needed to provide the resources to redress the deindustrialization of our inner cities and traditional blue-collar communities. The redistribution of resources and opportunities, such as job-training for high-value-added, high-wage jobs or adequately funded health care and day care for single-parent mothers who are supposed to break "the cycle of welfare," is a necessary, though by no means sufficient, condition for the restoration of a national, democratic, communal life. The decline of public intellectual life may mean it is unfair to demand that political theory have clear public political implications. But until political theory confronts politics as it is, and as it plausibly could be, it is likely to remain a peculiarly apolitical form of studying "the political." And indirectly, the absence of a critical, political edge to contemporary political theory contributes to the paucity of vision in our blocked political system.

Toward a Radical, Democratic, Pluralist Communitarianism; or, How Distinct Would It Be from a Liberal, Radical Rawlsian Politics?

The "democratic communitarian" aspects of Michael Walzer's work begins to develop a "situated" theory of rights derived from the shared understandings of membership in a democratic community.[12] It is such a "situated" theory of rights which I believe can end the unproductive impasse between rights-based and communitarian political theorists. Walzer insists that justice is inherently particularist, being dependent on the practices that members of a given community deem to be just. His normative commitment to democracy, however, pushes his theory of complex equality toward a universal commitment to social and political rights. Walzer is, after all, primarily a social democratic critic and not primarily an explicator of the dominant moral understandings of contemporary U.S. political practice. For example, he condemns the existing political practices of imperfect democratic polities that exclude immigrant "guest workers" from full citizenship and he rejects the U.S. practice of providing health care on the basis of need for some, the indigent and elderly, but not for the working uninsured. But what if these policies actually reflect a perhaps morally inconsistent but operative majoritarian political view in that society? Neither predominant German nor U.S. attitudes toward undocumented, immigrant "guest workers" conform to Walzer's democratic defense of their citizenship rights. Are these policies then just or unjust according to Walzer's particularist conception of justice?

That is, internally coherent social practices need not be logically or morally consistent. The antinomies between Walzer's commitment to the universalist claims of democracy and his defense of moral particularism have been widely addressed.[13]

But Walzer's conception of political and social rights as integral to a common commitment to a democratic community does point in the direction of a more political version of Rawls's "idea of an overlapping consensus." This idea contends that political justice is not a comprehensive theory of the good but a moral conception developed when groups holding different and even conflicting views of the good affirm "the publicly shared basis of political arrangements." Rather than advancing a comprehensive theory of the good, Rawls maintains that the overlapping consensus advances a moral conception of those cooperative virtues—tolerance, compromise—by which the plural communities of a democratic society are able to coexist and cooperate in the life of the "supracommunity of communities," a liberal democratic society and state. Rawls's conception of the overlapping consensus represents his most radical move away from the metaphysical grounding of "justice as fairness" in the unencumbered view of the self. Unfortunately, for those attracted to the democratic egalitarian implications of Rawls' earlier writings on justice, his latest book places much greater weight on the value of liberal procedural virtues, such as tolerance and compromise, than it does on the values of economic redistribution, democratic participation, and social rights.[14]

But the contemporary crisis of liberal democratic polities is not primarily characterized by a breakdown of procedural guarantees, as Rawls's recent work seems to imply. Rather, the crisis derives from an eviscerated political and social life that prevents citizens from establishing mutual identification. The absence of shared experience across barriers of class, gender, and in the United States, particularly race, has almost eliminated the concept of social solidarity from popular consciousness. Despite the complex class and social map of the inner-city United States, many white Americans (and even some of the middle-class minority residents in suburbs) share a racially constructed perception of inner-city residents as members of one homogenous, drug-infested "underclass." This conception of an all-pervasive culture of poverty, combined with the means-tested nature of our public health-care and child-care programs (Medicaid and AFDC), has weakened popular support for democratic public provision. Reconstructing a public philosophy and democratic politics committed to universal, decentralized public provision of basic human needs is a central challenge to theorists committed to the value of democratic community. The magnitude of that challenge is succinctly put by the following question: How many Americans would consciously embrace the third value in the classical liberal democratic triad of "liberty, equality, and fraternity," or in gender-neutral terms, solidarity?

One theme of this work has been the need for radical democrats to reject falsely posed dichotomies between centralization and decentralization, individuality and democratic community, and universality and particularity. I have emphasized the need for a radical democratic polity to guarantee and value social pluralism as integral to a free society. But as I have argued elsewhere at greater length, if a politics of democratic inclusiveness is to be revitalized, then a moral and political commitment to social solidarity—to the shared value of citizenship—must be reintroduced into our political life.[15]

If a commitment to rights can be "situated" in membership in a democratic community that values social pluralism and individual participation, then the disagreements about metaphysical conceptions of the self between egalitarian Rawlsian liberals and democratic communitarians may not need to result in significant operative political differences. Perhaps it is time to draw up articles of political, if not philosophical, reconciliation between egalitarian Rawlsian liberals and democratic communitarians, thus ending a seemingly never-ending debate that has yielded little new insight into the nature of politics in modern liberal democracies. Exploring the possibility of such a reconciliation, Charles Taylor queries whether even the most adamant of "proceduralist liberals," while opposing a polity adopting any specific conception of the good, would deny that such a liberal regime needs a noninstrumental commitment from its citizens to the good of procedural justice: "Society must be neutral on the question of the good life. But in the broader sense, where a rule of right can also count as 'good,' there can be an extremely important shared good."[16]

Taylor criticizes the liberal-communitarian debate for sloppily conflating a methodological debate about atomistic (methodological individualist) versus holistic (systemic) modes of social analysis with individualist versus collectivist visions of a good society. A liberal, Taylor argues, might prioritize the defense of individual liberties against the collectivity or state but also believe that society must share a holistic, moral commitment to such prioritization of individual liberty. Pointing toward the liberal-radical democratic synthesis advanced in this work, Taylor observes that any viable regime needs a critical mass of its members to be willing to make sacrifices on its behalf in times of crisis.[17] And, as has often been noted in critiques of liberal instrumental conceptions of the social contract, if citizens simply see the regime as a means for protecting their private interests, they will not be able to overcome "free riderism" and engage in collective action to defend the regime. This is obviously a vexing problem for Hobbesian liberals who state that it is irrational to risk one's life in order to preserve the polity.

It is a historical truism that all viable regimes necessitate, at critical moments, noninstrumental forms of patriotic behavior on the part of significant numbers of citizens. But those favoring a liberal, radical democratic politics, such as Taylor and myself, doubt that such patriotism can be sustained without opportunities for democratic, participatory self-rule. Of course such a thick sense of participatory community may not be necessary for developing certain patriotic sensibilities. The *sui generis* patriotism of the United States is grounded on a militant liberal individualist commitment to individual rights, equal treatment before the law, and the preservation of the ability of interest groups to influence decision makers. But such a liberal civic polity also suffers from an adversarial and fragmented, interest-based political culture. The United States, unlike most other democratic polities having a more collectivist sense of solidarity and social welfare, has made a civil religion out of liberal proceduralism. But even this most liberal of regimes defends its conception of the procedural republic as a moral good.[18] That is, our dominant ideology treats our liberal, self-interested culture as morally virtuous.

A major source of the communitarian-liberal conflict is the investment political philosophers have in believing that a radical disjunction exists between "deontological" and "teleological" political theories.[19] But democratic communitarians who adhere to the teleological "end" of a democratic community implicitly must be committed to those "deontological" political and social rights central to democracy. Advocates of "deontological," allegedly morally neutral theories of rights, when pressed about their substantive moral commitments, almost invariably develop a "thicker," quasi-teleological conception of a liberal democratic community that values equal respect and political autonomy. That both rights-based and communitarian theorists have made such intellectual moves in response to their respective critics demonstrates how all political theories, covertly or overtly, advance both a conception of what it is to be human and an outline of those institutional structures and social practices that foster the development of that humanity. In the case of theorists who are more pessimistic about the human condition, this relationship between judgment of human capacities and institutional structures yields the defense of a political system that aims to contain and channel negative human passions in productive directions (e.g., the social contract conceptions of a Hume or Hobbes).[20] But both Arendt and communitarian theorists, who claim to privilege the political, ultimately advance an impoverished conception of politics because they consciously reject consideration of those socioeconomic institutions that would best promote human development.

FALSE CHOICES: DIFFERENCE VERSUS UNIVERSALITY, FOUNDATIONALISM VERSUS ANTIFOUNDATIONALISM

In a conscious break with Marxism's totalizing tendencies, much of contemporary radical democratic theory, particularly in its postmodernist guise, has learned to value plurality and diversity, perhaps to a somewhat excessive degree. In frequently condemning citizenship and social solidarity as relying on implicit, dominant, male, heterosexual conceptions of humanity, advocates of a "politics of difference" stand the traditional radical antinomy on its head, by privileging the particular and denigrating the universal. But can the moral and cultural opportunities of oppressed groups be enhanced apart from the context of the shared citizenship of a radical democratic polity? Advocates of a "politics of difference," such as Judith Butler, Jane Flax, William E. Connolly, and Bonnie Honig, claim to eschew any commitment to an ontologically fixed, universal conception of human interests.[21] Individual identities are not only socially constructed but are so fraught with the anxious displacement of "difference" and "otherness" that efforts to stabilize the nature of individual identity thwart human freedom.

Thus William Connolly celebrates the agonal, individuated politics of "identity/difference" conflicts situated within each self. Such a critique, however, implicitly depends, as Seyla Benhabib argues, on a universal conception of the equal moral worth of human beings and of the value of open, democratic public dialogue.[22] In a world where everything is perpetually up for grabs, including the coherence of our own selves and the history of our aspirations and projects, the democratic project is rendered extremely problematic, if not unlikely. As Leslie Paul Thiel points out in an insightful review of Honig's book, democratic social movements involve as much the "consolidation" of shared identities as the "deconstruction" of traditional identities. This comment highlights the antinomy within much postmodern political theory between its celebration of particular group identity and its assertion that even a coherent individual identity is a myth of a dominant power/knowledge discourse.[23]

In *Identity/Difference* Connolly locates a liberating political potential in the "agonal respect" for the differences inherent to our own ever-shifting identities. Connolly evinces some uneasiness with the more authoritarian, individualist aspects of Nietzsche but believes we can appropriate "a politicized left-Nietzscheanism [which] unearths building stones in the democratic edifice all too easily buried under the rocks of identity, consensus, the common good, legitimacy, and justice also needed in its construction."[24] Even though Connolly believes these buried stones need not displace this other, more standard, nonfoundational "stonework" of democracy, he, like Honig, radically underestimates the tension between a Nietzscheian "will-to-power" of self-creation and the guarantee of individual rights and security necessary for democratic deliberation.

It is unfortunate that neither Honig nor Connolly wrestle fully with Charles Taylor's defense of the modernist conception of a situated but responsible self as central to the possibility of a shared moral culture.[25] Connolly responds briefly to Taylor's criticisms of his conception of fragmented identity but attempts to domesticate Taylor's insights for the purposes of his own argument. Connolly claims that Taylor's modernist belief that we are not fully free to reconstitute our self and must therefore take responsibility for our situated moral dilemmas is subverted by Taylor's idea of the "Augustinian" dependence of the finite self on belief in an infinite god. That is, Taylor's rationalist claim that the possibility of a moral way of life is grounded in our belief in a coherent, responsible self is undercut, Connolly believes, by his nonrational, spiritual faith.[26] Taylor only indirectly refutes extreme deconstructive views of the self as disjunctive "subject-positions" with no narrative coherence other than that established by power/knowledge discourses. But his *Sources of the Self* is a compelling, modernist defense of the role that the concept of the responsible, coherent self plays in our everyday commitment to individual agency, responsibility, and freedom.

"Postmodern" theorists also depend more on "modernist" conceptions of individual and group agency then they care to admit. For example, almost all these theorists assert that it is in the interest of subaltern groups to fight for greater control over their lives. Such a commitment is implicitly predicated on a belief in the universal, equal moral worth of human beings.[27] After all, why should a group protest if they have less access to social resources or life opportunities unless they believe that each member constituting the group is worthy of the same moral consideration as members of other groups? And why should members of other groups, oppressed or nonoppressed, solidarize with the claims of another subaltern group? In short, a commitment to a radical democratic pluralism is parasitic on Enlightenment beliefs in individual rights and the equality of democratic citizenship.

Contemporaneous to the decline of mass radical politics in the 1980s came a growing intellectual claim that epistemological critique, rather than concrete analysis of political institutions and practices, lay at the center of the radical theoretical project. (Whether such a turn partly derived from the closing of political opportunities for democratic reforms is an interesting issue in the sociology of knowledge which I cannot fully develop here.) Contemporary postmodern theorists, most notably Ernesto Laclau and Chantal Mouffe, as well as antifoundationalist "democratic pragmatists," explicitly Richard Rorty, implicitly Benjamin Barber, claim that a rejection of a foundationalist epistemology is central to a political commitment to the open structure of democratic societies.[28] Democrats, they claim, cannot believe that there exist certain *a priori* truths given by the structure of human reason or experience. A strong argument can be made, however, that no coherent theoretical or empirical relationship exists between epistemological approaches to political theory and operative political conclusions. There have been and will always be Kantian and pragmatist democrats, skeptical and naturalist conservatives. There does often exist a coherent relationship between a theorist's or a citizen's belief in the capacity and potentiality of human beings and the type of political order and institutions which they assert best fulfills those capacities.[29] These issues are at the heart of political theory and practice. But such conceptions can be founded on either teleological religious and ethical cosmologies (foundationalist) or on historicist and pragmatist observations (nonfoundationalist) about existing human practices. The theory of knowledge implicit in one's claims about the human condition does not determine one's political beliefs, nor does one's epistemological orientation determine the normative structure of institutional life which constitutes the core principles of one's political philosophy.

A quick review of contemporary theory provides striking *prima facie* evidence against any claim for a strict causal relationship between epistemological and political perspectives. Robert Nozick, John Rawls, and Susan Okin all work out of a post-Kantian tradition (Kant minus the metaphysics of the noumenal and phenomenal realms), but the first is a libertarian conservative, the second a liberal democrat, the third a feminist social democrat.[30] Jurgen Habermas and Seyla Benhabib both merge aspects of Kantianism and pragmatism in their development of an ethics of "universal pragmatics," yet Benhabib offers a feminist critique of Habermas's distinctions between public and private and between public interests and private moral norms.[31] Michael Sandel, Leo Strauss, and Alasdair MacIntrye all adhere to neo-Aristotelian conceptions of the social constitution of individual identities. Yet Sandel might loosely be described as a democratic communitarian and Strauss as a conservative communitarian, while MacIntyre is a nostalgic premodernist who claims to transcend left-right boundaries, contending that moral virtue can only be instantiated in small, noninstrumental communities.[32] Feminist postmodernists such as Judith Butler or Jane Flax are joined by Connolly in asserting that the epistemological skepticism of a Nietzscheian perspectivism has liberating implications for women and other oppressed individuals, because it rejects a fixed, logocentric, heterosexist notion of identity.[33] But allegedly democratic appropriators of Nietzsche might well heed Benhabib's warning in *Situating the Self* that the Nietzscheian will-to-power not only poses evident nihilist implications but also celebrates a traditional male conception of imposing one's will on the world.[34]

Does an antifoundationalist epistemology hostile to "metanarratives" about human nature and history yield a sounder commitment to democratic practices than do Enlightenment "foundational" claims about the rational capacities of humans? Claims as to the decentered nature of the self pose, in their own fashion, a new metanarrative: that antifoundational epistemology best grounds democracy. In response we might pose two queries: First, can democratic societies function on the basis of nonuniversalist or decentered conceptions of the self, or must members of a democratic culture share certain normative conceptions about the value of human agency and choice? Second, can the demands of particular groups for respect of their identity succeed in the absence of cross-group alliances based on a shared conception of democratic citizenship?

Regarding the first inquiry, do not defenders of democracy, implicitly or explicitly, contend that human beings are of equal moral worth and are the best judges of their own interests? Now this claim could be grounded religiously, historically, or pragmatically, as in the argument that democracy is the best of all imperfect political systems that our culture knows. Democratic practice involves a commitment to some narrative account of why democracy, as compared to nondemocratic regimes, is in the interest of human beings. Democracy cannot be agnostic as to its own moral worth. Such democratically defining moral commitments need not be grounded in grand metanarratives about human rationality or epistemological certitude. As Cornel West's philosophical pragmatist orientation puts it, democracy need not be "backed by noninferential, intrinsically credible elements in experience to justify claims about experience."[35] But the practice of democracy involves ethically treating each individual in accord with his or her moral worth. Of course, just who counts as a full citizen and how to guarantee the exercise of full citizenship rights is an issue confronted daily by antiracist and feminist movements.

As to the second query, a rejection of essentialist or fixed notions of human identity does not deny the possibility of communication or alliances across group identities that while internally diverse and relatively fluid are nonetheless socially and historically constructed realities. A belief in the possibility of cross-group communication implies that these groups share some common culture and system of meaning. We need not argue how extensive that shared sphere must be, but even communitarian and postmodern theorists, if they believe they are engaging in intellectual discourse, must recognize that they are writing for a heterogeneous, "multicultural" audience that shares sufficient cultural understandings to comprehend their arguments. The shared interests and identities of a democratic polity are not ontologically given or epistemologically certain; they develop through the concrete historical experience of an ongoing democratic society. If those experiences do not produce a sense of common interests and shared democratic practices, it is unlikely that the claims of marginal groups to be included will be heard. Given the absence of precisely these sorts of shared public experiences across the urban/suburban and racial divide of U.S. life, and the widespread belief among mainstream state and national political leaders of both parties that voters reside disproportionately "in the suburbs," it is far from certain that our society will address its growing racial, cultural, and socioeconomic apartheid. If not, the "politics of difference" are unlikely to be emancipatory.

LESSONS TO BE LEARNED: REJECTING THE RADICAL VISIONS OF
POSTSCARCITY, THE MONOLITHIC GOOD, AND
THE TRANSCENDENCE OF POWER

Three central lessons may be discerned from this examination of the radical tradition's failure to develop an adequate conception of politics, lessons that must inform contemporary attempts to develop a radical democratic vision of political life. *First*, radical democratic politics must reject the "sociological" assumption of the radical tradition that both scarcity and the division of labor can be completely transcended. *Second*, a radical democratic theory of politics must reject all monistic and fully comprehensive conceptions of the good life. *Third*, radical democratic political theory needs to develop both an adequate theory of power and a theory of political consent.

As to the first concern, scarcity regards far more than the absence of material well-being. Any advanced industrial society would involve a complex social structuring that necessitates democratic deliberation about the allocation of social roles—no matter how much the division of labor may be curtailed through job rotation, job retraining, shorter workweeks, sabbaticals, etc. Time itself is inherently scarce and even the materially affluent must choose among competing desires and values. Even if one brackets the complex relationship between politics and cultural issues and posits a materially abundant society, the political choices confined to socioeconomic concerns remain numerous—consumption versus savings, free time versus necessary labor, quantitative economic efficiency versus enrichment of the working life, how to relate justly to less economically advanced societies.

Second, even if the sociological assumption about the transcendence of material scarcity were achievable, there is no reason to think that there would be one conception of the good that would provide "true" answers to all human dilemmas. Aesthetic, moral, and social dilemmas would remain in even the most egalitarian democracy—e.g., the issues involved in surrogate motherhood, modes of child rearing, euthanasia, uses of public space, public versus private consumption, intergenerational allocation, social policy toward the aging, the teaching of values in public education—the list could go on. There exists no one true set of radical answers to these moral and political dilemmas. The only just solution to these dilemmas would result from democratic deliberation in the context of institutional guarantees of individual and group pluralism.

And it is far from evident why the achievement of one comprehensive conception of the good life should even be a desirable goal. Political life, which can play a fundamental role in enhancing the deliberative capacities of individuals, depends on the existence of diverse visions of the good life. Through political negotiation, confrontation, and reconciliation, citizens can enhance their powers of reasoning, imagining, and evaluating. Of course, not all conceptions of politics affirm these possibilities, but democracy provides the cultural and institutional context for potential individual and group self-realization through political participation.

The conception of democratic politics advanced in this work draws selectively on the radical tradition by insisting that structural economic, racial, and gender inequalities deny each citizen an equal potential voice in political deliberation. Certain left-liberal theorists might assert that the deepest reading of the liberal tradition yields a conception of politics that fulfills the inchoate desires of radical theory for democratic participation. Such a "radical liberalism" could definitively avoid the radical flirtation with the antipolitical.[36] Although the conception of civil society advanced in this work draws on the liberal tradition, that tradition is historically more contestable than "radical liberals" might wish it to be. The predominant liberal tradition advances the view that economic and gender relations are essentially "voluntary" and therefore should not be subject to democratic and public deliberation. If the liberal tradition were unambiguous in its willingness to subject economic power relations to democratic deliberation (to which certain liberals such as John Stuart Mill were amenable), then why does the European liberal tradition remain antiinterventionist in the economic sphere? Even the more social democratically tinged U.S. liberal tradition remains highly ambivalent toward democratic regulation of property rights, an attitude reflected in the Clinton administration's contention that "freedom of choice" in medical care depends on "market choice" of private insurance companies. As is well documented in Canada and elsewhere, socializing the private health insurance industry by establishing a government single-payer system would yield greater choice of private health-care providers, the choice that actually concerns consumers. Thus, at least in the United States, dominant liberal rhetoric still treats corporations as private entities rather than institutions of social power.

Although my project tries to "liberalize" the radical tradition, it still affirms the radical tradition's critique of the inequalities of power within the civil societies of liberal democracies. Thus, one of the remaining challenges facing democrats in relatively open but flawed democratic societies is how to achieve relatively equal power among different interests and communities when society is presently characterized by significant socioeconomic, political, and cultural inequalities among groups. If the system is so closed to a redress of those social inequalities that result in inequalities of political power, then an antisystemic, even revolutionary politics may be necessary. But if the system is somewhat open to social-movement organizing, which periodically has affected state policy and the balance of power in civil society, and if the core democratic social movements are committed to sustaining and expanding the openness of liberal rights, then the only choice for radical democrats is to struggle democratically on the uneven terrain of a flawed liberal democracy. This is the core of the argument as to why a "long march through the institutions" is the only viable—and moral—strategy for democratic radicals in imperfect liberal democracies. But if the governing regime depends on armed repression and the brutal suppression of the basic liberties of person, then covert, illicit organizing, and even armed resistance may be the only moral option for democrats. But given the powerful and technical nature of modern weaponry, revolutionary strategies are likely to be more dependent on popular mobilization and international efforts to delegitimize and isolate repressive regimes then they will be on classic strategies of armed, guerilla conflict. As the struggles against undemocratic and repressive rule in South Africa, Brazil, and Mexico have recently demonstrated, mass popular organizing forms the core of radical democratic politics, even if symbolic acts of violence against noncivilian targets may be salient to maintaining the morale of a repressed population experiencing a protracted popular struggle. In short, in the twentieth century, except for antiimperialist struggles against foreign occupiers, the traditional dichotomy between reform and revolutionary tactics has been an anachronism debated almost exclusively by isolated members of a left intelligentsia who rarely engage in effective political organizing.

PLURALIZING THE SITES OF POWER: THE TRANSCENDENCE OF
THE DEMOCRATIC SOCIALIST PROJECT?

The radical democratic prescriptive commitment advanced in this work is similar in spirit to Joshua Cohen and Joel Roger's effort in *On Democracy* to outline the essential principles of a "radical democratic" political order. A self-defined attempt to integrate the insights of Rawlsian liberalism with Rousseau and Marx's commitment to political and social autonomy, their conception of radical democracy grants priority to political liberty, while asserting that political equality and individual autonomy can only be realized if socioeconomic institutions are democratically and equitably structured. Despite the use of the term *democracy* to describe their desired social order, the reader is tempted to term their operative political philosophy "liberal democratic socialist," in that it stresses the centrality of both institutional guarantees of individual rights, and democratic control over capital, to a democratic order. Cohen and Rogers contend that democracy "cannot be satisfied merely through a proper arrangement of formal arenas of politics, if those arenas remain prey to the intrusions of private power. . . . The power of formal guarantees of freedom and equality is severely constrained by material inequalities in resource allocation and control."[37] One may choose to call such a political order "small d" democratic, but opponents of such a conception of the relationship between economic and political democracy will certainly brand such a regime socialist. Thus, whether or not a socialist society can also be both pluralist and economically viable is likely to remain a central question in radical theory and practice. No change in the semantics of radical democratic theory can change this reality.

Samuel Bowles and Herbert Gintis also claim to transcend democratic socialism in their vision of a "postliberal democracy" that incorporates the liberal tradition's concern with individual rights while applying democratic criteria of legitimacy to not only formal political institutions but also power relations in the spheres of economic and gender relations. They advance a heterogenous conception of power, which envisions structures of rules, language, customs, and laws simultaneously restraining and empowering actors in various sites of social activity (the workplace, the state, the family). Although eschewing an attempt to reduce all forms of domination to one archetype—be it class exploitation or gender or racial domination—they maintain that these diverse sites of power are bound together in "a common process of social reproduction."[38] But they fail to advance a comprehensive social theory of how these various sites of domination "bind together," perhaps because such a social theory would probably utilize terms such as capitalist patriarchy or liberal democratic capitalism.[39] Thus, "naming the system" might well associate Bowles and Gintis too closely with the socialist tradition from which they attempt to distance themselves. To their credit, Bowles and Gintis avoid the pessimistic, ultrapostmodern move of critiquing all authority relations, including democratic ones. (Bowles and Gintis term this position "Foucauldian.") Rather, they claim that although social structures constrain choice, they can be sites of collective resistance which move toward democratic relations of authority.[40] Their work makes a valuable contribution to a radical democratic theory of politics in that it pluralizes the sites of political conflict and seeks to democratize them. They reject attempting to transcend these sites for a future radical politics by refusing to offer a monistic, comprehensive view of the good life or a vision of an emancipated society beyond the need for rights and democratic deliberation.

My work, however, takes fraternal and sororal issue with the efforts of Bowles and Gintis (and other post-Marxists) to distance themselves from the democratic socialist commitment of their previous economic and social analysis.[41] In reality, their analysis of the relations of domination and exploitation within corporations advanced in *Democracy and Capitalism* remains neo-Marxist. A plausible claim can be made that the radical democratic project transcends the democratic socialist tradition, while also incorporating it, by extending the sites of democracy from the economic to the political, sexual, and cultural realms. One can also validly question, as do Bowles and Gintis, whether nonauthoritarian Marxists comprehend that interests are endogenously transformed through democratic collective action. Thus social interests cannot be simply "read off" from the structure of existing social relations and institutions. But Bowles and Gintis go much farther than distancing themselves from economistic forms of Marxism by contending that "the lingua franca" of contemporary democratic polities, "the discourse of rights," renders the democratic socialist project anachronistic and irrelevant. They hold that the struggle for democratizing a capitalist economy will be carried out under the banner of personal rights and democratic voice, not that of social ownership of the means of production.

The irony of this distancing is that most radical democrats, whether Bowles and Gintis, Cohen and Rogers, or Laclau and Mouffe, remain staunch advocates of "economic democracy" and "of the triumph of personal rights over property rights." Yet many recent post-Marxist or ex-socialist converts to "discourse analysis" seem to suggest that political actors voluntarily control the terrain of political discourse.[42] Politics, however, inherently involves the conflict of social interests occurring within the constraints of social structures and discourses that human action can transform, but only within certain structurally and historically determined limits. That is, the discourse of personal rights does not automatically trump the discourse of property rights. In fact, historically, most of the time it has failed to do so. The hegemonic liberal democratic capitalist ideology that equates the power to command of corporate owners and managers with the freedom of choice of individual exchange in the market cannot be simply challenged by speaking the language of personal rights against property rights. In the United States, corporate and political elites have mobilized the ideology of antisocialism not only against radical dissent, but, of greater historical import, against any modest reform that threatens corporate prerogatives. Integral to this antisocialist ideology is the claim that personal rights are guaranteed not only through freedom of individual choice in the market but also by the equation of corporate property rights with the personal rights of supposedly autonomous, small, individual shareholders. Not only are corporate property rights defended by denying the reality that large institutional investors (mutual funds, pensions, etc.) own the vast majority of capital (that is, capital is already socialized, but governed autocratically). The prerogatives of corporate managers are also defended by claiming that working people are incapable of efficiently governing the workplace through democratic means.

Thus, any mass movement that contends that corporate property rights impinge on personal rights would also have to make the case that corporations are social, not private, institutions and that they can and ought to be governed democratically. Even if one calls this alternative vision to democratic capitalism economic democracy, the opposition will certainly term it socialism. The discourse of rights has certainly been widely mobilized by U.S. democratic movements; but it is a contested discourse and has often been used to defend the prerogatives of not only corporate power but also husbands and slaveowners. Although the radical democratic project may be broader than that of democratic socialism, radical democracy needs to defend and incorporate the principled commitment of democratic socialism to economic and social democracy. There is no "discursive" short-cut to achieving a society of political, economic, and social democracy by simply appropriating the language of personal rights. The discourse of rights needs to be supplemented by a discourse and practice of democracy that critiques institutions of domination and exploitation by advancing feasible schemes (and concrete experiments) in democratic self-governance. Bowles and Gintis's faith that the discourse of personal rights will inexorably triumph over the logic of corporate property rights is eerily similar to Marx's teleology of the inevitable triumph of socialized forces of production over private relations of production.[43] By now we should have learned that nothing in politics is inevitable.

Political struggles for radical democracy cannot occur solely on the discursive terrain of rights; they also inevitably involve a struggle about the nature of democracy itself. In the immediate future, movements in the United States for economic justice are likely to focus on extending social rights, such as quality, publicly financed health care and child care, which have been achieved to a greater extent in all other advanced democratic societies. But it is the ideological weakness in the United States of the values of democracy and solidarity, as compared to the power of the values of individualism and market "choice" traditionally associated with the discourse of personal rights, which renders the struggle for minimal, humane reforms difficult. Until large segments of the U.S. public are able to say, "What's wrong with *socialized medical insurance*—or auto insurance or child care for that matter?" there will be little chance of developing quality, decentralized public provision. Thus, despite mainstream pundits' claims that the collapse of authoritarian communism renders all forms of socialism irrelevant to modern political life, the fight to legitimate socialized forms of provision and production remains integral to the revival of anticorporate politics, whether termed "liberal" or otherwise. In operative U.S. political terms, the fate of the "*l* word," *liberalism* (now almost as marginalizing a form of political identification as the "*s* word," *socialism*) remains intertwined with the fate of the socialist left.

The contestation over the discourse of rights partially outlines the rhetorical lines along which the battle for democracy in the United States has historically been fought. The vision of personal rights trumping corporate rights has been central to many of the demands of the labor, feminist, and civil rights movements. But the struggle for redefining personal rights away from its dominant corporate liberal form also involves convincing people that social institutions ought to—and can—be run both democratically and efficiently. That is, not just the rhetorical logic but also the practical expansion of democratic practice is needed to trump the false equation of corporate property rights with personal (and private property) rights. A restored faith in the possibilities of democratic practice, and not simply a discursive relocation of the concept of rights, is necessary to the achievement of radical democratic reform. The struggle is not simply discursive but involves a concrete social power struggle over who should control the means of discourse and communication.[44]

The conception of radical democratic pluralism defended here does not accept all interests or political decisions as legitimate. Radical democrats criticize the control private capital exercises over labor because workers have not freely deliberated over the structure of the economic institutions that govern the bulk of their lives. It also rejects as solely a matter of "private" choice the division of social roles between women and men in child rearing. The absence of public institutional support for child rearing renders unequal the socioeconomic opportunities and political power availabe to women and men. Nor would radical democrats conceive the institution of marriage as strictly a "private" relationship, because the historical construction of the marriage contract has conferred inordinate economic and legal power on men, which in turn contributes to the perpetuation of the physical domination of men over women. For example, in the United States several state legal systems still implicitly endorse the Victorian legal doctrine of male "coverture" of women by denying wives the legal standing to bring rape charges against husbands who physically coerce sex from them.[45] The above considerations need not imply that all radical democrats would concur on precisely how to draw the public/private distinction in conceptualizing democratic practices in child rearing or the family. The authoritarian potential of completely denying a public/private distinction has already been discussed. But where and how to draw such distinctions must be placed at the center of a radical democratic, antisexist politics.

Although many liberals would disagree that democracy necessitates democratic control over capital and the workplace or a radical reconceptualization of the family as a social institution, they would concur with radical democrats that the interests of slaveholders or of a majority in favor of dictatorship cannot be constitutionally tolerated by a democracy. Such interests or choices violate the system's commitment to every individual's capacity for deliberation and judgment. But this democratic intolerance of "undemocratic" interests does not preclude the existence of significant conflicts among interests and among competing conceptions of public policy in a radical democracy.

The need for a radical democratic theory of power and political consent partly arises from liberalism's failure to analyze adequately how disparities of power in civil society affect political power. Radical democrats can reaffirm this critique of liberalism. But radical democrats also need to specify what differentials in authority, expertise, and leadership might justly result from democratic deliberation. Conversely, radical democratic theory must confront the challenge posed by the rich, if diverse, liberal tradition regarding questions of political obligation and consent. A radical democratic politics must speculate as to what system of political organization rational and autonomous moral agents would find agreeable. Is such a system possible—and would it be stable and capable of reproducing itself freely and democratically?[46] A truly *political* theory of radical democracy would have to develop its own depth regarding questions of consent and power such as 1) How can democracy embrace tension and conflict among divergent social groups and conceptions of the public good and yet strive for an ever-shifting but operative, "thin" conception of the public good and for a restructuring of interests that yields a more equitable distribution of political power? and 2) How much social diversity can exist in a society that is relatively cohesive—in which there exists wide agreement on the common rules of the political game and relative equality in opportunities for political participation and power? Another way of positing this endemic dilemma for radical democracy is to ask, How can divergent social groups and interests be placed on a more equal social footing, regarding access to resources and opportunities, without homogenizing them or repressing them by forcing them to conform to dominant social norms?

Although postmodern and social movement theorists correctly highlight the culturally sustaining identities of "difference"—race, gender, ethnicity, sexual preference—as central to the life of a pluralist democracy, they frequently downplay the crucial role that the solidarity of common citizenship would play in a radical democracy. Contrary to the arguments of those postmodernists who counterpose particular identity with the "false universality" of citizenship, the radical democratic pluralist theory advanced herein contends that citizenship is not inherently a "homogenizing" category that reduces all to the pursuit of the same needs and interests. Nor must all forms of public provision conform to the "paternalistic," bureaucratic practices of some contemporary welfare states. Rather, if human beings and the particular communities to which they belong are to be accorded equal respect, then they must belong to a society where the decentralized, public provision of basic human needs guarantees the equal value of membership. Such "social rights" cannot be discovered by abstract philosophical arguments about the social contract. Rather, the nature and extent of public provision will depend on a community's shared understandings of the rights and obligations of its members and of what needs should be communally satisfied if each is to have an equal opportunity to function as a contributing member of the community.[47]

The False Antinomy of Universality versus Particularity: Toward a Radical Democratic Pluralist Politics of Citizenship

The above analysis assumes, of course, that we can distinguish among systems of power as being more or less democratic. An extreme Foucauldian reading of "power/knowledge discourses" denies that power can ever be redistributed in ways that lessen domination. In this view all that the establishment of a new system of power/knowledge or discursive practices does is rearrange the bars on the iron cage of domination.[48] If this be the case, however, why is it that movements for emancipation describe their own histories in terms of social gains and losses, retreats and advances? Is this false consciousness? And was not part of the postmodernist rejection of crude Marxism a skepticism regarding doctrines of false consciousness that enable radical intellectuals to impose their "correct" conception of interests on subaltern constituencies? Perhaps out of a desire to reject the most pessimistic reading of how power determines knowledge, Foucault in his last writings and interviews spoke more favorably of the spirit—if not the metaphysics—of the Enlightenment project and of the responsibility of truth to critique undemocratic institutional power.[49]

If disempowered communities are to strive for more democratic distribution of life opportunities, they inevitably will make claims on fellow citizens who do not fully share their racial, ethnic, sexual, or class identity. Doing so successfully involves a dialectic process of asserting the dignity of that particular group while demonstrating to others how the denial of that particular constituency's rights threatens universal rights. In transformative periods of insurgent democratic politics, the core constituency within a majoritarian, progressive coalition has performed the surrogate function of Marx's universal class, demonstrating how its particular grievances speak to the interests of the vast majority of citizens. For example, while the Congress of Industrial Organizations fought for the particular interests of industrial workers in the 1930s, it successfully contended that the absence of human rights in the workplace posed a threat to the dignity of all citizens. The civil rights movement asserted African-American dignity through contending publicly that the denial of African-American rights symbolized the failure of U.S. democracy to extend its promise to myriad groups and individuals. The recalcitrant nature of racism and the paternalist practices of whites within the civil rights movement engendered a Black Power movement that at times articulated a seemingly radical separatist ideology. But the mainstream of Black Power demanded the same opportunities for economic and political empowerment that other ethnic and immigrant groups had achieved through the interest group and machine politics of the urban United States.[50]

The crisis of the politics of emancipation of oppressed constituencies is not only ideological and discursive but also material. Conditions of stagnant economic restructuring lead not only advantaged groups but also middle strata fearing downward mobility, to reject the demands of the excluded for inclusion. Much of Reagan's and Thatcher's political appeal centered on obfuscating their defense of the deregulation of capital by an appeal to middle strata and working-class resentment against means-tested welfare programs that disproportionately benefit the poor. The ideological nature of this appeal is revealed by the fact that less than 20 percent of U.S. welfare-state expenditure and only 5 percent in the United Kingdom goes to means-tested programs. As to the distribution of the 20 percent of U.S. social-welfare expenditure that is means-tested, three-quarters goes to the relatively popular Food Stamp and Medicaid programs, while only one-fourth goes to the controversial Aid to Families with Dependent Children (AFDC) program. (Thus AFDC constitutes only slightly more than one percent of the federal budget.)

Working-class fear of downward social mobility, combined with an ideological hope that individual effort could avoid such a fate, lay the material basis for a majoritarian, mean-spirited politics of neoconservatism. With continued economic stagnation under conservative governments, it is now harder for the right to portray solidaristic social programs as handouts to the undeserving poor. Growing public support for universal health care and federally financed child care would radically decrease the 20 percent of U.S. social welfare expenditure that is means-tested, because AFDC and Medicaid are essentially nonuniversal child-support and health-care programs provided exclusively to poor children and mostly single parents. But the structural deficit consciously created by the Reagan and Bush administrations to curtail discretionary domestic social spending, combined with Democratic fears of appearing weak on defense or overly aggressive in restoring progressive taxation, severely limits the possibilities for social reform, as the likely punitive nature of Clinton's "welfare reform" well demonstrates.

Without a sustained depression (the 1930s), which eventually creates broad solidarity or a sustained period of rapid growth (the 1960s), which in turn facilitates middle-strata responsiveness to the demands of the marginalized for economic and social inclusion, a politics empowering the disenfranchised is difficult. The absence of concrete gains for excluded constituencies over the past two decades partly explains the resurgence of cultural celebrations of diversity, particularly in academic and intellectual circles. Undoubtedly a cultural and intellectual renaissance can aid the revitalization of communities in crisis; but cultural celebrations of, for example, a feminist ethic of care or an African-American aesthetic cannot by themselves reverse our polity's failure to provide progressively financed, quality child care for working parents or our polity's abandonment of the inner cities. A politics of resistance by besieged constituencies around particularist agendas may have been necessitated by recent conservative governments' attacks on past social gains. But the cost of this defensive politics of the left has come in terms of popular receptivity to the right's ideological claim that the feminist movement, the gay and lesbian movement, the trade union movement, and movements of communities of color represent narrow, "special interests." Even though these movements potentially represent the vast majority of Americans, they have yet to achieve this potential. Thus, even though it is difficult to give credence to the right's claim that mythical, hard-working, risk-taking individual capitalist entrepreneurs represent the true universal class, since the early 1970s the right has been popularly perceived as advancing a more unified, majoritarian approach to the national interest. The end of the Cold War, however, means that the red menace can no longer unite a right profoundly divided between predominantly middle-class, suburban economic libertarians and disproportionately working and lower- middle-class cultural conservatives who favor active state intervention to defend their besieged economic and cultural ways of life. Thus, not only the left, but also the right, faces an immediate future of fragmentation and crisis. We live in a peculiar interregnum where both the governing principles of the left and right stand discredited (Keynesianism-in-one-country for the left, military Keynesianism and deregulation for the right), but where no new majoritarian governing coalition and program has yet taken form. The November 1994 Republican congressional gain around a racially encoded agenda of being tough on criminals and welfare recipients does not mean that the right can build a stable majority around an unrealistic economic program all too reminiscent of a historically discredited "Reaganomics."

An Enlightenment Project without Enlightenment Metaphysics?

Can a radical democratic pluralist politics be adequately grounded in a "hard" postmodern worldview that conceives of society strictly through the prism of social fragmentation and a purely ideological, discursive politics? Or is the current democratic impasse more fruitfully examined (and strategized) as transpiring within an increasingly fragmented society where most individuals long to see themselves as "citizens" or "Americans," while fearing that centrifugal economic and social forces have denuded that concept of any substantive meaning. The longing for solidarity amidst diversity has taken predominantly right-wing, racist, sexist, and xenophobic populist forms in advanced industrial democracies. This longing for a homogeneous universality on the part of the right has been engendered by the unraveling of the symbiotic relationship between the ideal interest of social incorporation (redistribution on the margins) and the material interest of a high-wage, high-growth economy that underpinned the pre-1973 Keynesian "regime of accumulation."[51]

Central to a progressive response to this dialectic of disorienting, social fragmentation will be an intellectual and political recognition that particular identities can only flourish within democratic polities if sustained by a shared commitment to universal citizenship which neither transcends particular identities nor uncritically embraces chauvinist or anti-democratic aspects of such identities. Even Ernesto Laclau and Chantal Mouffe in their more democratic and socialist moments admit that the abandonment of the Enlightenment's epistemological position that there are foundational truths supported by the nature of humanity, god, or reason need not necessitate the abandonment of the Enlightenment project of radical democracy. That is, we can still strive to achieve the political goals of the Enlightenment minus its metaphysical trimmings. Group identity and interests can no longer be deduced from assumptions about the structure of society or the telos of history. But in their more postmodern moments, Laclau and Mouffe and others insist that the discursive self-constitution of groups in relationship to others implied by a postmodern epistemology can rekindle faith in an emancipatory project of self-definition. But to perform an immanent critique of the new radical orthodoxy, one might query whether this outlook has already emerged as a new "metanarrative" of "discursive" coalition-building?[52] The construction of democratic alliances among intertextually, discursively constituted groups will, Laclau and Mouffe contend, depend on the development of democratic practices in as many spheres of human activity as possible. Yet, given that they admit that democracy is itself an indeterminate, contestable concept, how can they believe there is any assurance that the democratic conceptions or interests of subaltern groups will coincide or that the multifaceted identities of members of these supposedly nonessentialized groups will cohere into group behavior?

Around what concrete beliefs, values, and social needs—however epistemologically grounded or not they may be—will such democratic alliances be constructed? Can such alliances transcend concrete intellectual and political investigation of the structural, ideological, and material basis for both shared and contested interests? Laclau and Mouffe might respond that the construction of a common practice of democracy can occur only through discursive interaction and contestation. But would not an essential part of that discourse be a political argument in defense of the equal moral worth of persons and thus the shared interests citizens have, across cultural and identity lines, in a democratic system? And would not part of that "discursive practice" be the discovery and institutionalization of those social programs that speak to the common needs of groups across lines of race, class, and gender domination? If this be the case, then postmodern advocates of "a politics of difference" cannot transcend the democratic dialectic of the universal and the particular, and the ideal and the material.[53] The classical radical tradition's Scylla centered on its granting primacy to the universal aspects of human identity; the new postmodern radical orthodoxy threatens to bring a Charybdis that grants primacy to the particularist aspects of human community. There is no "foundational" reason why intellectual balance and moderation cannot be associated with a radical politics.

The commitment to a purely "discursive" politics assumes both that there are infinite possibilities for political discourse and that subaltern groups share little, if any, common material interests—say in fair economic distribution or democratic control over production or child rearing. It also assumes that there can develop hegemonic alliances based on a normative conception of democracy, even if democratic self-determination for one community is in cultural or material tension with that of another. In the absence, however, of any theory of how social structure and institutional practices cohere to produce a governing political regime, how can a group or theorist strategize about how best to constitute and unite divergent social groups to fight a dominant ruling coalition? Without ascribing to social practices, institutions, and interests a meaning beyond the subjective interpretation of their participants, how can any political actor begin to construct the material and ideological basis for alliance politics? While this politics need not be rooted strictly in material needs, it is not surprising that the basic stuff of cross-cultural coalitions remains the bread-and-butter demands of economic justice (the necessary, but by no means sufficient conditions for human emancipation). Witness the program of Jesse Jackson's second, more inclusive 1988 "Rainbow Coalition" presidential campaign (although Jackson's plebiscitarian populist style may render him a problematic leader for a democratic coalition).

The normative value of democracy itself is sometimes predicated as the concrete basis for coalition.[54] This model for a primarily normative underpinning for a majoritarian radical movement assumes that the democratic interests of differently situated groups can be mediated by shared aspects of moral identity, if not material interest. But democracy as a value in-and-of-itself does not specify the practices or institutions around which groups can cohere. Democratic empowerment for divergent groups can yield political and economic demands that are quite divergent, and even in tension. Both within and among nonhomogenous, differentiated group identities, democratic mobilization is as likely to split as to unite constituencies. Thus, around what concrete social and economic policies such democratic mobilization occurs becomes crucial to majoritarian success or failure. The Gramscian "discursive" alliance politics advocated by Laclau and Mouffe, when stripped of its antiepistemological metanarrative is akin to a long-standing tradition of nonmaterialist, ethical socialism. This tradition has always asserted, regardless of its implicit epistemological orientation, that political struggle in democratic societies can produce shared, if not *a priori*, common interests across subaltern groups by increasing the role of democratic voice in determining the material and cultural conditions of their lives.[55]

CAN POSTMODERNISM GROUND A RADICAL DEMOCRATIC CONCEPTION OF JUSTICE?

Can a "politics of difference" adequately develop a politics of justice which can create operative political cooperation among diverse identities? Iris Marion Young's *Justice and the Politics of Difference* represents an ambitious theoretical attempt to do so. Yet its very effort to develop a postmodern conception of justice unconsciously illustrates the tension between the alleged postmodern proliferation of discourses and subject-positions and the democratic project of achieving a just social order grounded in the equal moral worth of persons. Young advances a trenchant critique of the inordinate focus of liberal theories of justice on the distribution of goods. Such theories, she argues, assume an atomistic, consumerist conception of the individual and fail to see how social goods are produced by decision-making institutions characterized by a structured division of labor. Young contends that a democratic theory of justice must analyze the structure of power within social institutions and the division of labor. She holds that justice as the overarching conception of a social order should be viewed as commensurate with both formal and substantive democratic political life.[56]

Young's argument represents a promising but problematic attempt to join the insights of postmodern theory with the universalist, post-Marxist ethics of Habermas. The virtue of Young's work is that it offers a more political and pluralist vision of Habermas's conception of communicative democracy and illustrates how institutional embodiment of the "ideal speech situation" would erode practices of domination and exploitation.[57] The problematic aspect, which I explore below, is that her unexamined assumption that an "urban" postmodern sensibility of "differences" suffices to create a common moral understanding among diverse identities leads her to gloss over the subversive implications of a postmodern politics for a democratic project such as her own which still embraces such a universal value as equality.

Young locates much of the insurgent activity in favor of democracy in new social movements based on identities of marginality and oppression which fight not so much for distributional reform and assimilation as for greater voice and respect for their particular identity within the polity. Her vision of a democratic community is not one of homogeneity and uniform rights of citizens, but rather of the heterogeneity and differentiated lifestyles of a modern but just city. In her view the diversity of urban life, in its ideal form, would foster the mutual toleration of diverse lifestyles rather than demand homogenous behavior on the part of equal citizens. This conception of communal diversity, in her view, mitigates against the inclination of traditional liberal and radical theories of justice to posit the autonomous and rational chooser of democratic society as a disembodied, gendered male voice of dispassionate reason and disinterestedness.[58]

While Young's critique of the disembodied or uniform voice of Kantian theories of justice reiterates an ontological critique by theorists as divergent as Sandel and Laclau and Mouffe, Young is too sensitive to the intolerant nature of parochial communities to opt for a traditional conception of community. Like Seyla Benhabib, she defends a participatory, diverse conception of community rather than the uniform public of republican and communitarian imagination (Barber, Sandel, MacIntyre). But Young does not adequately deal with the challenge posed by Benhabib's sympathetic critique, and thus more limited appropriation, of postmodernism.[59] New social movement advocates offer a powerful critique of the homogenizing and antipluralist aspects of the liberal and radical traditions. But in their metaphorical politics of rainbow coalitions or heterogenous, vibrant polities, they eschew the fundamental political question of what unites these divergent groups' conceptions of emancipation. An exploration of this problem needs to be centered not on metaphysical or ontological theoretical investigations but on the political sociology of everyday life. A simple posing of this problematic might start with the following example: Why would the end to the domination of gay men and lesbian women *necessarily* entail liberation for straight working-class men and women or inner-city straight (or gay) African Americans? Not that a relationship cannot be articulated between these emancipatory projects, but such relationships need to be openly aired and analyzed in all their cross-cutting cultural tensions. The simple assertion of the unity of the diverse but disempowered is not a suffcent political response to right-wing capturing of a majoritarian discourse.

It is by now a standard postmodern theoretical move to reject essentialist conceptions of group identity by acknowledging that individuals possess multiple, often conflictual, aspects to their identity. Individuals with the ascribed characteristics of a marginalized group do not necessarily act on or share that group identity. Ideological domination and repression plays a role in fostering this reality, but so does the complex nature of individual and group identity itself. In light of the proliferation of social groups mobilized around their particular identities, as well as the existence of many individuals who do not neatly identify with any politicized group, how does one construct a majoritarian democratic public that will support equal political and social rights for subaltern groups? And is there any guarantee that the vision of basic needs and democratic procedures will be exactly the same for each subaltern group?[60]

Thus any postmodern theory of justice cannot avoid the fact that when one critiques the discriminatory or repressive practices of any community—for example, a homogenous white working-class community that excludes people of color—one relies on quasi-universalist values. For justice itself is a universal standard of fairness, though articulated in culturally specific ways. The concept invariably involves making claims about the equal moral worth of persons within a community, though who is included as a member of the community differs radically across political cultures. The claim of equal moral worth need not be transcendentally defended—one can appeal to the democratic and liberal traditions of our own contested, multicultural society. Despite the homogenizing rhetoric of "new social movements," the social basis for many of these movements is not so "new" (i.e., postmaterial), nor are the bases for each postmaterial identity similar (nor even based on ascribed characteristics of race or gender). The ways in which identities are constructed are by no means uniform—an identity as a trade unionist, a woman, an African-American are not formed around the same exact ideal or material interests. And certainly the shared ethical concerns and worldview that unite the environmental and peace movements comprise a different form of shared identity than do the partly ascribed characteristics of ethnicity or race or the basis of identity for a community, of say, shared sexual preference. Thus, to bring together politically communities that not only differ from one another but are also internally diverse, necessitates the development of both a moral vision of radical democracy and a specific program to address shared needs across lines of group identity.

When a "rainbow coalition" seriously attempts to become a multiracial, cross-class coalition, it usually centers its politics on those universal social and economic demands historically associated with social democracy. Given the growing cultural import of insurgent identities, a renewed, majoritarian articulation of the social democratic tradition will, of necessity, be less economistic and more culturally pluralistic than its prior incarnations. But unless accompanied by a universalist commitment to democratic equality, an uncritical celebration of diversity can be easily domesticated and commodified as a post-melting pot ideology—the United States as a "stew" or "salad" of relatively autonomous, pluralist peoples. Such an uncritical pluralist vision, without a moral and political basis to critique inequalities in power, cannot ensure that each group within the stew will have an equal ability to develop the potentiality of its members. Any radical democratic defense of particular identities must also recognize that intolerant versions of nationalist and identity politics threaten the tolerant, democratic, and egalitarian values of pluralist democracy. Once these conceptual and strategic bridges are crossed, then those civil, political, and social rights that would constitute the core of a radical democratic pluralist program might well turn out to be a gender-and-racially sensitive version of Rawlsian liberalism. Unlike standard Rawlsian liberalism, a radical liberal democratic politics would include democratic participation as one of the "primary goods" to be maximized by society not only in the formal institutions of the state, but also in the workplace and community. But such an operative radical democratic politics is more likely to move along the path of a "thicker" democratic and egalitarian liberalism than to be an avant-garde, postmaterialist, postliberal "politics of difference."

TOWARD A RADICAL DEMOCRATIC POLITICS

In light of the demonstrated hostility of the radical tradition to politics, developing a coherent theory and practice of *radical democratic politics* will be no easy task. To be *political*, this vision must grant relative autonomy to the constituent interests, communities, and individuals that constitute a free society, while also comprehending that politics is the means by which these distinct groups work out a common public life. To be *democratic*, political life must be open to all members of society and social interests that obey the politically agreed-on constitutive rules of the polity. To be *radical*, such a political vision advocates within an imperfect democratic polity for a more egalitarian distribution of power and wealth and for a democratic restructuring of undemocratic social interests.

Developing a coherent radical democratic theory of politics will involve both rejecting and affirming aspects of the liberal tradition. Given the radical tradition's scant attention to the protection of both individual liberty and group autonomy, contemporary radical theorists must avoid a crude stereotyping of liberalism as simply an ideology of individual rights, or utilitarian interest-maximization, primarily aimed at protecting the rights of private property. Cohen and Rogers recommend that radical democrats draw on the liberal tradition's historical association "with the strong belief that individual liberties require some recognition not only in principle, but also in the institutional arrangements of political order."[61] Given the paucity of radical democratic thought on institutional guarantees for individual and group liberties, this aspect of the liberal tradition cannot be glibly demeaned as mere "bourgeois liberalism." Although some conceptions of liberalism contend that the existence of individual liberty depends on the sanctity of "free markets" and the unrestricted prerogatives of private property, others do not. The later writings of John Stuart Mill eloquently argued that individual liberty could be compatible with various forms of democratic and cooperative property ownership, coordinated by state-regulated markets.[62] That both contemporary libertarian capitalists and market socialists frequently claim to be the true heirs of the liberal tradition demonstrates just how contestable that tradition remains.

Democratic theory, beginning with de Tocqueville and Mill, moved beyond classical liberalism in emphasizing the development of citizens' self-governing capacities through public deliberation. It also emphasized that in a truly democratic regime sovereignty must be equally exercised. The views of each member of the democratic order must be accorded equal weight in the public arena—one person, only one vote. The democratic tradition, if pressed to its logical conclusion, yields a critique of the inequalities of power in civil society which much of the liberal tradition accepts as inherent to the life of a free society.

A democrat need not agree with all the tenets of Marxian political economy to concur that the ultimate logic of the capital-labor relationship structurally subordinates the interests of labor to capital, because that logic necessitates that capital achieve a private social surplus if the short-term well-being of both parties is to be assured. In a period of economic recession or economic restructuring in a democratic capitalist order, wage restraints are often agreed on by labor in collective bargaining in return for promises by capital to invest in plant modernization and job maintenance. The wage restraint will undoubtedly be imposed by capital on labor. But unless there is a further democratization of the investment process, there is absolutely no guarantee in today's capitalist democracies that the firm in question will fulfill its promise to increase investment at home rather than invest abroad in search of cheaper labor. Nor is there one specific radical democratic position in the debate between "difference" and "egalitarian" feminism, though any adequate radical democratic practice must critique those power dynamics, supported by a cultural, economic, and legal system, that defend patriarchal domination of economic, sexual, and child-rearing relationships. Thus, the struggle for democratic reforms that would expand women's power in the interdependent spheres of economic, sexual, and cultural production must be central to the radical democratic project. Antiracist scholars and activists differ as to how fluid and socially constructed those racial and ethnic identities are which in many cultures form powerful bases for community and culture, but also all too often racial and ethnic chauvinism. Any radical democratic politics must aim to dismantle those social and ideological institutions that reproduce racial and ethnic domination of some groups over others and preclude a democratic politics of difference.[63]

The achievement of such a radical theory and practice of politics necessitates an affirmation of the value of relatively autonomous cultural and social life within truly voluntary institutions of civil society. But such a defense of social pluralism should not be accompanied by an abandonment of the radical critique of the undemocratic nature of many allegedly "voluntary" relations in the civil society of liberal democratic capitalism. Participants in "voluntary" relationships who bring unequal economic, cultural, and intellectual resources to those relationships cannot be judged to be fully autonomous, democratic choosers. Thus, a truly liberal democratic socialism would appropriate the liberal tradition's affirmation of the value of individual civil and political rights but should not abandon the radical tradition's critique of liberalism as being insensitive to the ways that inequality of power in civil society thwarts both formal and informal democratic practices.

The collapse of authoritarian communism, the most blatant historical manifestation of the antipluralist radical tradition, has enabled the phoenix-like resurrection of a long-buried celebration of the market as a purely voluntary, contractual nexus of social relations—this at the very time that the global restructuring of capitalism subjects increasing numbers of people to the involuntary constraints of racial, class, and gender domination. Thus the rebirth of a radical democratic theory and practice is as imperative as ever, despite the momentarily eery, second-time-as-tragedy, reemergence of 1950s-esque theories of the end of ideology and history. Any cursory look at the contemporary United States, let alone the rampant inequalities characteristic of newly emerging "democracies," tells us that social injustice and political challenges remain and that only history will judge how well humanity faces up to those indignities. But in its reconstruction, a radical democratic pluralist politics must avoid the heterosexist and racist construction of allegedly universal practices that in reality instantiate the practices of particular, dominant identities. Conversely, a radical intellectual and activist community needs to be rebuilt which is sufficiently socially rooted in dominant culture that it can convince our fellow citizens that shared universal moral and material interests underpin our particular individual and group desires for democratic autonomy. If not, then the radical democratic project may no longer flounder on the shoals of a repressive, homogenizing, antipolitical universalism, but on those of a fragmenting, Nietzschean politics of the will which can only lead to the further entrenchment of powerful elites.

Radical democratic theory cannot abandon its critique of the material, social, and ideological structure of interests that confer undemocratic power on some over others. The critique of domination, of power relationships that have not been affirmed by free and autonomous moral agents, remains at the core of any radical democratic critique of liberal democracy. But if radical politics is to be democratic, then the restructuring of interests, in relatively open, liberal democratic societies, must result from free political debate and contestation.[64] A radical democratic politics cannot be imposed from above or from without. The messy stuff of conflicts between interests and between competing conceptions of the good will end only when politics and freedom end as well.

CHAPTER 1
INTRODUCTION:
THE RADICAL IMPULSE TO TRANSCEND POLITICS

1. For works of these authors relevant to contemporary democratic theory, see R. H. Tawney, *Equality* (London: Allen and Unwin, 1931) and *The Acquisitive Society* (New York: Harcourt, Brace and Howe, 1920). Tawney's vision of democratic planning did not fully anticipate the need for market mechanisms as a means for ascertaining consumer demand and relative costs of productions. See also G.D.H. Cole, *Self-Government in Industry* (London: G. Bell and Sons, 1919) and *Guild Socialism Restated* (London: Leonard Parsons, 1920). Cole did not adequately envision the relationship between workers' self-government in industry and the political desires of the broader polity, but he did take seriously the problems of national economic coordination among decentralized, worker-owned firms, unlike most others writing in the syndicalist tradition.

2. For a representative (but by no means inclusive) sample of contemporary works in radical democratic theory, see Carole Pateman, *Participation and Democratic Theory* (Cambridge: Cambridge University Press, 1970) and *The Sexual Contract* (Stanford: Stanford University Press, 1988); Robert Dahl, *Democracy and Its Critics* (New Haven: Yale University Press, 1989), *A Preface to Economic Democracy* (Berkeley: University of California Press, 1985), and *After the Revolution: Authority in a Good Society* (New Haven: Yale University Press, 1970); Michael Walzer, *Spheres of Justice* (New York: Basic Books, 1983); Jane Mansbridge, *Beyond Adversary Democracy* (New York: Basic Books, 1980); Benjamin Barber, *Strong Democracy: Participatory Politics for a New Age* (Berkeley: University of California Press, 1984); Amy Gutmann, *Liberal Equality* (Cambridge: Cambridge University Press, 1980); Iris Marion Young, *Justice and the Politics of Difference* (Princeton: Princeton University Press, 1990); Ernesto Laclau and Chantal Mouffe, *Hegemony and Socialist Strategy: Toward a Radical Democratic Politics* (London: Verso, 1985); Joshua Cohen and Joel Rogers, *On Democracy: Toward a Transformation of American Society* (New York: Penguin, 1983); Roberto Mangabeira Ungar, *Social Theory: Its Situation and Its Task*, Vol. 1: *A Critical Introduction to Politics: A Work in Constructive Social Theory* (Cambridge: Cambridge University Press, 1987); and Samuel Bowles and Herbert Gintis, *Democracy and Capitalism: Property, Community and the Contradictions of Modern Social Thought* (New York: Basic Books, 1986). Other works that have influenced this project include Charles Lindblom, *Politics and Markets* (New York, Basic Books, 1977); Norberto Bobbio, *Which Socialism?* trans. Roger Griffin (Minneapolis: University of Minnesota Press, 1987); Frank Cunningham, *Democratic Theory and Socialism* (Cambridge: Cambridge University Press, 1987); Susan Moller Okin, *Justice, Gender and the Family* (New York: Basic Books, 1989); Carol Gould, *Rethinking Democracy: Freedom and Social Cooperation in Politics, Economy and Society* (Cambridge: Cambridge University Press, 1988); and Carmen Sirianni, *Workers' Control and Socialist Democracy* (London: New Left Books, 1982).

3. For Laclau and Mouffe's philosophically "pragmatic" adoption of a commitment to rights, see Laclau, "Politics and the Limits of Modernity," in Andrew Ross,

ed., *Universal Abandon? The Politics of Postmodernism* (Minneapolis: University of Minnesota Press, 1988), pp. 63–83; and Mouffe, "Towards A Liberal Socialism," *Dissent* (Winter 1993): 81–87 Both essays contend that while each author rejects the Enlightenment, foundational, metaphysical assumption about the rational agency of the individual subject, each believes that an emancipatory, pluralist society would need constitutional guarantees of both individual rights and freedom of association. Hence, in a programmatic sense—but not in terms of their theoretical discourse—Laclau and Mouffe admit to being operatively indistinguishable from left Rawlsians or "radical democratic liberals." Despite Benjamin Barber's commitment to equal participation, *Strong Democracy* is so critical of the instrumental and atomized nature of traditional liberal politics that the book barely mentions the necessity of guaranteed rights and liberties if "strong democracy" is to avoid degenerating into the overly harmonious, excessively "solidaristic" democracy of Rousseau which Barber criticizes. Barber attempts to reconcile his commitment to a postliberal participatory democracy with guarantees of civil rights and liberties in his article "The Reconstruction of Rights," *The American Prospect* 5 (Spring 1991): 36–46. This essay is a representative case of what Amy Gutmann describes as democracy's potential to derive a commitment to individual rights not from any specific ontological or metaphysical commitment to an unsituated self, but from the situated commitment of democratic societies to the equality of each individual's opportunity to participate. See Amy Gutmann, "How Liberal Is Democracy?" in Douglas MacLean and Claudia Mills, eds., *Liberalism Reconsidered* (Totowa, N.J.: Rowman and Allanheld, 1983), pp. 25–50.

4. Roberto Mangabeira Ungar develops this insight in *Social Theory: Its Situation and Its Task*, vol. 1, esp. chap. 2, "The Conditional and the Unconditional." As argued below, Ungar's endorsement of a "politics of plasticity" in which all social structures are subject to permanent reconstruction excessively embraces the voluntarist side of this dichotomy. Ungar denies the need of human beings for some degree of secure routine in even the most democratic of societies. He also overlooks the role stable institutions play in a democracy through their promotion of social learning and efficient decision-making. Ungar would benefit from taking seriously the contribution that liberalism's commitment to institutional guarantees of freedom might make to a radical democratic theory of pluralist politics, as would Barber (*Strong Democracy*) and self-identified "postmodern" radical democrats such as William E. Connolly and Bonnie Honig. See Connolly, *Identity/Difference: Democratic Negotiations of Political Paradox* (Ithaca: Cornell University Press, 1991) and Honig, *Political Theory and the Displacement of Politics* (Ithaca: Cornell University Press, 1993).

5. On the importance of the ability of even small, solidaristic groups to shift from consensus-making decision mechanisms to adversary, majoritarian techniques when interests do conflict, see Jane Mansbridge, *Beyond Adversary Democracy*, esp. chap. 3, "The Inner Logic of Unitary Democracy," pp. 23–35.

6. See Charles Lindblom, *Politics and Markets*, esp. chap. 13, "The Privileged Position of Business," pp. 170–88.

7. See Alec Nove, *An Economic History of the Soviet Union*, rev. ed. (Hammondsworth, Middlesex: Penguin, 1982) and "Was Stalin Really Necessary?" *Problems of Communism* 25:4 (July-August 1976): 49–62. Alexander Erlich's *The Soviet Industrialization Debate 1924–1928* (Cambridge: Harvard University Press, 1967) is par-

ticularly insightful in its argument that the social chaos of the first Five Year Plan may have left the USSR more vulnerable to future German militarism than a more gradual industrialization strategy would have.

8. For a classic work in political science that argues that politics involves the "authoritative allocation of values," see David Easton, *The Political System: An Inquiry into the State of Political Science* (New York: Knopf, 1953).

9. For a definition of politics that comes close to imperiously equating politics with the production of all social goods, whether economic, cultural, ideological, social, or sexual, see Adrian Leftwich, *Redefining Politics: People, Resources and Power* (New York: Methuen, 1983).

10. Both Carl Schmitt in *The Concept of the Political*, trans. Carl Schwab (New Brunswick: Rutgers University Press, 1976) and Max Weber, throughout his work, equate politics with the use of force, particularly the legal monopoly of force held by a stable state. My interpretation of politics as the authoritative allocation of social values recognizes the role that force sometimes plays in political life, as its potential use by the state lurks in the background of all regimes to one degree or another. But as Gramsci's concept of hegemony powerfully illustrates, most liberal democratic societies derive their authority more from the tacit consent of the governed than from brute force. In fact, when force has to be overtly mobilized in a modern society, the legitimacy of the state has already been seriously challenged. Of course, even among self-identified left theorists, there is wide divergence as to whether the main causal factors producing such consent are the daily logic of economic and political institutions that act to reproduce themselves, the workings of ideological institutions such as the media and schools, the inertia of everyday life, or the social welfare benefits conferred on the governed that lead them to view radical transformation as either implausible, utopian, wrongheaded, or excessively risky.

11. Don Herzog's comments on the manuscript helped me clarify the relationship between politics and democratic politics which I advance in the work. My central concern is to investigate why the radical tradition did not unequivocally defend the role of democratic conflict in the authoritative allocation of values. By failing to outline a radical vision of democratic politics, theories aiming at an ineluctable "transcendence of politics" were mobilized in defense of the authoritarian, political repression of social and political diversity.

12. For defenses of Marx as an unambiguous democrat and of communism as a viable, postscarcity, postpolitical society, see John Ehrenberg, *The Dictatorship of the Proletariat* (New York: Routledge, 1992); Bertell Ollman, *Dialectical Investigations* (New York: Routledge, 1992); and Andrew Levine, *The General Will: Rousseau, Marx and Communism* (Cambridge: Cambridge University Press, 1993).

13. See Samuel Bowles and Herbert Gintis, *Democracy and Capitalism*, esp. chap. 1, "Present: Politics, Economics, and Democracy," pp. 3–26, for their analysis of the exogenous conception of interests of both the liberal and Marxist tradition.

14. For their conception of politics as more than a process of "getting" but also a process of "becoming," see Bowles and Gintis, *Democracy and Capitalism*, p. 9 and chap. 5, "Action: Learning and Choosing," pp. 121–51.

15. For the effect that political participation can have on transforming participants' conception of their group and public interests, see Benjamin Barber, *Strong Democracy*, particularly chap. 8, "Citizenship and Participation: Politics as Epistemology," pp. 163–212.

16. Barber downplays the role of rights because he fears they promote the instrumental individualism of liberalism and serve as barriers to the reflective transformation of "interests." For Barber an emphasis on "rights" encourages citizens only to "speak" and voice their particular interests. The adversarial culture of liberal rights, in Barber's view, does not encourage the democratic practice of "listening" to others and transforming one's conception of one's interests in light of the expressed needs of others. (See Barber, *Strong Democracy*, pp. 175–76.) But failing to protect individuals' conceptions of their interests—while understanding that interests are socially constructed and transformed through public life—may take away their necessary autonomy to both defend and reflectively transform their desires, projects, and interests. Thus, in order to "listen" democratically, individuals must also have the right to express needs and aspirations different from those of others. And in order to speak publicly, individuals must have some security that their interests will be respected and heard.

17. See Max Weber, "The Social Psychology of the World Religions," in *From Max Weber*, ed. Hans Gerth and C. Wright Mills (Oxford: Oxford University Press, 1952), p. 280.

18. On democracies prohibiting antidemocratic choices that do not respect "the capacity for reasoned choice itself," see Joshua Cohen and Joel Rogers, *On Democracy: Towards a Transformation of American Society*, pp. 146–47.

19. See Dahl, *Preface to Economic Democracy*, chap. 4, "The Right to Democracy within Firms," pp. 111–35; Dahl, *Democracy and Its Critics*, pp. 327–32; and Michael Walzer, *Spheres of Justice*, pp. 291–303.

20. For a provocative account of how the liberal discourse of "the rights of man" gave rise to radical democratic demands for suffrage, see Gareth Stedman Jones, *Languages of Class: Studies in English Working Class History* (Cambridge: Cambridge University Press, 1983). On the relationship between the breakdown of the aristocratic, status-determined hierarchy of seventeenth-century England and the emergence of concepts of individual choice and agency, see Don Herzog, *Happy Slaves: A Critique of Consent Theory* (Chicago: University of Chicago Press, 1989).

21. For the classic mainstream economic analysis of the decision-making process within corporate firms, see Ronald H. Coase, "The Nature of the Firm," *Economica* 4:16 (November 1937): 386–405.

22. Carole Pateman, *The Sexual Contract*, esp. chap. 6, "Feminism and the Marriage Contract," pp. 154–188. Pateman argues that laws of coverture have been eroded but not abolished in many democratic societies.

23. See Roberto Mangabeira Ungar, *Social Theory: Its Situation and Its Task*. My reading of Ungar has been influenced by Stephen Holmes's provocative "The Professor of Smashing," a review of Roberto Ungar, *Politics: A Work in Constructive Theory*, 3 vols., in *The New Republic*, October 19, 1987, pp. 30–38.

24. See Bruce Ackerman, "Neo-federalism?" in Jon Elster and Rune Slagstad, eds., *Constitutionalism and Democracy* (Cambridge: Cambridge University Press, 1988), pp. 153–94.

25. Leon Trotsky, *Literature and Revolution* (New York: Russell and Russell, 1957), pp. 230–31.

26. For this analysis of how vanguard revolutions have succeeded only where the working class was itself sociologically weak, see Michael Walzer, "A Theory of Revolution," *Marxist Perspectives* 5 (Spring 1979): 30–44.

27. See Tawney, *Equality* and *The Acquisitive Society*, George Orwell, *The Collected Essays, Journalism and Letters*, 3 vols., ed. Sonia Orwell and Ian Angus (New York: Harcourt, Brace and World, 1968); and Harold Laski, *The State in Theory and Practice* (New Haven: Yale University Press, 1917) and *Studies in the Problem of Sovereignty* (New York: Viking, 1935).

28. See Perry Anderson, *Arguments within English Marxism* (London: Verso, 1980).

29. See Ernesto Laclau and Chantal Mouffe, *Hegemony and Socialist Strategy: Towards a Radical Democratic Pluralism*. This work, despite its relative inaccessibility to those not schooled in discourse theory, has had a profound impact on post-Marxist theory. It has aided post-Marxism in taking seriously the relative autonomy of politics and the authoritarian implications of totalistic conceptions of identity. But, as I analyze further in Chapter 7, Laclau and Mouffe's argument for the construction of a radical democratic, hegemonic political bloc implicitly relies on Enlightenment conceptions of shared interests and democratic citizenship. As their writing is rather coy about those commitments, their sincere commitment to radical democracy has often been subverted by readers who infer from the work that no majoritarian coalitions are possible across "incommensurable" discourses of identity. Also, their work's emphasis on the discursive construction of reality has been used by postmodern enthusiasts to criticize any analysis of how social structures and institutions constrain individual choice and how material interests continue to play a role in politics, particularly in an era of economic stagnation and global capitalist restructuring.

30. See Jacob Talmon, *The Origins of Totalitarian Democracy* (New York: Praeger, 1960); Bernard-Henri Lévy, *Barbarism with a Human Face*, trans. George Holoch (New York: Harper and Row, 1979); and André Glucksmann, *The Master Thinkers*, trans. Brian Pearce (New York: Harper and Row, 1980).

31. See Trotsky, *Literature and Revolution*, p. 256.

32. See Hannah Arendt, *The Human Condition* (Chicago: University of Chicago Press, 1958); John Gunnell, *Political Theory: Tradition and Interpretation* (Cambridge: Winthrop, 1979); Sheldon Wolin, *Politics and Vision* (New York: Little, Brown, 1960); Benjamin Barber, *The Conquest of Politics* (Princeton: Princeton University Press, 1988); and Bonnie Honig, *Political Theory and the Displacement of Politics*. Loosely grouped, Arendt, Wolin, and Gunnell hold that political theory has been displaced by mass society's prioritization of instrumental, private ends over the public ends of the good life. The means-ends logic of corporate and governmental bureaucracy has displaced public discourse about the proper goals of society.

Barber and Honig are less sociological in their explanation of theory's alleged fall from political grace, finding a more theoretical origin for the displacement of political considerations from contemporary political thought. They believe that theorists have tried to "fix" or "delimit" the political and thus have driven politics from theory. Their arguments imply that contemporary Rawlsian liberals attempt a litigious end to political deliberation through a consensus theory of distributive justice, whereas the communitarians engage in an antipolitical longing for communal adherence to a monistic conception of virtue. Honig argues against the intellectual closure imposed by fixed concepts such as authority, law, sex/gender, and community. Rather, she favors an agonal politics, which would combine and transcend the distinction between Machiavellian *virtù* (skill) and classical moral virtue by realizing that nothing is fixed in politics—all human activities are social, including the creation of the self. Honig locates this potential for self-creation in a fluid, postmodern conception of the self.

This conception of the self, she argues, creates the potential for a disruption of the dominant political order through newly valued political sites of personal struggles for freedom and identity.

Honig's argument that both Rawlsian liberals and communitarian theorists of virtue search for a postconflictual, closed notion of the political has influenced my own work. But her prescriptive recommendation for the retrieval of politics rests, in my view, too heavily on a Nietzschean conception of self-creation and an Arendtian "politics of performativity" (which, to Honig's credit, abandons Arendt's fixed conception of the public/private distinction). Thus Honig takes too lightly the necessity for rights and democratic equality if a world of self-realizing, self-transforming individuals is not to engender the Nietzschean domination of "the strong" over the weak. Her conception of agonal self-creation ignores the reality that the egalitarian social terrain on which a democratic, individualistic agonal politics could occur necessitates a thoroughgoing critique of existing structures of socioeconomic and cultural domination. Nietzsche (or Dewey, a more attractive figure) may be referenced for the belief that there are no ultimate ontological or epistemological guarantees of a stable, fixed personal identity. But if individuals feel that their own self-definition is constantly open to challenge not only by themselves but by others—particularly, but not exclusively, the state—the possibility for democratic collective action, and the individual risk-taking that such action inherently involves, will be severely reduced.

33. For the traditional radical view of the instrumental, contractual nature of classical liberalism, see C. B. Macpherson, *The Political Theory of Possessive Individualism* (Oxford: Clarendon Press, 1962). Although there remains some merit to Macpherson's interpretation, it too crudely reduces different social strata's complex and diverse motivations for the critique of absolutism to a common defense of private property rights in an emerging capitalist marketplace.

34. See Richard Ashcraft, *Revolutionary Politic and Locke's "Two Treatises of Government"* (Princeton: Princeton University Press, 1986), esp. chap. 4, "The Basis of Radical Politics," pp. 128–80; see also James Tully, *A Discourse on Property: John Locke and His Adversaries* (Cambridge: Cambridge University Press, 1990). Herzog's *Happy Slaves* is particularly useful on the diverse historical and political positions of early and modern liberalism regarding conceptions of freedom, autonomy, participation, and consent. I tend to agree with Joshua Cohen's argument that Locke's theory of the social contract does not preclude the institutionalization of a society in which only property owners are enfranchised (Cohen terms this regime a "property-owning democracy"). That is, there are certain conditions, in accord with Locke's initial assumptions, in which it might be theoretically rational for the propertyless to enter into a social contract in which they defer the right to make the laws to only those with property. Cohen argues that Rousseau's conception of the social contract precludes such a class-based suffrage because the property system is not, as is the case in Locke, merely a background of the agreement on the contract but is itself central to the subject matter of the agreement. Thus, I agree with Cohen that although Lockeian liberalism does not eliminate the possibility of representative democracy without property qualifications for suffrage, neither does its conception of the social contract require such a state. See Joshua Cohen, "Structure, Choice and Legitimacy: Locke's Theory of the State," *Philosophy and Public Affairs* 15:4 (Fall 1986): 301–24.

35. In reading the manuscript, Don Herzog suggested this similarity between the conservative and radical longing for social unity. But his comment leaves open the

possibility that "there are different understandings of unity at stake," and I believe there are. The key difference is that conservative unity depends on deference to social hierarchy while radical unity depends on spontaneous and mutual cooperation that transcends the need for any permanent social organization, let alone social hierarchy. Thus, in answer to Herzog's rhetorical question to the author of "Lenin Is the Real Inheritor of Thomas Hooker?" I maintain that their lineages are quite distinct, but their operative postpolitical conclusions express both a crucial affinity and a salient difference.

36. See Barber, *The Conquest of Politics*, esp. chap. 3, "Justifying Justice: John Rawls and Thin Theory," pp. 54–90; Honig in *Political Theory and the Displacement of Politics* argues that Rawls's difference principle fails to silence those who are alienated by its justification of some inequality (chap. 5, "Rawls and the Remainders of Politics," pp. 126–61). Whereas Michael Walzer is politically sympathetic to some of the policy outcomes derivable from Rawls's theory of justice, Walzer contends that such principles of justice can only be established through contingent democratic argument rather than analytic philosophical speculation. Nor does he believe that Rawls's "primary goods" are self-evident; different cultures consider different goods as central to citizenship and life opportunity. See Michael Walzer, *Spheres of Justice*, pp. xiv, 79–82.

37. For an extended argument that true individuality can only be fulfilled through participation in a democratic community, see Alan Gilbert, *Democratic Individuality* (Cambridge: Cambridge University Press, 1990).

38. For an argument of this sort, see Barber, "The Reconstruction of Rights," *The American Prospect* 5 (Spring 1991): 36–46. Sandel has also identified himself as a "pluralist communitarian" in some of his popular writings and academic talks.

39. See John Rawls, "Justice as Fairness: Political, Not Metaphysical," *Philosophy and Public Affairs* 14:3 (Summer 1985): 223–52.

40. See Seyla Benhabib, *Situating the Self: Gender, Community and Postmodernism in Contemporary Ethics* (New York: Routledge, 1992), p. 22.

41. The political implications of some "canonical" postmodernist writings come dangerously close to rejecting all forms of moral discourse and "universal" concepts such as citizenship because they are based on Cartesian, "rationalist" conceptions of the self which are inherently "male" and "repressive." These postmodernists argue in favor of rejecting all universal concepts of identity and for conceiving subjectivity as "decentered," "particular," and "in process." For example, see Julia Kristeva, *Polylogue* (Paris: Seuil, 1977); Sandra Harding, *The Science Question in Feminism* (Ithaca: Cornell University Press, 1986), esp. chap. 7; Jane Flax, *Thinking Fragments: Psychoanalysis, Feminism and Postmodernism in the Contemporary West* (Berkeley: University of California Press, 1990); Judith Butler, *Gender Trouble: Feminism and the Subversion of Identity* (New York: Routledge, 1990); and Chris Weedon, *Feminist Practice and Post-Structuralist Theory* (Oxford: Polity Press, 1987).

For socialist-feminist and radical pluralist conceptions of feminism that reject the extremes of both postmodern and classical liberal views of the self and that strive to develop a sophisticated understanding of the relationship between universal and particular forms of identity, see the introductory essay by Seyla Benhabib and Drucilla Cornell in their collection *Feminism as Critique* (Oxford: Polity Press, 1987); Sabina Lovibond, "Feminism and Postmodernism," *New Left Review* 178 (1989): 5–28; Susan Moller Okin, *Justice, Gender and the Family*; Iris Marion Young, *Justice and the Politics of Difference*; and Seyla Benhabib, *Situating the Self*.

42. As David Plotke has argued in "What's So New about New Social Movements," *Socialist Review* 90:1 (Jan.–March 1990): 81–102, interpreting contemporary social movements as strictly "postmodern" not only ignores the reality that few social movement activists have ever heard of or understand the private language of postmodern intellectuals; such an interpretation also fails to recognize that most social movements not only demand respect for their particular identities but also make claims on fellow citizens for a greater material share of the polity's social and economic resources. That is, social movements may not be so "new" and "postmaterial" or antiuniversal as postmodern theory claims them to be.

CHAPTER 2
THE THREAT OF INTERESTS TO THE GENERAL WILL:
ROUSSEAU'S CRITIQUE OF PARTICULARISM

1. Joshua Cohen's "Reflections on Rousseau: Autonomy and Democracy," *Philosophy and Public Affairs* 15:3 (Summer 1986): 275–97 persuasively analyzes Rousseau's social contract as an attempt to delineate the type of social order human beings conscious of their interdependence would construct if they aimed to maximize their individual autonomy: "What form of association would *socially interdependent individuals* agree to if they were interested in protecting their person and goods and in *being free*?" (pp. 283–84) Note that Cohen rejects the view that all social contract theorists must assume that deliberators are "asocial and purely self-interested." Cohen correctly implies that both Rawls and Rousseau seek to solve collective choice problems involving individuals who are socially interdependent. But, as I will argue shortly, Cohen's interpretation downplays Rousseau's belief that in order to solve this collective choice problem, the importance of particular interests to social life must be radically curtailed by solidaristic cultural mores and practices.

2. See Cohen, "Reflections on Rousseau"; Carole Pateman, *Participation and Democratic Theory* (Cambridge: Cambridge University Press, 1970), esp. pp. 20–26; and Jim Miller, *Rousseau: Dreamer of Democracy* (New Haven: Yale University Press, 1964).

3. Richard Ashcraft and Richard Tuck hold that a careful reading of John Locke indicates that he not only defended liberal rights but also implicitly advanced a case for popular sovereignty and democratic voice in creating those rights. See Richard Ashcraft, *Revolutionary Politics and Locke's "Two Treatises of Government"* (Princeton: Princeton University Press, 1986) and Richard Tuck, *Natural Rights Theories* (Cambridge: Cambridge University Press, 1979). Ashcraft makes a convincing argument that Locke defended the virtues of the labor of the gentry and artisans against the indolence of much of the landed aristocracy. But he admits that Locke disdains the "undeserving poor" and does not provide for representation for those without property. See Ashcraft, *Revolutionary Politics*, chap. 6, "Class Conflict and Electoral Politics," pp. 228–85. It is hard to read Locke as an unqualified democratic theorist, because he only advances the right of property owners to have a voice in those laws that affect the status of their property. Locke did not view democracy as a positive expression of self, but as a prophylactic means for protecting rights in civil society. That is, for Locke, civil and political rights are in accord with an innate human nature that defines acquisition, sociability, and freedom of expression as, hypothetically, characteristic of human society before the existence of government. For Rousseau, the very structure of modern civil society—and property rights—is a conven-

tional creation of democratic sovereignty rather than a product of a static human nature. In an interpretation of Locke closer to my own, Joshua Cohen emphasizes that the internal logic and assumptions of his social contract do not preclude the defense of a "property-owners democracy"; see Joshua Cohen, "Structure, Choice, and Legitimacy: Locke's Theory of the State," *Philosophy and Public Affairs* 15:4 (Fall 1986): 301–24.

4. See Patrick Riley, *Will and Political Legitimacy* (Cambridge, Mass.: Harvard University Press, 1982). Riley contends that there is a profound tension within Rousseau between his commitment to social contract "voluntarism" and to an objective, perfectionist conception of "common good morality" that denies the possibility of free human agency. Riley argues that Rousseau believes the conception of the common good is acquired through a nonvoluntary process of socialization; yet Rousseau, Riley holds, justifies this common good by claiming that truly free citizens would voluntarily will it. Riley describes this tension as "the greatest paradox in all of Rousseau: the paradox created by the fact that in the original contractual situation the motives needed by individuals to relinquish particular will and self-interest to embrace a general will and the common good cannot exist at the time the compact is made but can only be the result of the socialization and common morality that society alone can create" (p. 110).

5. See Cohen, "Reflections on Rousseau," pp. 280–84.

6. Jean-Jacques Rousseau, *The Social Contract*, trans. Gerard Hopkins, in *Social Contract: Essays by Locke, Hume and Rousseau*, ed. Ernest Barker (New York: Oxford University Press, 1962), Book 2, section 3, p. 194: "Where subsidiary groups do exist their numbers should be made as large as possible, and none should be more powerful than its fellows."

7. Richard Fralin, *Rousseau and Representation* (New York: Columbia University Press, 1978).

8. John Dewey, *The Public and Its Problems* (New York: Henry Holt, 1927). I am indebted to Jeffrey Isaac for pointing this out to me.

9. Benjamin Barber in *Strong Democracy* (Berkeley: University of California Press, 1984) frequently cites Rousseau's critique of representative government as paralleling Barber's desire to locate not only sovereignty but also legislative political life in neighborhood or local assemblies. But Barber never cites any passages in Rousseau that outline the deliberative content of local political life—perhaps because there is little evidence to cite. Barber makes a powerful argument for the import of locally based deliberation (neighborhood and workplace councils, etc.), but, as with many "Rousseauian" proponents of "direct democracy," he does not adequately outline the nature of the relationship between national, and perhaps in the future, international, representative institutions and local institutions of popular sovereignty. In an increasingly global economy, the preconditions for local democracy would necessarily involve greater democratic state and international regulation of the movement of capital.

Too often, advocates of participatory democracy advance syndicalist or almost anarchist conceptions of decentralized authority, free of all integrative regulation by a centralized government authority. But the particular associations of a pluralist democratic society need to be regulated by comprehensive national or international institutions of popular sovereignty, if the overall polity is to address existing inequalities of economic and social resources among devolved authorities and interests. On the other hand, conceiving of a democracy without a vigorous political life in the internal workings of neighborhood associations, the workplace, and advocacy groups, as well as vigorous efforts by these associations to influence national political life, would be to envision a polity without meaningful participation by its constituent parts.

10. Rousseau, *The Social Contract*, Book 4, sect. 2, p. 271.

11. Ibid., Book 2, sect. 11, p. 217.

12. Rousseau's belief that women's concerns are inherently limited to the personal and familial leads him to deny their potential to be citizens. In fact, Rousseau believes that women's concerns for the particular interests of their children and husbands is inherently subversive of the public spirit necessary for virtuous political regimes. Thus, women should be excluded from the public sphere as much as possible. I subsequently discuss only the cultural transformations that Rousseau believed civilized men needed to undergo in order to become virtuous citizens only because of Rousseau's sexist assumption that women could never be virtuous citizens.

13. Rousseau, *The Social Contract*, Book 1, sect. 6, p. 181.

14. Ibid., Book 2, sect. 3, p. 194.

15. See Allan Bloom's essay "Rousseau," in Leo Strauss and Joseph Cropsey, eds., *The History of Political Philosophy*, 2nd ed. (Chicago: Rand-McNally, 1972), pp. 532–53; and Bloom's introductory essay in Jean-Jacques Rousseau, *The Emile or "On Education,"* trans. Alan Bloom (New York: Basic Books, 1979), pp. 3–20.

16. Ernst Cassirer, *The Question of Jean-Jacques Rousseau*, trans. Peter Gay (New York: Columbia University Press, 1954).

17. In *Rousseau Juge de Jean-Jacques*, Rousseau wrote: "But human nature does not turn back. Once man has left [the state of nature], he can never return to the time of innocence and equality," as quoted in Cassirer, *The Question of Jean-Jacques Rousseau*, p. 53.

18. Roger Masters, *The Political Philosophy of Rousseau* (Princeton: Princeton University Press, 1968), p. 165.

19. Jean-Jacques Rousseau, *Discourse on the Origin of and Foundation of Inequality among Men* (hereafter referred to as *The Second Discourse*) in *The First and Second Discourses*, trans. Roger D. and Judith R. Masters (New York: St. Martin's Press, 1964), p. 64.

20. Rousseau, *The Second Discourse*, p. 95.

21. Ibid., pp. 95–96.

22. Ibid., p. 113.

23. Jean-Jacques Rousseau, *The Government of Poland*, trans. Willmore Kendall (New York: Bobbs-Merrill, 1972), p. 11.

24. Ibid., p. 14.

25. See Friedrich Wilhelm Nietzsche, *The Use and Abuse of History*, 2nd ed., trans. Adrian Collins (Indianapolis: Bobbs-Merrill, 1957).

26. Rousseau, *The Second Discourse*, p. 115.

27. Ibid., pp. 151, 156.

28. Rousseau, *The Social Contract*, Book 1, sect. 6, p. 180.

29. Rousseau, *The Second Discourse*, p. 130.

30. On this point see Judith Shklar, *Men and Citizens: A Study of Rousseau's Social Theory* (Cambridge: Cambridge University Press, 1969), p. 29.

31. Rousseau, *The Government of Poland*, p. 30.

32. Emile Durkheim, *The Division of Labor in Society*, trans. George Simpson (Glencoe, Ill.: The Free Press, 1947), chap. 2, "The Mechanical Solidarity through Likeness," pp. 70–110.

33. Rousseau, *The Second Discourse*, p. 149.

34. Ibid., p. 154.

35. Ibid., p. 157.

36. Ibid., p. 159.

37. Ibid., p. 162.

38. Ibid., pp. 162, 163.

39. Ibid., p. 177.

40. Ibid.

41. Ibid., p. 170.

42. Ibid., note S, pp. 227–28.

43. Ibid., p. 227.

44. Rousseau, *The Social Contract*, Book 2, sect. 7, p. 207.

45. Shklar, *Men and Citizens*, p. 165.

46. Rousseau, *The Social Contract*, Book 1, sect. 4, p. 170.

47. Ibid., Book 1, sect. 7, pp. 175 and 184, and Book 1, sect. 6, p. 180.

48. Ibid., pp. 180–81.

49. Ibid., Book 2, sect. 5, p. 199.

50. Ibid., Book 1, sect. 7, p. 184.

51. Ibid., Book 2, sect. 3, p. 194.

52. Ibid., Book 2, sect. 3, p. 194.

53. Ibid., pp. 193–94.

54. For Durkheim's optimistic assessment of "organic solidarity," the bonds formed by modern citizens through the comprehension of their mutual dependence on a highly developed division of labor, see Emile Durkheim, *The Division of Labor*, chap. 3, "Organic Solidarity due to the Division of Labor," pp. 111–32.

As Durkheim came to doubt the ability of citizens to comprehend how an advanced division of labor makes them mutually dependent, he increasingly emphasized the need to combat anomie by state-encouraged membership in functionally based corporatist institutions and by state promotion of a civic religion of republican virtue and social solidarity. See his essay "Individualism and the Intellectuals," in Emile Durkheim, *On Morality and Society*, ed. Robert Bellah (Chicago: University of Chicago Press, 1973), pp. 43–57.

55. Rousseau, *The Social Contract*, p. 194.

56. Ibid., p. 196.

57. See Amy Gutmann, "How Liberal Is Democracy?" in Douglas MacLean and Claudia Mills, eds., *Liberalism Reconsidered* (Totowa, New Jersey: Rowman and Allanheld, 1983), pp. 25–50.

58. Rousseau, *The Social Contract*, Book 4, sect. 2, p. 273.

59. Shklar, *Men and Citizens*, p. 29.

60. Rousseau, *The Social Contract*, Book 3, sect. 8, p. 243.

61. Ibid., Book 3, sect. 6, pp. 237–38.

62. Ibid., sect. 10, p. 251.

63. Ibid., sect. 15, p. 262.

64. Ibid.

65. For an excellent historical analysis of the origins of the antinomy in radical thought and practice between representative and direct democratic institutions see Carmen Sirianni, "Councils and Parliaments: The Problem of Dual Power and Democracy in Comparative Perspective," *Politics and Society* 12, no. 1 (1983): 83–123, as well as Carmen Sirianni, "Production and Power in a Classless Society: A Critical

Analysis of the Utopian Dimensions of Marxist Theory," *Socialist Review* 59 (September-October 1981): 33–82. The sections in "Production and Power in a Classless Society" on "Paradoxes of Democracy" and "Expertise and Bureaucracy," (pp. 57–70) are particularly relevant here and to my subsequent discussion of the Marxist tradition's inability to deal creatively with the tensions between participation and expertise and representative and direct forms of participation.

66. Rousseau, *The Social Contract*, Book 3, sect. 1, p. 221; and Book 2, sect. 5, p.197.

67. Ibid., Book 3, sect. 1, pp. 221 and 226.

68. Ibid., Book 3, sect. 17, pp. 264 and 265.

69. Ibid., Book 3, sect. 4, p. 233, and sect. 18, p. 269.

70. For example, Rousseau's distinction between the government and the sovereign people, and his critique of democratic government, is never mentioned in Carole Pateman, *Participation and Democratic Theory*.

71. See Rousseau, *The Social Contract*, Book 3, sect. 4, p. 231.

72. Ibid., Book 3, sect. 10, p. 251, and sect. 18, p. 267.

73. Ibid., Book 3, sect. 18, p. 266.

74. Ibid., p. 267.

75. Ibid.

76. Ibid., Book 4, sect. 1, p. 270.

77. Ibid., Book 4, sect. 2, p. 271.

78. Ibid., p. 272.

79. Ibid., p. 273.

80. Ibid.

81. Ibid., Book 4, sect. 1, p. 269.

82. See Jacob Talmon, *The Origins of Totalitarian Democracy* (New York: Praeger, 1952).

83. Rousseau, *The Social Contract*, Book 2, sect. 3, p. 194.

84. Ibid., Book 4, sect. 8, p. 305.

85. Ibid., Book 4, sect. 2, p. 272.

86. Ibid., Book 2, sect. 7, pp. 204–5.

87. Ibid., p. 205.

88. Ibid., p. 208.

89. Ibid., p. 207.

90. Rousseau, *The Government of Poland*, p. 30.

91. Rousseau, *The Social Contract*, Book 4, sect.8, p.306.

92. For Mansbridge's basic definitions of "unitary" and "adversary" democracy, see Jane Mansbridge, *Beyond Adversary Democracy* (New York: Basic Books, 1980), chap. 2, "Unitary versus Adversary Democracy," pp. 8–22.

93. For representative works see Claude Lefort, *Democracy and Political Theory*, trans. David Macy (Minneapolis: University of Minnesota Press, 1988); Andrew Arato and Jean Cohen, *Civil Society and Political Theory* (Cambridge: MIT Press, 1992); Alan Wolfe, *Whose Keeper: Social Science and Moral Obligation* (Berkeley: University of California Press, 1989); and Jurgen Habermas, *The Structural Transformation of the Public Sphere: An Inquiry into a Category of Bourgeois Society*, trans. Thomas Burger with the assistance of Frederich Lawrence (Cambridge: MIT Press, 1989).

94. The predominantly liberal conception of the social contract in the contemporary United States becomes apparent when one teaches an introductory political

theory course. To define democracy, invariably students' initial, uncoaxed responses focus on individual liberties and equality of economic opportunity. With some prodding reminders about the etymology of the word *democracy*, one might then solicit a vague reference or two to popular sovereignty and self-government. But in the post-Cold War era of "the triumph of the market," rarely will students argue that meaningful democratic participation is predicated on certain limits to social inequality. Nor will it strike them as intuitively plausible that the original justification for many public goods, such as the public education the students may be benefiting from at that very moment, is that they promote reflective membership in the political community. When they are told that the democratic revolutions of the eighteenth and nineteenth centuries were fought for the values of "liberty, equality and fraternity," they usually are not able to define *fraternity*—or, in its gender-neutral form, *solidarity*. This reflects the devaluation of shared membership in a democratic polity by the rampant individualism of the dominant, conservative libertarian ideology of the 1980s.

CHAPTER 3
THE HEGELIAN STATE:
MEDIATING AWAY THE POLITICAL

1. See Zbignew Pelczynski, ed., *Hegel's Political Writings*, trans. T. M. Knox (Oxford: Oxford University Press, 1964), selections on British constitutional reform; and Shlomo Avineri, *Hegel's Theory of the Modern State* (Cambridge: Cambridge University Press, 1972), chap. 11, "The English Reform Bill—The Social Problem Again," p. 208. Avineri points out that although Hegel argued that the British should not adopt universal suffrage but rather a differentiated franchise that would represent legitimate interest groups, he did warn the British that serious economic inequality, the failure to extend the franchise significantly, and the absence of a strong professional civil service threatened the stability of Great Britain.

2. See in particular Stephen Smith, *Hegel's Critique of Liberalism: Rights in Context* (Chicago: The University of Chicago Press, 1989); and also Andrew Arato and Jean Cohen, *Civil Society and Political Theory* (Cambridge: MIT Press, 1992); Alan Wolfe, *Whose Keeper?* (Berkeley: University of California Press, 1989); and Keith Tester, *Civil Society* (New York: Routledge, 1992).

3. See the sections on the decadent particularity of bourgeois privatized culture prior to the revolutionary establishment of the bourgeois state in G.W.F. Hegel, *The Phenomenology of Mind*, trans. J. B. Baillie (New York: Harper Torchbooks, 1967), chap. 6, "Spirit," sect. B1, "Spirit in Self-Estrangement: The Discipline of Culture and Civilization," pp. 541–64.

4. This process culminates in the universal pagan state of Alexander the Great in which there is no autonomy to the private life of the citizen because all must serve the privatized state power of Alexander. Thus the particular, the family, revolts against enslavement to the privately controlled, falsely universal state, thereby subverting the Roman Empire. See Hegel, *The Phenomenology of Mind*, Part C, chap. 6, pp. 494–95.

5. See Alexander Kojève, *Introduction to the Reading of Hegel: Lectures on "The Phenomenology of Spirit,"* assembled by Raymond Queneau, trans. James Nichols, Jr. (New York: Basic Books, 1969), especially chap. 2, "Summary of the First Six Chapters of the *Phenomenology of Spirit*," pp. 31–70.

6. See the section on the master-slave dialectic in Hegel, *The Phenomenology of Mind*, Part B, chap. 4A, "Independence and Dependence of Self-Consciousness: Lordship and Bondage," pp. 228–40.

7. Hegel endorses the initial motivating principles of the French Revolution in which ordinary people abused by the ancien régime risk their lives on behalf of universal laws made by representatives of the citizenry and which treats all citizens as equals: "Freedom demands that the individual recognize himself in such acts, that they should be veritably his, it being his interest that the result in questions should be attained." It is only when the regime attempts to institute a subjective politics of virtue that the freedom of a legal, rational order dissipates. See G.W.F. Hegel, *The Philosophy of History*, trans. J. Sibree (London: The Colonial Press, 1900), Part IV, sect. 3, chap. 3, "The Eclaircissement and Revolution," p. 447.

8. The liberal, legal state includes all male citizens, women being viewed by Hegel as inherently the bearers of the particularism of the family and therefore not capable of the universal behavior necessary for citizenship.

9. Hegel, *The Phenomenology of Mind*, Part C, chap. 6, B3, "Absolute Freedom and Terror," p. 610.

10. See George Lichtheim, "Introduction to the Torchbook Edition," in G.W.F. Hegel, *The Phenomenology of Mind*, esp. pp. xxx-xxxi.

11. For an interpretation of Hegel as a liberal pluralist, see George Armstrong Kelly, *Hegel's Retreat from Eleusis* (Princeton: Princeton University Press, 1978), especially chap. 4, "The Problem of the Modern State." Stephen Smith's *Hegel's Critique of Liberalism* frames Hegel more as a pluralist communitarian whose state promotes and defends the particular ethical identities constructed in civil society.

12. See Bernard Yack, *The Longing for Total Revolution: Philosophic Sources of Social Discontent from Rousseau to Marx to Nietzsche* (Princeton: Princeton University Press, 1986), especially chap. 5, "Hegel: The Longing Tamed," pp.185–223. Yack's reading is closer to Hegel's actual text than is Kojève's. Kojève is clearly involved in a project of reconstructing Hegel's argument in a materialist direction.

13. Hegel, *The Phenomenology of Mind*, Part C, chap. 8, "Absolute Knowledge," p. 807. See also Yack, *The Longing for Total Revolution*, pp. 211–15.

14. For the role of death in maintaining the possibility of individuality in a self-comprehending world where free citizens all have the same status, see Hegel, *The Phenomenology of Mind*, Part C, Chap. 6, sect. B3, "Absolute Terror and Freedom," p. 609: "It is universal will, which in this last abstraction has nothing positive, and hence can give nothing positive for the sacrifice. But just on that account this will is in unmediated oneness with self-consciousness, it is the pure positive because it is the pure negative; and that meaningless death, the unfilled, vacuous negativity of self, in its inner constitutive principle, turns round into absolute positivity."

15. For Kojève's interpretation of the Hegelian end-of-history as the achievement of a self-governing state, see *Introduction to the Reading of Hegel*, pp. 231–36. Kojève emphasizes the transformative role of work and action in achieving the end of history more than Hegel does. That is, Kojève extends the master-slave dialectic across historical epochs. The following quote is fairly typical of Kojève's materialistic appropriation of Hegel: "It is Work, and only Work, that transforms the World in an *essential* manner, by creating truly new realities. . . . Work is what transforms the purely natural World into a technical World inhabited by Man—that is, into a historical World." (pp. 144–45) Hegel would have probably substituted the

concept of spirit for Kojève's concept of work as the means by which humans achieve self-realization.

16. Hegel, *The Philosophy of History*, Introduction, p. 33.

17. Ibid., p. 32.

18. Ibid., p. 21.

19. Alexander Kojève, *Introduction to the Reading of Hegel*, p. 190.

20. Though that victory undoubtedly owed more to the patriotism and nationalism of the Soviet peoples—and efficient production during the war—than to Stalin's brutal collectivization policies and abolition of all dissent within even the Communist Party leadership.

21. For an analysis of the implications for democratic theory of the United States government's attempt in the 1970s and 1980s to include citizen groups in developing and implementing environmental regulations, see an unpublished paper by Carmen Sirianni, "Citizenship, Civic Discovery and Discourse Democracy: Social Movements and Civic Associations in Citizen Participation Programs," proceedings of the September 1993 American Political Science Association Convention, University of Michigan Microfilms.

22. See Shlomo Avineri, *Hegel's Theory of the Modern State*; Charles Taylor, *Hegel and Modern Society*; and Stephen Smith, *Hegel's Critique of Liberalism*.

23. The most influential and persuasive statement of this position is found in Michael Sandel, *Liberalism and the Limits of Justice* (Cambridge: Cambridge University Press, 1982), although Sandel does not explicitly emphasize his affinity with Hegel. Sandel acknowledges, however, that his analysis of the constitutive concept of personal identity draws on that of Charles Taylor, the most astute contemporary interpreter of Hegel. Alasdair MacIntyre's *After Virtue* (Notre Dame: University of Notre Dame Press, 1981) derives its communal conception of identity from the Aristotelian conception of virtue, but although MacIntyre does not explicitly discuss it, the affinity between Aristotle's conception of personal identity and Hegel's has been often noted.

24. See MacIntyre, *After Virtue*, esp. pp. 256–263; and Amitai Etzioni, *The Spirit of Community: Rights, Responsibilities and the Communitarian Agenda* (New York: Crown Publishers, 1993).

25. In addition to Arato and Cohen, *Civil Society and Political Theory*, two other noteworthy examples of this tendency are Norberto Bobbio, "Gramsci and the Concept of Civil Society," and Zbigniew Pelczynski, "Solidarity and 'The Rebirth of Civil Society,' " both in John Keane, ed., *Civil Society and the State* (London: Verso, 1988), pp. 73–100 and 361–380, respectively. Bobbio claims that Gramsci derives his concept of the relative autonomy of civil society more from Hegel than from Marx. Pelczynski, who should be credited with doing much to rescue Hegel from simplistic readings as an authoritarian political conservative, claims that Hegel's concept of associational life in civil society, which influenced Gramsci, ironically came to fruition not in Italy, but in the Solidarity movement in Poland.

26. Smith advances the interpretation that Hegel's corporatist theory of the state aims at promoting "institutions of ethical life, or *Sittlichkeit* . . . to preserve and enhance our right to mutual recognition and esteem" in *Hegel's Critique of Liberalism*, Preface, p. xi.

27. Avineri, *Hegel's Theory of the Modern State*, p. 102.

28. Smith, *Hegel's Critique of Liberalism*, p. 143.

29. See Bernard Yack, *The Longing for Total Revolution*, especially chap. 5, "Hegel: The Longing Tamed," pp. 185–223.

30. Hegel's corporatist regulation of civil society prefigures Durkheim's late-nineteenth-century fears as to the growing anomie of societies characterized by a complex division of labor. In his early work, *The Division of Labor In Society*, Durkheim contends that the functional interdependence of the division of labor will promote a sense of organic unity among the citizens. But the emphasis in his late writings on civil religion, corporatist integration, and public, civic education stems from Durkheim's growing recognition that the modern division of labor hinders individuals from conceiving how their specialized tasks sustain the lives of increasingly differentiated fellow citizens. For the optimistic early view, see Emile Durkheim, *The Division of Labor in Society*, trans. George Simpson (Glencoe, Ill.: Free Press, 1947), chap. 3, "Organic Solidarity due to the Division of Labor," pp. 111–32. For his later corporatist schemes for promoting social solidarity, see *The Division of Labor*, Preface to the Second Edition, pp. 1–31. On the role of civil religion and democratic education in promoting a conscious awareness of the interdependence of functionally differentiated societies, see Emile Durkheim, *Professional Ethics and Civil Morals*, ed. Robert Bellah (Glencoe, Ill.: Free Press, 1958), p. 63, and the essay "Individualism and the Intellectuals" in Emile Durkheim, *On Morality and Society*, ed. Robert Bellah (Chicago: University of Chicago Press, 1973), pp. 43–57.

31. On this point see Smith, *Hegel's Critique of Liberalism*, p. 91.

32. For an insistence on the radical implications of Hegel's political thought, see Richard Dien Winfield's introduction in Joachim Ritter, *Hegel and the French Revolution*, trans. Richard Dien Winfield (Cambridge: MIT Press, 1982), pp. 1–34. David MacGregor also interprets Hegel to be a radical critic of capitalism who argued for greater property rights for workers and a voice in production. MacGregor believes Hegel's reformist vision is more realistic than Marx's because it prefigured both the welfare state and the class compromises embodied in it. See David MacGregor, *The Communist Ideal in Hegel and Marx* (Toronto: University of Toronto Press, 1983), esp. chap. 1, "Hegel and Marx," pp. 11–38.

Although Herbert Marcuse may overestimate the centrality of the critique of the capitalist labor process to Hegel's early political writings, Marcuse argues, in contrast to MacGregor, that Hegel drops this critique in his mature writings. See Herbert Marcuse, *Reason and Revolution: Hegel and the Rise of Social Theory* (Oxford: Oxford University Press, 1941).

33. G.W.F. Hegel, *The Philosophy of Right*, trans. T. M. Knox (Oxford: Oxford University Press, 1952), par. 245, p. 150.

34. Ibid., par. 258, pp. 156–57.

35. Charles Taylor points this out in *Hegel and Modern Society*, p. 79.

36. Hegel, *The Philosophy of Right*, par. 5, p. 22.

37. Ibid., addition to par. 5, pp. 227–28.

38. Although as Patrick Riley has argued, the second formulation of Kant's categorical imperative—that humans should treat each other as if they were ends-in-themselves—can plausibly be read to imply a substantive commitment to the social relations of democratic equality. See Patrick Riley, *Kant's Political Philosophy* (Totowa, N.J.: Rowman and Littlefield, 1982), p. 49.

39. Hegel, *The Philosophy of Right*, pars. 71 and 72, pp. 57–58.

40. Ibid., addition to par. 75, p. 242.

41. Ibid., addition to par. 41, p. 235.

42. Ibid., addition to par. 49, p. 237.

43. Jeremy Waldron, *The Right to Private Property* (Oxford: Oxford University Press, 1988), chap. 10, "Hegel's Discussion of Property," pp. 343–89, esp. part 5, "Poverty and Inequality," pp. 377–86 and Chap. 12, "Property for All," pp. 422–55. Waldron distinguishes between special rights (SR) and general rights (GR) arguments for private property: "The former, associated with Lockeian political theory, sees private property as a right that someone may have rather in the way that he has certain promissory or contractual rights; he has it because of what he has done or what has happened to him. The latter, associated in the last hundred years with Hegelian political theory, sees private property as a right that all men have rather in the way they are supposed to have the right to free speech or to elementary education . . . GR generates a requirement that private property . . . is something all men must have." (pp. 443–44)

44. Hegel, *The Philosophy of Right*, par. 144, p. 105.

45. Taylor develops this point in *Hegel and Modern Society*, p. 82.

46. The same questions may be asked of Frances Fukuyama's argument in *The End of History and the Last Man* (New York: Free Press, 1992). One might term "world historical," without much exaggeration, the ideological and political conflicts that characterize the problematic transition to liberal democracy in the former Soviet republics and Eastern Europe, as well as the newly industrializing, democratizing nations in the Third World. Neither Brazilian, Mexican, nor South African politics are the realm of the materialist, self-satisfied, conformist "last man" of Fukuyama's allegedly hegemonic liberal democracy. Nor do the political and social conflicts of liberal industrial democracies, engendered in part by the globalization of capital, represent an end to politics, material conflict, ideology, or history.

47. Hegel, *The Philosophy of Right*, Preface, p. 10.

48. For a related discussion of Hegel's view of the relationship between modernity and the decline of tragedy, see Judith Shklar, " 'Hegel's Phenomenology': An Elegy for Hellas," in Z. A. Pelczynski, ed., *Hegel's Political Philosophy: Problems and Perspectives* (Cambridge: Cambridge University Press, 1971), pp. 73–89.

49. Hegel, *The Philosophy of Right*, par. 140, p. 102.

50. Yack, *The Longing for Total Revolution*, p. 222.

51. See Fukuyama, *The End of History and the Last Man*.

52. Obviously the Hegelian corporatist state involves more government regulation of civil society than envisioned by classical liberalism. But Hegel's state may be termed liberal in the one sense that it promotes the equal legal and property rights of citizens, regardless of their social status.

53. Hegel, *The Philosophy of Right*, par. 185, p. 123.

54. Steven Smith insightfully describes Hegel's belief in the rationality of the modern state as deriving from his view that the modern state is the first in which the universal good of the state is integrally bound up with the freedom of its particular members. See Smith, *Hegel's Critique of Liberalism*, p. 113, and Hegel, *The Philosophy of Right*, addition to part. 260A, p. 280.

55. See Hegel on the ancient world in *The Phenomenology of Mind*, Part C, chap. 6, sect. A, "Objective Spirit: The Ethical Order," pp. 462–506.

56. *Polizei* is often mistranslated as police; its true meaning is closer to that of the Greek *politeia*, or "regime." This interpretation of *Polizei* is effectively made by Bernard Cullen in *Hegel's Social and Political Thought: An Introduction* (New York: St. Martin's Press, 1979), p. 83.

57. Hegel, *The Philosophy of Right*, par. 199, p. 130 and par. 198, p. 129.

58. Ibid., par. 200, p. 130.

59. Ibid., par. 195, p. 128 and addition to par. 185, p. 267.

60. Hegel's conception of the corporation is similar to the feudal guilds that allegedly united the interests of all those working at a specific craft—whether apprentices, journeymen, or master craftsmen.

61. Hegel, *The Philosophy of Right*, addition to par. 201, p. 270.

62. Ibid., pars. 207 and 209, p. 134.

63. Ibid., par. 207, p. 133.

64. Ibid., par. 294, p. 192.

65. Ibid., par. 296, p. 193.

66. Ibid., par. 297, p. 193. My argument is in certain ways sympathetic with Marx's critique. See Karl Marx, *Critique of Hegel's Philosophy of Right*, ed. Joseph O'Malley (Cambridge: Cambridge University Press, 1972). For a provocative alternative account to Marx's, which claims that Hegel succeeds in defining an attractive "neutral" state that promotes the "common good" among competing particular interests, see George Armstrong Kelly, *Hegel's Retreat from Eleusis*, particularly chap. 4, "The Problem of the Modern State." Hegel contends that the sovereign on the top and the corporations below serve as effective checks-and-balances on the civil service's authority: "The sovereign working on the middle class at the top, and Corporation-rights working on it at the bottom, are the institutions which effectively prevent [the middle class civil servants] from acquiring the isolated position of an aristocracy and using its education and skill as a means to arbitrary tyranny." (*The Philosophy of Right*, par. 297, p. 193.) My argument questions whether, in Hegel's actual schema, either the sovereign or the corporations exercise substantive political power in the context of the highest decisions of state.

67. Hegel argues that the civil servants naturally lose any subjective perspective through their experience as servants of the common good: "In those who are busy with the important questions arising in a great state, these subjective interests automatically disappear, and the habit is generated of adopting universal interests, points of view, and activities." (*The Philosophy of Right*, par. 296, p. 193.)

68. Hegel, *The Philosophy of Right*, par. 292, pp. 190–91.

69. Weber's "ideal type" of modern bureaucrat does not own his office or "means of administration" and can be removed for failure to act according to rules set by those higher in the administrative hierarchy.

70. Hegel, *The Philosophy of Right*, par. 291, p. 190.

71. Weber advocates the reintroduction of values into modern politics through plebiscitary leadership in "Parliamentary Government and Democratization," pp. 1442–62 (particularly the section on "Plebiscitary Leadership and Parliamentary Control," pp. 1451–58) in Max Weber, *Economy and Society: An Outline of Interpretative Sociology*, trans. Ephraim Fischoff et al., ed. Guenter Roth and Claus Wittich (Berkeley: University of California Press, 1978).

72. Hegel, *The Philosophy of Right*, par. 279, p. 183.

73. For a discussion of the role of the working class in the Jena manuscripts, see Herbert Marcuse, *Reason and Revolution: Hegel and the Rise of Social Theory*, chap. 3, pp. 62–90. The lectures relevant to Marcuse's argument were delivered by Hegel at the University of Jena and collected in G.F.W. Hegel, *Jenenser Realphilosophie II*, ed. J. Hoffmeister (Leipzig: Felix Meiner, 1931), esp. pp. 211, 221, and

237–40. Jenaer Systementwürfe III: *Realphilosophie. Gesammelte Werke*, vol. 8, ed. Johann Heinroch Trede (Hamburg: Felix Meiner, 1968), esp. pp. 243–45; 266–67.

74. Translation from G.W.F. Hegel, *Jenaer Systementwürfe* III: *Realphilosophie, Gesammelte Werke*, vol. 8, p. 244.

75. Hegel, *The Philosophy of Right*, par. 243, pp. 149–50.

76. For this analysis see Hegel, *The Philosophy of Right*, par. 245–46, pp. 150–51.

77. See David MacGregor, *The Communist Ideal in Hegel and Marx*, chap. 7, "The External Capitalist State," pp. 195–235.

78. Hegel, *The Philosophy of Rights*, addition to par. 236, p. 276; par. 245, p. 150.

79. *Ibid.*, addition to par. 244, p. 278; par. 242, p. 149; addition to par. 244, p. 278.

80. Ibid., par. 242, p. 149.

81. Ibid., addition to par. 244, p. 278; addition to par. 290, p. 290.

82. Ibid., par. 258, p. 156.

83. Ibid., par. 253, p. 153.

84. Ibid., par. 253, p. 154.

85. Ibid., addition to par. 255, p. 278.

86. This analogy is made by Michael Walzer in *Obligations* (Cambridge: Harvard University Press, 1970), pp. 219–21.

87. Hegel, *The Philosophy of Right*, par. 288, p. 189.

88. Ibid., addition to par. 265, p. 281; par. 278, pp. 180–81; and par. 289, p. 189.

89. Bernard de Mandeville was the only classical liberal theorist who came close to endorsing what is today's stereotypical view of the invisible hand. In contrast, Adam Smith openly acknowledged numerous negative externalities of the unregulated market, including the drudgery of many jobs defined by a rigid division of labor. Smith advocated state action, such as the funding of public education, to address these externalities.

90. See Steven Smith, *Hegel's Critique of Liberalism*, pp. 129–31.

91. Hegel, *The Philosophy of Right*, par. 272, p. 174; par. 273, p. 176; par. 299, p. 194; and par. 273, p. 178.

92. Ibid., par. 302, p. 197; and par. 301, p. 196.

93. Ibid., par. 301, p. 196.

94. Hegel obviously did not envision the future, intensive commercialization and capitalization of agriculture in industrial societies.

95. Hegel, *The Philosophy of Right*, par. 302, p. 197.

96. Ibid., par. 289, p. 190.

97. Ibid., par. 302, p. 197.

98. Radicals who reject national representative democracy in favor of local participatory institutions often speak laudably of the revolutionary bloc councils of Castro's Cuba. These committees may facilitate deliberation about how localities can organize block cleanups and how to make registration of draft-age men more efficient. But do these citizens have an equal voice in determining national environmental or AIDS policy or whether Cuban soldiers should or should not have fought in Angola? Such is the price for posing an either/or proposition between national representative institutions and local, "direct" democratic institutions.

A good indicator of just how free a society is politically is whether borders are open (both ways—for travel and for communication) and whether or not peaceful political opposition can be organized openly and legally at all levels of society. That is, in a society of mass communications, if a citizen cannot locate oppositional political organizations in the phone book—whether the opposition takes the form of parties, factions within parties, or mass organizations independent of state control—then political freedom cannot be said to exist. It is a false juxtaposition to pose economic and social freedoms as superior to (or in tension with) political freedoms, as the empirical evidence indicates that the more government's must be responsible to democratic political pressure the more they will be responsive to people's social needs. That is, Mexico is partly a socially and economically inequitable society because it is not a full political democracy. Nevertheless, there remain some American leftists who would concur with the above statement about the synergistic relationship between political and social democracy in Mexico but argue that the absence of political democracy in Cuba (or under Maoism in China) is excusable because of the greater social and economic equality that exists in these societies as compared to developing capitalist nations. It is now evident, however, that party elites, even in Cuba and Nicaragua, garnered social and economic privileges for their families. Nor is there any compelling evidence that greater political freedoms would threaten social welfare programs. What is certain is that the collapse of the Soviet empire and its economic subsidy of Cuba to the tune of $4 billion a year in subsidized trade relations has severely damaged such programs.

99. Hegel, *The Philosophy of Right*, par. 324, p. 210.

CHAPTER 4
THE ORIGINS OF MARX'S HOSTILITY TO POLITICS:
THE DEVALUATION OF RIGHTS AND JUSTICE

1. The now classic exploration of the problem of aggregating potentially nontransitive individual preference functions into coherent social choices remains Kenneth Arrow, *Social Choice and Individual Values* (New York: Wiley, 1951).

2. Alan Gilbert in his thoughtful comments on a draft of this manuscript suggested the tension between Marx's own methodological self-conception as an analyst of economic laws of motion and the nuanced observations in his journalistic and historical writings on the role of politics in social transformation.

3. Uncritical defenders of Marx might contend that I am imposing twentieth-century conceptions of civil and political rights on a nineteenth-century theorist and activist who fought against an authoritarian Prussia and, at best, a liberal but nondemocratic Great Britain. But, as the work of Gareth Stedman Jones, E. P. Thompson, and Marx's own writings on Chartism demonstrate, demands for civil and political rights were central to the political discourse of the British working-class movements of Marx's own time. See Gareth Stedman Jones, *Languages of Class: Studies in English Working Class History* (Cambridge: Cambridge University Press, 1983); and E. P. Thompson, *The Making of the English Working Class* (New York: Vintage Books, 1963). Marx defended the Chartists' organizing on behalf of universal suffrage against attacks by Owenites and other utopian socialists that the suffrage was irrelevant to revolutionary working-class interests. See Marx, *The Communist Manifesto*, in Robert C. Tucker, ed., *The Marx-Engels Reader*, 2nd ed. (New York: Norton, 1978), p. 499.

4. See Roberto Mangabeira Ungar, *Social Theory: Its Situation and Its Task: A Critical Introduction to Politics: A Work in Constructive Theory* (Cambridge: Cam-

bridge University Press, 1987), esp. chap. 8, "Conclusion: The Radical Project and the Criticism of False Necessity," pp. 199–227.

5. Jon Elster makes a similar point that Marx, in his criticism of abstract theories of justice, ironically (and probably unconsciously) invokes a theory of justice—distribution according to need. See Jon Elster, *Making Sense of Marx* (Cambridge: Cambridge University Press, 1985), p. 222.

6. Carmen Sirianni has written extensively and convincingly on the implausibility of Marx's undefended assumption that scarcity can be completely transcended in any society. In his generous comments on a draft of this manuscript, he argued that even "a classless society must organize an economy of (scarce) time, and every decision to allocate resources implies a specific use of that time." See Carmen Sirianni, "Production and Power in a Classless Society: A Critical Analysis of the Utopian Dimensions of Marxist Theory," *Socialist Review* 59 (September-October 1981): 33–82, particularly pp. 48–56, and Sirianni, "Economies of Time in Social Theory: Three Approaches Compared," *Current Perspectives in Social Theory* 8 (1987): 161–95. "Production and Power in a Classless Society" especially influenced my initial thinking as to how suspending Marx's assumption of the complete transcendence of scarcity has profound implications for a socialist theory of postrevolutionary politics, particularly on the subjects of the tensions between participation and expertise, enrichment of skill versus rotation of jobs, representative versus direct democracy, etc.

7. Hegel and Marx may be somewhat unfair to Kant. The *Critique of Judgment* indicates that Kant is aware that universal moral maxims will produce divergent applications depending on the historical and material circumstances.

8. Marx, *The German Ideology*, in *The Marx-Engels Reader*, pp. 173–74.

9. Allen Wood advances this provocative interpretation of Marx conceiving freedom and autonomy to be nonmoral goods in "The Marxian Critique of Justice," in Marshall Cohen, Thomas Nagel, and Thomas Scanlon, eds., *Marx, Justice and History* (Princeton: Princeton University Press, 1980), pp. 3–41. In "Freedom and Private Property in Marx" in *Marx, Justice and History*, pp. 80–105, George G. Brenkert offers a counterinterpretation of Marx embracing freedom as the highest moral good. Wood's interpretation is probably more in accord with Marx's self-understanding of freedom as a nonmoral "fact" about human needs. But, as I will argue, this self-understanding stands in tension with the obvious moral indignation expressed in much of Marx's condemnation of capitalism.

As my argument develops, it will become evident that I partly sympathize with Marx scholars such as Norman Geras and Jon Elster who, although acknowledging Marx's explicit rejection of moral discourse, read him to be a moral critic of capitalism who incorrectly denies that he is engaging in moral criticism. I stress the debilitating consequences of this self-denial for subsequent Marxian moral and political theorizing even more than does Geras or Elster. See Norman Geras, "The Controversy about Marx and Justice," *New Left Review* 150:2 (March-April 1985): 47–85, and Jon Elster, *Making Sense of Marx*, chap. 4, "Exploitation, Freedom and Justice," pp. 166–233.

10. See Alan Gilbert, *Democratic Individuality* (Cambridge: Cambridge University Press, 1990), p. 203. I am grateful to Gilbert for clarifying his own position in the course of commenting on a draft of the manuscript.

11. Wood's analysis is found in "The Marxian Critique of Justice" in Cohen, Nagel, and Scanlon, *Marx, Justice and History*, pp. 3–41, as well as his *Karl Marx* (New York: Routledge and Kegan Paul, 1981).

12. Marx, *The German Ideology*, in *The Marx-Engels Reader*, p. 171.

13. For the possibility that certain members of the bourgeois intelligentsia will support the communist movement, see Marx, *The Communist Manifesto*, in *The Marx-Engels Reader*, p. 481.

14. Karl Marx, *Capital*, vol. 1, trans. Ben Fowkes (New York: Vintage, 1977), chap. 7, "The Labour Process and the Valorization Process," p. 301.

15. That Marx's specific materialist "science" reduces all morality to class domination does not necessarily mean that alternative realist views of science that attempt to develop a theory of objective human interests of ethical import are inherently flawed. In generous and extensive comments on an earlier draft, Jeffrey Isaac pointed out to me that Marx's problem may not be his scientism, but his particular historicist and class-reductionist "scientific" explanation of ethics. My intuitive response to Isaac, who is both more knowledgeable of and more sympathetic to "realist" conceptions of social science than I, is that all realist views of morality confront the problem that conceptions of objective human needs, beyond the most minimal physical ones, are inherently contestable and do not by themselves produce political agreement. Only political contestation can establish an ever-shifting conception of basic human needs. For an initial attempt at developing a realist account of ethics, see the concluding chapter of Ian Shapiro, *Political Criticism* (Berkeley: University of California Press, 1990).

16. Karl Marx, *Capital*, vol. 1, chap. 10, "The Working Day," p. 375.

17. Ibid., chap. 24, "The Transformation of Surplus Value Into Capital," p. 728.

18. For arguments that Marx condemned capitalism as unjust, see Norman Geras, "The Controversy about Marx and Justice," and Jon Elster, *Making Sense of Marx*, chap. 4, "Exploitation, Freedom and Justice," particularly section 4.3, "Is Exploitation Unjust?" pp. 216–33. Both Geras and Elster contend that although Marx implicitly believed that capitalism was morally unjust, he did not think he thought so. That is, he consciously stated that his condemnation of capitalism was based on amoral, scientific grounds, although his critique simultaneously manifests moral indignation.

Ziyad I. Husami argues that Marx condemns capitalism from the moral perspective of first-stage communism's rewarding of labor according to its contribution. Husami recognizes that Marx believed this was a flawed conception of justice, as compared to the distribution according to need of second-stage or full communism. But, Husami contends, Marx believed that first-stage communism's concept of justice was superior morally to that of capitalist justice. See Ziyad Husami, "Marx on Distributive Justice," in Cohen, Nagel and Scanlon, *Marx, Justice and History*, pp. 42–79.

19. Interpreters who see Marx as condemning capitalism on nonmoral, "scientific" grounds include Allen Wood, "The Marxian Critique of Justice"; Richard Miller, *Analyzing Marx* (Princeton: Princeton University Press, 1984), chaps. 1 and 2, pp. 15–100; and Allen Buchanan, *Marx and Justice* (London: Methuen, 1982), chap. 4, pp. 50–85.

20. G. A. Cohen, Review of Allen Wood, *Marx*, in *Mind* 92:367 (1983): 443.

21. Steven Lukes, *Marxism and Morality* (Oxford: Oxford University Press, 1985), pp. 48–59.

22. Allen Wood, "The Marxian Critique of Justice," and Robert C. Tucker, *The Marxian Revolutionary Idea* (New York: Norton, 1969), pp. 37–53.

23. Gary Young, "Doing Marx Justice," in Kai Nielsen and S. C. Patten eds., *Marx and Morality* (Guelph, Ontario: Canadian Association for Publishing in Philosophy, 1981), pp. 251–68.

24. Marx, *Capital*, vol. 1, chap. 6, "The Sale and Purchase of Labour-Power," p. 280.

25. Of course, the individual's wage, which is proportional to the worker's relative productivity, deducts the individual's contribution to the collective proceeds of labor needed for reinvestment and social insurance. Marx criticizes Lasalle for arguing that communism rewards the worker with the "undiminished proceeds of his labor." See Marx, "The Critique of the Gotha Programme," in *The Marx-Engels Reader*, pp. 528–29.

26. Husami, "Marx on Distributive Justice," in *Marx, Justice and History*, pp. 42–79.

27. Elster, *Making Sense of Marx*, p. 223.

28. See Allen Wood, "Marx on Right and Justice," in *Marx, Justice and History*, pp. 132–33.

29. See Miller, *Analyzing Marx*, chaps. 1 and 2, pp. 15–100.

30. Gilbert, *Democratic Individuality*, particularly pp. 1–18; 197–238; 292–304.

31. Alan Gilbert contends that a process of historical "moral learning" has created a broad liberal and radical consensus on the objective capacity of each individual for moral personality. This consensus is evidenced by the universal condemnation of slavery, genocide, and fascism as subversive of moral personality. What liberals and radicals disagree about, in Gilbert's conception of "moral realism," are not core moral values but only the empirical facts about what society best fulfills such values.

Bracketing the question of whether there are conservatives in our culture who endorse a more hierarchical conception of the distribution of human moral capacity, does Gilbert firmly believe that significant normative disagreements are usually "solvable" by appeal to alleged empirical evidence? Doesn't an observers' normative outlook influence how he or she "empirically" views the world? As Thomas Kuhn's work has shown, aren't "facts" themselves "theory-laden?" Perhaps the relationship between facts and values is even more "dialectical" than this. Within distinct limits, observers may be open to new "empirical" evidence that may influence their moral conception of the world. But what "evidence" can influence them is clearly determined, at least in part, by the normative outlook they currently embrace.

For example, don't those who hold classical libertarian conceptions of freedom interpret the data about alleged disincentive effects of welfare provision extremely differently than do those adhering to social democratic conceptions of substantive equality of opportunity? Most right-wing observers contend that "welfare" (Aid to Families with Dependent Children—AFDC) creates employment disincentives, while most left-wing observers argue that it is not AFDC but the absence of decent-paying jobs and publicly funded, universal health care and child care that create disincentives for AFDC mothers to enter the formal labor market. The right points to the growing number of AFDC beneficiaries as evidence of the disincentive effect, while the left argues that the right's argument is illogical. The left contends that the 40 percent drop in the real, inflation-adjusted value of AFDC benefits in the past fifteen years should have, according to the right's logic of market incentives, significantly increased the attractiveness of work relative to welfare. Yet welfare rolls have expanded, the left argues, because of decreasing inner-city job opportunities and the disincentive effects that loss of Medicaid and child support have on people who consider entering the formal workforce. Are these two normative positions bridgeable through empirical arguments? Or is our perception of the "factual" world affected by our different normative outlooks? "Moral realists" have yet to address this point adequately.

32. See Marx's summer 1853 journalistic pieces in *The New York Daily Tribune* on British imperialism in India, excerpted as "On Imperialism in India" in *The Marx-Engels Reader*, pp. 653–64.

33. See Leszek Kolakowski, *Towards a Marxist Humanism*, trans. Jane Peel (New York: Grove Press, 1968), particularly "Conscience and Social Progress," pp. 128–42.

34. See John Dewey, "Means and Ends," in George Novack, ed., *Their Morals and Ours: Marxist and Liberal Views on Morality* (New York: Pathfinder Press, 1968), pp. 51–58.

35. See Alan Gilbert, *Democratic Individuality*; Peter Railton, "Moral Realism," *Philosophical Review* 95:2 (Spring 1986): 163–207; and Joshua Cohen, "Do Values Explain Facts—The Case of Slavery," *American Political Science Association Proceedings* (University of Michigan Microfilms, 1986).

36. On Marx's mistrust of all forms of market transactions precluding his development of a plausible economic and political vision of a socialist society, see Alec Nove, *The Economics of Feasible Socialism* (London: Allen and Unwin, 1983).

37. See Marx, *Capital*, vol. 1, chap. 10, "The Working Day," pp. 411–16.

38. Admittedly the phrase "free association of producers" is drawn from the French syndicalist tradition, which was concerned with workplace democracy. See Michael Harrington, *Socialism: Past and Future*, (New York: Arcade, 1989), p. 32.

39. Jeffrey Isaac's comments on this section of the manuscript convinced me that an earlier draft overemphasized the democratic aspects of Marx's emancipatory vision. What is striking about Marx's vision of "free association" is that it hardly describes any concrete issues for democratic deliberation which might confront socialist workers or citizens.

40. Andrew Levine, *The End of the State* (London: Verso, 1987), p. 175.

41. Jeffrey Isaac first pointed out to me that it was not only Marx's moral agnosticism but also his perfectionist vision that contributed to many Marxists defending Stalinist terror.

42. See Leon Trotsky, "Their Morals and Ours," in George A. Novack, ed., *Their Morals and Ours: Marxist versus Liberal Views on Morality* (New York: Pathfinder Press, 1968), pp. 1–50, and Maurice Merleau-Ponty, *Humanism and Terror: An Essay on the Communist Problem*, trans. John O'Neill (Boston: Beacon Press, 1969).

43. As mentioned in the Introduction, Alec Nove's and Alexander Erlich's work on 1930s Soviet industrialization demonstrates that there was a tremendous waste of resources under Stalinist "planning" and forced collectivization. It is quite possible that a more moderate industrialization strategy would have yielded superior results. In any event, if Stalin was consciously preparing to defeat fascism, as his apologists argued, why did he squander the two years "gained" by the Hitler-Stalin pact, during which he purged his top military staff and made little, if any, preparations for the ensuing conflict? See Alexander Erlich, *The Soviet Industrialization Debate 1924–1928* (Cambridge: Harvard University Press, 1967), and Alec Nove, *An Economic History of the Soviet Union*, rev. ed., and "Was Stalin Really Necessary?" *Problems of Communism* 25:4 (July-August 1976): 49–62.

44. This is not an *ad hominem* attack on Merleau-Ponty, because he later condemned the immorality of his earlier historicist justification of Stalinism in *Humanism and Terror*.

45. John Dewey, "Means and Ends," in George Novack, ed., *Their Morals and Ours: Marxist versus Liberal Views on Morality*, pp. 51–58.

46. As "shock therapy" exacts its costs, the bloom is increasingly off the rose of the alleged wonders of the (never-existing) free market capitalism of Milton Friedman.

47. Don Herzog correctly pointed out in his reading of the manuscript that my critique of Marx's desire to transcend politics does not in any way prove that politics inherently involves moral judgment. Absent an explicit defense of the role of morality in democratic politics, my critique of Marx could be read to defend a "realpolitik" of pure interest-group competition or could be rejected by Marxists as simply moralizing on behalf of the particular interest of reformist pseudo-radicals. Although the relationship between morality and politics is obviously a large issue, I begin to address it in the brief remarks that follow in the main text.

48. I first heard this term to describe this structure of Marxist moral argument in a lecture on Marxism and morality by Michael Walzer.

49. Sheldon Wolin persuasively interprets Machiavelli as a moral utilitarian theory of "an economy of violence," in Sheldon Wolin, *Politics and Vision* (New York: Little, Brown, 1960), chap. 7, "Machiavelli: Politics and the Economy of Violence," pp. 195–238.

50. As I discuss in Chapter 6, this is also true of the contemporary communitarian critique of rights.

51. Karl Marx, *On the Jewish Question*, in *Writings of the Young Marx on Philosophy and Society*, ed. Loyd D. Easton and Kurt H. Guddat (Garden City, N.Y.: Doubleday, 1967), p. 239.

52. Ibid.

53. Ibid., p. 240.

54. Ibid., p. 228.

55. In commenting on the manuscript, Alan Gilbert argued that Marx's commitment to a social revolution that went beyond mere political changes at the top may have led him to theoretically downplay his operative political commitment to those rights associated with the "bourgeois" political revolutions.

56. In part this explains the intellectual attraction for ex-Marxist, Third World, and Eastern European elites of IMF-inspired, "free market" strategies that essentially promote development for a small upper and middle class at the expense of impoverishment for the vast majority.

57. See Friedrich Engels's introduction to Marx, *The Civil War in France*, in *The Marx-Engels Reader*, p. 629.

58. Marx, *The Civil War in France*, p. 633.

59. Marx, *The Critique of the Gotha Programme*, in *The Marx-Engels Reader*, p. 537.

60. Marx's analysis of the state and his concept of the dictatorship of the proletariat is discussed at greater length in the Chapter 5 section comparing Marx's and Lenin's views on the state and revolution. See pp. 162–77.

61. As to how Marx reduced liberal theories of rights to a narrow defense of private property and how he failed to see how rights might protect other democratic individual and group endeavors, see Steven Lukes, *Marxism and Morality*, pp. 65–70.

62. Shlomo Avineri develops this argument in *The Social and Political Thought of Karl Marx* (Cambridge: Cambridge University Press, 1968).

63. Marx, *On the Jewish Question*, in *The Marx-Engels Reader*, pp. 41–46.

64. Marx, *The Eighteenth Brumaire of Louis Bonaparte* (New York: International Publishers, 1969), p. 66.

65. Marx, *The Critique of the Gotha Programme*, in *The Marx-Engels Reader*, p. 538.

66. After barely surviving, by clandestine means, under lengthy periods of right-wing, repressive rule in the twentieth century, the Italian Communist Party, the Chilean Socialist Party, and the democratic wings of the Spanish and Greek Communist Parties became staunch defenders of civil liberties as goods-in-themselves.

67. For Berlin's now-classic (and much debated) distinction between "freedom from" and "freedom to" see Isaiah Berlin, "Two Concepts of Liberty," in *Four Essays On Liberty* (Oxford: Oxford University Press, 1969), pp. 118–72.

68. See Marx, *The German Ideology*, in *The Marx-Engels Reader*, pp. 161–62.

69. For a fuller discussion of these issues, see Bernard Williams, "The Idea of Equality," in Williams, *Problems of the Self* (Cambridge: Cambridge University Press, 1973), pp. 230–49. Michael Walzer's *Spheres of Justice* (New York: Basic Books, 1983) fully explores the "pluralist" theory of justice implied in Williams's succinct essay.

70. G. A. Cohen, *Karl Marx's Theory of History: A Defence* (Oxford: Oxford University Press, 1978), p. 305.

71. Ungar's essential argument is that "human empowerment depends on diminishing the distance between context-preserving routine and context-transforming conflict," *Social Theory: Its Situation and Its Task*, p. 7. Although he occasionally cautions against the "modernist mistake" by holding that "true human freedom cannot be repeated defiance of all established institutions and conventions," (p. 13) he fails to outline the shared moral practices and institutional procedures that would provide a minimalist social framework for a democratic society that would not have to reinvent, moment to moment, its basic democratic structure. That is, as I argue at greater length against Ungar in Chapter 7, democratic societies need to be committed to some relatively stable forms of democratic procedures and norms.

72. For interesting essays on how constitutional limits on political behavior can promote democracy, see Stephen Holmes's essay and Jon Elster's introduction in Jon Elster and Rune Slagstad, eds., *Constitutionalism and Democracy* (Cambridge: Cambridge University Press, 1988). Elster's introductory essay argues that the traditional posing of the question as the inherent tension between liberal constitutionalism and democracy misperceives the role that self-imposed constitutional limits on majority decisions may play in promoting a stable democratic society. Elster contends that the "expected stability and duration of political institutions is an important value in itself, since it allows for long-term planning. . . . Democracy must rest on popular participation, but on the other hand, it must be protected from the particularism and myopia which can easily result from unchecked popular rule." (p. 14) Neither Elster nor I argue that the current constitutional structure of liberal democracies is fully democratic; the argument that institutionalized corporate property should not be treated as "private," but subject to democratic social regulation, is central to any radical democratic critique of a liberal democratic capitalist order. But that critique does not obviate the need for institutionalized democratic principles and norms in a more just society. On this point see Elster's essay, "Arguments for Constitutional Choice: Reflections on the Transition to Socialism," in *Constitutionalism and Democracy*, pp. 303–323.

Stephen Holmes in "Precommitment and the Paradox of Democracy" argues that self-binding constitutional constraints can be enabling, by constructing constitutive rules for a democratic society, provided that these democratic ground rules can be altered by specified supramajorities: "If we take certain procedures and institutions fixed in the past for granted, we can accomplish more in the current generation by not having to be sidetracked by creating a new basic framework for political life." (p. 217) Ungar's core insight that radical democrats believe in the capacity of human beings to democratically transform the institutional structures that govern their lives can be readily affirmed. But his desire that radical democratic societies be so "plastic" that they would be in a state of constant flux perhaps reflects the social theorist's attraction to permanent theoretical revolution. Ungar radically underestimates the need for relative stability and certainty of expectations which rank-and-file citizens would need in order to engage fully in the plurality of life projects which a radical democratic society seeks to promote.

73. Marx, *The Economic and Philosophical Manuscripts*, in *The Writings of the Young Marx on Philosophy and Society*, p. 312.

74. Ibid., p. 307–8.

75. For Marx's description of "primitive communism" in *The German Ideology*, see *The Marx-Engels Reader*, pp. 160 and 165.

76. In that sense, the stageist theory of the Mensheviks, who believed the Russian Revolution could only establish a bourgeois democracy, was closer to Marx's views than Lenin's voluntarist belief in communist revolution. Marx, in a famous 1881 letter to the Russian Marxist revolutionary Vera Zasulich, did speculate that a form of socialism might develop out of the rural, collectivist traditions of the Russian peasant *mir*: "[The mir] is the mainspring of Russia's social regeneration, but it . . . would first have to eliminate the deleterious influences which assail it from every quarter and then to ensure the conditions normal for spontaneous development" (Marx, letter to Vera Zasulich, excerpted in *The Marx-Engels Reader*, p. 675). The qualifications in his remarks indicate that Marx concurred with the judgment of a lengthy letter Engels sent in 1874 to a Russian populist, Pyotr Tkachov (and which Marx read before its transmission) that the *mir* was no longer farmed communally and was being divided up into nonviable small plots by the commercialization of Russian agriculture. Engels is quite explicit that "spontaneous economic development" toward socialism in Russia would depend on a proletarian revolution in capitalist Western and Central Europe and economic aid to a revolutionary Russian government that, on its own, could not achieve full socialism: "Communal ownership in Russia is long past its period of florescence. . . . Raising it [to collective rather than private cultivation] without it being necessary for the Russian peasants to go through the intermediate stage of bourgeois small holdings . . . can only happen, if, before the complete breakup of communal ownership, a proletarian revolution is carried out in Western Europe, creating for the Russian peasant the [material] conditions requisite . . . to save Russian communal ownership and give it a chance of growing into a new, really viable form" (Friedrich Engels, "On Social Relations in Russia," open letter to Pyotr Tkachov, 1874, excerpted in *The Marx-Engels Reader*, p. 673).

77. Marx, *The Economic and Philosophical Manuscripts*, in *Writings of the Young Marx*, p. 302.

78. Ibid., p. 303.

79. Marx, *The German Ideology*, in *The Marx-Engels Reader*, p. 161. The Tucker volume rather politely translates this phrase as "all the old filthy business would necessarily be reproduced."

80. Lenin's prerevolutionary writings, including *State and Revolution*, explicitly stated that a communist transformation of Russia would depend on a successful communist revolution in Western Europe. Thus it is not surprising that after the failures of the German communist insurrections of 1919 and 1923, Lenin unveiled his New Economic Program that argued that an unaided, long-term transition to socialism in Russia would have to take place on the terrain of a mixed, capitalist economy.

81. Marx, *The Critique of the Gotha Programme*, in *The Marx-Engels Reader*, p. 530.

82. Ibid., p. 531.

83. Ibid.

84. For a more extensive, stimulating analysis of the implications for socialist theorizing of abandoning Marx's vision of completely transcending scarcity (including the inherent scarcity of time and of the life-course), see Sirianni, "Production and Power in a Classless Society."

85. Karl Marx, *The German Ideology*, in *The Marx-Engels Reader*, p. 160.

86. Karl Marx, *Capital*, vol. 3, excerpted in *The Marx-Engels Reader*, p. 441.

87. Karl Marx, *Economic and Philosophical Manuscripts*, as quoted in Erich Fromm, *Marx's Concept of Man* (New York: Frederick Ungar, 1971), pp. 141–42.

88. Barber argues for the democratic, participatory implications of epistemological "uncertainty," as compared to notions of *a priori* or other forms of certitude, in *Strong Democracy* (Berkeley: University of California Press, 1984), pp. 166–69. Barber's "antifoundationalism" may lead him to underestimate the need for a social consensus on one common value—the good of democracy itself and of those individual rights that preserve the ability of each individual to participate in communal deliberation.

89. John Rawls, *A Theory of Justice* (Cambridge: Harvard University Press, 1971), p. 11.

90. See Jon Elster, "Self-Realisation in Work and Politics: The Marxist Conception of the Good Life," in Jon Elster and Karl Ove Moene, eds., *Alternatives to Capitalism* (Cambridge: Cambridge University Press, 1989), p. 127–58.

91. Keynes already demonstrated how the uncertainties of a market capitalist society necessitated such planning, which every democratic capitalist regime engages in to this day. The question remains, On behalf of whose interests do capitalist governments "steer" their economies?

92. Elster, "Self-Realisation in Work and Politics," p. 153.

93. Ibid.," p. 140. Elster argues that because the ideal of self-ownership should govern the principles of socialist distributive justice, then some economic inequalities can be morally justified. But obviously they must be limited if the socialist moral principles of equal respect for persons and equal political power are also to be respected. The extent to which the less able should benefit from the productivity of the more able is a political decision, in his view, that cannot be made according to a neutral, objective standard.

94. Marx, *The Grundrisse*, trans. Martin Nicolaus (Baltimore: Penguin, 1973), p. 705.

95. Karl Marx, *Capital*, vol. 1, chap. 15, "Machinery and Large-Scale Industry," p. 549.

96. Ibid., p. 618.

97. There is an intense contemporary debate about whether information-age technology will "upskill" or "deskill" work. As technology is not simply technological but highly political, the manner in which it is applied in the workplace and in society depends heavily on political factors. That is, computer technology can be used by management to routinize the tasks of workers, making it easier for them to be monitored by management, or it can increase the autonomy and input of individual employees. The intentions of management and the balance of power between management and labor critically affect the application of computer technology. See Shoshana Zuboff, *In the Age of the Smart Machine* (New York: Basic Books, 1988).

98. Marx, *The Grundrisse*, trans. Martin Nicolaus, p. 705–6.

99. Daniel Bell, "The 'Rediscovery' of Alienation," in Shlomo Avineri, ed., *Marx's Socialism* (New York: Lieber-Atherton, 1973), pp. 59–79.

100. Marx, *Capital*, vol. 1, chap. 13, "Cooperation," pp. 448–49.

101. Marx, *The Grundrisse*, p. 706.

102. Marx, *Economic and Philosophical Manuscripts*, in *The Writings of the Young Marx*, p. 306.

103. Marx, *The Grundrisse: Selections*, ed. David McClelland (New York: Harper and Row, 1971), p. 124.

104. Marx, *Economic and Philosophical Manuscripts*, in *The Marx-Engels Reader*, p. 82.

105. Ibid., p. 83.

106. Marx, *Economic and Philosophical Manuscripts*, in *Writings of the Young Marx*, p. 307.

107. Marx, *Economic and Philosophical Manuscripts*, in *The Marx-Engels Reader*, p. 82.

108. Elster, "Self-Realisation in Work and Politics," p. 138.

109. For Marx's conception of "true human suffering" under communism, see Marx, *The Economic and Philosophical Manuscripts*, in *The Marx-Engels Reader*, pp. 87–89.

110. See Yack, *The Longing for Total Revolution* (Princeton: Princeton University Press, 1986), pp. 251–309.

111. See Lukes, *Marxism and Morality*, pp. 86–99.

112. Some readers, depending on recreational and aesthetic preferences, might prefer as an example the problem of how to distribute scarce, skilled ice-skating coaches to aspiring skaters pursuing their People's Olympics dream. (There will also be readers who object to any metaphors of competition. The problem with competition under capitalism is that qualities of respect, monetary reward, and fame which are nonintrinsic to the beauty of, for example, figure skating or playing basketball above the rim, overwhelm the intrinsic value of the performative act. But to say there would be no performance—athletic or aesthetic—nor comparative judgment of that performance under communism is to fulfill the conservative vision of a drab, grey, pseudo-egalitarian vision of communist anti-individuality.) Those who react completely negatively to the pursuit of automotive speed may well reflect a middle-class, intellectual radicalism that disdains mass culture (but these same people probably have enjoyed taking a tight curve). Not that stock car racing would necessarily be a popular spectator sport in a more democratic, egalitarian society (can we know for sure about mass culture in a more democratic society?). Nor need automobiles necessarily be associated with sexist aspects of populist, predominantly working-class white, dispropor-

tionately Southern, culture. But that few contemporary U.S. leftists could correctly identify stock car racing as this country's most popular spectator sport only demonstrates how marginal the left is to U.S. culture. This aside is not meant to argue for a romantic conception of a stereotyped view of white, male, blue-collar culture (urban hip-hop and rap music might be used to prove the same point). The point to be made is that contentious and political issues of preference-development would remain in a relative postscarcity society. Questions of whether or how to subsidize "high culture" and "popular culture," however socially constructed in a radical democracy, would not wither away after the revolution.

113. See G. A. Cohen, "Self-Ownership, World-Ownership and Equality," in Frank S. Lucash, ed., *Justice and Equality: Here and Now* (Ithaca: Cornell University Press, 1986), pp. 108–35, and also "Self-Ownership, World-Ownership and Equality: Part II," *Social Philosophy and Policy* 3:2 (Spring 1986): 77–96.

114. Cohen, "Self-Ownership," p. 113.

115. G. A. Cohen, "Self-Ownership, Part II," p. 88.

116. For the analysis of the nonviability of the "intermediate constitution," see G. A. Cohen, "Self-Ownership," pp. 113–18. For Cohen's hesitancy about Hillel Steiner's "starting gate theory of justice" but his willingness to endorse a reformed version thereof, see G. A. Cohen, "Self-Ownership, Part II," pp. 92–96.

117. Ibid., p. 96. See also Cohen, "Self-Ownership," particularly pp. 112–20 on the tensions between the socialist ethic of autonomous labor (self-ownership) and the socialist commitment to collective control over capital and natural resources.

118. See Ian Shapiro, "Resources, Capacities and Ownership: The Workmanship Idea and Distributive Justice," *Political Theory* 19:1 (February 1991): 47–72.

119. On the theories of justice advanced by Rawls and Dworkin being closer to the tradition of European social democracy (agnostic on the organization of the economy, but radically egalitarian in distributional implications) and to the "left of Marx" in rejecting the self-ownership thesis, see Cohen, "Self-Ownership, " pp. 113–15.

120. Rawls argues for the morally arbitrary nature of individual abilities and of upbringing's influence on their development in *A Theory of Justice*, pp. 12, 15, 72–73, 101–3. For his statement that people should still be held responsible for their preferences, see "Social Unity and Primary Goods" in Amartya Sen and Bernard Williams, eds., *Utilitarianism and Beyond* (Cambridge: Cambridge University Press, 1982), pp. 168–69. Rawls does countenance limited material incentives—those necessary to get the talented to contribute their talents and efforts to an extent that advantages the least well off group.

121. Dworkin makes the case for compensating those with inferior personal endowments and abilities in "What is Equality? Part II: Equality of Resources," *Philosophy and Public Affairs* 10 (Fall 1981): 300–301.

122. See Shapiro, "Resources, Capacities and Ownership," p. 64.

123. On a theory of justice being "ambition sensitive" by rewarding the benefits that individuals' choice of pursuits and diligence in pursuing them brings to others, see Dworkin, "What is Equality? Part II: Equality of Resources," pp. 288, 302, 311.

124. See Rawls, "Social Unity and Primary Goods," pp. 168–69.

125. See Shapiro, "Resources, Capacities and Workmanship," p. 60.

126. See Elster, "Self-Realization in Work and Politics," p. 132.

127. Shapiro, "Resources, Capacities and Ownership," p. 63.

128. See Jon Elster, "Self-Realisation in Work and Politics," p. 149.

129. Shapiro's concluding section is particularly astute in its defense of the inherently democratic nature of any fair distributive theory of justice. See Shapiro, "Resources, Capacities and Ownership," part 6, "Productive Fictions? Consequentialist and Democratic Considerations," pp. 63–66.

130. Marx, *The Economic and Philosophical Manuscripts*, in *The Marx-Engels Reader*, p. 81.

CHAPTER 5
LENIN (AND MARX) ON THE SCIENCES OF
CONSCIOUSNESS AND PRODUCTION:
THE ABOLITION OF POLITICAL JUDGMENT

1. See Leon Trotsky, *The History of the Russian Revolution*, trans. Max Eastman (Ann Arbor: University of Michigan Press, 1967).

2. Adam Ulam, *The Bolsheviks* (New York: MacMillan, 1969), p. 462.

3. The famous summation of *State and Revolution*'s view of postrevolutionary governance is actually not from the text itself but from an indirect commentary on it in a satirical poem by Mayakovsky. See V. Mayakovsky, "Vladimir Ilyich Lenin," in *Mayakovsky*, trans. and ed. Herbert Marshall (New York: Hill and Wang, 1965), p. 305.

4. See Jurgen Habermas, *Knowledge and Human Interests*, trans. Jeremy Shapiro (Boston: Beacon Press, 1971), chaps. 2 and 3; also *Towards a Rational Society*, trans. Jeremy Shapiro (Boston: Beacon Press, 1970), pp. 80–122. Albrecht Wellmer also develops this theme in *A Critical Theory of Society*, trans. John Cumming (New York: Herder and Herder, 1971), esp. chap. 2, pp. 67–119.

5. For a fuller exploration of this point, see Carmen Sirianni, *Workers Control and Socialist Democracy* (London: New Left Books, 1982), chap. 7, pp. 245–60.

6. See A. J. Polan, *Lenin and the End of Politics* (Berkeley: University of California Press, 1984).

7. See David Lovell, *From Marx to Lenin: An Evaluation of Marx's Responsibility for Soviet Authoritarianism* (Cambridge: Cambridge University Press, 1984).

8. Ibid., p. 63.

9. See Polan, *Lenin and the End of Politics*, p. 109. He relies on a distinction between *techne* and *phronesis* first made by Aristotle in *The Politics* and modernized by Habermas in *Towards a Rational Society*, chap. 1.

10. Certainly one can be a democrat and believe that certain political truths are discoverable. As Don Herzog has pointed out to me, John Stuart Mill certainly argued in *On Liberty* that open political debate was valuable, in part, because it promoted the discovery of truth. And I contend (in both the introduction and conclusion to this work) that democrats cannot be agnostic as to the moral validity of the equal worth of persons. Beyond a minimal, "thin" institutional and moral conception of democracy, however, democrats—whether epistemologically anti-foundational or not—must believe that it is undemocratic to impose "objectively true policies" on citizens. Democratic public policy, as distinct from democratic institutions and basic rights, cannot be viewed by a consistent democrat as embodying permanent, immutable truths. Rather, policies must stand the tests of time and popular support and adapt to changing circumstances.

11. See Ralph Miliband, "The State and Revolution," in *Lenin Today*, ed. Paul Sweezy and Harry Magdoff (New York: Monthly Review Press, 1970), pp. 77–90,

and *Marxism and Politics* (Oxford: Oxford University Press, 1977), chap. 5, "Class and Party," pp. 118–53.

12. V. I. Lenin, *State and Revolution* (New York: International Publishers, 1932), p. 43.

13. Ibid., p. 80.

14. Karl Kautsky, *The Dictatorship of the Proletariat* (Ann Arbor: University of Michigan Press, 1964), pp. 120–28.

15. Rosa Luxemburg, "Leninism or Marxism," in her *The Russian Revolution and Leninism or Marxism* (Ann Arbor: University of Michigan Press, 1961), p. 96. This pamphlet was originally published in 1904 in *Iskra* and *Neue Zeit*—the theoretical journals, respectively, of the Russian Social Democratic and German Social Democratic parties—under the title of "Organizational Questions of Russian Social Democracy."

16. Lenin, *What Is to Be Done?* (New York: International Publishers, 1961), p. 11

17. One could argue that the historical materialist Karl Kautsky was as epistemologically committed to a "science of history" as Lenin was; thus Lenin's antidemocratic attitudes might not be due solely to his commitment to a "science of history." Kautsky, however, offers a different criterion of legitimacy than does Lenin as to whether or not a political opinion, whether derived from a "scientific" analysis or not, should be held by a democratic movement (i.e., Kautsky argues that the position should be adopted only if a majority of the movement voluntary accepts it). As Dewey argued in "Means and Ends," his response to Leon Trotsky's *Their Morals and Ours*, a democratic political activist could believe that there is a natural structure to the universe or scientifically discernible laws of history. But if they are to act democratically, these activists cannot dogmatically assert that their scientific theory gives them omniscient knowledge of the future. Therefore, they cannot justify their undemocratically imposing their views on others based on the mere allegation that "scientifically" discerned beneficial consequences will occur in the distant future. I am sympathetic to Dewey's epistemological pragmatism. But the central issue of what constitutes democratic practices is not determined by our ontological or epistemological conception of the world. Rather, it is set by whether we politically relate to others according to the principles of democratic openness. Both antifoundationalists and foundationalists, skeptics and objectivists, have acted in both democratic and undemocratic ways.

18. From *The Economic and Philosophical Manuscripts*, in Marx, *The Early Writings*, ed. Tom Bottomore (London: Penguin, 1963), p. 176.

19. Marx's address to the meeting of the Central Authority of the Communist League, September 15, 1850, in *Marx-Engels Collected Works* (Moscow: Progress Publishers, 1975), vol. 10, p. 626.

20. From Marx, *The Poverty of Philosophy*, as quoted in *Karl Marx: Selected Writings in Sociology and Social Philosophy*, ed. T. Bottomore and M. Rubel (London: Penguin, 1963), pp. 194, 195.

21. Marx, *The Communist Manifesto*, in *The Marx-Engels Reader*, 2nd. ed., ed. R. C. Tucker (New York: W. W. Norton, 1978), p. 481.

22. Marx, "Instructions for the Delegates to the Geneva Congress," in *Karl Marx, Political Writings*, vol. 3, ed. D. Fernbach (New York: Random House, 1974), p. 91.

23. Karl Marx, *The Eighteenth Brumaire of Louis Bonaparte* (New York: International Publishers, 1969), p. 124.

24. Marx, *The Communist Manifesto*, in *The Marx-Engels Reader*, p. 481.

25. Marx, *The Holy Family*, in *Writings of the Young Marx*, ed. L. Easton and K. Guddat (Garden City, N.Y.: Doubleday, 1967), p. 368.

26. Ibid.

27. Marx, *The Communist Manifesto*, in *The Marx-Engels Reader*, p. 481.

28. Ibid., p. 484.

29. Ibid., p. 499.

30. Whether those opinions would be as in accord with revolutionary Marxism, as Luxemburg assumes, is highly problematic, particularly given the reality that in the October-December 1917 Constituent Assembly elections in Russia, the Bolsheviks achieved only 25 percent of the vote, whereas the populist, peasant-based Social Revolutionary party garnered over 40 percent.

31. See Marx, *On the Jewish Question*, in *The Marx-Engels Reader*, p. 36.

32. See Neil Harding, *Lenin's Political Thought*, vol. 1 and 2 (New York, St. Martin's Press, 1977 and 1981), esp. vol. 1, chaps. 7–9, pp. 161–212.

33. See Lenin, *The Development of Capitalism in Russia* (Moscow: Progress Publishers, 1974). Written in 1899, Lenin's most ambitious analytic work may have overestimated the degree of capitalization of Russian agriculture. After the abortive 1905 revolution, which witnessed peasant demands for the nationalization of all landed estates, Lenin stated that the extent of feudalism in the countryside was greater than he had previously believed. The legacy of feudal dependency on the aristocracy, he argued, led peasants to be more willing to support the nationalization of land, because the majority were not commercial farmers and still depended on an aristocracy whom the peasantry desired to abolish. If both the peasantry and the aristocracy had become landowning, capitalist, commercial farmers, then the peasantry would have been less supportive of land nationalization. See Lenin, *Collected Works*, vol. 13, pp. 291–92, for this 1907 critique of *The Development of Capitalism in Russia*. Sirianni correctly points out that down to 1917 Lenin vascillated between viewing Russia as a nascent capitalist society, with anachronistic feudalistic social remnants and viewing it as a state and society so shot through with precapitalist elements and feudal bureaucratic vestiges that it could not be deemed a capitalist society. See Carmen Sirianni, *Workers Control*, esp. chap. 5, "The Peasantry in Revolution," pp. 159–97.

34. Lenin, *What Is to Be Done?* p. 80.

35. Ibid., p. 31.

36. Ibid., p. 63.

37. Ibid., p. 19.

38. Ibid., p. 72.

39. See Lenin, *Imperialism: The Highest Stage of Capitalism* (New York: International Publishers, 1967). The original publication date was mid-1916.

40. Karl Marx, "Letter to Bolte," in *The Marx-Engels Reader*, p. 520.

41. Those who would eventually become the Menshevik wing of the Russian Social Democratic Party saw Lenin's rejection of the central political import of immediate working-class struggles as his major deviation from Marxist orthodoxy. The future Menschevik leaders Axelrod and Martov agreed with Lenin that intellectuals played a seminal role in bringing socialist consciousness to the proletariat, and their vision of democratic centralism *initially* was not far different from Lenin's (see Harding, *Lenin's Political Thought*, vol. 1, chap. 7). In analyzing the split of the Russian Social Democratic Party into its Bolshevik and Menshevik wings after the 1902 Party Congress, historians have paid inordinate attention to the issue of internal party rules

and party structure, which involved the question of whether or not the party should consist solely of full-time revolutionaries and whether the decisions of higher bodies should be binding on lower bodies—democratic centralism. Although those questions were to grow in salience as the movement developed, becoming particularly crucial after the February 1917 revolution, the initial 1902 split centered on differing evaluations of the centrality of the trade union movement to revolutionary socialist strategy. From 1902 onward the Menshevik leadership stressed the building of strong political links between the party and the trade unions. After the failed 1905 revolution, the Mensheviks focused on the re-creation of the soviets as an arena for political resistance, while most Bolsheviks mistrusted their "spontaneity," except for a temporary period of enthusiasm on Lenin's part in 1907.

But it is worth noting that neither the Mensheviks nor the Bolsheviks, until 1917, ever discussed the soviets as an arena of sole and direct democratic governance. In fact, no Russian socialist faction before or after 1918 ever engaged in any serious theorizing about the relationship between workers' councils and parliamentary government. Not until workers' councils were created in Germany in 1918, a nation with strong trade union and socialist parliamentary traditions, did any serious analysis of this problematic relationship occur. (See Sirianni, *Workers' Control and Socialist Democracy*, chaps. 10–11 and "Workers' Control in Europe: A Comparative Sociological Analysis," in James Cronin and Carmen Sirianni, eds., *Work, Community and Power* [Philadelphia: Temple University Press, 1983], pp. 254-310.)

The Mensheviks' adherence to the traditions of European social democracy led them to embrace civil liberties and parliamentary democracy as ends-in-themselves. But it also led them, *unlike Lenin*, to underestimate the role the peasantry would play in the revolution against the autocracy. The populist, peasant-based Social Revolutionary Party's failure to oppose World War I enabled Lenin, particularly as the war dragged on, to appropriate their slogan of "bread and land" and to gain peasant support for a revolution led by a working class that represented under 10 percent of Russia's population. For a fuller discussion of the theoretical basis of the Menshevik-Bolshevik split, see Kolakowski, *Main Currents of Marxism*, vol. 2, chaps. 16 and 17, pp. 381–486, and Lovell, *From Marx to Lenin*, chap. 6, pp. 142–62.

42. See Lenin, "'Left-Wing' Communism: An Infantile Disorder," in Lenin, *Selected Works*, vol. 10 (New York: International Publishers, 1938), pp. 55–158.

43. Lenin, *What Is to Be Done?* p. 31.

44. Ibid., pp. 31–32.

45. Ibid., p. 26.

46. Marx, *The Communist Manifesto*, in *The Marx-Engels Reader*, p. 483.

47. Karl Kautsky, as quoted in Lenin, *What Is to Be Done?* p. 40.

48. Ibid., pp. 40–41, 94.

49. Georg Lukacs, *History and Class Consciousness*, trans. Rodney Livingstone (Cambridge: MIT Press, 1971), p. 51.

50. Either Lukacs's neo-Hegelian teleological conception of Marxism as the unfolding of true reason or a more traditional economic determinist conception of consciousness as a reflection of objective material interests yields a Marxism with a closed, antipolitical conception of working class agency.

51. *What Is to Be Done?* served as the *Iskra* group's manifesto for the 1902 Russian Social Democratic Party Congress. The group, whose leaders included the future Mensheviks Martov and Axelrod, was united in its opposition to the narrowly trade-union-oriented "economists." Martov and Axelrod would initially break ranks with

Lenin over the dropping of Axelrod, Zasulich, and Potresov from the editorial board of *Iskra*. The dispute between Martov and Lenin over the strictness of the membership clause in the constitution, though producing the original Bolshevik (majority) and Menshevik (minority) factions, struck most foreign observers at the time, including Kautsky, as a splitting of hairs.

Lenin's Article I membership clause defined a party member as one who "recognizes the party's program and supports it by material means and by personal participation in one of the Party's organizations." Martov's membership clause defined a party member as one who "recognizes the party's program and supports it by material means and by regular personal assistance under the direction of the party organizations." At the 1906 "Unity Congress" of the Russian Social Democratic Party, the Mensheviks accepted Lenin's definition of party membership. But by that time differences in attitudes toward the trade unions and soviets had transplanted questions of party organization as the central issues of dispute between the Bolshevik and Menshevik factions. Even if there was a temporary agreement on constitutional language, it was clear to the Mensheviks that Lenin favored a much stricter form of democratic centralism than even the repressive conditions of Tsarist Russia justified. The two factions split into two parties in 1912.

52. See Rosa Luxemburg, *The Russian Revolution*, p. 79.

53. Lenin, *What Is to Be Done?* p. 109.

54. Ibid., p. 118.

55. Left-wing critics of the social democratic tradition correctly point out that social democracy has also had its statist, technocratic exponents. But the commitment of most social democrats to civil liberties, social pluralism, and representative government undoubtedly contributed to its infinitely less repressive, though by no means unblemished, history as compared to that of Leninist regimes.

56. Lenin, *What Is to Be Done?* p. 138.

57. Ibid., p. 138.

58. Rosa Luxemburg, "Leninism or Marxism," in her *The Russian Revolution and Leninism or Marxism*, p. 107.

59. See Marx, *The Eighteenth Brumaire*, p. 62; for a fuller development of these images of the "servile" and "dominant" state in Marx, see John M. Maguire, *Marx's Theory of Politics* (Cambridge: Cambridge Univ. Press, 1978), esp. chap. 1, pp. 6–27.

60. Marx, *The Critique of the Gotha Program*, in *The Marx-Engels Reader*, p. 537.

61. I take the term "sorcerer's apprentice" from a lecture by Michael Walzer on Marx's theory of the state.

62. Marx, *The Critique of Hegel's Philosophy of Right*, in *Writings of the Young Marx*, p. 186.

63. Marx, *On the Jewish Question*, in *Writings of the Young Marx*, p. 228.

64. According to Althusser's influential interpretation, Marx's *German Ideology* represents a break with his early writings' immature, nonscientific, "humanistic" critique of capitalism in favor of a mature materialist and "scientific" analysis of the structural laws of capitalism. See Louis Althusser, *For Marx*, trans. Ben Brewster (New York: Vintage, 1970). Although outside of his notes for *Capital* in *The Grundrisse*, the mature Marx abandons explicit use of the concept of alienation, any coherent reading of *Capital*, particularly the sections on the fetishism of commodities, must acknowledge that the critique of capitalism as a system that workers create but do not control—the essence of the theory of alienation—remains.

65. Marx, *The German Ideology*, in *Writings of the Young Marx*, p. 228.

66. Marx, *The Communist Manifesto*, in *The Marx-Engels Reader*, p. 490.

67. Ibid., pp. 490–91.

68. Ibid., p. 491.

69. Engels termed the Commune "the dictatorship of the proletariat" in his 1891 introduction to *The Civil War in France*. See Engels's introduction to *The Civil War in France*, in *The Marx-Engels Reader*, p. 629. But Marx himself never used the term to describe the Paris Commune.

70. Marx, *The Civil War in France*, in *The Marx-Engels Reader*, p. 635.

71. Marx, "Letter to F. Domela-Nieuwenhuis," in *Marx and Engels: Basic Writings on Politics and Philosophy*, ed. Lewis Feuer (New York: Doubleday, 1959), pp. 390–91.

72. For Marx's analysis of the Commune as a democratic but nonsocialist form of government that implemented moderate reforms, see Marx, "First Draft of 'The Civil War in France,'" in *The First International and After, Political Writings*, vol. 3, pp. 236–42.

73. Marx, *The Civil War in France*, in *The Marx-Engels Reader*, p. 635.

74. Ibid., p. 635.

75. Ibid., p. 633.

76. See Marx, *Capital* (trans. Ben Fowkes, New York: Vintage, 1977), vol. 1, chap. 1, "The Commodity," pp. 169–73.

77. See Karl Kautsky, *The Dictatorship of the Proletariat* (Ann Arbor: University of Michigan Press, 1964), esp. chap. 5, "Dictatorship," pp. 42–58.

78. Marx is often charged with being an unambiguous authoritarian because of his use of the expression "the dictatorship of the proletariat." But this argument is too simple an answer to the complex question of Marx's attitude toward democracy. The term *dictatorship* only acquired the definition of an authoritarian state, ruled by one person or one party employing state terror, in the twentieth century. When Marx used the term, *dictatorship* still held its classical Roman connotation of a constitutional emergency regime summoned by a republic primarily for the purpose of military defense. The *dictator* could suspend laws but could not alter any existing statutes nor introduce new ones. The "dictator" was appointed for a specified, limited time and held accountable for his actions afterward by the republican Senate (although cases of unconstitutional usurpation obviously occurred). The modern equivalent to the conception of dictatorship which Marx employed is martial law or a state of siege implemented by a democratic, constitutional regime. For an expansion on this point, see Lovell, *From Marx to Lenin*, pp. 36–41.

79. Marx, "After the Revolution," in *The Marx-Engels Reader*, p. 545. Because "After the Revolution" is usually referred to in other collections of Marx's work as Marx's "Conspectus on Bakunin," I will subsequently refer to these marginal notes on the Russian anarchist's Mikhail Bakunin's *Statehood and Anarchy* as "Conspectus on Bakunin." A significant but overlooked aspect of the "Conspectus" is its demonstration of Marx's sensitivity to the peasantry's attachment to private property and his recognition that a socialist revolution must avoid coercion by using voluntary economic incentives to promote more cooperative forms of agricultural production. Marx cautions against "stunning" the peasantry and urges a socialist government not to proclaim by political fiat "the abrogation of the right of inheritance or of his property." (Marx, "Conspectus on Bakunin," p. 545, emphasis added)

80. Marx, "Conspectus on Bakunin," in *The Marx-Engels Reader*, p. 546.

81. Ibid., p. 545.

82. Ibid., p. 546.

83. Friedrich Engels, *Socialism, Utopian and Scientific*, in *The Marx-Engels Reader*, p. 713.

84. Despite Lenin's attempt to equate the direct democratic institutions of workers' councils with the Commune, the Commune itself was a representative municipal democracy of eighty-six representatives elected by districts. Although workers did participate in decision-making in some of the municipalized firms seized from emigrés, such participation was not counterposed to the need for a representative body to govern the municipality of Paris as a whole.

85. Lenin, *State and Revolution*, p. 5.

86. For a discussion of the influence of Pannekoek's and Bukharin's writings on the state on Lenin's *State and Revolution* see Marian Sawer, "The Genesis of *State and Revolution*," in Ralph Miliband and John Saville, eds., *The Socialist Register 1977* (New York: Monthly Review Press, 1977), pp. 209–27.

87. Pannekoek as quoted in Sawer, "The Genesis of State and Revolution," p. 211.

88. Nikolai I. Bukharin, *Imperialism and the World Economy* (New York: Monthly Review Press, 1973).

89. Bukharin as quoted in Sawer, "The Genesis of State and Revolution," p. 215.

90. Lenin on Bukharin in "Letter to Shliapnikov, March 1916," in *The Bolsheviks and the World War*, ed. O. Gankin and H. Fisher (Stanford: Stanford University Press, 1960), p. 241.

91. Lenin's reply to Bukharin's "Towards a Theory of the Imperialist State," in *The Bolsheviks and the World War*, p. 239.

92. Lenin, as quoted in Sawer, "The Genesis of State and Revolution," p. 218.

93. See Neil Harding, *Lenin's Political Thought*, vol. 2, esp. chap. 9, pp. 201–19. Harding offers a highly sophisticated analysis of the relationship between Lenin's theory and practice, but Harding is overly optimistic in his assertion of the democratic implications of Lenin's turn toward the soviets in 1916–17 (and very briefly in 1907).

94. The spring 1921 revolt of the Kronstadt naval base outside of Leningrad was led by sailors who had spearheaded the October 1917 Bolshevik revolution under the slogan of "all power to the soviets." By the spring of 1921, many of these same individuals revolted in defense of democratic soviets against Bolshevik domination.

95. Carmen Sirianni, *Workers Control and Socialist Democracy*, particularly Part Two, "Discourses of Democracy," chaps. 7–9, pp. 243–305, offers the richest account of the theory and practice of workers' control in the October revolution and its aftermath. Sirianni documents the impressive spontaneous organization and coordination of factory councils during the revolution, often led by Bolsheviks who ignored the party leadership's favoring of (a fragile) central government's control of planning. He also illustrates how Lenin's productivism, both in theory and practice, as well as the exigencies of civil war, led the Bolshevik regime to crush independent experiments in workers' councils by 1919. Although Sirianni's work takes seriously the democratic impulses and accomplishments of Russian revolutionary workers—Menshevik, Bolshevik, and Social Revolutionary—unlike most sympathetic accounts of the revolution, it does not gloss over the antidemocratic aspects of Bolshevik ideology and practice.

Sirianni's comparative work on workers' councils movements in Europe in the post-World War I era is particularly instructive in analyzing the theoretical and practical tensions between representative and direct forms of democracy. Most of the sympathetic literature on workers' councils contributes to the "myth of the council" that direct democratic institutions are both inherently more democratic than representative forms and spontaneously supported by radical workers who reject parliamentary and electoral forms of political representation. But Sirianni's work convincingly demonstrates that many Western and Central European workers who vigorously participated in the short-lived post-World War I council movement also favored the development of representative parliamentary institutions and civil liberties. This was particularly true of the German working class, which supported the council movement but rejected the appeals of the Spartacists (those who would later found the German Communist Party) to revolt against the social democratic-dominated parliamentary government. Thus the practical political impulses of the mass working class, though inchoate at times, were more sophisticated than the simplistic Leninist dichotomy between representative and direct political institutions. For an analysis of the workers' council movement in a comparative historical perspective, see Part Three of Sirianni, *Workers Control,* "The Russian Experience in Comparative Perspective," pp. 312–68, "Councils and Parliaments: The Problems of Dual Power and Democracy in Comparative Perspective," *Politics and Society* 12: 1 (1983): 83–123, and "Workers' Control in Europe: A Comparative Sociological Analysis," in Cronin and Sirianni, eds., *Work, Community and Power,* pp. 254–310.

96. Lenin, *State and Revolution,* pp. 29–30.

97. Ibid., pp. 38, 42.

98. Ibid., p. 10.

99. Ibid., p. 11.

100. Lenin, *State and Revolution,* p. 14. Lenin strikingly does not quote Engels's subsequent remarks that the suffrage is more than just a gauge of working-class strength but also a means for working-class parties to force through reforms that would alter the structure of the previously "bourgeois" state: "It was found that the state institutions, in which the rule of the bourgeoisie is organized, offer the working class still further opportunities to fight these very state institutions." (Engels, "The Tactics of Social Democracy," in *The Marx-Engels Reader,* p. 566.)

In this article, "The Tactics of Social Democracy," an 1895 introduction to a new edition of Marx's *The Class Struggles in France,* Engels clearly viewed universal suffrage as a grave threat to bourgeois power. Threatened by the growth of working-class political power under democratic rule, the bourgeoisie, Engels believed—and not the working class—would likely be the first to resort to armed force to preserve its rule against an imminent working-class electoral majority. Engels urged the proletariat not to respond to bourgeois provocations aimed at producing an insurrection, although he defended the working class's right to armed self-defense. In Engels's opinion the advent of modern weaponry meant that armed struggle would probably lead to the mutual ruin of the contending classes: "The irony of world history turns everything upside down. We, the 'revolutionists,' the 'overthrowers'— we are thriving far better on legal methods than on illegal methods and overthrow. The parties of Order, as they call themselves, are perishing under the legal conditions created by themselves." ("The Tactics of Social Democracy," in *The Marx-Engels Reader,* p. 569.) Engels was certainly no pacifist. But before his death he clearly argued that the working class in liberal democracies would have the best chance of coming to power by achieving such hegemony in civil society that counterrevolutionary resistance by the army would be impossible because of rank-and-file troop support for the revolution. If it came to civil war, social democracy would fight fiercely. But

Engels predicted the left would fight on extremely unfavorable terrain, given the increasing professionalization of armies and the sophistication of modern weaponry. See Engels, "The Tactics of Social Democracy," in ibid., pp. 556–73. For Engels's doubts as to the efficacy of armed struggle and his defense of the importance of first demonstrating electoral majority support in bourgeois democracies, see ibid., pp. 566–73.

101. Lenin, *State and Revolution*, p. 14. Tsereteli, Chernov, and Palchinsky were Menshevik and Social Revolutionary ministers in Kerensky's Provisional Government of February 1917 to October 1917, a government characterized by considerable bureaucratic corruption.

102. Ibid., p. 22.

103. Ibid., p. 25.

104. Lenin, quoting from Marx's *The Poverty of Philosophy*, in *State and Revolution*, p. 21.

105. That Marx should have rejected a stageist conception of communism and solely advanced the potentially more pluralist and political vision of socialism (i.e., first-stage communism) is the theme of an admirably concise and insightful work by the philosopher Stanley Moore, *Marx on the Choice between Socialism and Communism* (Cambridge: Harvard University Press, 1980).

106. Lenin, *State and Revolution*, p. 83.

107. Ibid., p. 23.

108. Ibid., p. 24.

109. Ibid., p. 31.

110. Ibid., p. 37.

111. Ibid., p. 43.

112. Ibid., pp. 83, 42–43.

113. Lenin, *State and Revolution*, p. 43.

114. Weber most fully develops this analysis of the relationship between political leadership and the bureaucracy in "Parliament and Government in a Reconstructed Germany," in his *Economy and Society; An Outline of Interpretive Sociology*, vol. 2, ed. Guenther Roth and Claus Wittich (Berkeley: University of California Press, 1978), pp. 1,381–1,469.

115. See Erik Olin Wright, *Class, Crisis and the State* (London: New Left Books, 1978), chap. 4, "Bureaucracy and the State," esp. pp. 194–204.

116. Ibid., pp. 183–94.

117. Ibid., pp. 213–25.

118. In his last work, Michael Harrington argued that a truly democratic socialist society would have to aim to socialize both ownership and knowledge. He suggests, "There have to be [public] funds that allow workers and communities to hire the experts who can translate their intuitive desires into the requisite equations and computer printouts" (*Socialism: Past and Future* [New York: Arcade, 1989], p. 199).

Both Harrington and Robert Dahl stress that many decisions that elites claim to be technical are ultimately determined by implicit or explicit political values that should be set as democratically as possible. Dahl contends, for example, that United States nuclear armaments policy was driven more by the political inclinations of the foreign policy and defense establishment than by technical decisions that were beyond the comprehension of publicly elected representatives and an informed public. (see Dahl, *Democracy and Its Critics* [New Haven: Yale University Press, 1989], pp. 69–70.)

Because Dahl contends that most critical decisions in society are not technological but involve basic judgments about how we view the world (our ontology) and how we wish to live (our moral judgment), these decisions should be subject to democratic deliberation. But to ensure as informed a participating public as possible and to lessen the gap between political representatives and the political public, Dahl suggests that a manageable, demographically representative "minipopulus" of one thousand citizens be randomly selected to deliberate for one year on each critical agenda item coming up before the representative elected legislature. To ensure that these "minipopuli" serve as "attentive publics," their members would serve in a full-time, paid capacity (why not a sabbatical-policy for all citizens?) and each "minipopulus" would have sufficient public funding to hire administrative staff and academic and technical advisors. The "minipopuli" would publicly report their decisions, though democratically elected representatives would continue to make final national policy decisions (see Dahl, *Democracy and Its Critics*, pp. 339–40).

119. Neither Lenin nor Weber delineated democratic political means by which to determine the role of technical expertise in modern administration. On this issue both political theorists and political scientists have had surprisingly little to say. Technology is not purely technologically determined; it is partly a social and political construct. On the other hand, to assert glibly, as some "postmodernists" do, that technology is strictly a discursive and political construct and has nothing to with relatively stable (though always evolving) laws of physics and mechanics, for example, is to totalize the conception of politics to such an extent that any distinction between politics and science (or politics and anything else) is rendered meaningless. For a work that exhibits such tendencies, see Stanley Aronowitz, *Science as Power: Discourse and Ideology in Modern Society* (Minneapolis: University of Minnesota Press, 1988).

That is, politics cannot encompass all of human existence if it is to be either democratic or efficacious. Political deliberation must determine broad social priorities and oversee technical and bureaucratic management. But practitioners of a democratic politics must also understand that there are certain technical imperatives to modern social and economic institutions—and these imperatives are best not politicized. To politicize all bureaucratic and technological decisions would yield massive inefficiency because managers and technicians would be unwilling to take risks out of fear of political penalties. Or it might produce fawning technocrats who strive only to please the mass public or political elites. Workers and consumers should obviously have a strong voice in the choosing of managers and in evaluating their overall performance (a meaningful power to hire and fire can significantly increase this voice). But if workers are to grant no powers of discretionary judgment to their fellow worker-managers, it is hard to imagine how democratic managers could make effective decisions. Finally, and perhaps most dangerously, the total politicization of all social practices could drive technocrats and bureaucrats to strive for political dominance in order to shore up their threatened "relative" autonomy. Politics should be in "command" as the "master science"; but it should not attempt to supplant all other social practices.

120. Lenin, *State and Revolution*, pp. 41–42.

121. Ibid., p. 40.

122. Ibid., p. 70–71. The original quote from *The Critique of the Gotha Program* can be found in *The Marx-Engels Reader*, p. 538.

123. Lenin, *State and Revolution*, p. 73.

124. Ibid.

125. Ibid., p. 80. Pomyalovsky's *Seminary Sketches* depicted a group of spoiled, aristocratic student-ruffians who destroyed things solely for the pleasure it gave them.

126. Ibid., p. 82.

127. Ibid.

128. Ibid., p. 83.

129. Ibid., p. 91. This passage is Lenin paraphrasing Kautsky.

130. Ibid., p. 92.

131. Ibid., p. 93.

132. Ibid., p. 96.

133. In the Constituent Assembly elections of November-December 1917, the Bolsheviks won close to 25 percent of the over 800 seats contested in the first and only fully free nationwide election ever held in Russia or the Soviet Union, until the relatively free elections for the last Supreme Soviet of the USSR in 1990. The Social Revolutionaries (the SRs), the predominantly peasant party (who would in early 1918 split into the Left and Right SRs—pro- and anti-war factions) garnered close to 50 percent of the seats in the 1917 Constituent Assembly elections, with perhaps one-fifth of these delegates (or an additional 10 percent of the entire Assembly) eventually aligning with the Left SRs, who backed the Bolshevik desire to withdraw from World War I.

In January 1918, when the Constituent Assembly first convened, Lenin and the Bolshevik Party dismissed it (permanently), arguing that the elections were not truly representative of the will of the people because many voters in outlying provinces had not heard news of the October 1917 revolution before casting their ballots and because the SRs only split into two factions after the elections. See Lenin's December 1917 "Theses on the Constituent Assembly" in Lenin, *The Proletarian Revolution and the Renegade Kautsky* (Moscow: Progress Publishers, 1934), pp. 94–98. Both Rosa Luxemburg (no enemy of the Bolshevik revolution) and Karl Kautsky pointed out in, respectively, *The Russian Revolution* and *The Dictatorship of the Proletariat*, that Lenin's arguments could justify proroguing the Constituent Assemblies and then immediately holding new elections (which, of course, were never held). Luxemburg and Kautsky contended that Lenin's argument could never justify permanently abolishing the first representative democratic body ever elected in Russia or the Soviet Union.

CHAPTER 6
HANNAH ARENDT'S POLITICS OF "ACTION":
THE ELUSIVE SEARCH FOR POLITICAL SUBSTANCE

1. Although theorists referred to in contemporary debates as "republicans" or "communitarians" are sufficiently diverse that they cannot be categorized as a unified school of political thought, the theorists and works cited here share a certain tendency to celebrate "political discourse" at the expense of theorizing about concrete political and socioeconomic dilemmas. They include Hannah Arendt, *The Human Condition* (Chicago: University of Chicago Press, 1958); J.G.A. Pocock, *The Machiavellian Moment* (Princeton: Princeton University Press, 1975); Alasdair MacIntyre, *After Virtue* (Notre Dame:University of Notre Dame Press, 1981); Michael Sandel, *Liberalism and the Limits of Justice* (Cambridge: Cambridge University Press, 1982); Benjamin Barber, *Strong Democracy: Participatory Politics for a New Age* (Berkeley: University of California Press, 1984); and Sheldon Wolin, *Politics and Vision* (Boston: Little, Brown, 1960).

2. See Sheldon Wolin, "Hannah Arendt and the Ordinance of Time," *Social Research* 44:1 (Spring 1977): 100–105, and "Hannah Arendt: Democracy and the Political," *Salamagundi* 60 (Spring-Summer 1983), esp. pp. 15–19. For Wolin's ambivalence toward the domination of contemporary politics by instrumental, socioeconomic conflict, see his editorials and other writings in the journal he edited, *democracy*, 1981–84.

3. Arendt develops these themes in all her work, but they are most succinctly advanced in *Between Past and Future: Six Exercises in Political Thought* (Cleveland: World, 1963), particularly in the essays "What is Authority?" pp. 114–20, and "What is Freedom?" pp. 151–65.

4. See MacIntyre, *After Virtue*, pp. 146–48.

5. Sandel offers a tentative vision of a good society of "shared commitments" in the final chapter of *Liberalism and the Limits of Justice*, pp. 175–83. In some of his more recent journalistic writings it is evident that he attempts to develop a democratic communitarianism that, although rejecting an atomized, instrumental liberal conception of the self, values plurality and difference, but in the context of a limited but substantive local and national communal solidarity. See Michael Sandel in "Roundtable: The Politics of Meaning," *Tikkun* 8:5 (September-October 1993): 19–26, 87–88. Sandel laments the absence of community in U.S. political life, but he also warns against those, such as *Tikkun* editor Michael Lerner, who wish for a "politics of meaning" that can tend to the individual psyche's need for communal identity. Sandel in the "Roundtable" warns of trying to locate in the political realm the virtues of psychological connectedness and dependence better found in personal and family relationships.

6. For a provocative argument as to why political discourse, though informed by one's overall moral perspective, has to affect concrete social problems if it is to be truly self-realizing for its participants, see Jon Elster, "Self-Realisation in Work and Politics: The Marxist Conception of the Good Life," in Elster and Moene, eds., *Alternatives to Capitalism* (Cambridge: Cambridge University Press, 1989), pp. 148–49. Elster implies that our ultimate moral judgment of a political community involves not just an evaluation of how democratic its political deliberations may be but also how democratic the actual results are of the regime's public policy.

7. For an insightful alternative reading of Arendt as prefiguring a "postmodern" democratic politics centered in autonomous communities in civil society resisting instrumental economic domination and bureaucratic state domination, see Jeffrey C. Isaac, *Arendt, Camus and Modern Rebellion* (New Haven: Yale University Press, 1992). My operative difference with Isaac's reading is that he is much less skeptical of Arendt's celebration of the periodic upsurge of worker and community "councils" as the best site for democratic participation. I argue for a more dialectic conception of the relationship between representative and direct democratic institutions and am skeptical that local councils could ever completely supplant representative political institutions. As Norberto Bobbio points out in his writings on the relationship between liberalism and socialism, most institutions of direct democracy eventually incorporate critical aspects of representative democracy because of the problems of numbers, representativeness of debate, and scarcity of time. See Norberto Bobbio, "What Alternatives Are There to Representative Democracy?" in Bobbio, *Which Socialism?* trans. Roger Griffin (Minneapolis: University of Minnesota Press, 1987), pp. 65–84.

Whereas Isaac makes the most compelling account of Arendt as a realistic, radical thinker and activist, my reading of the antidemocratic implications of Arendt's intellectual outlook is closer in sympathy to Claude Lefort's interpretation (See Lefort, *Democracy and Political Theory*, trans. David Macey [Minneapolis: University of Minnesota Press, 1988]).

8. Arendt develops the philosophical basis for these political arguments in the chapter on "Action" in *The Human Condition*, pp. 175–247 and regarding the question of motives and intent in Chapter 2, "The Social Question," in her *On Revolution* (New York: Viking, 1963), esp. pp. 91–100. Arendt most succinctly discusses these themes in the essays in *Between Past and Future*, particularly in "On History," pp. 61–63; "What is Authority?" and "What is Freedom?"

9. See Chapter 2, "The Social Question," in Arendt, *On Revolution*, esp. pp. 53–60 and 83–87.

10. Ibid. Arendt's argument about the social question and "American exceptionalism" is on pp. 62–64.

11. Ibid. On the ideological nature of the European politics of the "social question," see pp. 116–21.

12. For Arendt's hostility to Cartesian metaphysical doubt and her belief in its link to utilitarian politics, see Chapter 5, "The *Vita Activa* and the Modern Age," in *The Human Condition*, esp. pp. 273–80 and 305–20. A remaining vestige of the Kantian tradition in Arendt's work is her hostility to weighing motives or consequences when judging the worth of political deliberation. For this aspect of her thought, see esp. ibid., pp. 206–8 and "What is Freedom?" in *Between Past and Present*, pp. 151–55. The following passage is typical: "[Political] action to be free must be free from motive on one side [and] from its intended goal as a predictable effect on the other. . . . They are [an acts] determining factors, and action is free to the extent that it is able to transcend them" (ibid., p. 151).

Arendt, however, differs from Kant in believing that moral action should not be guided by the free will but by what she terms "principles": "Honor, or glory, love of equality, which Montesquieu called virtue, or distinction or excellence . . . [or] Machiavelli's concept of *virtu*" (ibid., pp. 151–52). Contemporary "republican" theorists are attracted to Arendt's conception of "virtue" and "practice" as the highest end of politics. But "republican" theorists, who believe they hold to a substantive or teleological conception of political virtue that has clear implications for political outcomes as well, often fail to see Arendt's opposition to a politics with fixed, final ends. Political excellence, for Arendt, is in the acting, not in the "making." This anticonsequentialism and concern more with "acting" than "intentions" can jibe with a Machiavellian, republican conception of *virtù* as skill. But Machiavelli also held to a substantive conception of what goals those skills should serve. The Prince should follow a form of utilitarian calculus, a just war theory applied to the domestic and international front, which benefits the people of the republic. For this analysis see Sheldon Wolin, *Politics and Vision*, chap. 7, "Machiavelli: The Economy of Violence," pp. 195–238.

13. See Benjamin Schwartz, "The Religion of Politics: Reflections on the Thought of Hannah Arendt," *Dissent* (Spring 1979): 144–61.

14. George Kateb, *Hannah Arendt: Politics, Conscience, Evil* (Oxford: Martin Robertson, 1983), pp. 16–18. In comments on the manuscript, Jeffrey Isaac pointed out that Kateb's analysis cannot explain Arendt's deeming the post-World War II peace movement a "supremely political" movement. But a peace movement's politics involves the grand questions of war or peace, just as civil rights movements and,

according to her definition, the council movements deal with basic constitutional questions of the nature of the polity. My central point is that Arendt defines movements and issues that focus on socioeconomic concerns out of politics. Along these lines she praises workers' councils for being concerned with national political questions but condemns whatever interest they demonstrate in issues concerning economic justice in the workplace.

15. Arendt, "What is Freedom?" p. 155.

16. Ibid.

17. Ibid., p. 153.

18. On Arendt's hostility toward the worldliness of the Jewish religion, see Schwartz, "The Religion of Politics," 151–54. Schwartz does not mention that Arendt also credited Judaism's theological concern for worldly action as a factor in the laudable Jewish passion for justice.

19. Arendt, *The Human Condition*, p. 188.

20. Peter Fuss, "Hannah Arendt's Conception of Political Community," in Melvyn A. Hill, ed., *Hannah Arendt: The Recovery of the Public World* (New York: St. Martin's Press, 1979), p. 155.

21. For Arendt's "self-selected aristocracy" of council democracy, see *On Revolution*, pp. 279–85.

22. Michael Walzer makes this point in his essay "A Day in the Life of a Socialist Citizen," which is written from the perspective of a committed participatory democrat who worries seriously about the activist tendency to ignore or dismiss the opinions of the less active. See Walzer, "A Day in the Life of a Socialist Citizen," in his *Obligations: Essays on Disobedience, War and Citizenship* (Cambridge: Harvard University Press, 1970), pp. 229–38.

23. For a clear statement of Arendt's belief that modernity's utilitarian, instrumental concerns obliterate the public realm, see *The Human Condition*, p. 220.

24. Ibid., p. 5.

25. Ibid., p. 155.

26. The above summary of Arendt's distinction between "work" and "labor" is drawn from her discussion in Chapter 4, "Work," in *The Human Condition*, esp. pp. 136–59.

27. Arendt, *The Human Condition*, p. 8.

28. Ibid., p. 176.

29. Ibid., p. 180.

30. Arendt contends that Plato and Aristotle "elevated lawmaking and city-building to the highest rank in political life . . . because to the Greeks [these activities] were pre-political" (ibid., p. 195). Arendt argues that Plato and Aristotle abandon the pre-Socratic and Roman emphasis on politics as legislation and foundation and supplant it with a craftsman's (*homo faber's*) vision of "making" (*poiesis*) rather than "action" (*praxis*). Plato and Aristotle emphasize the making of laws and voting because in them "men 'act like craftsmen' [i.e., as *homo faber*]: the result of their action is a tangible product, and its process has a clearly recognizable end" (ibid., p. 195). *Praxis*, though the only true form of politics for Arendt, is in her view inherently uncertain, boundless, and usually futile. Not even Plato and Aristotle, Arendt claims, were strong enough to live with this glorious uncertainty.

31. Ibid., p. 191.

32. Ibid.

33. Ibid., p. 206.

34. Ibid.

35. See Kateb, *Hannah Arendt: Politics, Conscience, Evil*, p. 15.

36. Arendt, *The Human Condition*, p. 182.

37. Schwartz, "The Religion of Politics," p. 146.

38. See Wolin, "Hannah Arendt: Democracy and the Political," p. 8. Moses I. Finley argues, in direct contradiction of Arendt's position, that participants in the Greek polis were very concerned with policy outcomes and often chose not to participate actively at a given moment if they deemed the polis's policies just and knew they could denounce and replace ineffective leaders: "The *demos* recognized the instrumental role of political rights and were more concerned in the end with substantive decisions, were content with the power to dismiss and punish their leaders." See Moses I. Finley, "The Freedom of the Citizen in the Greek World," in his *Economy and Society in Ancient Greece* (London: Chatto and Windus, 1981), pp. 77–94.

39. Jurgen Habermas, "Hannah Arendt's Communications Concept of Power," *Social Research* 44:1 (Spring 1977): 21.

40. For Arendt's idiosyncratic conception of power, see *The Human Condition*, pp. 200–205 and "On Violence," in *Crises of the Republic* (New York: Harcourt Brace Jovanovich, 1973), pp. 139–55.

41. See Judith Shklar, "Rethinking the Past," in *Social Research* 44:1 (Spring 1977): 80–90.

42. Arendt, *The Human Condition*, p. 221.

43. For Arendt's view that "the greater part of political philosophy since Plato could easily be interpreted as various attempts to find theoretical foundations and practical ways for an escape from politics altogether," see ibid., p. 222.

44. Ibid.

45. For Arendt's conception that post-Socratic politics subordinates the political to other ends and "interests," see ibid., pp. 228–30. Central to her argument that post-Socratic politics has been degraded into the utilitarian handmaiden of "interests" is her belief that violence has supplanted "action" (verbal promise-making) as the basis of political legitimacy. She develops this argument at length in "On Violence," in *Crises of the Republic*, esp. pp. 134–40 and 152–55.

46. Arendt, *The Human Condition*, p. 28. "On Violence" further develops the argument that the unhealthy political concern with the economic and social has engendered modern bureaucracies—the rule of "no man." See "On Violence" in *Crises of the Republic*, esp. p. 137.

47. For Arendt's view on the relationship between property and political freedom, see *The Human Condition*, pp. 58–66.

48. Ibid., p. 33.

49. Ibid., p. 42.

50. Ibid., p. 40.

51. For Arendt on Marx as a "philosopher of labor" opposed to the public esteem accorded to the objects produced by work, see ibid., pp. 85–90 and 162–67.

52. Ibid., pp. 145–52.

53. For Arendt's conception of labor and modern science's devaluation of objects and nature, see ibid., pp. 305–10. Jeffrey Isaac pointed out in comments on the manuscript that Arendt rejects Kant's categorical imperative for its "monological nature" but "retains Kant's idea that each person is a universal, entitled to dignity and respect."

54. In Arendt's view, Marx denigrates work and the objects (i.e., commodities) it creates while embracing "labor" and the possibility of machines "transcending" labor. Embracing the transcendence of labor denies Marx, according to Arendt, the possibility of envisioning the abolition of one's subordination to a mechanized labor process. Arendt advances this argument in *The Human Condition*, pp. 126–35. For a perceptive argument that Arendt radically misreads Marx by failing to comprehend that his distinction between alienated and nonalienated labor is quite similar to her distinction between "labor" and "work" (the conscious creation of objects), see Mildred Bakan, "Hannah Arendt's Concepts of Labor and Work," in Melvyn A. Hill, ed., *Hannah Arendt: The Recovery of the Public World*, pp. 49–66.

55. Arendt, *The Human Condition*, p. 133.

56. Ibid., p. 135.

57. Ibid., pp. 323–24.

58. Ibid., pp. 324–25.

59. Not only does Jeffrey Isaac perceive Arendt this way—as he makes clear both in his book and in comments on this manuscript—but her role as a public intellectual is a major theme of Elisabeth Young-Bruehl's biography, *Hannah Arendt: For Love of the World* (New Haven: Yale University Press, 1982).

60. Arendt, *On Revolution*, pp. 143, 149.

61. For further discussion of the relationship between Arendt's concept of work and Marx's concept of free labor, see Mildred Bakan, "Hannah Arendt's Concept of Labor and Work," and Bikhu Parekh, "Hannah Arendt's Critique of Marx," both in Melvyn A. Hill, ed., *Hannah Arendt: The Recovery of the Public World*, pp. 49–66 and 67–100, respectively.

62. Arendt, *The Human Condition*, p. 118.

63. Karl Marx, *The Grundrisse: Selections*, ed. David McLellan (New York: Harper and Row, 1971), p. 142.

64. For this pessimistic conclusion, see the end of *The Human Condition*, pp. 320–25.

65. Ibid., p. 216.

66. For Arendt's view of the central role of the working class in spontaneously fighting for a council system that placed politics above economic "interests," see *The Human Condition*, pp. 218–20. On this point Arendt was clearly influenced by Rosa Luxemburg, the Marxist revolutionary who placed the greatest faith in the spontaneous capacities of the working class. Luxemburg was also one of the few Marxists to take seriously the role for democratic politics after the revolution. Luxemburg held to a more sophisticated view of the need for both workplace councils and democratic representative institutions in a postrevolutionary society than did Arendt.

67. Arendt could not envision the widespread insecurity that would visit the working and middle strata of the advanced industrial economies with the global restructuring of the world capitalist economy beginning in the early 1970s and the subsequent demise of tens of millions of high-wage industrial jobs throughout liberal democratic societies.

68. Arendt blames the incorporation of the working class into society, largely due to the emergence of the welfare state, for ending the revolutionary political role of that class. For this analysis, see *The Human Condition*, pp. 218–20. Here Arendt offers an analysis quite similar to those of left-wing critiques of welfare state reforms. Like these left-wing criticisms, Arendt fails to see that it is not only elite concessions but also working-class political struggle that created the modern welfare state. It is

also now evident that popular majoritarian political mobilization is necessary to protect public provision from evisceration. Such mobilization becomes more problematic with the increasing segmentation and fragmentation of late-capitalist society. As John Stephens argues in *The Transition from Capitalism to Socialism* (Champaign-Urbana: University of Illinois Press, 1988), labor movements that have demanded greater political control over capital, such as the Swedish, are generally in nations with the most advanced welfare states, not the least. So the historical record does not support the view that increased economic equity demobilizes working-class political radicalism. If that were the case, then the U.S. working class would be more politically conscious than its Northern European counterparts who live in more egalitarian welfare states.

69. For an example of this trend within radical democratic thought, which is also evidenced at times in Sandel's and MacIntyre's discussions of contemporary politics, see Sheldon Wolin, "Hannah Arendt: Democracy and the Political," pp. 17–19, and Wolin's *democracy* magazine editorials from 1981 to 1984.

70. For this reading of Marx see Arendt, *On Revolution*, pp. 260–62.

71. Ibid., pp. 59–60.

72. Ibid., p. 55.

73. Ibid., pp. 108–9.

74. Ibid., p. 122.

75. Ibid., p. 121.

76. On the American "genius" of resting authority and sovereignty not in the people but in the Constitution itself, see Arendt, *The Human Condition*, pp.155–56 and 200.

77. Ibid., p. 206.

78. Arendt, "What Is Authority?" in *Between Past and Future*, p. 106.

79. Arendt, *On Revolution*, p. 65.

80. Ibid., p. 66.

81. John Adams quoted in ibid., p. 63.

82. Robert Nisbet in "Hannah Arendt and the American Revolution," *Social Research* 44:1 (Spring 1977): 66–69, succinctly summarizes the work of such historians as Carl Bridenbaugh, Jackson Turner Main, Bernard Bailyn, R. R. Palmer, and Richard Morris on the role of social conflict in the American Revolution.

83. For Arendt on Montesquieu, see *On Revolution*, pp. 148–53.

84. Arendt, *On Revolution*, p. 187.

85. Ibid., pp. 161–62.

86. Ibid., p. 162.

87. Ibid p. 166.

88. Ibid., p. 167.

89. Ibid., p. 171.

90. For this analysis of the relationship between power and authority, see Arendt, *On Revolution*, p. 176–78.

91. Arendt describes the tension between individual rights and democratic participation in a manner that strikingly prefigures the communitarian critique of liberalism in *On Revolution*, p. 131.

92. Ibid., p. 238.

93. Ibid.

94. Ibid., p. 134.

95. Ibid., p. 252.

96. After Arendt wrote *On Revolution* in 1958, the council communist experiments of 1918–19 were cited by many 1960s new left intellectuals as an attractive, if somewhat utopian, revolutionary tradition.

97. For Arendt's analysis of the hostility of professional and statist revolutionaries to the council tradition and the willingness of statist revolutionaries to use violence to smash the councils, see *On Revolution*, pp. 261–69.

98. For Arendt's disdain for modern political parties, see *On Revolution*, pp. 269–79. In a comment on the manuscript, Jeffrey Isaac suggested that Arendt's negative attitudes toward political parties derives, in part, from her formative political experience in the Weimar Republic. That is definitely the case; but Arendt was a sophisticated enough political observer to realize that not all party systems are as fragmented and ideological as that of Weimar Germany.

99. Arendt, *On Revolution*, pp. 272–75.

100. Ibid.

101. Ibid., p. 273. For Sandel's most explicit critique of the failure of New Deal and welfare state liberalism to achieve political community, see his article "The Procedural Republic and the Unencumbered Self," *Political Theory* 12:1 (February 1984): 81–96. Sandel argues that both the New Deal and Great Society social welfare programs were justified by a rhetoric of rights which assumed the willingness of a national political community to share talents and redistribute economic benefits. Sandel claims that such an adequate national sense of community was never achieved (or could be achieved?) to sustain such national redistributive programs. Social welfare liberals tried to ground such programs on a procedural conceptions of rights, rather than on the substantive, communal moral commitments that alone could sustain them. Sandel appears to argue that moral and political identities are best sustained in local, solidaristic communities. But if such identities are based not only on situated, but also fairly parochial identities, then is Sandel implying that creating a democratic, pluralist America that both sustains and goes beyond particular identities is impossible? Can adequate redistribution of social and economic power be achieved without a revived sense of national citizenship and community? On these issues Sandel has yet to articulate a clear position.

For MacIntyre's critique of the instrumental, bureaucratic nature of the welfare state, see *After Virtue*, chap. 16, "From the Virtues to Virtue and After Virtue," esp. p. 212. One can defend the importance of situated identities and local moral communities to a pluralist democracy without viewing as antithetical to diversity those social rights that guarantee the value of equal citizenship. Universal political, civil, and social rights, as well as national and international economic and social policies that promote the greatest opportunities for life planning (job retraining, sabbaticals, flexible career paths, etc.), are necessary if diverse forms of communities are to have an equal opportunity to pursue their conception of the good life. On the relationship between universal conceptions of justice and norms of democratic procedure to the development of particular moral and localist democratic communities, see Carmen Sirianni, "Learning Pluralism: Democracy and Diversity in Feminist Organizations," in *Nomos XXXV: Democratic Community*, ed. Ian Shapiro (New York, New York University Press, 1992), pp. 283–312.

102. Michael Walzer contends that democratizing social provision would be as essential to a radical democratic society as is the infinitely more theorized, but practically more problematic, democratization of production. That is, much of social provision is already public under welfare state capitalism whereas production obvi-

ously is not. But social provision's conceptualization and delivery is essentially bureaucratic and administrative rather than democratic. Unlike many advocates of
greater social provision through voluntary associations in civil society, Walzer recognizes that democratic state funding and regulation would be necessary to guarantee
basic minimal levels of equality of provision. See Michael Walzer, "The Idea of Civil
Society," *Dissent* (Spring 1991): 293–304, and "Socializing the Welfare State," in
Amy Gutmann, ed., *Democracy and the Welfare State* (Princeton: Princeton University Press, 1988), pp. 13–26.

103. Arendt, *On Revolution*, p. 276.

104. Ibid., pp. 277–79.

105. Ibid., p. 279.

106. For a description of the German *Räte*'s concern with workplace affairs and
the belief of the majority of rank-and-file workers that broader political concerns were
better dealt with by representative parliamentary politics, see Carmen Sirianni,
"Workers Control in Europe: A Comparative Sociological Analysis," in James Cronin
and Carmen Sirianni, eds., *Work, Community and Power* (Philadelphia: Temple University Press, 1983), pp. 254–310; for Germany 1918–23, which is the most instructive case, see esp. pp. 260–64, 278–87. See also Sirianni, "Councils and Parliaments:
The Problems of Dual Power and Democracy in Comparative Perspective," *Politics
and Society* 12:1 (1983): 83–123.

107. Arendt, *On Revolution*, p. 278.

108. For an argument that a commitment to the principles of political democracy
implies a commitment to economic democracy, see Robert Dahl, *A Preface to Economic Democracy* (Berkeley: University of California Press, 1985). Dahl, being a sophisticated analyst of the diversity of interests in civil society, is well aware of the need
for consumers and the broader polity to have influence over the behavior of large-
scale enterprises. This input can be partially achieved by allowing the market to register consumer demand, while government macroeconomic, monetary, trade, and industrial policy would place broad policy constraints on a firm's choices. But these
broader influences on the behavior of worker-owned or worker-managed firms does
not negate a major participatory role for workers as citizens and worker-managers of
the enterprises in which they work. Any sophisticated projection of a socially owned
economy cannot advance a strictly syndicalist model of workers' control which treats
a given enterprise as the collective private property of the workers in that firm. Such
a decentralized, simplistic model of workers' control threatens to produce a type of
people's capitalism in which workers in highly capitalized firms and/or rapidly growing economic sectors would have inordinate economic and social power.

109. Arendt, *On Revolution*, p. 278.

110. Ibid. p. 279.

111. As noted earlier, Arendt's conception of council democracy is strikingly—
and admittedly—that of a self-selected, democratic "aristocracy." See *On Revolution*,
p. 284.

112. See Norberto Bobbio, *Which Socialism?* trans. Roger Griffin (Minneapolis:
Univ. of Minnesota Press, 1987), esp. chap. 3, "What Alternatives Are There to Representative Democracy?" pp. 65–84, and chap. 4, "Why Democracy?" pp. 85–102.

113. Arendt, *On Revolution*, pp. 283–84.

114. Ibid., p. 281.

115. Ibid., p. 284.

116. Ibid.

117. This conception of national (or perhaps international) political society as a democratic allocator of authority among different social groups is similar to John Rawls's view in *A Theory of Justice* of society as a whole as the "super union" among particular "social unions." See John Rawls, *A Theory of Justice* (Cambridge: Harvard University Press, 1971), p. 527.

118. Mary McCarthy in "Hannah Arendt: On Hannah Arendt," in Melvyn A. Hill, ed., *Hannah Arendt: The Recovery of the Public World*, pp. 315–16.

119. Hannah Arendt in "Hannah Arendt: On Hannah Arendt," p. 316.

120. Ibid., pp. 317–18.

121. Hannah Arendt, "Reflections on Little Rock," *Dissent* (Winter 1959): 45–56. Given the centrality of race and racism to U.S. political discourse, politics, and social policy, it is hard to imagine how problems of racial equality could be solved by "experts" as nonpolitical, "technical" matters.

CHAPTER 7
CONCLUSION: REDRESSING THE RADICAL TRADITION'S
ANTIPOLITICAL LEGACY

1. See Jacob Talmon, *The Origins of Totalitarian Democracy* (New York: Praeger, 1960).

2. Michael Sandel's description of individual identity is strikingly akin to Hegel's description of individual identity being "constituted" by his or her communally cooperative activities. Sandel writes, "To say that the members of a society are bound by a sense of community is not simply to say that a great many of them profess communitarian sentiments and pursue communitarian aims, but rather that they conceive their identity . . . as defined to some extent by the community of which they are a part" (Michael Sandel, *Liberalism and the Limits of Justice* [Cambridge: Cambridge University Press, 1982], p. 147).

3. Bernard Yack in *The Problems of a Political Animal: Community, Justice, and Conflict in Aristotelian Political Thought* (Berkeley: University of California Press, 1993) criticizes the communitarian misappropriation of Aristotle as an alleged advocate of virtuous, morally homogenous communities. Yack reads Aristotle as conceiving political conflict and social difference to be central to the life of all political communities, even virtuous ones.

4. See Benjamin Barber, *Strong Democracy: Participatory Politics for a New Age* (Berkeley: University of California Press, 1984), pp. 252–54. Barber correctly rejects the more economic deterministic aspects of the Marxist tradition that subordinates relatively autonomous cultural, gender, and political phenomenon to the economic. But in arguing in this section and elsewhere that politics must come before economics (and thus "strong democracy" is agnostic as to what sort of economic system best fulfills its claims), Barber makes the converse error of ignoring how structural economic and cultural constraints (the distribution of economic and educational resources) curtail what is politically feasible and demand political transformation. That is, one can abandon reductionist Marxism without rejecting the value of political economy as a mode of social analysis.

To bring this discussion down to the real-world level, Barber and other political theorists concerned with the value of community (William Galston, most notably) are now involved in a project within and around the Clinton administration to propose means to revitalize citizen participation in grassroots, associational, and governmental life. Bracketing the reality that creating the necessary leisure time for working parents to participate in such activities would require a substantial reallocation of state funds to child care, how can ordinary citizens possess political resources comparable to those of major corporate lobbying institutions if political campaign financing, for example, is not taken head-on? The inexorably interwined nature of politics and economics will soon become highly evident in the fight over welfare reform. The Clinton administration's unwillingness to take on the lasting ideological remnants of the Reagan-Bush era by seriously cutting defense spending and reinstituting progressive income and corporate taxation means that the adminsitration will not have the revenues to provide child care, health care, and meaningful job retraining and placement for women forced to leave the welfare rolls. Thus, the supposedly empowering, democratic "welfare reform" may degenerate, despite the good intentions of David Ellwood, Donna Shalala, and others around Health and Human Services, into a punitive measure against poor women and their children. That is, the Clinton administration's "pragmatic" desire to separate out political symbolism from issues of economic and social policy demonstrates the bankruptcy of putting politics first rather than realizing the interdependent nature of political, economic, and ideological realities.

5. See Alasdair MacIntyre, *After Virtue* (South Bend: University of Notre Dame Press, 1981), esp. chap. 18, "After Virtue: Nietzsche or Aristotle, Trotsky and St. Benedict," pp. 256–63.

6. See Jean Cohen, *Class and Civil Society: The Limits of Marxian Critical Theory* (Amherst: The University of Massachusetts Press, 1982); Andrew Arato and Jean Cohen, *Civil Society and Political Theory* (Cambridge: MIT Press, 1992); and Ernesto Laclau and Chantal Mouffe, *Hegemony and Socialist Strategy* (London: Verso, 1985).

7. While Arendt's emphasis on pluralism places her closer to the republican tradition of de Tocqueville than the more monolithic conceptions of community advanced by communitarians, her hostility to social interests and social conflict moves her back toward a unitary conception of social virtue similar in tone to that advanced by communitarians.

8. Will Kymlicka, "Liberalism and Communitarianism," *Canadian Journal of Philosophy*, 18:2 (June 1988): 181–204.

9. Amy Gutmann, "How Liberal is Democracy?" in Douglas MacLean and Claudia Mills, eds., *Liberalism Reconsidered* (Totowa, N.J.: Rowman and Allanheld, 1983), pp. 25–50. See also Amy Gutmann, "Communitarian Critics of Liberalism," *Philosophy and Public Affairs* 14:3 (Summer 1985): 308–22.

10. For Rawls's response to communitarian and other criticisms of his work, see his "Kantian Constructivism in Moral Theory: The Dewey Memorial Lectures 1980," *Journal of Philosophy* 77 (September 1980): 515–72, and "Justice as Fairness: Political Not Metaphysical," *Philosophy and Public Affairs* 14:3 (Summer 1985): 223–52. These responses and others constitute much of the material for his recent book *Political Justice* (New York: Columbia University Press, 1993).

11. See Rawls, *Political Justice*. For a review that critiques the retreat from the more radical, social democratic implications of the earlier *A Theory of Justice*, particularly for distributive justice, see Perry Anderson, "On John Rawls," a review of Rawls, *Political Justice*, in *Dissent* (Winter 1994): 139–44.

12. See Michael Walzer, "Philosophy and Democracy," *Political Theory* 9:3 (August 1981): 379–99, and "Liberalism and the Art of Separation," *Political Theory* 12:3 (August 1984): 315–30.

13. For a provocative exploration of Walzer's "universal" commitment to democracy and the superiority of societies that allow the practice of social criticism, see William Galston, "Community, Democracy, Philosophy: The Political Thought of Michael Walzer," *Political Theory* 17:1 (February 1989): 119–30. Walzer's critique of the existing practices of most democratic polities toward the political rights of "guest workers" is advanced in *Spheres of Justice* (New York: Basic Books, 1983), pp. 52–63. His criticism of the existing practice of the United States regarding the distribution of health care is in ibid., pp. 86–91.

Walzer might claim that he does not impose a "universal" or "external" critique on the distribution of health care in the United States because there already exists a politically contested internal contradiction in U.S. practice between providing health care for the indigent and elderly based on need (Medicaid and Medicare) while leaving the working class and middle class to the vagaries of private insurance. But would not Walzer also criticize a society with a stable political consensus behind distributing health care strictly by private market mechanisms as violating the just, democratic moral principle that health care ought to be distributed according to need?

In his chapter on political power, Walzer appears to offer a universal defense of democracy as the sole just practice for distributing the good of political power: "Once we have located ownership, expertise, religious knowledge, and so on in their proper places and established their autonomy, there is no alternative to democracy in the political sphere. . . . Democracy is a way of allocating power and legitimating its use—or better, it is *the political way* of allocating power. Every extrinsic reason is ruled out. What counts is argument among the citizens" (ibid., pp. 303–4). Walzer himself emphasizes that democracy is the only proper *political* way of distributing power. Would he defend other "nonpolitical" ways of distributing political power as just, if they appeared to be the consensus practices of a stable but nondemocratic society? Or does Walzer believe that a seemingly legitimate, widely supported, but undemocratic political system is to be rejected as a just, "particularist" form of political power because such a regime's stability inevitably depends on some combination of repression of discontent, ideological domination, and/or the writing of history by the dominant who excise actual subaltern resistance from their accounts? If Walzer opts for any of these three explanations, then he is committing himself to some sort of universal, democratic conception of the nature of a free and just polity.

14. Rawls, "The Idea of an Overlapping Consensus, *Oxford Journal of Legal Studies* 7:1 (Spring 1987): 10n.17. His latest book, *Political Justice*, analyzes at greater length the cooperative political practices and constitutional structure that are essential to liberal democracy.

15. For an exploration of the sociological and political origins of the collapse of social solidarity in the United States and reflections on theoretical and political possibilities for a renewal of a solidaristic politics, see Joseph Schwartz, "Coalition Politics in a Three Speed Society," *Socialist Review* 90:2 (April-June 1990), pp. 67–79. See also my "Democratic Solidarity and the Crisis of the Welfare State," in John P. Burke, Lyman H. Letgers, and Arthur DiQuattro, eds., *Critical Perspectives on Democracy* (Lanham, Md.: Rowman and Littlefield, 1994), pp. 87–111.

16. See Charles Taylor, "Cross-Purposes: The Liberal-Communitarian Debate," in Nancy Rosenblum, ed., *Liberalism and the Moral Life* (Cambridge: Harvard University Press, 1989), p. 173.

17. Ibid., pp. 170–76.

18. Ibid., pp. 180–82.

19. See Ian Shapiro, *The Evolution of Natural Rights* (Cambridge: Cambridge University Press, 1986), pp. 301–5.

20. For a sophisticated argument as to how a coherent liberal political system can be based on nonteleological assumptions about the negative potential of human character, see Charles Larmore, *Patterns of Moral Complexity* (Cambridge: Cambridge University Press, 1987). Don Herzog, in comments on the manuscript, pointed out how the Humean tradition of liberal thought rejects the view that political theory must center on a picture of human flourishing. Rather, he states that a "Humean tradition casts human nature as a set of problems and threats and institutions as offering the possibility of thwarting human nature." For a more extensive treatment of this view and how an antifoundationalist epistemology can yield a coherent conception of liberal politics, see Don Herzog, *Without Foundations: Justification in Political Theory* (Ithaca: Cornell University Press, 1985). Aryeh Botwinick's work argues that an antifoundationalist, postmodern epistemology offers the best "grounds" on which to base a moral argument for participatory democracy; see Aryeh Botwinick, *Skepticism and Political Participation* (Philadelphia: Temple University Press, 1990) and *Postmodernism and Democratic Theory* (Philadelphia: Temple University Press, 1993). Unlike Botwinick, Herzog does not claim that an antifoundationalist epistemology is inherently democratic. In his view and my own, there can be foundationalist or antifoundationalist democrats, as well as foundationalist or antifoundationalist defenders of undemocratic regimes.

21. See Judith Butler, *Gender Troubles: Feminism and the Subversion of Identity* (New York: Routledge, 1990); Jane Flax, *Thinking Fragments: Psychoanalysis, Feminism and Postmodernism in the Contemporary West* (Berkeley: University of California Press, 1990); William E. Connolly, *Identity/Difference: Democratic Negotiations of Political Paradox* (Ithaca: Cornell University Press, 1991); and Bonnie Honig, *Political Theory and the Displacement of Politics* (Ithaca: Cornell University Press, 1993).

22. See Seyla Benhabib, *Situating the Self: Gender, Community and Postmodernism in Contemporary Ethics* (New York: Routledge, 1992).

23. See Leslie Paul Thiel, "Review of Bonnie Honig, *Political Theory and the Displacement of Politics*," *American Political Science Review* 88:1 (March 1994): 214–15.

24. Connolly, *Identity/Difference*, p. 190.

25. See Charles Taylor, *Sources of the Self: The Making of the Modern Identity* (Cambridge: Harvard University Press, 1989).

26. See Connolly, *Identity/Difference*, pp. 107–12.

27. Theorists of a "politics of difference" adopt a rather schizophrenic position toward the intellectually radical implications of postmodern theory for the concept of group identity. If oppressed groups can share certain identities based on common historical experiences, then individual identity cannot be as fragile and decentered as the most radical advocates of postmodernism claim. If we cannot even know who we are—constantly moving from "subject-position" to "subject-position" thus, constantly reconstituting the intertwined complex of the self and "others"—then how can we possibly identify other human subjects as sharing our identity? On the integral relationship between belief in the concept of a coherent, self-critical, self-conscious self to arguments for individual freedom and autonomy, see Charles Taylor, *Sources of the Self*.

The obverse danger, of course, is that group identity can essentialize individuals. To cite just one prominent example, not all "people of color" conceive themselves to be "people of color;" nor do they all believe they share a common ethnic, racial, gender, linguistic, class, or sexual preference identity. In the context of the United States, the term "people of color" refers to the experience of subordination that nonwhite groups have shared at some point in their experience here. But there are obviously diverse experiences across and within non-European groups in the United States. (Just think of the diversity of the Latino community in the United States and disputes over whether *Latino, Spanish-speaking, Hispanic-American*, or no unifying term should be used to identify an alleged common experience of Cuban-Americans, Mexican-Americans, Puerto Ricans, recent Dominican immigrants, etc.). This is not to deny that certain cultural and historical experiences, such as a common language, shared Ibero-Caribbean culture, and shared experience of colonialist displacement or conquest, constitute a certain form of shared group identity among Spanish-speaking peoples in the Americas. But such an identity should not be essentialized by denying that there are often cross-cutting cultural, socioeconomic, regional, and sexual differences within the collectivity that is being identified.

28. See Laclau and Mouffe, *Hegemony and Socialist Strategy*; Richard Rorty, *Contingency, Irony and Solidarity* (Cambridge: Cambridge University Press, 1989); Benjamin Barber, *Strong Democracy*.

29. I consciously avoid using the term "human nature," as one can have a theory of what it is to be human which conceives of human beings as the one species that is, within limits, capable of transforming its nature. That is, human beings are the only historically defined and self-transforming species. This belief does not necessarily mean that there are no aspects of human behavior that are shared across cultures and historical epochs.

30. See Robert Nozick, *Anarchy, State and Utopia* (New York: Basic Books, 1974); John Rawls, *A Theory of Justice* (Cambridge: Harvard University Press, 1971); and Susan Moller Okin, *Justice, Gender and the Family* (New York: Basic Books, 1989).

31. See Jurgen Habermas, *The Theory of Communicative Action*, vol. 2, *Lifeworld and System*, trans. Thomas McCarthy (Boston: Beacon Press, 1987); and Benhabib, *Situating the Self*.

32. For representative works see Sandel, *Liberalism and the Limits of Justice*; Leo Strauss, *Natural Right and History* (Chicago: University of Chicago Press, 1953); and MacIntyre, *After Virtue*.

33. See Butler, *Gender Troubles*; Flax, *Thinking Fragments*; and Connolly, *Identity/Difference*. Flax's work demonstrates how a "strong" version of postmodern theory cannot be uncritically appropriated by those committed to democratic political transformation. Her unrestrained "Foucauldian" analysis of how power/knowledge matrixes construct human subjects and truth so denudes the possibility of individual agency (or coherent individual selves) that it is hard to imagine how normative and political critiques of domination remain possible. If there is no "doer behind the deed" other than "subject-positions" constructed by discursive practices, then the possibility for democratic agency become as pessimistic in postmodern thought as it is in the structuralist analysis that postmodernism critiqued as overly deterministic. "Smashing the metaphysics of presence" can be as politically disabling a "metanarrative" as any teleology generated by the Enlightenment tradition.

34. See Benhabib, *Situating the Self*, pp. 22, 195, 202n.

35. Cornel West, in Andrew Ross, ed., *Universal Abandon? The Politics of Postmodernism* (Minneapolis: University of Minnesota Press, 1988), p. 269.

36. This discussion is, in part, a response to the comments of Don Herzog, who believes my argument is more in accord with the liberal tradition than my radical political identity enables me to acknowledge openly. Although he is correct to point out that certain members of the liberal tradition hold normative and political positions close to those advanced in this work, I do not believe, as argued below in my response to the work of Samuel Bowles and Herbert Gintis, that such "radical liberal" politics reflects the dominant liberal ideological, and even theoretical, tradition. Nor can such "radical liberal" politics be consistently held without embracing the systemic, radical critique of liberal democratic capitalist societies historically associated with the democratic socialist tradition.

37. Joshua Cohen and Joel Rogers, *On Democracy: Toward a Transformation of American Society* (New York: Penguin, 1983), p. 150. Combining Rawls's two principles of justice with a commitment to economic democracy, Cohen and Rogers advance seven institutional requirements for democracy: "civil rights and civil liberties, public subsidy for organized competitive political groups, egalitarian distributional measures, public control of investment, workplace democracy, equality of opportunity, and a foreign policy informed by the principles of democratic legitimacy," ibid., p. 167.

38. See Samuel Bowles and Herbert Gintis, *Democracy and Capitalism: Property, Community, and the Contradictions of Modern Social Thought* (New York: Basic Books, 1986), pp. 92–97.

39. See Frank Cunningham, *Democratic Theory and Socialism* (New York: Cambridge University Press, 1987), p. 340n.4.

40. Bowles and Gintis, *Democracy and Capitalism*, p. 97.

41. For prior work that is not only democratic socialist but neo-Marxist in its orientation, see Samuel Bowles and Herbert Gintis, *Schooling in Capitalist America* (New York: Basic Books, 1973) and Bowles, David Gordon, and Thomas Weisskopf, *Beyond the Wasteland* (Garden City, N.J.: Anchor, 1983).

42. In their well-intentioned effort to move beyond structuralist Marxism's denigration of the relatively autonomous import of ideological and cultural contestation, Laclau and Mouffe, and the many cultural and social theorists influenced by them, come perilously close to granting a primacy to purely "discursive practices" as the engine-room of a nonteleological history. It is as if they have dropped the second clause of Marx's famous dictum in *The Eighteenth Brumaire* that "human beings make history, but not under conditions of their own choosing." See Ernesto Laclau and Chantal Mouffe, *Hegemony and Socialist Strategy*, esp. chap. 3, "Beyond the Positivity of the Social: Antagonisms and Hegemony," pp. 93–148.

43. Jeff Goodwin makes this point about Bowles and Gintis's unproven teleological faith in the triumph of personal rights over property rights in an insightful review of their *Democracy and Capitalism*. He also advances a similar argument to the one made here that utilizing the term *economic democracy* instead of *democratic socialism* does not erase the antisocialist bogey-person from the realities of U.S. politics. See Jeff Goodwin, "The Limits of 'Radical Democracy,'" *Socialist Review* 90:2 (April-June 1990): 131–44.

44. Thus my initial prescriptive argument for radical democracy is more in line with the efforts of democratic socialist theorists who defend the socialist analysis of domination and exploitation in the economic sphere while incorporating the insights

of feminist and some postmodern theorists regarding the centrality in a radical democracy of pluralism and a civil society relatively autonomous from state interference. In this sense I am in closer sympathy with the efforts of Carol C. Gould, *Rethinking Democracy: Freedom and Social Cooperation in Politics, Economy, and Society* (New York: Cambridge University Press, 1988); Frank Cunningham, *Democratic Theory and Socialism*; Philip Green, *Retrieving Democracy: In Search of Civic Equality* (Totowa, N.J.: Rowman and Allanheld, 1985); and Benhabib, *Situating the Self*. And despite some methodological and theoretical differences discussed elsewhere, my work relies significantly on Iris Marion Young's *Justice and the Politics of Difference* (Princeton: Princeton University Press, 1990), and Michael Walzer's *Spheres of Justice* and his essays on political and economic democracy. It is not an accident that almost all of these theorists would probably be comfortable with the label "liberal socialist-feminists," "liberal democratic socialists," etc. That is, all would agree that significant aspects of both the liberal and democratic socialist tradition should be incorporated into any successful reconstruction of a radical democratic pluralist theory and practice.

45. See Carole Pateman, *The Sexual Contract* (Stanford: Stanford University Press, 1988), esp. chap. 5, "Wives, Slaves and Wage Slaves," pp. 116–53.

46. For one of the few serious contemporary attempts to develop a radical theory of consent and obligation drawing on the best of the liberal tradition, see Cohen and Rogers, *On Democracy*.

47. For a description of how a society's "social contract" is not the product of abstract philosophical arguments but of the actual social and political construction—and contestation—of common moral meanings in regard to the distribution of social goods and social roles, see Walzer, *Spheres of Justice*, esp. pp. 82–83.

48. For a critique of the pessimism of the Foucauldian perspective, see Michael Walzer, "The Lonely Politics of Michel Foucault," in his *The Company of Critics: Social Criticism and Political Commitment in the Twentieth Century* (New York: Basic Books, 1988), pp. 191–209.

49. See Michel Foucault, "What is Enlightenment?" pp. 32–50; and "Polemics, Politics and Prolematizations," pp. 381–90 in *The Foucault Reader*, ed. Paul Rabinow (New York: Pantheon, 1984).

50. For a classic statement of the initial Black Power movement and the argument that its alleged separatist desire for power was no different than that of previous ethnic insurgencies in U.S. urban politics, see Stokely Carmichael and Charles V. Hamilton, *Black Power: The Politics of Liberation in America* (New York: Vintage, 1967).

51. The "regulatory school" of political economy argues that every stage of capitalist development is characterized by a hegemonic "social structure of accumulation," the economic, moral, and political principles of a viable socioeconomic order. This "social structure of accumulation" consists of a "regime of accumulation," a particular stragegy of economic development, and a "mode of regulation," the particular set of economic, political, and moral/ideological policies that enable the "regime of accumulation" to function smoothly. Thus, in the regulatory school's analysis, the contemporary political impasse facing both the traditional left and right in advanced industrial democracies results from the breakdown of the old "Keynesian/Fordist" "social structure of accumulation." (The Keynesian "social structure of accumulation" rested on a high-value-added, industrial "regime of accumulation" centered in the core Western countries that provided the tax-revenues and economic growth necessary to support the gradual expansion of public provision

and working-class living standards characteristic of the "mode of regulation" of the welfare state.)

This postwar Keynesian "social structure of accumulation" has been supplanted, since around 1973, by a "post-Fordist" global "regime of accumulation," in which the core capitalist economies now must compete against the newly industrializing societies. But there has yet to develop a new "mode of regulation," comparable to the Keynesian welfare state from 1945 to 1973, which can stably govern democratic polities by offsetting corporate downsizing and declining living standards. The ideology of Reagan-Thatcherism (deregulation, social welfare cuts accompanied by military Keynesianism) represented the first effort at a "post-Fordist" political "mode of regulation." But its failure to deter downward global presures on living standards in the advanced industrial polities led to the erosion by the end of the 1980s of its previous decade-long dominance of Western politics (though by no means exhausting its political power). The democratic left is in an even weaker ideological position than this semi-exhausted "conservatizing modernizing" project, because the revival of a high-wage economy that could support a growth in public provision awaits a global Keynesian strategy of raising living standards in both the First and Third Worlds. Building the transnational social movements and political institutions capable of implementing such a "global Keynesian" "mode of accumulation" may well be an epochal project for the left.

For representative works of "the regulatory school," see Michael Aglietta, *A Theory of Capitalist Regulation* (London: New Left Books, 1979) and Alain Lipietz, *Mirages and Miracles: The Crisis of Global Fordism* (London: Verso, 1987). For an attempt to apply the concept of a "social structure of accumulation" to the U.S. "post-Fordism," see Samuel Bowles, David Gordon, and Thomas Weisskopf, *Beyond the Wasteland: A Democratic Alternative*.

52. For Laclau and Mouffe's argument as to how distinct social movements must extend a "logic of equivalence" to other struggles of oppressed groups and "construct a chain of democratic equivalences" grounded in a vision of a new, contingent, democratic "social order" if these groups are to achieve social hegemony, see Laclau and Mouffe, *Hegemony and Socialist Strategy*, esp. chap. 4, "Hegemony and Radical Democracy," particularly pp. 176–93. Their two essays in *Universal Abandon* demonstrate their ambivalence about whether democracy can survive apart from the universal values of the Enlightenment, particularly regarding rights and pluralism, even while democratic movements can no longer depend on the metaphysics and ontology of Enlightenment reason. See Mouffe, "Radical Democracy: Modern or Post-Modern?" trans. Paul Holdengraber, pp. 31–45, and Laclau, "Politics and the Limits of Modernity," pp. 63–82, both in Andrew Ross, ed., *Universal Abandon?*

53. The resurgence of the new right in the late 1970s and 1980s has often been cited by Laclau and Mouffe and the British journal *Marxism Today* as an example of the power of discourse in defining political alternatives. But the decline of left-identified, Keynesian welfare states and social democratic parties had as much to do with the material crisis of Keynesianism-in-one-country as it did with the discovery by the right of a "new hegemonic discourse" of the efficiency of the market and of entrepreneurs as the universal class. The broadly defined left has recently made modest recoveries in both the West and East largely due to the failure of the new right to bring economic security to the vast majority. Whether or not the left can develop a new majoritarian "social structure of accumulation" is both a question of economic strategy and of a cultural or "discursive" response to the new right's ideology of competitive individualism.

54. See Cohen and Rogers, *On Democracy*, pp. 173–83, for a compelling, non-postmodern version of the argument that the moral commitment to democracy should transcend the coalition-model of radical politics which is too dependent on divergent and ever-shifting material interests among diverse identities. Although concurring that a normative commitment to the value of democracy is part of the glue that must hold together any pluralist, majoritarian democratic movement, I give more emphasis in this work to what Cohen and Rogers do admit is another necessary task, that of forging a common identity of citizenship and a common material, political agenda.

55. Stanley Aronowitz interprets Laclau and Mouffe to be "closet ethical socialists" in his essay "Postmodernism and Politics," in Ross, ed., *Universal Abandon?* pp. 46–62.

56. See Iris Marion Young, *Justice and the Politics of Difference*, chap. 1, "The Distributive Paradigm," pp. 15–38.

57. For Young on Habermas, see ibid., pp. 117–18. Young defines domination as the absence of democratic voice in institutional life, and exploitation as absence of control over one's labor (see chap. 2, "Five Faces of Oppression," pp. 39–65).

58. Ibid., chap. 8, "City Life and Difference," pp. 226–56.

59. See Benhabib, *Situating the Self*, esp. chap. 7, "Feminism and the Question of Postmodernism," pp. 202–41.

60. For example, as Cornel West has noted on numerous occasions, although many gay and lesbian people are African-American, the dominant political and cultural institution in the African-American community—the church—has a tradition, though by no means a monolithic one, of homophobia. See bell hooks and West's discussion of gay and lesbian liberation and the African-American community in bell hooks and Cornel West, *Breaking Bread: Insurgent Black Intellectual Life* (Boston: South End Press, 1990), pp. 83–84, 122–24.

61. Cohen and Rogers, *On Democracy*, p. 148.

62. See John Stuart Mill, *Principles of Political Economy, Books IV and V* (London: Penguin, 1985), Book 4, chap. 7, "On the Probable Future of the Labouring Classes," pp. 118–44.

63. My semiconscious tendency to group examples of racial and gender hierarchy with those of class domination is not intended to deny the relatively autonomous logic of diverse forms of oppression. Nor is it meant to ignore the complex interactions of forms of oppression which render the question of "identity" far more complex than acknowledged by essentialist readings of group identity. But my examples do imply that although racism, sexism, and homophobia both predated, and unfortunately will probably postdate, liberal democratic capitalist societies, these specific forms of oppression in our society are influenced by the logic of late capitalist society.

Some may find the implicit belief that economic democracy must serve as a necessary but not sufficient condition for overcoming racial and gender domination an anachronistic "democratic socialist, economistic" throwback to a past, historical juncture of contingent anticapitalist struggle. But it is impossible to envision how a globalized economy's incorporation and accentuation of race, class, and gender hierarchies into the international division of labor can be tackled without the creation of transnational labor, antiracist, and feminist organizations. To hold that "identity politics" transcends the "traditional" material realm is to ignore the complex interaction between race, class, gender, and sexual preference in the social construction of identity. On the other hand, noneconomic identities of ethnicity, citizenship, and com-

munity have played a central role in the construction of class solidarity. If the conception of identity offered here appears overly "dialectic" and unwilling to grant
primacy to either economic or cultural factors, a possible reason is that social reality
denies any simplistic either/or choice. If the analysis evidences a latent "soft" materialism, the reason is that I believe we are still living in a "material world." (So perhaps
the "postmodern" commodification of a Madonna is not such a postmaterialist
phenomenon.)

64. There has been a perennial debate within radical movements as to how open
and nonrepressive liberal democratic polities truly are. The covert, nonmajoritarian
means that revolutionary movements in repressive societies are forced to employ are
often poor preparation for governing democratically in a postrevolutionary period.
This problem, one of the great challenges, and tragedies, of revolutionary movements, is increasingly acknowledged by revolutionary movements in the Third World
today who have recently abandoned orthodox Marxist-Leninism.

But what of the argument that the power of dominant ideology and establishment
control over the mass media renders liberal democracies more insidiously repressive—
"repressively tolerant" in Marcuse's famous phrase—than nonliberal societies? (See
Herbert Marcuse, "Repressive Tolerance," in Marcuse, Barrington Moore, Jr., and
Robert Paul Wolff, *Critique of Pure Tolerance* [Boston: Beacon Press, 1969], pp.
81–117.) Adherents of such a view rarely ask themselves how they came to be radicalized under such allegedly repressive conditions. Is their perspective specially privileged, or if they could come to a radical critique of the system, could not their political efforts convince others? Nor do they investigate why the left is stronger in some
liberal democratic polities than in others. Undoubtedly the structural inequalities of
liberal democratic capitalist societies render these democracies seriously imperfect,
with unequal access to the mass media and private financing of political campaigns
involving significant distortions of liberal democracy's commitment to egalitarian
politics. But there exists no shortcut around mass democratic politics—both extra-
parliamentary and parliamentary—to fight those structural inequalities. Adam
Przeworski and others have described how it is "rational" for subordinate groups
normally to opt for short-term gains within the democratic capitalist system rather
than risk long-term transformative strategies. (see Adam Przeworski, *Capitalism and
Social Democracy* [Cambridge: Cambridge University Press, 1985], esp. chap. 5,
"Material Interests, Class Compromise, and the State," pp. 171–204). But no one
promised that the terrain of political struggle in democratic capitalist societies would
be "fair" to popular forces. The challenge facing social movements in liberal democracies is how to organize on an admittedly nonlevel playing field.

Subordinate groups are often less dismissive of "mere bourgeois civil liberties"
than are small, elite vanguards that speak in the name of the subordinated. A possible
explanation is that democratic social movements understand that civil liberties were
not paternalistically granted to them by elites aiming to coopt them. Rather, they
were won by costly popular struggle. Such an understanding underpins the critique
by "Minority Legal Scholars" of Critical Legal Studies' dismissal of the value of rights
in a democratic society. See Patricia Williams, "Alchemical Notes: Reconstructing
Ideals from Deconstructed Rights," 22 *Harvard Civil Rights-Civil Liberties Law
Review* 401.

Ackerman, Bruce. "Neo-federalism?" In Jon Elster and Rune Slagstad, eds., *Constitutionalism and Democracy*. Cambridge: Cambridge University Press, 1988, pp. 153–94.

Aglietta, Michael. *A Theory of Capitalist Regulation*. London: New Left Books, 1979.

Alford, Robert B., and Roger Friedland. *Powers of Theory: Capitalism, the State and Democracy*. Cambridge: Cambridge University Press, 1985.

Althusser, Louis. *For Marx*. Translated by Ben Brewster. New York: Vintage, 1970.

Anderson, Perry. *Considerations on Western Marxism*. London: New Left Books, 1976.

———.*Arguments within English Marxism*. London: Verso, 1980

———."On John Rawls," *Dissent* (Winter 1994): 139–44.

Arato, Andrew, and Jean Cohen. *Civil Society and Political Theory*. Cambridge: MIT Press, 1992.

Arendt, Hannah. *The Human Condition*. Chicago: University of Chicago Press, 1958.

———. "Reflections on Little Rock." *Dissent* (Winter 1959): 45–56.

———. *Between Past and Future: Six Exercises in Political Thought*. Cleveland: World, 1963.

———. *On Revolution*. New York: Vintage, 1963.

———. *Crises of the Republic*. New York: Harcourt Brace Jovanovich, 1973.

Aronowitz, Stanley. "Postmodernism in Politics." In Andrew Ross, ed., *Universal Abandon? The Politics of Postmodernism*. Minneapolis: University of Minnesota Press, 1988, pp. 46–62.

———. *Science as Power: Discourse and Ideology in Modern Society*. Minneapolis: University of Minnesota Press, 1988.

Ashcraft, Richard. *Revolutionary Politics and Locke's "Two Treatises of Government."* Princeton: Princeton University Press, 1986.

Avineri, Shlomo. *The Social and Political Thought of Karl Marx*. Cambridge: Cambridge University Press, 1968.

———. *Hegel's Theory of the Modern State*. Cambridge: Cambridge University Press, 1972.

———, ed. *Marx's Socialism*. New York: Lieber-Atherton, 1973.

Bakan, Mildred. "Hannaah Arendt's Concept of Labor and Work." In Melvyn A. Hill, ed., *Hannah Arendt and the Recovery of the Public World*. New York: St. Martin's Press, 1979, pp. 49–66.

Barber, Benjamin. *Strong Democracy: Participatory Politics for a New Age*. Berkeley: University of California Press, 1984.

———. *The Conquest of Politics*. Princeton: Princeton University Press, 1988.

———. "The Reconstruction of Rights." *The American Prospect* 5 (Spring 1991): 36–46.

Bell, Daniel. "The 'Rediscovery' of Alienation." In Shlomo Avineri, ed., *Marx's Socialism*. New York: Lieber-Atherton, 1973, pp. 59–79.

Benhabib, Seyla. *Situating the Self: Gender, Community and Postmodernism in Contemporary Ethics*. New York: Routledge, 1992.

———Benhabib, Seyla, and Druscilla Cornell, eds. *Feminism as Critique*. Oxford: Polity Press, 1987.

Berlin, Isaiah. *Four Essays on Liberty*. Oxford: Oxford University Press, 1969.

Berman, Marshall. *The Politics of Authenticity: Radical Individualism and the Emergence of Modern Society*. New York: Atheneum, 1970.

Bloom, Alan. Introduction to *The Emile or "On Education,"* by Jean-Jacques Rousseau. Translated by Alan Bloom. New York: Basic Books, 1979, pp. 3–20.

———. "Rousseau." In Leo Strauss and Joseph Cropsey, eds., *The History of Political Philosophy*, 2nd ed. Chicago: Rand-McNally, 1972, pp. 532–53.

Bobbio, Norberto. *Which Socialism?* Translated by Roger Griffin. Minneapolis: University of Minnesota Press, 1987, pp. 73–100.

———. "Gramsci and the Concept of Civil Society." In John Keane, ed., *Civil Society and the State*. London: Verso, 1988, pp. 73–100.

Botwinick, Aryeh. *Skepticism and Political Participation*. Philadelphia: Temple University Press, 1990.

———.*Postmodernism and Democratic Theory*. Philadelphia: Temple University Press, 1993.

Bowles, Samuel, and Herbert Gintis. *Schooling in Capitalist America: Educational Reform and the Contradictions of Economic Life*. New York: Basic Books, 1976.

———.*Democracy and Capitalism: Property, Community, and the Contradictions of Modern Social Thought*. New York: Basic Books, 1986.

Bowles, Samuel, David Gordon, and Thomas Weisskopf. *Beyond the Wasteland: A Democratic Alternative to Economic Decline*. Garden City, N.J.: Anchor Press, 1983.

Brenkert, George G. "Freedom and Private Property in Marx." In Marshall Cohen, Thomas Nagel, and Thomas Scanlon, eds., *Marx, Justice and History*. Princeton: Princeton University Press, 1980, pp. 80–105.

Buchanan, Allen. *Marx and Justice*. London: Metheun, 1982.

Bukharin, Nicholai. *Imperialism and the World Economy*. New York: Monthly Review Press, 1973.

Butler, Judith P. *Gender Troubles: Feminism and the Subversion of Identity*. New York: Routledge, 1990.

Carmichael, Stokely, and Charles V. Hamilton. *Black Power: The Politics of Liberation in America*. New York: Vintage, 1967.

Cassirer, Ernst. *The Question of Jean-Jacques Rousseau*. Translated by Peter Gay. New York: Columbia University Press, 1954.

Coase, Ronald H. "The Nature of the Firm." *Economica* 4:16 (November 1937):386–405.

Cohen, G. A. *Karl Marx's Theory of History: A Defence*. Oxford: Oxford University Press, 1978.

———. Review of Allen Wood, *Marx. Mind* 92:367 (1983): 443.

———. "Self-Ownership, World-Ownership and Equality." In Frank S. Lucash, ed., *Justice and Equality: Here and Now*. Ithaca: Cornell University Press, 1986, pp. 108–35..

———. "Self-Ownership, World-Ownership and Equality: Party II." *Social Philosophy and Policy* 3:2 (Spring 1986): 77–96.

Cohen, Jean. *Class and Civil Society: The Limits of Marxian Critical Theory.* Amherst: University of Massachusetts Press, 1982.

Cohen, Joshua. "Reflections on Rousseau: Autonomy and Democracy." *Philosophy and Public Affairs* 15:3 (Summer 1986): 275–97.

———. "Do Values Explain Facts—The Case of Slavery." Paper delivered at the American Political Science Association Convention, 1986. University of Michigan Microfilms, 1986.

———. "Structure, Choice, and Legitimacy: Locke's Theory of the State." *Philosophy and Public Affairs* 15:4 (Fall 1986): 301–24.

Cohen, Joshua, and Joel Rogers. *On Democracy: Toward a Transformation of American Society.* New York: Penguin, 1983.

Cohen, Marshall, Thomas Nagel, and Thomas Scanlon, eds. *Marx, Justice and History.* Princeton: Princeton University Press, 1980.

Cole, G.D.H. *Self-Government in Industry.* London: G. Bell, 1919.

——— *Guild Socialism Restated.* London: Leonard Parsons, 1920.

Coletti, Lucio. *Marxism and Hegel.* Translated by Lawrence Garner. London: New Left Books, 1973.

Connolly, William E. *The Terms of Political Discourse*, 2nd ed. Princeton: Princeton University Press, 1983.

———.*Identity/Difference: Democratic Negotiations of Political Paradox.* Ithaca: Cornell University Press, 1991.

Crick, Bernard. *In Defence of Politics*, 2nd ed. London: Penguin, 1972.

Cronin, James, and Carmen Sirianni, eds. *Work, Community, and Power.* Philadelphia: Temple University Press, 1983.

Cullen, Bernard. *Hegel's Social and Political Thought: An Introduction.* New York: St. Martin's Press, 1979.

Cunningham, Frank. *Democratic Theory and Socialism.* Cambridge: Cambridge University Press, 1987.

Dahl, Robert. *After the Revolution: Authority in a Good Society.* New Haven: Yale University Press, 1970.

———. *A Preface to Economic Democracy.* Berkeley: University of California Press, 1985.

———. *Democracy and Its Critics.* New Haven: Yale University Press, 1989.

Dewey, John. *The Public and Its Problems.* New York: Henry Holt, 1927.

———. "Means and Ends." In George A. Novack, ed., *Their Morals and Ours: Marxist and Liberal Views on Morality.* New York: Pathfinder Press, 1968, pp. 51–58.

Durkheim, Emile. *The Division of Labor in Society.* Translated by George Simpson. Glencoe, Il.: Free Press, 1947.

———. *Professional Ethics and Civil Morals.* Ed. Robert Bellah. Glencoe, Il.: Free Press, 1958.

———. *On Morality and Society.* Ed. Robert Bellah. Chicago: University of Chicago Press, 1973.

Dworkin, Ronald. "What Is Equality: Part II: Equality of Resources." *Philosophy and Public Affairs* 10 (Fall 1981): 283–345.

Easton, David. *The Political System: An Inquiry into the State of Political Science.* New York: Alfred Knopf, 1953.

Ehrenberg, John. *The Dictatorship of the Proletariat: Marxisms's Theory of Socialist Democracy.* New York: Routledge, 1992.

Elster, Jon. *Making Sense of Marx.* Cambridge: Cambridge University Press, 1985.

————."Arguments for Constitutional Choice: Reflections on the Transition to Socialism." In Jon Elster and Rune Slagstad, eds., *Constitutionalism and Democracy.* Cambridge: Cambridge University Press, 1988, pp. 303–26.

————. "Self-Realisation in Work and Politics: The Marxist Conception of the Good Life." In Jon Elster and Karl Ove Moene, eds., *Alternatives to Capitalism.* Cambridge: Cambridge University Press, 1989, pp. 127–58.

Elster, Jon, and Karl Ove Moene, eds. *Alternatives to Capitalism.* Cambridge: Cambridge University Press, 1989.

Elster, Jon, and Rune Slagstad, eds. *Constitutionalism and Democracy.* Cambridge: Cambridge University Press, 1988.

Engels, Friedrich. Introduction to *The Civil War in France,* by Karl Marx. In *The Marx-Engels Reader.* 2nd ed. Ed. Robert C. Tucker. New York: Norton, 1978, pp. 618–29.

————. "On Authority." In *The Marx-Engels Reader,* pp. 730–33.

————. *Socialism: Utopian and Scientific.* In *The Marx-Engels Reader,* pp. 683–717.

————. "The Tactics of Social Democrcy." In *The Marx-Engels Reader,* pp. 556–73.

Erlich, Alexander. *The Soviet Industrialization Debate 1924–1928.* Cambridge: Harvard University Press, 1967.

Etzioni, Amitai. *The Spirit of Community: Rights, Responsibilities and the Communitarian Agenda.* New York: Crown, 1993.

Finley, Moses I. "The Freedom of the Citizen in the Greek World." In his *Economy and Society in Ancient Greece.* London: Chatto and Windus, 1981.

Flax, Jane. *Thinking Fragments: Psychoanalysis, Feminism and Postmodernism in the Contemporary West.* Berkeley: University of California Press, 1990.

Foucault, Michel. "Polemics, Politics and Problematizations: An Interview with Michel Foucault." In *The Foucault Reader.* Ed. Paul Rabinow. New York: Pantheon, 1984, pp. 381–90.

————. "What is Enlightenment?" In *The Foucault Reader,* pp. 32–50. New York: Pantheon, 1984.

Fralin, Richard. *Rousseau and Representation.* New York: Columbia University Press, 1978.

Fukuyama, Frances. *The End of History and the Last Man.* New York: Free Press, 1992.

Furét, François. *The French Revolution and the Creation of Modern Political Culture.* New York: Pergamon Press, 1982.

Fuss, Peter. "Hannah Arendt's Conception of Political Community." In Melvyn A. Hill, ed., *Hannah Arendt: The Recovery of the Public World.* New York: St. Martin's Press, 1979, pp. 157-76.

Galston, William. "Community, Democracy, Philosophy: The Political Thought of Michael Walzer." *Political Theory* 17:1 (February 1989): 119–30.

Geras, Norman. "The Controversy about Marx and Justice." *New Left Review* 150:2 (March-April 1985): 47–85.

Gilbert, Alan. *Marx's Politics: Communists and Citizens.* New Brunswick: Rutgers University Press, 1981.

————.*Democratic Individuality.* Cambridge: Cambridge University Press, 1990.

Gildin, Hillel. *Rousseau's Social Contract.* Chicago: University of Chicago Press, 1983.

Glucksmann, André. *The Master Thinkers.* Translated by Brian Pearce. New York: Harper and Row, 1980.

Goodwin, Jeff. "The Limits of 'Radical Democracy.'" *Socialist Review* 90:2 (April–June 1990): 131–44.

Gould, Carol C. *Rethinking Democracy: Freedom and Cooperation in Politics, Economy, and Society*. Cambridge: Cambridge University Press, 1988.

Green, Philip. *Retrieving Democracy: In Search of Civil Equality*. Totowa, N.J.: Rowman and Allanheld, 1985.

Gunnell, John. *Political Theory: Tradition and Interpretation*. Cambridge: Winthrop, 1979.

Gutmann, Amy. *Liberal Equality*. Cambridge: Cambridge University Press, 1980.

———. "How Liberal Is Democracy?" In Douglas MacLean and Claudia Mills, eds., *Liberalism Reconsidered*. Totowa, N.J.: Rowman and Allanheld, 1983, pp. 25–50.

———. "Communitarian Critics of Liberalism." *Philosophy and Public Affairs*. 14:3 (Summer 1985): 308–22.

Gutmann, Amy, ed. *Democracy and the Welfare State*. Princeton: Princeton University Press, 1988.

Habermas, Jurgen. *Towards a Rational Society*. Translated by Jeremy Shapiro. Boston: Beacon Press, 1970.

———. *Knowledge and Human Interests*. Translated by Jeremy Shapiro. Boston: Beacon Press, 1971.

———. "Hannah Arendt's Communications Concept of Power." *Social Research*. 44:1 (Spring 1977): 3–24.

———. *The Theory of Communicative Action*. Vol. 1: Reason and the Rationalization of Society. Translated by Thomas McCarthy. Boston: Beacon Press, 1984.

———. *The Theory of Communicative Action*. Vol. 2: *Lifeworld and System*. Translated by Thomas McCarthy. Boston: Beacon Press, 1987.

———. *The Structural Transformation of the Public Sphere: An Inquiry into a Concept of Bourgeois Society*. Translated by Thomas Burger with the assistance of Frederich Lawrence. Cambridge: MIT Press, 1989.

Harding, Neil. *Lenin's Political Thought*. Vol.1. New York: St. Martin's Press, 1977.

———. *Lenin's Political Thought*. Vol.2. New York: St. Martin's Press, 1981.

Harding, Sandra. *The Science Question in Feminism*. Ithaca: Cornell University Press, 1986.

Harrington, Michael. *Socialism: Past and Future*. New York: Arcade, 1989.

Hegel, G.W.F. *The Philosophy of History*. Translated by J. Sibree. London: The Colonial Press, 1900.

———. *Jenenser Logik, Metaphysik under Naturphilosophie*. Ed. G. Lasson. Leipzig: Felix Meiner, 1923.

———. *Jenenser Realphilosophie II*. Ed. J. Hoffmeister. Leipzig: Felix Meiner, 1931.

———. *The Philosophy of Right*. Translated by T. M. Knox. Oxford: Oxford University Press, 1952.

———. *Hegel's Political Writings*. Translated by T. M. Knox. Ed. Z. A. Pelczynski. Oxford: Clarendon Press, 1964.

———. *The Phenomenology of Mind*. Translated by J. B. Baillie. New York: Harper Torchbooks, 1967.

———. *Jenaer Systementwürfe* II: *Logik, Metaphysick under Naturalphilosophie*. In *Gesammelte Werke*, Vol. 7. Ed. Johann Heinrich Trede. Hamburg: Felix Meiner, 1968.

———. *Jenaer Systementwürfe* III: *Realphilosophie*. In *Gesammelte Werke*, Vol. 8. Ed. Johann Heinrich Trede. Hamburg: Felix Meiner, 1968.

Herzog, Don. *Without Foundations: Justification in Political Theory.* Ithaca: Cornell University Press, 1985.

———. "Some Questions for Republicans." *Political Theory* 14:3 (August 1986):473–91.

———. *Happy Slaves: A Critique of Consent Theory.* Chicago: University of Chicago Press, 1989.

Hill, Melvyn A., ed. *Hannah Arendt: The Recovery of the Public World.* New York: St. Martin's Press, 1979.

Holmes, Stephen. "The Professor of Smashing." Review of Roberto Mangabeira Ungar, *Politics: A Work in Constructive Theory. The New Republic,* Oct. 19, 1987, pp. 30–38.

———."Precommitment and the Paradox of Democracy." In Jon Elster and Rune Slagstad, eds., *Constitutionalism and Democracy.* Cambridge: Cambridge University Press, 1988, pp. 195–240..

Honig, Bonnie. *Political Theory and the Displacement of Politics.* Ithaca: Cornell University Press, 1993.

hooks, bell, and Cornel West. *Breaking Bread: Insurgent Black Intellectual Life.* Boston: South End Press, 1990.

Hume, David. *A Treatise on Human Nature.* Oxford: Oxford University Press, 1960.

Husami, Ziyad. "Marx on Distributive Justice." In Marshall Cohen, Thomas Nagel, and Thomas Scanlon, eds., *Marx, Justice and History.* Princeton: Princeton University Press, 1980, pp. 42–79.

Isaac, Jeffrey. *Arendt, Camus and Modern Rebellion.* New Haven: Yale University Press, 1992.

Jones, Gareth Stedman. *Languages of Class: Studies in English Working Class History.* Cambridge: Cambridge University Press, 1983.

Kamenka, Eugene. *The Ethical Foundations of Marxism.* New York: Frederick A. Praeger, 1962.

Kariel, Henry. *The Promise of Politics.* Englewood Cliffs, N.J.: Prentice Hall, 1966.

Kateb, George. *Hannah Arendt: Politics, Conscience, Evil.* Oxford: Martin Robertson, 1983.

Kautsky, Karl. *The Dictatorship of the Proletariat.* Ann Arbor: University of Michigan Press, 1964.

Keane, John, ed. *Civil Society and the State.* London: Verso, 1988.

———. *Democracy and Civil Society.* London: Verso, 1988.

Kelly, George Armstrong. *Hegel's Retreat from Eleusis: Studies in Political Thought.* Princeton: Princeton University Press, 1978.

Kojève, Alexander. *Introduction to the Reading of Hegel: Lectures on "The Phenomenology of Spirit."* Assembled by Raymond Queneau. Translated by James H. Nichols, Jr. Edited by Allan Bloom. New York: Basic Books, 1969.

Kolakowski, Leszek. *Toward a Marxist Humanism: Essays on the Left Today.* Translated by Jane Zielonko Peel. New York: Grove Press, 1968.

———. *Main Currents of Marxism.* Vol. 2: *The Golden Age.* Oxford: Oxford University Press, 1981.

Kristeva, Julia. *Polylogue.* Paris: Seuil, 1977.

Kymlicka, Will. "Liberalism and Communitarianism." *Canadian Journal of Philosophy* 18:2 (June 1988): 181–204.

Laclau, Ernesto. "Politics and the Limits of Modernity." In Andrew Ross, ed., *Universal Abandon? The Politics of Postmodernism*. Minneapolis: University of Minnesota Press, 1988, pp. 63–82.

Laclau, Ernesto, and Chantal Mouffe. *Hegemony and Socialist Strategy: Towards a Radical Democratic Politics*. London: Verso, 1985.

Larmore, Charles. *Patterns of Moral Complexity*. Cambridge: Cambridge University Press, 1987.

Lasch, Christopher. Introduction to special issue on "Politics and the Social Contract." *Salmagundi*. 60 (Spring-Summer 1983): iv–xvi.

Laski, Harold. *The State in Theory and Practice*. New Haven: Yale University Press, 1917.

———. *Studies in the Problem of Sovereignty*. New York: Viking Press, 1935.

Lefort, Claude. *Democracy and Political Theory*. Translated by David Macy. Minneapolis: University of Minnesota Press, 1988.

Leftwich, Adrian. *Redefining Politics: People, Resources and Power*. New York: Methuen, 1983.

———, ed. *What Is Politics? The Activity and Its Study*. Oxford: Basil Blackwell Ltd., 1984.

Lenin, V. I. *State and Revolution*. New York: International Publishers, 1932.

———. *Left Wing Communism: An Infantile Disorder*. In *Selected Works*, vol. 10. New York: International Publishers, 1938, pp. 55–158.

———. *The Proletarian Revolution and the Renegade Kautsky*. Moscow: Progress Publishers, 1934.

———. "Letter to Shlyapnikov." In *The Bolsheviks and the World War*. Ed. O. Gankin and H. Fisher. Stanford: Stanford University Press, 1960, p. 241.

———. *What Is to Be Done?* New York: International Publishers, 1961.

———. *Collected Works*. 45 vols. Moscow: Progress Publishers, 1965.

———. *Imperialism: The Highest Stage of Capitalism*. New York: International Publishers, 1967.

———. *The Development of Capitalism in Russia*. Moscow: Progress Publishers, 1975.

Levine, Andrew. *The End of the State*. London: Verso, 1987.

———. *The General Will: Rousseau, Marx and Communism*. Cambridge: Cambridge University Press, 1993.

Lévy, Bernard-Henri. *Barbarism with a Human Face*. Translated by George Holoch. New York: Harper and Row, 1979.

Lichtheim, George. Introduction to *The Phenomenology of Mind*, by G.W.F. Hegel. New York: Harper Torchbooks, 1967.

Liebman, Marcel. "Lenin in 1905: A Revolution That Shook a Doctrine." In *Lenin Today*. New York: Monthly Review Press, 1970, pp. 57–76.

Lindblom, Charles. *Politics and Markets*. New York: Basic Books, 1977.

Lipietz, Alain. *Mirages and Miracles: The Crisis of Global Fordism*. London: Verso, 1987.

Lovell, David. *From Marx to Lenin: An Evaluation of Marx's Responsibility for Soviet Authoritarianism*. Cambridge: Cambridge University Press, 1984.

Lovibond, Sabina. "Feminism and Postmodernism." *New Left Review* 178 (November-December 1989): 5–28.

Lukacs, Georg. *History and Class Consciousness*. Translated by Rodney Livingstone. Cambridge: MIT Press, 1971.

Lukes, Steven. *Marxism and Morality.* Oxford: Oxford University Press, 1985.

Luxemburg, Rosa. *The Russian Revolution and Leninism or Marxism.* Ann Arbor: University of Michigan Press, 1961.

McCarthy, Mary. "Hannah Arendt: On Hannah Arendt." In Melyvn A. Hill, ed., *Hannah Arendt: The Recovery of the Public World.* New York: St. Martin's Press, 1979, pp. 301–39.

MacGregor, David. *The Communist Ideal in Hegel and Marx.* Toronto: University of Toronto Press, 1983.

MacIntyre, Alasdair. *After Virtue.* Notre Dame: University of Notre Dame Press, 1981.

McLennan, Gergor. *Marxism, Pluralism and Beyond.* Cambridge: Polity Press, 1989.

Macpherson, C. B. *The Political Theory of Possessive Individualism.* Oxford: Clarendon Press, 1962.

Maguire, John. *Marx's Theory of Politics.* Cambridge: Cambridge University Press, 1978.

Mansbridge, Jane J. *Beyond Adversary Democracy.* New York: Basic Books, 1980.

Marcuse, Herbert. *Reason and Revolution: Hegel and the Rise of Social Theory.* Oxford: Oxford University Press, 1941.

———. "Repressive Tolerance." In Robert Paul Wolff, Herbert Marcuse and Barrington Moore, Jr., *The Critique of Pure Tolerance.* Boston: Beacon Press, 1965, pp. 81–117.

Marx, Karl. *Marx and Engels: Basic Writings in Politics and Philosophy.* Ed. Lewis Feuer. Garden City: Doubleday, 1959.

———. *The Economic and Philosophical Manuscripts.* In *Karl Marx: The Early Writings.* Ed. Tom Bottomore. New York: McGraw-Hill, 1964, pp. 61–219.

———. *Karl Marx: Selected Writings in Sociology and Social Philosophy.* Ed. Tom Bottomore and Maximillian Rubel. London: Penguin, 1963.

———. *Writings of the Young Marx on Philosophy and Society.* Ed. Loyd Easton and Kurt Guddat. Garden City, N.Y.: Doubleday, 1967.

———. *The Eighteenth Brumaire of Louis Bonaparte.* New York: International Publishers, 1969.

———. *Grundrisse: Selections.* Ed. David McClellan. New York: Harper and Row, 1971.

———. *Critique of Hegel's Philosophy of Right.* Ed. Joseph O'Malley. Cambridge: Cambridge University Press, 1972.

———. *Grundrisse.* Translated by Martin Nicolaus. Baltimore: Penguin, 1973.

———. "First Draft of 'The Civil War in France.'" In *Karl Marx: Political Writings.* Volume 3: *The First International and After.* Ed. David Fernbach. New York: Random House, 1974, pp. 236–42.

———. *Karl Marx: Political Writings.* Vol. 3: *The First International and After.* Ed. David Fernbach. New York: Random House, 1974.

———. *Marx-Engels Collected Works.* Moscow: Progress Publishers, 1975.

———. *Capital.* Translated by Ben Fowkes. 3 vols. New York: Vintage 1977.

———. *The Civil War in France.* In *The Marx-Engels Reader,* pp. 629–52.

———. *The Marx-Engels Reader,* 2nd ed. Ed. Robert C. Tucker. New York: Norton, 1978.

Masters, Roger D. *The Political Philosophy of Rousseau.* Princeton: Princeton University Press, 1968.

Mayakovsky, V. "Vladimir Ilyich Lenin." In *Mayakovsky*. Translated and edited by Herbert Marshall. New York: Hill and Wang, 1965, pp. 249–330.

Medvedev, Roy. *Leninism and Western Socialism*. London: New Left Books, 1981.

Merleau-Ponty, Maurice. *Humanism and Terror: An Essay on the Communist Problem*. Translated by John O'Neill. Boston: Beacon Press, 1969.

Meszaros, Istvan. *Marx's Theory of Alienation*. New York: Harper and Row, 1972.

Miliband, Ralph. *Marxism and Politics*. Oxford: Oxford University Press, 1977.

———. "The State and Revolution." In *Lenin Today*. Ed. Paul Sweezy and Harry Magdoff. New York: Monthly Review Press, 1970, pp. 77–90.

Mill, John Stuart. *On Liberty*. Indianapolis: Hackett Publishing Co. 1978.

———. *Principles of Political Economy*. London: Penguin, 1985.

Miller, Jim. *Rousseau: Dreamer of Democracy*. New Haven: Yale University Press, 1984.

Miller, Richard. *Analyzing Marx*. Princeton: Princeton University Press, 1984.

Moore, Stanley. *Marx on the Choice between Socialism and Communism*. Cambridge: Harvard University Press, 1980.

Mouffe, Chantal. "Radical Democracy: Modern or Post-Modern?" Translated by Paul Holdengraber. In Andrew Ross, ed., *Universal Abandon? The Politics of Postmodernism*. Minneapolis: University of Minnesota Press, 1988, pp. 31–45.

———. "Towards a Liberal Socialism," *Dissent* (Winter 1993): 81–87.

Nietzsche, Friedrich Wilhelm. *The Use and Abuse of History*. 2nd ed. Translated by Adrian Collins. Indianapolis: Bobbs-Merrill, 1957.

Nisbet, Robert. "Hannah Arendt and the American Revolution." *Social Research* 44:1 (Spring 1977):63–79.

Nove, Alec. "Was Stalin Really Necessary?" *Problems of Communism* 25:4 (July-August 1976): 49–62.

———. *An Economic History of the Soviet Union*, rev. ed. Hammondsworth, Middlesex: Penguin, 1982.

———. *The Economics of Feasible Socialism*. London: Allen and Unwin, 1983.

Nozick, Robert. *Anarchy, State and Utopia* . New York: Basic Books, 1974.

Okin, Susan Moller. *Justice, Gender and the Family*. New York; Basic Books, 1989.

Ollman, Bertell. *Alienation: Marx's Conception of Man in Capitalist Society*. Cambridge: Cambridge University Press, 1971.

———. *Dialectical Investigations*. New York: Routledge, 1992.

Orwell, George. *The Collected Essays, Journalism and Letters*. 3 vols. Ed. Sonia Orwell and Ian Angus. New York: Harcourt Brace and World, 1968.

Parekh, Bikhu. "Hannah Arendt's Critique of Marx." In Melvyn A. Hill, ed., *Hannah Arendt: The Recovery of the Public World*. New York: St. Martin's Press, 1979, pp. 67–100.

Pateman, Carole. *Participation and Democratic Theory*. Cambridge: Cambridge University Press, 1970.

———. *The Sexual Contract*. Stanford: Stanford University Press, 1988.

Pelczynski, Z. A., ed. *Hegel's Political Philosophy: Problems and Perpsectives*. Cambridge: Cambridge University Press, 1971.

———. "Solidarity and 'The Rebirth of Civil Society.'" In John Keane, ed., *Civil Society and the State*. London: Verso, 1988, pp. 361–80.

Perez-Diaz, Victor M. *State, Bureaucracy and Civil Society: A Critical Discussion of the Political Theory of Karl Marx*. London: MacMillan, 1977.

Plamenatz, John Petrov. *Man and Society: Political and Social Theory.* Vol. 1: *Machiavelli through Rousseau.* New York: McGraw Hill, 1963.

———. *Man and Society: Political and Social Theory.* Vol. 2: *Bentham through Marx.* New York: McGraw Hill, 1963.

———. *Karl Marx's Philosophy of Man.* Oxford: Oxford University Press, 1975.

Plotke, David. "What's So New about New Social Movements?" *Socialist Review* 90:1 (Jan.–March 1990): 81–102.

Pocock, J.G.A. *The Machiavellian Moment.* Princeton: Princeton University Press, 1975.

Polan, A. J. *Lenin and the End of Politics.* Berkeley: University of California Press, 1984.

Poulantzas, Nicos. *State, Power, Socialism.* London: New Left Books, 1978.

Przeworski, Adam. *Capitalism and Social Democracy.* Cambridge: Cambridge University Press, 1985.

Railton, Peter. "Moral Realism." *Philosophical Review* 95:2 (Spring 1986): 163–207.

Rawls, John. *A Theory of Justice.* Cambridge: Harvard University Press, 1971.

———. "Kantian Constructivism in Moral Theory: The Dewey Memorial Lectures 1980." *Journal of Philosophy* 77 (September 1980): 515–72.

———. "Social Unity and Primary Goods." In Amartya Sen and Bernard Williams, eds., *Utilitarianism and Beyond.* Cambridge: Cambridge University Press, 1982, pp. 159–85.

———. "Justice as Fairness: Political Not Metaphysical." *Philosophy and Public Affairs* 14:3 (Summer 1985): 223–52.

———. "The Idea of an Overlapping Consensus." *Oxford Journal of Legal Studies* 7:1 (Spring 1987): 1–25.

———. *Political Justice.* New York: Columbia University Press, 1993.

Riley, Patrick. *Kant's Political Philosophy.* Totowa, N.J.: Rowman and Littlefield, 1982.

———. *Will and Political Legitimacy.* Cambridge: Harvard University Press, 1982.

Ritter, Joachim. *Hegel and the French Revolution.* Translated by Richard Dien Winfield. Cambridge: MIT Press, 1982.

Rorty, Richard. *Philosophy and the Mirror of Nature.* Princeton: Princeton University Press, 1979.

———. *Consequences of Pragmatism* (Essays: 1972–80). Minneapolis: University of Minnesota Press, 1982.

———. *Contingency, Irony, and Solidarity.* Cambridge: Cambridge University Press, 1989.

Rosenblum, Nancy L. *Another Liberalism: Romanticism and the Reconstruction of Liberal Thought.* Cambridge: Harvard University Press, 1987.

———, ed. *Liberalism and the Moral Life.* Cambridge: Harvard University Press, 1989.

Ross, Andrew, ed. *Universal Abandon? The Politics of Postmodernism.* Minneapolis: University of Minnesota Press, 1988.

Rousseau, Jean-Jacques. *The Social Contract: Essays by Locke, Hume and Rousseau.* Translated by Gerard Hopkins. New York: Oxford University Press, 1962.

———. *The First and Second Discourses.* Translated by Roger D. Masters and Judith R. Masters. New York: St. Martin's Press, 1964.

———. *The Government of Poland.* Translated by Willmore Kendall. New York: Bobbs-Merrill, 1972.

————. *The Emile or On Education*. Translated by Allan Bloom. New York: Basic Books, 1979.

Sandel, Michael. *Liberalism and the Limits of Justice*. Cambridge: Cambridge University Press, 1982.

————. "The Procedural Republic and the Unencumbered Self." *Political Theory* 12:1 (February 1984): 81–96.

————. "Roundtable: The Politics of Meaning." With Michael Lerner, Charles Derber, Mary Edsall, Peter Gabel, and Ruth Rosen. *Tikkun* 8:5 (September-October 1993): 19–26; 87–88.

Sawer, Marian. "The Genesis of State and Revolution." In Ralph Miliband and John Saville, eds., *The Socialist Register 1977*. New York: Monthly Review Press, 1977, pp. 209–27.

Schmitt, Carl. *The Concept of the Political*. Translated by George Schwab. New Brunswick: Rutgers University Press, 1976.

Schwartz, Benjamin. "The Religion of Politics: Reflections on the Thought of Hannah Arendt." *Dissent* (Spring 1970): 144–61.

Schwartz, Joseph. "Coalition Politics in a Three Speed Society." *Socialist Review* 90:2 (April–June 1990): 67–79.

————. "Democratic Solidarity and the Crisis of the Welfare State." In John P. Burke, Lyman H. Letgers, and Arthur DiQuattro, eds., *Critical Perspectives on Democracy*. Lanham, Md.: Rowman and Littlefield, 1994, pp. 87–111..

Seligman, Adam. *The Idea of Civil Society*. New York: Free Press, 1992.

Shapiro, Ian. *The Evolution of Natural Rights*. Cambridge: Cambridge University Press, 1986.

————. *Political Criticism*. Berkeley: University of California Press, 1990.

————. "Resources, Capacities and Ownership: The Workmanship Idea and Distributive Justice." *Political Theory* 19:1 (February 1991): 47–72.

Shklar, Judith. *Men and Citizens: A Study of Rousseau's Social Theory*. Cambridge: Cambridge University Press, 1969.

————. "Hegel's Phenomenology: An Elegy for Hellas." In Z. A. Pelczynski, ed., *Hegel's Political Philosophy: Problems and Perspectives*. Cambridge: Cambridge University Press, 1971, pp. 73–89.

————. *Freedom and Independence: A Study of the Political Ideas of Hegel's Phenomenology of Mind*. Cambridge: Cambridge University Press, 1976.

————. "Rethinking the Past." *Social Research*. 44:1 (Spring 1977):80–90.

Sirianni, Carmen. "Production and Power in a Classless Society: A Critical Analysis of the Utopian Dimensions of Marxist Theory." *Socialist Review* 59 (September-October 1981): 33–82.

————. *Workers Control and Socialist Democracy*. London: New Left Books, 1982.

————. "Councils and Parliaments: The Problem of Dual Power and Democracy in Comparative Perspective." *Politics and Society* 12:1 (1983): 83–123.

————. "Workers Control in Europe: A Comparative Sociological Analysis." In James Cronin and Carmen Sirianni, eds., *Work, Community, and Power*. Phildelphia: Temple University Press, 1983, pp. 254–310.

————. "Economics of Time in Social Theory: Three Approaches Compared." *Current Perspectives in Social Theory* 8 (1987): 161–195.

————. "Learning Pluralism: Democracy and Diversity in Feminist Organizations." In Jan Shapiro, ed., *Nomos XXXV: Democratic Community*. New York: New York University Press, 1993, pp. 283–312.

Siriamni, Carmen. "Citizenship, Civic Discovery and Discourse Democracy: Social Movements and Civic Associations in Citizen Participation Programs." Paper delivered at the September 1993 American Political Science Association Convention.

Smith, Steven B. *Hegel's Critique of Liberalism: Rights in Context.* Chicago: University of Chicago Press, 1989.

Stephens, John. *The Transition from Capitalism to Socialism.* Rev. ed. Champaign-Urbana: University of Illinois Press, 1988.

Strauss, Leo. *Natural Right and History.* Chicago: University of Chicago Press, 1953.

Strauss, Leo, and Joseph Cropsey, eds. *The History of Political Philosophy*, 2nd ed. Chicago: Rand-McNally, 1972.

Sweezy, Paul, and Harry Magdoff, eds. *Lenin Today.* New York: Monthly Review Press, 1970.

Talmon, Jacob. *The Origins of Totalitarian Democracy.* New York: Praeger, 1960.

Tawney, R. H. *The Acquisitive Society.* New York: Harcourt, Brace and Howe, 1920.

———. *Equality.* London: G. Allen and Unwin, 1931.

Taylor, Charles. *Hegel.* Cambridge: Cambridge Universty Press, 1975.

———. *Hegel and Modern Society.* Cambridge: Cambridge University Press, 1979.

———."Cross-Purposes: The Liberal-Communitarian Debate." In Nancy L. Rosenblum, ed., *Liberalism and the Moral Life.* Cambridge: Harvard University Press, 1989, pp. 159–82.

———. *Sources of the Self: The Making of the Modern Identity.* Cambridge: Harvard University Press, 1989.

Tester, Keith. *Civil Society.* New York: Routledge, 1992.

Thiel, Leslie Paul. Review of Bonnie Honig, *Political Theory and the Displacement of Politics. American Political Science Review* 88:1 (March 1994): 214–15.

Thompson, E. P. *The Making of the English Working Class.* New York: Vintage, 1962.

Trotsky, Leon. *Literature and Revolution.* New York: Russell and Russell, 1957.

———. *The History of the Russian Revolution.* Translated by Max Eastman. Ann Arbor: University of Michigan Press, 1967.

———. "Their Morals and Ours." In George Novack, ed., *Their Morals and Ours: Marxist versus Liberal Views on Morality.* New York: Pathfinder Press, 1968.

Tuck, Richard. *Natural Rights Theories.* Cambridge: Cambridge University Press, 1979.

Tucker, Robert C. *The Marxian Revolutionary Idea.* New York: Norton, 1969.

———, ed. *The Marx-Engels Reader.* 2nd ed. New York: Norton, 1978.

Tully, James. *A Discourse on Property: John Locke and His Adversaries.* Cambridge: Cambridge University Press, 1990.

Ulam, Adam. *The Bolsheviks.* New York: Macmllan, 1969.

Ungar, Roberto Mangabeira. *Social Theory: Its Situation and Its Task.* Vol. 1: *A Critical Introduction to Politics: A Work in Constructive Social Theory.* Cambridge: Cambridge University Press, 1987.

———.*Politics: A Work in Constructive Theory.* 3 vols. Cambridge: Cambridge University Press, 1987.

Waldron, Jeremy. *The Right to Private Property.* Oxford: Oxford University Press, 1988.

Walzer, Michael. "A Day in the Life of a Socialist Citizen." In his *Obligations* (listed below), pp. 229–38.

———. *Obligations: Essays on Disobedience, War, and Citizenship.* Cambridge: Harvard University Press, 1970.

———. "A Theory of Revolution." *Marxist Perspectives* 5 (Spring 1979): 30–44.

———. "Philosophy and Democracy." *Political Theory* 9:3 (August 1981): 379–99.

———. *Spheres of Justice: A Defense of Pluralism and Equality.* New York: Basic Books, 1983.

———. "Liberalism and the Art of Separation." *Political Theory* 12:3 (August 1984): 315–30.

———. *The Company of Critics: Social Criticism and Political Commitment in the Twentieth Century.* New York: Basic Books, 1988.

———. "The Lonely Politics of Michel Foucault." In his *The Company of Critics* (cited above), pp. 191–209.

———. "Socializing the Welfare State." In Amy Gutmann, ed., *Democracy and the Welfare State.* Princeton: Princeton University Press, 1988, pp. 13–26.

———. "The Communitarian Critique of Liberalism." *Political Theory* 18:1 (February 1990), pp. 6–23.

———. "The Idea of Civil Society." *Dissent* (Spring 1991): 293–304.

Weber, Max. "The Social Psychology of World Religions." In *From Max Weber.* Ed. Hans Gerth and C. Wright Mills. Oxford: Oxford University Press, 1952, pp. 267–301.

———. *Economy and Society: An Outline of Interpretive Sociology.* 2 vols. Translated by Ephraim Fischoff et al. Ed. Guenther Roth and Claus Wittich. Berkeley: University of California Press, 1967.

Weedon, Chris. *Feminist Practice and Post-Structuralist Theory.* Oxford: Polity Press, 1987.

Wellmer, Albert. *A Critical Theory of Society.* Translated by John Cumming. New York: Herder and Herder, 1971.

West, Cornel. Interview with Anders Stephanson. In Andrew Ross, ed., *Universal Abandon? The Politics of Postmodernism.* Minneapolis: University of Minnesota Press, 1988, pp. 269–86.

West, Cornel, and bell hooks. *Breaking Bread: Insurgent Black Intellectual Life.* Boston: South End Press, 1991.

Williams, Bernard. *Problems of the Self.* Cambridge: Cambridge University Press, 1973.

Williams, Patricia. "Alchemical Notes: Reconstructing Ideals from Deconstructed Rights." 22 *Harvard Civil Rights-Civil Liberties Law Review* 401.

Winfield, Richard Dien. Introduction to Joachim Ritter, *Hegel and the French Revolution.* Translated by Richard Dien Winfield. Cambridge: MIT Press, 1982.

Wolfe, Alan. *Whose Keeper: Social Science and Moral Obligations.* Berkeley: University of California Press, 1989.

Wolin, Sheldon. *Politics and Vision.* Boston: Little, Brown, 1960.

———. "Hannah Arendt and the Ordinance of Time." *Social Research.* 44:1 (Spring 1977):91–105.

———. "Hannah Arendt: Democracy and the Political." *Salmagundi* 60 (Spring-Summer 1983): 3–19.

Wood, Allen. "The Marxian Critique of Justice." In Marshall Cohen, Thomas Nagel, and Thomas Scanlon, eds., *Marx, Justice and History.* Princeton: Princeton University Press, 1980, pp. 3–41.

———. *Karl Marx.* New York: Routledge and Kegan Paul, 1981.

Wright, Erik Olin. *Class, Crisis and the State*. London: New Left Books, 1978.

Yack, Bernard. *The Longing for Total Revolution: Philosophic Sources of Social Discontent from Rousseau to Marx to Nietzsche*. Princeton: Princeton University Press, 1986.

———. *The Problems of a Political Animal: Community, Justice and Conflict in Aristotelian Political Thought*. Berkeley: University of California Press, 1993.

Young, Gary. "Doing Marx Justice." In Kai Nielsen and S. C. Patten, eds., *Marx and Morality*. Guelph, Ontario: Canadian Association for Publishing in Philosophy, 1981, pp. 251–68.

Young, Iris Marion. *Justice and the Politics of Difference*. Princeton: Princeton University Press, 1990.

Young-Bruehl, Elisabeth. *Hannah Arendt: For Love of the World*. New Haven: Yale University Press, 1982.

Zuboff, Shoshannah. *In the Age of the Smart Machine*. New York: Basic Books, 1988.

Ackerman, Bruce, 19
"administration of things," 147, 167, 170, 203–4, 210, 215. *See also* bureaucracy; Lenin; planning
Aglietta, Michael, 307n.51
Alexander the Great: and Hegel's concept of the privatized state, 263n.4
Althusser, Louis, 149, 285n.64
amour de soi-même, 38
amour propre, 38
Anderson, Perry, 301n.11
antidiscrimination: and universal values, 246
antifoundationalism, relationship to democracy, 229–30, 303n.20
Arendt, Hannah, 21, 28, 189–216; on "action" as politics, 190, 194, 195, 206; on "administration of things," 203–4, 215; on American versus French Revolution, 204–7, 297n.76, 297n.82; on apolitical, technical solutions to social problems, 203, 210–12, 215, 227, 300n.121; on barriers to politics, 190, 193, 199, 203, 207, 209, 211, 295n.46; on constitutions and freedom, 191, 201, 204, 207; critique of "instrumental," economic concerns, 190, 191, 192, 194, 197, 198, 203, 210–12, 216, 293–94n.14; critique of natural rights, 205, 206, 297n.91; critique of representative democracy, 193, 201, 207, 208, 213, 214–15; elitism of, 193, 194, 212–14; on emancipation from labor, 200–201; on federalism, 205, 206; on freedom, 189, 190, 191, 195; on founding fathers, 203, 204, 205, 207, 208; hostility to particular interests, 31, 194, 209; on Judaism, 193, 294n.18; on Kant, 192, 200, 293n.12; on "labor" versus "work," 194–95, 199, 202, 296n.54; misreading of Marx, 202, 296n.54; on "natality," 201, 202, 207; opposition to political parties, 208, 209, 298n.98; on political theory as antipolitical, 24, 198, 206, 295n.43; on politics as contingent, antiteleological, 191, 195, 294n.30; on politics as "performance," 192, 193, 196, 216; on power as 'promise-making among equals,' 196, 197; on pre-Socratic theory as political, 197, 198, 295n.45; on "public happiness" and direct democracy, 207, 209; on republican-ism and communitarianism, 207, 216, 293n.12, 301n.7; on sovereignty, 204, 205, 206; threat of "social question," 192, 205, 207; on virtue of politics, 31, 189, 192–93, 200, 204, 205; on war and found-ing, 102, 192, 216; on welfare state versus "public happiness," 209–11; on working-class depoliticization, 203, 209, 296–97n.68; on working-class revolt, 201–3; on workers' councils, 26, 193, 202, 203, 207–14, 221, 296n.66. *See also* communi-tarianism; political theory; soviets; workers' councils
Aristotle, 15, 24, 132, 294n.30; on politics as 'master science,' 15; on politics as stable equilibrium, 24, 294n.30; on *techne* versus *phronesis*, 281n.9
Aronowitz, Stanley, 290n.119, 308n.55
Arrow, Kenneth, 270n.1
Ashcraft, Richard, 25, 258n.3
associations: relative autonomy of in demo-cratic society, 144–45
Athens: class-conflict within, 197
automation: and deskilling of work in Marx, 135; and transcendence of necessary labor, 135
autonomy: and freedom in Rousseau, 46, 63; and solidarity in Rousseau, 46. *See also* democratic individuality; freedom; Kant
Avineri, Shlomo, 76

Bakan, Mildred, 296n.54, 296n.61
Bakunin: versus Marx, 168–70
Barber, Benjamin, 4, 24, 28, 189, 229, 245; on agonal politics, 26, 255n.32, 257n.36; critique of rights, 14, 252n.3, 254n.16, 257n.38; on democratic deliberation, 132, 229, 278n.88; on democratic socialism, 221; on participation and transformation of interests, 14, 253n.15, 254n.15; versus political control of the economy, 221, 300–301n.4; versus representative govern-ment, 221, 259n.9; on search for fixed laws of politics, 24, 255n.32
Bell, Daniel, on division of labor, 135
Benhabib, Seyla, 228, 230, 257n.41, 306n.44; on dangers of Nietzsche, 228, 230; on postmodernism, 28, 228, 245
Black Power movement, 240, 306n.50

Bloom, Allan, 37

Bobbio, Norberto: on direct and representative democracy, 213, 292n.7; reading of Hegel, 265n.25

Bolshevik Party, 8, 209; on political power, 155; and socialist revolution, 186–87; on trade unions and soviets, 283–84n.41, 285n.51. *See also* Lenin; vanguard party

Botwinick, Aryeh, 303n.20

Bowles, Samuel, 4, 13, 234–35, 254n.14, 307n.51; on agency and choice, 13, 235; on democratic socialism, 235; on "learning and choosing," 14; on "postliberal democracy," 234–35; on rights and radical democracy, 234; and teleology of rights, 236, 305n.43

Brenkert, George, on freedom in Marx, 171n.9

Buchanan, Allen, 272n.19

Bukharin, Nikolai, 8, 116, 172

bureaucracy: in Hegel, 75; in democratic theory, 75–76; in Lenin and Weber, 181–82. *See also* "administration of things"; expertise; Hegel; Lenin; technology; Weber

Burke, Edmund, 25

Butler, Judith, 227, 257n. 41, 303n.33

Capital, 104, 108–11, 130–31, 135–36, 168, 285n.64

capitalism, 10, 248, 306–7n.51, 308n.63; and economic insecurity, 296n.67, 307n.53; and inequalities, 249, 308n.63; and privatization of economic relations, 11, 248. *See also* liberalism

Cassirer, Ernst, 37

Chinese Communist Party: and "authoritarian capitalism," 8, 115; and political pluralism, 8, 115

citizenship, 4, 210, 231, 241; and diversity, 31, 238, 239, 242; and "subaltern" claims on others, 239. *See also* difference; solidarity

civil religion, 34, 64, 227, 261n.54. *See also* Durkheim; Rousseau

civil society, 210; democracy and autonomy of, 11, 16, 248; theorists of, 76–77, 94. *See also* democracy; "difference"; solidarity

The Civil War in France, 114, 120, 162, 165–67

class consciousness: "imputed" versus actual, 159–60; objective versus subjective, 149, 151, 160; structuralist versus culturalist, 149, 151. *See also* "false consciousness"; ideology

"class-for-itself": versus "class-in-itself," 149–51

Clinton, Bill, on the "politics of meaning," 223–24

coalition politics, and material interests, 243, 246

Cohen, G. A., 140–41

Cohen, Joshua, 4; on banning of undemocratic interests, 254n.18; on guarantee of rights, 247; on Locke, 256n.34; on Rousseau and Rawls, 33, 256n.34, 258n.1; as theorist, 234, 235, 305n.37, 306n.46, 308n.54. *See also* radical democracy; Rogers

Cole, G.D.H., 4, 251n.1

common good: as consistent with particular interests, 115, 249, 298n.101; as political, 24, 115, 216, 222, 249. *See also* general will

communism, 4; and antipluralist left, 4, 32, 115, 116, 218–19, 249; as democratic individuality and collective autonomy, 107; Marx's conception of, 4, 7, 111–14, 134–35, 165–68; as postscarcity anarchism, 6, 10, 106; as spontaneous mutuality, 27; theory of "crude" or "primitive" (Marx), 126; and transcendence of politics, 10; and "true human suffering," 138–39. *See also* first-stage communism; "dictatorship of the proletariat"; Lenin; Marx

Communist Manifesto, The (Marx), 108, 120, 149, 151–54, 170, 171–72, 178

Communist regimes: collapse of, 6, 249, 275n.56; and radical democratic theory, 22; suppression of civil society in, 218–19

communitarianism, 189, 212, 218, 220, 298n.101; on community and "the good," 191, 222; critiques of, 22, 27, 189, 190, 216, 220; as "disinterested," academic theory, 222–23, 228; as excessively solidaristic, 220, 222, 245, 301n.7; hostilities of, 22, 189, 221, 223; and politics, 21, 220; on Rawlsian liberalism, 27–28, 222, 223, 226, 228, 245, 246. *See also* community; MacIntyre; Sandel; self; Taylor; Walzer; Young

community: exclusionary nature of, 222, 245; and need for rights, 28, 222

conflict, radical transcendence of, 3, 21, 249

Connolly, William E., 227–28, 252n.4, 304n.33; and conflicts within self, 228

conservatism: and concept of "universal class," 241; in current U.S. politics, 241; exhaustion of Reagan-Thatcher model, 32;

hostility to politics, 24–25, 257n.35; "naturalization" of market, 31; resurgence of, 240, 307n.53

Constituent Assembly (Russian), 187, 208–9, 283n.30, 291n.133

constitution: democratic stability and, 276–77n.72; in radical democracy, 19, 125, 276n.32; in social contract, 33

Cornell, Druscilla, 257n.41

corporations, 4; in Hegel, 95–97; as public entities, 235–36; as structures of power, 17; subject to social regulation, 248; workers' control of, 16, 248

Critique of the Gotha Programme, The (Marx), 120, 122, 127–29, 167, 176, 183–84, 273n.25

Cuba: economic versus political freedom in, 269–70n.98; participation and elitism in, 269–70n.98

culture, "high" versus "low," 279–80n.112

Cunningham, Frank, 306n.44

Dahl, Robert, 4; on democratic control of technology, 182, 289–90n.118; on economic democracy, 299n.108; for workers' control of corporations, 16, 299n.108

de Mandeville, Bernard, 269n.89

democracy, 3, 230–31; and citizenship, 230; and coalition politics, 243, 245; and concept of liberty in American ideology, 226–27, 233, 262–63n.94; and delimiting of politics, 10–11; on direct/participatory versus representative forms, 34, 165–67, 185–86, 207–9, 213, 261–62n.5, 284n.41, 287–88n.95, 299nn.106 and 108; and distance from particular identities within, 57, 223; on equal moral worth of persons, 230–31, 242, 247, 281n.10, 302n.13, 308n.54; and Paris Commune, 165–67; and participation, 14, 232, 246, 254n.15; on process and minimal values, 11, 12, 14, 23, 222, 230, 281n.10; and relationship to rights, 25, 278n.88; role of general will in establishing, 33–34; on tension between universal and particular, 13, 35, 79, 230–31, 249; versus undemocratic interests, 12, 15, 238, 246, 249; and the workplace, 135–39, 299n.108. *See also* Dahl; liberalism; participation; radical democracy; Walzer; workers' councils; workplace democracy

democratic centralism, 160, 162, 285n.51

democratic individuality, 25, 26, 257n.37; in Marx, 26, 138–40. *See also* Gilbert

democratic left, 31; need for global Keynesian program, 32

democratic socialism, 4, 234–35, 305n.36, 308–9n.63; as allegedly anachronistic, 234; centrality of politics to, 123–24; and liberalism, 248, 305n.36, 306n.44; and radical democracy, 235–36, 305n.36, 305–6n.44. *See also* Cole; Tawney; Walzer

deontology, and liberal rights, 227

development, equitable, 116, 120

Dewey, John, 34, 282n.17; critique of Marx, 113, 116; on sovereignty and government, 34

"dictatorship of the proletariat," 120, 275n.60; in Lenin, 148, 173, 175, 183; as martial law, 168, 286n.78; and Paris Commune, 165–67, 286n.69

"difference," 23, 219; as constructed by power, 220; and critique of citizenship, 22, 228, 249; and fragmentation of left, 32, 241; and politics of, 11, 227–28, 231, 244; and solidarity, 68, 238, 244, 249; and tension with citizenship and solidarity, 11, 68, 219–20, 227, 238, 244, 249. *See also* diversity; identity; identity politics; postmodernism; social movements

diversity: and dialectic with unity, 27; as "post-melting pot" ideology, 246

division of labor, 231; under communism, 129, 134; in complex societies, 12, 231; radical democratic construction of, 13, 129–130, 231. *See also* expertise; Lenin; management; Marx

Durkheim, Emile, 43; on division of labor, 261n.54; on mechanical solidarity and Rousseau's Golden Age family, 43–44, 51; relationship to Hegel's corporatism, 266n.30

Dworkin, Ronald, on human talents, 141–42, 280n.119

Easton, David, 253n.8

Economic and Philosophical Manuscripts, The (Marx), 125–26, 132, 134, 137; and theory of socialist justice, 138–40, 143–44; and transcendence of institutions, 125

efficiency, tension with participation, 106, 136, 162

Ehrenberg, John, 253n.12

Eighteenth Brumaire of Louis Bonaparte, The (Marx), 163–64, 176–77

Ellwood, David, 301n.4

Elster, Jon: on justice based on need, 271n.5; on Marx as moral critic, 271n.9, 272n.18; on need for concrete results, 292n.6; on risk and self-realization, 133; on self-ownership and socialist justice, 142, 278n.93

"end-of-history": in Fukuyama, 86, 249, 267n.46; in Hegel, 70, 86

Engels, Friedrich: on armed struggle, 288–89n.100; on socialist production, 170–71, 215; on socialist revolution in Russia, 277n.76; on suffrage, 288–89n.100

Enlightenment, 4, 5, 241–44, 252n.3; determinism versus freedom within, 5, 105; and Marx on planning and abundance, 130, 134; postmodernism's critique of, 228, 230, 241, 304n.33

epistemology, and politics, 117, 229–30, 281nn.10 and 17, 303n.20. See also ontology; philosophy

equality: as "crude levelling" in Marx, 126–28; and postmodernism, 229; in radical democracy, 238, 248; socialist justice and various conceptions of, 139–40

Erlich, Alexander, 7, 274n.43

ethical socialism, 22, 117, 121–24, 244; need for description of, 114

Etzioni, Amitai, 76

expertise: relationship to democracy, 162, 170, 182, 289–90n.118, 290n.119. See also bureaucracy; efficiency; management; technology; workplace democracy

"false consciousness," 121, 151, 152–54, 157, 159, 284n.50, 309n.64. See also Herbert; ideology; Lenin; Marcuse; Marx

family, 16, 238; in Rousseau, 43–44

feminism, 16, 231, 240, 241, 257n.41, 306n.44

Finley, Moses I., 197; on conflict in Athenian democracy, 295n.38

"first-stage communism": and bourgeois distributive principles, 127–28, 168; in Lenin as compared to Marx, 147, 162–63, 177–78, 184; as persistence of state and division of labor, 127; and politics in Marx, 171, 177, 184, 289n.105; role of state within, 164–65. See also communism; "dictatorship of the proletariat"; Lenin; Marx; socialism

Flax, Jane, 227, 257n.41, 304n.33

Foucault, Michel, and "power/knowledge" discourses, 235, 239, 304n.33, 306n.48

foundationalism: critique of, 4, 230, 278n.88; and "thin conception" of democracy, 230, 281n.10. See also antifoundationalism; philosophy

"free association of producers," 104, 114, 165; and democratic freedom, 121, 271n.39. See also communism; Marx; workplace democracy

freedom: and liberalism, 256n.34; in Marx, 23, 27, 104, 114, 121, 165; and rights, 121; in Rousseau, 40–43. See also autonomy; democratic individuality

"freedom from," versus "freedom to," 123

"full communism": Lenin's doubts about, 183; in Marx, 23, 75, 104, 106, 134–35, 167, 169; as transcending justice, 129. See also "free association of producers"; Lenin; Marx

Fukuyama, Frances: on "end of history," 86, 249, 267n.46; hostile to reform, 86. See also "end-of-history"

Galston, William, 300–301n.4, 302n.13

gay and lesbian movement, 241, 308n.60; and African-American community, 308n.60

gender, 222, 225, 237, 246, 248, 249, 308n.63

general will, 18, 33, 41; as constitutional rules and public goods, 60; and democratic culture, 63, 259n.4; as majority, 62; as restraint on self-interest, 55, 68; as social solidarity, 36, 64; as "thin" set of democratic procedures, 53–54. See also common good; Rousseau

Geras, Norman, on Marx as moral critic, 271n.9, 272n.18

German Ideology, The (Marx), 108, 126–27, 164, 175–76, 285n.64

Gilbert, Alan, 255n.37, 273n.31, 275n.55; on Marx as moral realist, 112–13; on tensions in Marx, 107, 114, 270n.2. See also democratic individuality

Gintis, Herbert, 4, 13, 234–35, 254n.13, 305n.43. See also Bowles

Glucksmann, André, 22

good, the, 4; as liberal proceduralism, 226–27; plural conceptions of, 20, 217, 222, 226, 232, 298n.101; public, 5, 222, 298n.101; radicalism's conception of, 5, 231, 232. See also communitarianism; Sandel

goods: politics and distribution of, 8; plural nature of, 124–25. See also Walzer

Goodwin, Jeff, 305n.43

Gordon, David, 307n.51

Gould, Carole C., 306n.44

government, versus sovereignty in Rousseau, 34

Government of Poland, The (Rousseau), 40; on promoting solidarity, 42, 66; and Rousseau as reformer, 66

Gramsci, Antonio, 149

Green, Philip, 306n.44

groups, 231. *See also* identity; social movements

Grundrisse, The (Marx), 130–31, 134–35, 137, 143–44

Gunnell, John, 24, 255n.32

Gutmann, Amy, 4; on democracy and rights, 53, 223, 252n.4

Habermas, Jurgen, 230, 308n.57; critique of Arendt, 197; on Marx, 147; and theory of justice, 244

Hall, Stuart, 149

Harding, Neil, 287n.93

Harding, Sandra, 257n.41

Harrington, Michael, on democratic control over technology, 182, 289–90n.118

health care: democracy and provision of, 233, 236–37

Hegel, George Wilhelm Friedrich, 4, 21; on ancient world and particularity, 86, 263n.4; on autonomous civil society, 70, 76, 218, 265n.25; on bureaucracy as arbiter, 100–103; and contemporary communitarianism, 29, 70, 76, 83, 218, 300n.2; on corporations, 79, 83, 88, 94, 95–97, 99–100; as critic of liberal individualism, 70, 76, 77, 79–80, 86, 263n.3; on "cunning of history," 73; on diversity in civil society, 69, 77, 102, 218; on "end-of-history," 70, 86; on freedom and contract, 79–81; on freedom of property, 80, 82, 84, 87, 88, 93–94; on the French Revolution, 84, 101, 102, 264n.7; on historicism and moral relativism, 73, 74; on *Klasse* (class) as way of life, 88–89; on legislature and bureaucracy, 98–99, 102–3; on liberal state, 70–73, 78, 83, 94, 267n.52; on Marx's universal class, 74, 91; and neutral state bureaucracy and common good, 14, 69, 71, 73, 77, 89; on political participation within corporations, 96–97, 99–100; on *Polizei* (public authority), 86, 93, 266n.32; as postpolitical statist, 76, 101; and role of state, 97–103, 222; on self-

comprehending reason (*Geist*/Spirit), 78, 84; on teleology of freedom, 70, 84; on war as transcending particularism, 101–2; on will and contract, 79–81; on working class in early writings, 91–92, 268–69n.73

Herzog, Don, 254n.10, 275n.47, 281n.10, 304n.36; and diversity of liberal tradition, 256n.34, 305n.36; on search for postpolitical unity, 256–57n.35; on social contract theory, 303n.20

historicism, 8; and "moral agnosticism," 8, 73, 74, 117

Hobbes, Thomas, 38; on social contract, 227; on sovereign as final arbiter of disputes, 38; theory of obligation, 38–39

Holmes, Stephen, 276–77n.72

Honig, Bonnie, 24, 28, 228, 252n.4; absence of theory of power in, 256n.32; critique of communitarianism, 255n.32; critique of Rawls, 26, 255n.32, 257n.36; defense of Machiavellian *virtù* and flux, 255–56n.32; on identity and displacement of "difference," 228; on Nietzsche's theory of self-creation, 255n.32; political theory as antipolitical search, 255n.32; as postmodern radical theorist, 228. *See also* Connolly; postmodernism; self

Hooker, Thomas, and search for conservative unity, 257n.35

hooks, bell, 308n.60

Human Condition, The (Arendt), 194–201, 294n.23

human needs: as socially constructed, 272n.15, 304n.29; as subject to political debate, 124, 132; as "true" and objective in Marx, 119, 132

Hume, David, on social contract, 227, 303n.20

Husami, Ziyad, 272n.18

ideas, and independent role in politics, 15

identity, 5, 228, 231, 246, 248, 303n.27; and dialectic of universal/particular, 243; material basis of, 307n.53, 308–9n.63; postmodern, essentialist conceptions of, 303–4n.27; religious and national in Marx, 104. *See also* "difference"; postmodernism; social movements

identity politics, 5, 246, 303–4n.27. *See also* "difference"; identity; postmodernism; social movements

ideology, 114, 116–18, 120–23, 132, 150–55, 157–60, 164, 175–77, 272n.15, 273n.31, 275nn.47 and 61, 281n.10,

ideology, *(cont.)*
282n.17, 284n.50, 285n.65, 309n.64. *See also* "false consciousness"; Lenin; Lukacs; Marcuse; Marx
India, and moral relativism in Marx, 113
individuality: and democracy, 236; in Marx, 26, 138–40
institutions, 19, 27, 106
interests, 5, 227; assumed endogenous, 13, 235; democratic versus undemocratic, 8, 231, 238; ideal, 15, 153–54, 167, 216, 242–43; liberal, instrumental conception of, 13; radical conception of, 5, 10, 167; transformation through, 8, 12, 231, 238, 242, 254n.15; universal, 167. *See also* groups; identity; pluralism
Isaac, Jeffrey, 272n.15, 274n.39, 296n.59; on Arendt, 292n.7, 293–94n.14

Jackson, Jesse, 243
Jacobins, 217; Marx's critique of, 118–19, 167
On the Jewish Question (Marx), 118–19, 122, 123, 164
Jones, Gareth Steadman, 149, 254n.20, 270n.3
justice: and capitalism in Marx, 110–14; as democratically determined, 144–45, 281n.129; and holding others accountable, 133–34; in Marx, 107–8; and Rawls, 26, 28, 223, 226, 229; relationship to radical democracy, 128–34; and self-development, 139; socialist theory of, 134–45; as standard of fairness, 246. *See also* democracy; equality

Kant, Immanuel: Arendt on, 192, 293n.12, 295n.53; on categorical imperative, 140, 229, 266n.38, 271n.7; on Hegel, 79–81; on Rousseau, 63; and theories of justice, 245
Kateb, George, 192
Kautsky, Karl: on democracy under socialism, 185–86, 291n.133; on Lenin's vanguard theory, 158, 159; on revolutionary consciousness, 158; on Soviet Union as "state capitalism," 148
Kelly, George Armstrong, on Hegel, 264n.11, 268n.66
Keynesianism, 307n.53; need for global version of, 32, 242, 307nn.51 and 53
King, Martin Luther, 153
Koestler, Arthur, 74
Kojeve, Alexander, on Hegel, 71, 264n.15

Kolakowski, Leszek, early writings, 117
Kronstadt rebellion, 287n.95
Kuhn, Thomas, 273n.31
Kymlicka, Will, 223

labor: "free versus necessary" in Marx, 130–31, 137; under communism, 131, 137. *See also* work
labor theory of value, 135
Laclau, Ernesto, 4, 229, 235, 251n.3., 255n.29; and "democratic alliances," 242, 307n.52; on Enlightenment values or "mood," 242, 251–52n.3, 307n.52; as implicit ethical socialist, 244, 308n.55; as philosophical pragmatist, 251–52n.3; and rejection of Enlightenment metaphysics, 228, 252n.3; and rejection of structuralist Marxism, 22; on social reality, 305n.42, 307n.53. *See also* "difference"; Enlightenment; Mouffe; philosophy; postmodernism; social movements
Larmore, Charles, 303n.20
LaSalle, Ferdinand, 122
Laski, Harold, 22
Lefort, Claude, 293n.7
Leftwich, Adrian, 253n.9
Legislator: and democratic social contract, 46; as founder, not reformist, 66; inculcating democratic mores, 65; in Rousseau's Social Contract, 34
Lenin, Vladimir Ilyich, 4, 14, 21; on absence of political deliberation under communism, 147, 172, 173–74, 177, 184, 187–88; on "armed workers," 148, 173, 180, 187; on bureaucratization of revolution, 187–88; and class consciousness, 30, 146, 149, 154, 159, 179; on communist administration, 147, 163, 172, 173–74, 177, 179–80, 182, 184; on democracy, 161, 173, 176–77, 184–85; on democratic centralism, 160, 162; on division of labor under communism, 147, 151, 153, 155–57, 161, 174, 179–80, 182; on "factory discipline" under communism, 147, 173, 179; and NEP, 8, 146, 162, 278n.80; on the Paris Commune 146, 148–49; on party organization and postpolitical vision, 147; on the peasantry, 156, 283n.33; on postrevolutionary repression, 175, 183; on revolutionary consciousness, 158; on science as planning, 146, 179; on "smashing the state," 148, 174–75, 186; on soviets, 143, 146, 149, 173, 182, 186–87; on state under capitalism, 171–72; on the vanguard

party, 10, 146, 152–54, 158, 159, 178, 180; on withering away of the state under "first-stage" communism, 177–78. *See also* Bolshevik Party; class consciousness; Leninism; Marx; vanguard party

Leninism, 119, 309n.64

Lerner, Michael, 292n.5

Levine, Andrew, 253n.12

Lévy, Bernard-Henri, 22

liberal democracy, 233, 309n.64

liberalism: as critique of absolutism and established religion, 25, 256n.34; diverse forms of, 232–33, 247; dominant conception of, 25, 232–33; and economic and gender relations, 10, 16, 232, 238; and instrumental conception of interests, 13; radical critique of, 4, 9, 21, 25, 217, 219, 232; and undemocratic structure of power, 16–17, 232, 238, 248; value for radical democracy, 16, 226, 232, 256n.34. *See also* democracy; freedom; liberal democracy; liberalism; Locke; pluralism

Lipietz, Alain, 307n.51

Locke, John, social contract theory of, 25, 256n.34, 258n.3

love, 44, 144

Lovell, David, 147

Lukacs, Gyorgy, 159, 284n.50

Lukes, Steven, 110–12, 139–40, 275n.61

Luxemburg, Rosa, 4, 160, 296n.66; critique of Lenin, 148, 162; on democratic politics after the revolution, 154, 291n.133; opposition to democratic centralism, 162

MacGregor, David, on Hegel, 86, 93, 266n.32

Machiavelli, 29, 56, 255–56n.32, 275n.49, 293n.12

MacIntyre, Alasdair, 21, 28, 189, 209, 210, 230, 245, 298n.101; and Aristotelian conception of virtue, 190, 265n.24; as premodern, romantic communitarian, 76, 190

Macpherson, C. B., theory of possessive individualism, 256n.33

Madison, James, and Federalist Ten, 52

management, 136–37. *See also* bureaucracy; expertise; technology; workplace democracy

Mansbridge, Jane, 4; on democracy, 6, 252n.5; on Rousseau, 67

Marcuse, Herbert: on Hegel, 266n32; on "repressive tolerance," 309n.64. *See also* ideology

markets: and externalities, 106; romanticization of, 6, 123–24, 249, 275n.56; as measure of relative costs, 7, 17, 106, 251n.1, 299n.109; and planning, 251.n1; and risk and self-realization, 133, 275n.46

market socialism, 133, 299n.108; and self-ownership, 140

marriage, 18, 23, 237

Marx, Karl, 3, 4, 21; on abolition of classes, 14, 30, 104, 163, 165; on "administration of things," 75, 167, 169; as alleged democrat, 253n.12; on automation and labor theory of value, 134–35; and Bakunin, 168–70; on "bourgeois democracy," 122, 176; on capitalism as "wage-slavery," 109, 110–11; on communism as humane, 111–14, 134–35; on communist revolutionaries and vanguardism, 153, 156, 158; on creative labor, 143–44; critique of equality, 105, 127–28; critique of Jacobin terror, 118–19, 167; critique of rights, 17, 105, 108, 117–21, 167–70, 217, 270n.3; on crude, "primitive communism," 126–27; and "dictatorship of the proletariat," 120, 165–70; on the division of labor, 23, 105, 109, 126; emancipatory impulse within, 23, 114, 156; Enlightenment faith of, 105, 114, 167, 169; on "first-stage communism," 126–28, 163–67; on freedom and autonomy, 110, 114, 271n.9; on "full communism," 23, 104, 106, 109, 115, 134–35, 218; hostility to markets, 114, 274n.35; as implicit moral theorist, 105, 106, 109; on India and historicist relativism, 113; on intelligentsia in revolution, 108; and justice under capitalism, 110–14; and Lenin's theory of class consciousness, 152–54; and material prerequisites for communism, 119–20, 218; as moral realist theorist, 107, 109, 113; on "necessary" versus "free labor," 130–31, 137, 202; on Paris Commune, 30, 158, 162–63, 165–67; as "scientist," 104–5, 107, 109, 114; on social mediation, 105, 122; on "social" versus political revolution, 118–19; on surplus-value, 108, 109; and theory of the state, 162–68; on the universal class, 150; on working-class interests, 107, 151–52, 167; on working-class self-transformation, 150; works of (*See under individual titles*). *See also* communism; "dictatorship of the proletariat"; freedom; justice; Lenin; radical tradition

"Marxism and morality" debate, 110–17

Marxist-Leninism. *See also* Leninism

Mayakovsky, Vladimir, 281n.3

McCarthy, Mary, 215

Mensheviks, 156, 277n.76; differences with Bolsheviks, 283–84n.41, 285n.51; and underestimation of peasantry, 284n.41

Merleau-Ponty, Maurice: on critique of Koestler's *Darkness at Noon*, 74; on defense of Stalin as ethical, 74; on Marx's "perfectionism," 115–16

Mill, John Stuart, 15, 139, 213, 232, 247, 281n.10

Miller, James, on Rousseau as democratic theorist, 33

Miller, Richard, on Marx and human freedom, 112–14

mir, 277n.76

money, Marx's critique of, 138–40

Montesquieu, 204

Moore, Stanley, 289n.105

moral realism, 273n.31; in Hegel, 84; in Marx, 111–14. *See also* Gilbert; Miller, Richard; Wood

Mouffe, Chantal, 4, 229, 235, 242, 244, 305n.42, 307n.52. *See also* Laclau

nationalism: affinity with democracy, 40; as postpolitical vision, 6

needs, theory of: and socialist theory of justice, 128

New Economic Program (NEP), 7, 8, 278n.80; as economic pluralism, 7, 115, 162; and exclusion of peasantry, 7, 162

Nietzsche, Friedrich, 40; on postmodern theory, 26, 228, 230; undemocratic, misogynist dangers of, 26, 228, 230, 249. *See also* Benhabib; postmodernism; self

Nisbet, Robert, 297n.82

Nove, Alec: and market socialism, 274n.36; and Soviet industrialization debate, 7, 274n.43

Nozick, Robert, 141–42, 229

obligation, in radical democratic politics, 15, 43, 231, 238

Okin, Susan Moller, 229, 257n.41

Ollmann, Bertell, 253n.12

On Revolution (Arendt), 201–14

ontology, and politics, 94, 117, 223, 227. *See also* epistemology; philosophy

original position, 28, 57, 223

Orwell, George, 22

"overlapping consensus," 28, 225

Parekh, Bikhu, 296n. 61

participation, value of, 14, 232, 246, 254n.15

participatory democracy, 34, 135–39, 165–67, 185–87, 207, 213, 259n.9, 287–88n.99, 299nn.100, 106; and ignorance of centralized power, 259–60n.9, 299n.108, 300n.4. *See also* democracy, representative versus direct; soviets; Walzer; workers' councils; workplace democracy

particular identity, reflective distance from, 35, 298n.101. *See also* "difference"; identity; particularism

particularism: hostility to, 5; role in democratic politics, 8; and universality in radical thought, 239

Pannekoek, Anton, 172

Paris Commune, 158, 162–63, 165–67, 208, 287n.84; Marx's analysis of, 166, 286n.71. See also *The Civil War in France*; democracy, dictatorship of the proletariat

Pateman, Carole, 4; democracy and the "marriage contract," 18, 23, 237; on Rousseau as democratic theorist, 33

patriarchy, 225, 237, 248

patriotism, 34, 226. *See also* Rousseau

peasantry, in Russia, 7, 208–9

Pelczynski, Z. A., 265n.25

"personal as political," and social pluralism, 12. *See also* "public/private distinction."

Phenomenology of Mind, The, 70–77; on conceptions of history, 73–77; on death and individuality, 264n.14; as interpreted by Kojeve, 72

philosophy, and political perspective, 94, 117, 223, 227, 229–30, 281nn.10 and 17, 303n.20. *See also* epistemology; ontology

Philosophy of Right, The: on "absolute freedom," 81; on civil society, 86–88; on corporations, 95–97; on freedom through private property, 81; on state mediation of particular interests, 77–83; on working class and the poor, 91–94

planning: and corporate investment, 18; inefficiency of under communism, 274n.43; and markets, 251n.1; and politics in Marx, 131, 168; as science in Marx and Lenin, 131, 146, 168; and tension with self-ownership, 140

Plato, 24; and politics as antipolitical, 24, 294n.30

Plotke, David, 258n.42

pluralism, 3, 4, 12, 218, 222, 238; radicals versus liberals on, 17, 67, 238, 246; and relationship to rights, 121

Pocock, J.G.A., 189
Polan, A. J., 281n.9
polis, 189
political economy: "regulatory school of,"
    306–7n.51
political judgment: in democratic justice,
    143, 179; as practical skill, 90, 281n.10
political theory, 8, 227; as apolitical, 8, 24,
    190, 215, 222, 224; need for theory of
    agency and power, 29; and reflection on
    political practice, 28, 190–92, 222, 224; as
    search for fixed laws of politics, 24
politics, 3; absence of under communism
    (Marx), 121; as all social activity, 253n9;
    as allocation of goods and values, 8, 9,
    20, 212, 253n.8; democratic versus non-
    democratic, 3, 254n.11; as determining
    socialist justice, 143–45; and force,
    253n.10; Hegel's hostility to, 70; Lenin's
    hostility to, 146, 179, 182, 184; Marx's
    hostility to, 75, 104–5, 122, 167, 169;
    pluralism within, 218; proper delimitation
    of, 11, 290n.119; radical democratic,
    3, 4, 8, 290n.119; radical transcendence
    of, 3, 9, 10, 217–19; Rousseau's hostility
    to, 67–69
polyarchy, 20
positional goods, 124
"possessive individualism," as liberalism, 13,
    25. *See also* Macpherson
postcommunist societies: and absence of left
    tradition, 116; as postpolitical, 6; and
    romanticization of market, 6, 123–24,
    249, 275n.56
post-Fordism, 307n.51
postmodernism, 234–35, 242; and "differ-
    ence"/particularity, 11, 219, 227, 241;
    as parasitic on the Enlightenment, 229,
    242; and radicalism, 219, 227, 252n.4,
    306n.44; as "superliberalism," 28, 227,
    229; tensions in, 22, 28, 31, 227, 228–29,
    244, 245, 257n.41, 303n.27; and theory of
    justice, 244–47; and undemocratic power
    relations, 11, 29, 234–35, 243, 255n.29.
    See also Connolly; "difference"; Honig;
    identity; self
postrevolutionary politics, necessity of, 124,
    138–45
Poulantzas, Nicos, 149
power, 3, 235; Arendt's conception of,
    196–97; and construction of "difference,"
    220, 235; egalitarian distribution of, 3;
    "Foucauldian" conception of, 235, 239,
    304n.33, 306n.48; and radical democratic

theory, 231, 235, 238; undemocratic na-
    ture of, 11, 235
pragmatism, and democracy, 229
"primitive accumulation," 7
"primitive communism," 127
property, 4, 217, 235; and freedom in Hegel,
    80; as natural in Locke, 258n.3; and role in
    U.S. liberalism, 233; as social in Marx, 109,
    118–19; as state-created in Rousseau,
    258n.3
Przeworksi, Adam, 309n.64
public goods, in radical democracy, 11, 33,
    238–39, 298n101
"public/private distinction," 9, 10, 210,
    237; as politically determined, 10, 11

race, 222, 225, 240, 241, 246, 248, 249,
    303–4n.27, 308n.63
racism: and inclusive citizenship, 231, 240,
    241, 308n.63; and overcoming capitalism,
    308n.63
radical democracy: and democratization of
    social decisions, 20, 237, 248; and equality
    among interests, 20, 217, 238, 246, 249;
    on inequalities of power in civil society, 97,
    217, 247, 248, 249; and liberal concept of
    pluralism and rights, 16, 17, 217, 218,
    226, 233, 237, 247, 248; on patriarchy and
    racism, 248, 305–6n.44; and pluralism, 4,
    5, 20, 31, 226, 238, 246, 249; politics of,
    4, 219, 231, 239–41, 247–49; and prob-
    lem of obligation in, 15, 231, 238; rela-
    tionship to democratic socialism, 235–36;
    and theory of consent and power, 231,
    238, 306n.46; theory of, 5, 8, 234–39,
    247–49. *See also* democracy; politics; radi-
    cal liberalism; radical tradition
radical liberalism, 232–33, 305n.36
radical tradition: and conception of demo-
    cratic people, 53, 245; and false antino-
    mies, 27, 71, 219, 220, 225, 239, 249,
    269n.98; hostilities, 18, 21, 70, 217, 219,
    249; and inequality of power in civil soci-
    ety, 16, 232–33, 238; and liberal, instru-
    mental conception of politics, 13, 14, 21,
    219; and liberalism, 232–33; and vision as
    postpolitical, 3, 9, 25, 218, 219. *See also*
    democracy; liberalism; politics; radical de-
    mocracy; radical liberalism
Rainbow Coalition, 243, 246
Rawls, John, 26, 223, 226, 229, 256n.32,
    257n.36; and communitarians, 28, 225; on
    "original position" as heuristic for fairness,
    28, 57, 223; and "overlapping consensus,"

Rawls, John, *(cont.)*
28, 225; and politics of economic redistribution, 223, 225, 301n.11; radical democratic potential of, 246; on social contract,
50, 225, 300n.117; on talents as socially
owned, 141, 280nn.119,120. *See also* communitarianism; justice; liberalism
reason: in Hegel, 78, 85; in Rousseau, 67
reform, and revolution in democratic societies, 233
repression, 233, 309n.64
republicanism, 216; and conflict, 189; as political theory, 189; and war and founding,
102
responsibility: and equal worth of persons,
134; versus intuition of talents, 142–43
revolution: in advanced industrial societies,
233, 309n.64; and power relations in civil
society, 123; versus reform, 233, 309n.64
rights, 3, 251.n.3; centrality of, 270n.3,
309n.64; and democratic community, 52,
221–22, 237, 238, 239, 298n.101; in just
socialist society, 145; Marx's critique of,
117–21, 128, 275n.61; need to incorporate, 5, 12, 17, 144–45, 168, 217,
276n.66; personal versus property, 235–
37; vague in Rousseau, 53; as valued by
minority struggles, 309n.64. *See also*
democracy; liberalism
Riley, Patrick: on Kant's categorical imperative, 266n.38; on socialization and voluntary choice in Rousseau, 258n.4
risk: relationship to meaningful work and self-
realization, 133, 138–39
Rogers, Joel, as radical democratic theorist,
234, 235, 247, 304n.37, 308n.54
Rorty, Richard, 229
Rousseau, Jean-Jacques, 3, 4, 21, 29, 33–69;
on absence of conflict, 61–63; as alleged
totalitarian, 64, 217; on *amour de soi-
même*, 38, 39, 49; on artisanal, economic
self-sufficiency, 27; on civil freedom and interdependent autonomy, 41, 43, 44, 49–
50; defense of parochialism, 39, 40; on direct democracy, 35, 56–57; on division of
labor, 40, 41, 44; on the family, 43–44;
and freedom, 40–43; and the general will,
14, 33, 36, 41, 51, 54–55, 59, 60, 217; on
government versus sovereignty, 34, 60; on
historical versus just social contract, 45–46;
hostility to political influences, 23, 33–35,
50, 51, 52, 67; hostility to politics, 65–69;
on inequality, 33–34, 47; on Legislator and
democratic mores, 34, 35, 39, 42, 47–48;

65–67; on liberal social contract, 33, 43;
on market society, 23, 27, 33, 44, 217; on
natural versus civil freedom, 36, 37, 40, 41,
49; on particularism versus the general will,
29, 34, 36, 42; on patriotism and civil religion, 34, 35, 39, 41, 42, 43; on politics as
"unnatural," 38, 39; on property as state-
created, 258n.3; on public service as service
to state, 47; on representative democracy,
56, 259n.9; on solidarity and particular
identities, 18, 36, 51, 53; on sovereign assemblies, 36, 54, 58–64; on theory of obligation, 38–39; as "unitary democrat," 67.
See also common good; democracy; general
will; Legislator

Sandel, Michael, 21, 28, 189, 209, 220, 245,
298n.101; as democratic, pluralist communitarian, 230, 257n.38, 292n.5, 298n.101;
and Hegel for personal identity, 265n.23,
300n.2; on "the politics of the good," 190.
See also communitarianism
scarcity, transcendence of, 231–32
Schmitt, Carl, on politics and force, 253n.10
Schwartz, Benjamin, 192, 197, 294n.18
Schwartz, Joseph M., 302n.15
The Second Discourse (Rousseau), 37, 43, 44–
48; Golden Age family in, 45; on historical
social contract, 45; and humans in state of
nature, 37; on inequality as social creation,
45; as prefiguring *Social Contract*, 46; on
state of nature as heuristic, 37
security, and interests in democracy, 252n.4
self: and democracy, liberalism, 222–23, 225,
252n.4; and moral responsibility, 229; as
"power/knowledge" discourse, 228; as
"situated" in democratic community, 224,
226; as situated/unsituated, 222–23, 225,
252n.4, 298n.101, 300n.2, 303n.27. *See
also* communitarianism; Connolly; Hegel;
Honig; Sandel; Taylor
self-ownership: and socialist theory of justice,
140–43, 278n.93; versus collective ownership, 140, 143
self-realization, and risk, 133, 138–39
Serge, Victor, 4
sexuality, politics of, 222, 240, 249, 308n.60
Shalala, Donna, 301n.4
Shapiro, Ian, on democratic justice, 141–42,
142–43, 281n.129
Shklar, Judith, 48, 197
Sirianni, Carmen: on abandoning assumption of post-scarcity, 278n.84; on citizen
participation, 265n.11; on false radical

antinomies, 261–62n.65, 287–88n.95; on universal identities and democracy, 298n.101

"smashing the state," 148, 171, 174–75, 186

Smith, Adam, 13, 269n.89

Smith, Stephen, on Hegel as liberal communitarian, 25, 76, 86, 264n.11, 265

social choice: absence of perfect solution to, 104, 232, 270n.1; "transcendence" under communism of, 134, 232

social contract, 5; as democratic procedures, 23, 27, 226; and human nature, 227, 303n.20; liberal American conception of, 226, 262–63n.94; as politically constructed, 306n.47

Social Contract, The, 48–67; on "forced to be free," 50; as prefigured in *The Second Discourse*, 46; as solution to free-rider problem, 50, 226; on sovereignty as conventional, 48

social democracy, as evolutionary determinism, 119; form of in United States, 233; as less repressive than Leninism, 285n.55; and postmaterialism, 246; as statist, technocratic, 285n.55

social fragmentation, 241–42

socialism: competition within, 279n.122; and democratic rhetorical claims, 121–24; as pregnant within capitalism, 104; role of state in construction of, 164–65; and theory of justice, 134–45; thought on crime and punishment, 133. *See also* democratic socialism; first-stage communism; Marx

social movements, 5, 22, 231, 240, 244; bases for unity among, 307n.53, 308nn.54, 63; and concern for pluralism, 222; and expansion of rights, 233; as not exclusively postmaterial, 240, 245, 258n.42, 308n.63; and "universal class," 239. *See also* citizenship; "difference"; identity; identity politics

Social Revolutionary Party, 8, 291n.133

solidarity, 9, 225; collapse of in United States, 249, 302n.15; and "difference," 68, 238; and individual autonomy in Rousseau, 47; overvalued in radical tradition, 219–20; as radical democratic value, 9, 238, 249; as shared values of democratic community, 65, 225, 249; source of radical postpolitical vision, 9, 18, 22

sovereignty, 248; in Rousseau, 34

soviets, 146, 179, 186–87, 207–8, 209–14, 296n.66, 298n.98; and vanguard party, 149, 173

spontaneity, and radical social organization, 18

Stalin, Joseph, 162

Stalinism, left-liberal tolerance of, 116

state: and construction of socialism, 164–67; "dominant" versus "servile" in Marx, 162–63, 285n.59; in Hegel, 97–103, 267n.54; as legal monopoly of force, 253n.10; Lenin's conception of, 173, 174–75, 183, 186; Marx's analysis of, 163–68, 173

State and Revolution, The, 146–48, 155, 162, 171–88; as allegedly participatory and democratic, 146; *leitmotiv* of factory discipline in, 147; vanguard party in, 148, 178

Stephens, John, 297n.68

Strauss, Leo, 230

subaltern groups, and solidarity, 239

subject: as "decentered," 28, 257n.41; as socially constructed, 304n.33

Talmon, Jacob, 22, 217–18

Tawney, R. H., 4, 22, 251n.1

Taylor, Charles: and Hegel on personal identity, 265n.23; and liberal-communitarian debate, 226; on modernist, situated self, 228–29, 303n.27

technology, and democratic control, 136–37, 182, 289–90n.118, 290n.119; as political, not "technological," 182, 279n.97, 290n.119. *See also* bureaucracy; efficiency; expertise; management

teleology: and conceptions of the good, 227; as historical declension in Rousseau, 46, 47; and historicist relativism in Hegel, 70, 84; in Marx, 113–17

Thiel, Leslie Paul, 228

Thompson, E. P., 149

time: scarcity of, necessitates politics, 12, 19, 23, 232; "transcendence" under communism, 134–35

Tocqueville, Alexis de, 15, 199, 206, 213, 247, 301n.7

totalitarianism, and radical tradition, 22, 217–18

transcendence, of politics, 3, 9, 10, 25, 217–19. *See also* politics; radical tradition

Trotsky, Leon: on Lenin as political tactician, 146; and Marxism's postpolitical vision, 19–20; on Marx's "perfectionism," 115–16; and suprahuman communist individuals, 23–24

"true human suffering," and Marx's conception of communism, 138–40

Tucker, Robert C., 110

Tully, James, 25

Ulan, Adam, 146

Ungar, Roberto, 4; "antinecessitarian politics of," 125; politics of "plasticity," 18–19, 252n.4, 276n.71, 277n.72

unity: and diversity in radical democracy, 27, 31, 220; tension of diversity with, 37. *See also* "difference"; particularity; universality

"universal class": in Hegel, 29, 30, 74, 91; in late industrial societies, 239; in Marx, 150–52

universality, 23; heterosexist and racist construction of, 249; and radical tradition, 27, 220, 239, 249, 298n.101; as "thin" norms, 19, 23

vanguard party, 10, 152, 158, 187, 309n.64

virtù, 28, 29, 56, 255–56n.32

virtue, 189–90. *See also* communitarianism; good, the; MacIntyre; Sandel

Waldron, Jeremy; on Hegel and "property-owning democracy," 82–83, 267n.43

Walzer, Michael, 4, 224–25, 306n.44; as democratic communitarian, 224; on democratization of social provision, 298–99n.102; on Foucault, 306n.48; on justice, 124–25, 225, 257n.36; on rights, 194, 224–25, 294n.22; on social contract as politically constructed, 306n.47; on universal commitment and particularist theory, 224–25, 302n.13; on vanguardism and working class, 22, 254n.26; and workers' control of corporations, 16

Webb, Sidney and Beatrice, 185

Weber, Max: on civil servant, 90; in contrast with Hegel, 90–91, 268n.69; on ideas and interests in politics, 15; on meaning in bureaucratic societies 90–91, 268n.69; on political control of bureaucrats and experts, 181, 289n.114, 290n.119; on political judgment as inherently value-laden, 90; on relationship of iron cage to Arendt, 200; on the state and force, 175, 253n.10

Weedon, Chris, 257n.41

Weisskopf, Thomas, 307n.51

welfare debate, 240, 301n.4; and relation of facts to values, 273n.31

welfare state, 209–10; communitarian critique of, 298n.101; as creation of working-class struggle, 296–97n.68; and means-tested programs in U.S., 225, 240

West, Cornel, 308n.60

What Is to Be Done?, 155–62; relationship to *State and Revolution*, 155

Winfield, Richard Dien, on Hegel, 80, 86, 266n.32

Wolin, Sheldon, 24, 189, 197, 209, 295n.38; on Machiavelli, 275n.49; on politics and instrumental, private ends, 189, 255n.32, 292n.2; and "welfare/warfare" state, 189, 203

women: in Hegel, 264n.8; in Rousseau, 260n.12. *See also* gender; sexuality

Wood, Allen: on capitalism as just, 110; on freedom and autonomy in communism, 107, 112–14; on Marx, 107–8, 114

work: as meaningful, 138–39; and justice, 133; reward to contribution of, 142–43; as true need in Marx, 125, 129, 137

workers' councils: in Arendt, 202–3, 209–11, 298n.96; and representative democracy, 209, 211, 284n.41, 287–88n.95, 299n.106; in *State and Revolution*, 143, 146, 149, 173, 182, 186–87. *See also* democracy; participatory democracy; soviets; workplace democracy

working-class: in Arendt, 202–3; and divisions of race, religion, ethnicity, 149; as reformist in advanced industrial societies, 22, as revolutionary in less developed societies, 22; as universal class, 150–52, 239

workplace democracy, 16, 133, 135–39, 251n.1; control of technology and management, 182, 290n.119

Wright, Erik Olin: on bureaucracy and political power, 181–82

Yack, Bernard: on communitarian reading of Aristotle, 300n.3; critique of Nietzsche and Marx, 85, 139; on Hegel and reason and reality, 72, 85, 264n.12

Young, Iris Marion, 4, 257n.41, 306n.44; on domination and exploitation, 308n.57; and parochial communitarianism, 245; and postmodern theory of justice, 244–47

Young-Bruehl, Elisabeth, 296n.59

Zasulich, Vera: on socialism in Russia, 277n.76

Zuboff, Shoshana, 279n.97